旅游英汉互译

朱 华 编著

图书在版编目(CIP)数据

旅游英汉互译/朱华编著. —北京：北京大学出版社，2022.10
ISBN 978-7-301-33303-7

Ⅰ.①旅… Ⅱ.①朱… Ⅲ.①旅游－英语－翻译－教材 Ⅳ.①F59

中国版本图书馆CIP数据核字（2022）第160178号

书　　　名	旅游英汉互译 LÜYOU YINGHAN HUYI
著作责任者	朱　华　编著
责任编辑	刘　爽
标准书号	ISBN 978-7-301-33303-7
出版发行	北京大学出版社
地　　　址	北京市海淀区成府路205号　100871
网　　　址	http://www.pup.cn　　新浪微博：@北京大学出版社
电子信箱	nkliushuang@hotmail.com
电　　　话	邮购部 010-62752015　发行部 010-62750672　编辑部 010-62759634
印 刷 者	天津中印联印务有限公司
经 销 者	新华书店 720毫米×1020毫米　16开本　24.75印张　478千字 2022年10月第1版　2022年10月第1次印刷
定　　　价	89.00元

未经许可，不得以任何方式复制或抄袭本书之部分或全部内容。
版权所有，侵权必究
举报电话：010-62752024　电子信箱：fd@pup.pku.edu.cn
图书如有印装质量问题，请与出版部联系，电话：010-62756370

内容简介

《旅游英汉互译》是一部内容、结构、体例与众不同的旅游翻译著作,完全摒弃了传统翻译著作以字、词、句、篇章为主要内容的写作方式。本书将旅游者在客源地、目的地和旅游通道中的空间活动作为翻译对象,将旅游翻译行为与旅游活动置于雷柏尔旅游系统模型,形成一个旅游活动与旅游翻译相融合的学习框架,以便读者、译者在旅游活动和旅游时空中正确理解旅游翻译的本质、方法和作用。游前翻译包括旅游广告、旅游网站、旅游指南、旅游手册;游中翻译包括旅游景点介绍、景点导游词和途中导游词;游后翻译包括游记、博客、旅游评论等。诗歌、楹联等翻译则散见于不同旅行阶段和文本之中。本书构建了一个全新的旅游翻译实践知识体系,提供了丰富的译文分析和案例研究,配有演示,适用于高等学校旅游翻译、导游翻译、企业外宣、本地化翻译的教学和研究。

前　言

《旅游英汉互译》是一部内容、结构、体例与众不同的旅游翻译著作，摒弃了传统的翻译著作以字、词、句、篇章为主要内容的写作方式。笔者按照雷柏尔旅游系统模型，将旅游者在客源地、目的地和旅游通道中的空间活动作为翻译对象，将旅游活动与旅游翻译活动联系起来，分为游前、游中、游后三段式翻译，即旅游者从客源地到目的地"离""经""到"全过程翻译，形成一个旅游翻译与旅游活动相融合的学习框架，便于读者、译者在旅游时空中理解旅游活动与旅游翻译活动的关系，以及旅游翻译的本质、作用和方法。

一、旅游活动与旅游翻译的关系

无论是出境旅游还是入境旅游，旅游者都需要经历游前、游中以及返程的过程，而旅游翻译实际上就是对旅游活动的三个阶段所包含的各类文本、材料的翻译行为（包括口译和笔译），比如游前（客源地）对广告、指南、网站等的翻译；游中（旅游通道）对途中景点的翻译以及到达旅游目的地对旅游景点的翻译；游后对游记、博客、评论等的翻译。

根据雷柏尔旅游系统模型，笔者从旅游时间和空间两个维度构建了旅游翻译的过程和翻译实践体系：游前——旅游客源地的翻译；游中（1）——旅游通道的翻译；游中（2）——旅游目的地的翻译；游后——返回旅游客源地的翻译。旅游活动并非简单的线性活动，由于时空交叉，同一种文本会在不同旅游阶段出现，如旅游景点介绍的翻译既可出现在旅游网站（游前），也可出现在途中导游词（游中），还可能出现在旅行后文本的游记、博客、旅游评论中（游后）。

二、中、英旅游文本的特点

中、英思维方式不同，由此对旅游文本的翻译策略和方法产生重要影响。多数中国人追求客观与主观情感融合，"一切景语皆情语"，景物描写呈现出一种"浑然"之美、"意境"之美。因此，汉语用词大多华丽缥缈，表达华丽妍美，主观色彩浓厚（马松梅，2003：109）。英语景物描写则相对客观，主张"模仿"或"再现"自然，不刻意在言辞上作过多的情景、意象渲染（连淑能，2010：272—275），呈现出真实自然的"简约"之美、"理性"之美。英文"以形统意"，造句用各种形式的连接词、分句或从句，注重结构完整；中文"以意统形"，大量使用四字词、叠词，同义反复，凭经验、语境和悟性从整体上领会意义。翻译中、英旅游文本应注意"形象"与"意象"、"形合"与"意合"、"静态"与"动态"、"简约"与"华美"之间的相互转换。

三、旅游翻译的本地化

本地化翻译对旅游翻译的效果具有重要影响，旅游网站本地化的翻译更是如此。按照功能翻译理论，成功的旅游文本翻译主要取决于是否能实现文本预先设定的目标和功能，而译文与源语在语言、体裁、篇章上保持一致是次要的。如果要实现预先设定的文本功能，离不开对文本符合目的的创造性改写，既可以采取"等功能翻译"，也可以采取"异功能翻译"。由于中外旅游文本受不同哲学和审美的影响，中、英旅游文本存在诸多差异，这给旅游本地化翻译带来诸多挑战。旅游文本的翻译在于成功激发旅游者的旅游动机和行为，在内容取舍、篇章重构等方面，译者有较大的决定权，旅游文本的本地化翻译尺度之大，可能会颠覆一般读者的想象。

四、主体意识与翻译行为

翻译本质是承担传播主体的功能，承载国家意志、国家价值，是国家文化和文明建构的全球化叙事。任何翻译行为都是译者主体意识的体现，表达译者的政治倾向和思想观点，反映译者所处的政治立场、意识形态和个体选择，彰显译者参与文化调停的身份(黄艳群、项凝霜，2016：109)。由于旅游翻译涉及大量人文历史、宗教文化等内容，无论是译者对翻译内容的选择（"译"与"不译"），采用不同的翻译策略（"异化"与"归化"），抑或是对文本的历史背景、风情民俗、典章制度、新奇语言特征等做出的注解和阐释（译者注），其主体意识都会在译文中以不同方式表现出来。因此，新时期的译者应将译者的主体意识与国家意识融为一体（朱义华，2019：118），在旅游文本中突显译文在国际社会中的中国价值、中国话语。

综上所述，旅游翻译是应用性翻译，但与一般的应用性翻译不同，既有文学翻译，也有非文学翻译，涉及多个翻译领域、不同的翻译文本和体裁。由于中、英思维不同、审美观照不同，中、英旅游文本存在较大差异，体现在"主观"与"客观"、"形象"与"意象"、"形合"与"意合"、"动态"与"静态"、"简约"与"华美"等各个方面，旅游翻译应当注意这种差异，采取不同的翻译策略和方法，使译文符合目标语读者的审美心理，满足不同文化背景游客的审美需求，使他们获得更美好的旅游体验，并在旅游翻译实践中不断探索中国核心价值观在不同国家和民族地区的传播途径和方法，发挥旅游翻译在构建人类命运共同体话语体系中的特殊作用。

本书配有PPT和翻译实践及参考答案，适用于高等学校旅游翻译、导游翻译、企业外宣、本地化翻译等的教学和研究，也适用于高等院校MTI翻译特色课程的建设。如有需要，可致函ernestzhu@126.com申请。

朱　华

2022年5月22日

成都，龙湖

目 录

第一篇 旅游翻译基础

第一章 旅游翻译概论 ……………………………………………… 3
一、旅游活动与旅游翻译 ………………………………………… 3
二、中、英旅游文本对比 ………………………………………… 7
三、旅游文本的语言特点 ………………………………………… 11
四、旅游文本的体裁和类型 ……………………………………… 23

第二章 旅游翻译策略和方法 ……………………………………… 39
一、功能翻译理论与旅游翻译 …………………………………… 39
二、旅游翻译的策略 ……………………………………………… 41
三、旅游翻译的方法 ……………………………………………… 47

第二篇 游前文本翻译

第三章 旅游广告翻译 ……………………………………………… 67
一、旅游广告概论 ………………………………………………… 67
二、旅游广告的用词特点 ………………………………………… 69
三、旅游广告的句法特点 ………………………………………… 72
四、旅游广告对话性的特点 ……………………………………… 75
五、旅游广告的修辞特点 ………………………………………… 76
六、旅游广告的翻译策略和方法 ………………………………… 84

第四章 旅游网站翻译 ……………………………………………… 91
一、旅游网站的结构和内容 ……………………………………… 94

二、旅游网站的文本功能···101
三、旅游网站的语言特点···104
四、旅游网站的本地化翻译···108

第五章　旅游指南翻译···128
　　一、旅游指南文本的特点···128
　　二、旅游指南信息分类···133
　　三、旅游指南信息处理···142
　　四、旅游指南翻译原则···147
　　五、旅游指南翻译方法···151

第六章　旅游手册翻译···159
　　一、旅游手册与指南对比···159
　　二、旅游手册的文本结构···162
　　三、旅游手册的文本功能···167
　　四、旅游手册的语言特点···169
　　五、旅游手册的体裁···179
　　六、旅游手册的翻译···183

第三篇　游中文本翻译

第七章　旅游景点介绍翻译···193
　　一、中西思维与旅游景物描写···193
　　二、中西语言差异与旅游景物描写·······································200
　　三、景物描写性文本的翻译···211
　　四、景物说明性文本的翻译···217

第八章　景点导游词翻译···229
　　一、导游词风格类型···229

二、导游词翻译原则 ……………………………………………… 236
三、导游词翻译方法 ……………………………………………… 245
四、面中取点、点面结合 ………………………………………… 251
五、以点带面、以小博大 ………………………………………… 257

第四篇 游后文本翻译

第九章 旅行后文本的翻译 …………………………………………… 271
一、旅行后文本的分类 …………………………………………… 271
二、旅行后文本的特点 …………………………………………… 276
三、旅行后文本的翻译 …………………………………………… 286
四、游记翻译欣赏 ………………………………………………… 295

第十章 旅游文本中的诗歌、楹联翻译 ……………………………… 311
一、诗歌、楹联在旅游文本中的作用 …………………………… 312
二、诗歌、楹联的翻译策略 ……………………………………… 316
三、诗歌、楹联的翻译方法 ……………………………………… 321
四、旅游文本中的诗歌翻译 ……………………………………… 326
五、旅游文本中的楹联翻译 ……………………………………… 328

第十一章 旅游文本中典故、专用名词等的翻译 …………………… 334
一、旅游文本中特殊的语言表达 ………………………………… 334
二、旅游文本中典故、俗语的翻译 ……………………………… 338
三、旅游文本中地名、景点名称的翻译 ………………………… 345
四、旅游文本中概念文化词的翻译 ……………………………… 350

参考文献 ………………………………………………………………… 361
后　　记 ………………………………………………………………… 380

第一篇

旅游翻译基础

第一章　旅游翻译概论

何谓"旅游"？人们普遍将"旅游"和"旅行"画上等号，认为两者是同义词，表达的概念是一样的，但事实上两者只能算作近义词，概念上有重合之处，更有相异之处。倘若要给旅游一个准确的定义，那必然要先理清"旅游"与"旅行"之间的共同点以及区别。

"旅游"和"旅行"，二者都有"旅"字，其形在甲骨文、金文、小篆，尤其是在甲骨文中明显可以看到这个字所要传达的意思，两个人跟着一面旗，而这面旗是军旗，两人代表的是一群人，其身份为士兵，也就是一群士兵跟随着军旗，因此"旅"本意为军队。而《说文·仒部》写道："军之五百人为旅"（许慎、汤可敬，1997：924），所以"旅"本意为军队编制单位，据此"旅"字引申出军令、驻扎等与军队有关的意思，后又引申为路途，再后又引申出旅游、旅行等。

"旅游"与"旅行"的差别在于"游"与"行"之异。"游"作动词，意为游逛，到各地从容地行走、观看，也表嬉戏、玩乐，因此"游"不仅要产生行走的动作，还要产生玩耍的动作。而"行"作动词，意为走路，因此，"行"只产生行走的动作。据此可知，"旅游"与"旅行"的区别在于二者所涵盖的范围和侧重点不同，前者包含且强调玩乐之意，译为"tourism"；后者重在行，重在出发，而非一定要娱乐，故译为"travel"。所有的旅游都要经历旅行的过程，但不是所有的旅行都是旅游。

一、旅游活动与旅游翻译

旅游学家雷柏尔（1995）根据旅游活动制订了一个旅游模型（见图1.1），人们称之为雷柏尔旅游系统模型。旅游活动涉及旅游地理空间的时空转移，从客源地出发，途经一个或若干过境之地即旅游通道抵达目的地，再从目的地返回客源地，形成一个旅游的地理空间系统。从空间角度观察，旅游活动涉及客源地和目的地两类场所以及两者之间的旅游通道，客源地与目的地两大场所在大多数情况下是不重叠的，并且各自有自己的运行规律（朱华，2014：11）。但是，如果旅游者从客源地抵达目的地后，前往下一个目的地，或经其他旅游通道返回客源地，便会形成更复杂的旅游系统。

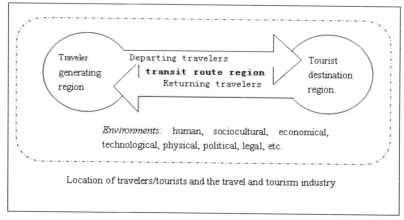

图1.1 雷柏尔旅游系统模型

雷柏尔旅游系统模型突出了客源地、目的地和旅游通道三个空间要素，旅游活动实际上就是旅游者从客源地到目的地的流动，从而形成旅游流（tourist flow）。如果中国旅游者到国外观光旅游，便形成了出境旅游市场；如果外国旅游者到中国来观光旅游，便形成了入境旅游市场。无论是出境旅游还是入境旅游，旅游活动都需经历游前、游中以及到达目的地后返程三个阶段，而旅游翻译就是对旅游活动的三个阶段所包含的各类文本、材料的翻译行为（包括口译和笔译），比如游前（客源地）对广告、指南、网站等的翻译；游中（旅游通道）对途中景点的翻译以及到达旅游目的地对旅游景点的译介；游后对游记、博客、评论等的翻译（见图1.2）。

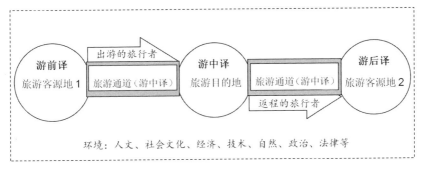

图1.2 雷柏尔旅游系统与旅游翻译

由此可见,旅游翻译是一种跨时空、跨语言、跨社会、跨文化、跨心理的交际活动,受旅游环境,如模型中人文、社会文化、经济、技术、自然、政治、法律等环境的影响,与其他类型的翻译相比,它在跨文化、跨心理交际特点上表现得更为直接、更为突出、更为典型、更为全面(陈刚,2009:10)。需要指出的是,旅游语言服务涉及旅游客源地(游前)、旅游通道(游中)和旅游目的地(游中,尚未返回客源地)。但是,当旅游者从旅游目的地返回客源地(居住地)之后,旅游者的旅游行为就变成游后行为,而旅游翻译也就成为(游后)翻译行为,如游记、博客、旅游评论等的翻译。

本书摒弃了以字、词、句、篇章为主要内容的写作方式,以系统论规范旅游翻译研究,将旅游活动和旅游翻译行为置于模型中。按照雷柏尔旅游系统模型,本书将旅游者在客源地、目的地和旅游通道中的空间活动作为翻译对象,分为游前、游中、游后翻译,即旅游者从客源地到目的地"离""经""到"全过程翻译,形成一个旅游活动与旅游翻译相融合的学习框架,构建起一个全新的旅游翻译实践知识体系,以便读者、译者能够在旅游时空中更好地理解旅游翻译的本质、方法和作用。

译者的旅游翻译行为在雷柏尔旅游系统模型中的两个维度中进行。时间维度:游前、游中、游后;空间维度:旅游客源地、旅游通道、旅游目的地。游前翻译包括旅游广告、旅游网站、旅游指南、旅游手册;游中翻译包括旅游景点介绍、景点导游词和途中导游词;游后翻译包括游记、博客、旅游评论等。由于旅

游活动并非简单的线性活动,旅游流呈现双向或多向特点,时空交叉,同一种文本会在不同旅游时空出现,如诗歌、楹联既可能出现在途中导游词(游中),也会出现在景点导游词(游中)或旅行后文本的游记、博客、旅游评论(游后)。

表1 旅游活动与旅游翻译

旅游活动与旅游翻译	翻译文本/材料	备注
旅游客源地的翻译（游前）	✓旅游广告 ✓旅游网站 ✓旅游指南 ✓旅游手册	以下文本也可能在旅游客源地出现： ✓游记 ✓博客 ✓旅游评论
旅游通道的翻译（游中）	✓旅游景点介绍 ✓旅游公示语 ✓旅游文本中的诗歌、楹联 ✓旅游文本中的典故、专用名词	以下文本也可能在旅游通道中出现： ✓旅游广告 ✓旅游指南 ✓旅游手册
旅游目的地的翻译（游中）	✓旅游景点介绍 ✓景点导游词 ✓旅游公示语 ✓旅游文本中的诗歌、楹联 ✓旅游文本中的典故、专用名词	以下文本也可能在旅游目的地中出现： ✓旅游广告 ✓旅游指南 ✓旅游手册
返回客源地的翻译（游后）	✓游记 ✓博客 ✓旅游评论	以下文本也可能在返回的客源地出现： ✓旅游网站 ✓旅游文本中的诗歌、楹联 ✓旅游文本中的典故、专用名词

综上所述,旅游翻译是一种跨语言、跨文化的交际活动,既包含非文学翻译(如应用文、社交、日常生活等翻译),也包含文学翻译(诗歌、楹联、散文等翻译)(傅燕,2007:17),文本类型、体裁多样,涉及历史、文化、地理、宗教、民俗、自然科学等知识,其翻译难度并不亚于纯文学翻译。无论翻译什么样的旅游文本,译者都应照顾译文读者的审美需求,不能只停留在字、词、句的表象,拘泥于原文的句法结构,否则就会导致译文晦涩难懂,出现死译、错译、乱译等问题(赵红军,2014:168—169)。

二、中、英旅游文本对比

汉语和英语是两种不同的语言体系,语言和文化存在某种"不可通约性"(incommensurability),表现在词语搭配、句型结构、写作风格和文化内容的差异性(贾文波,2012:20—33)。由于不同的语言文化和思维习惯,中、英旅游文本的行文习惯与行文规范不同,读者对译文的期待也不一样。从本质上讲,中、英旅游文本的差异是中、英不同的哲学思想、逻辑思维、审美方式、文化传统所致,主要体现在形合与意合、华美与简约、作者视角与读者视角的不同。从宏观上了解中、英旅游文本的这些差异,能更好地处理中、英旅游文本在用词、句法、语篇、修辞上的异同,在旅游文本英汉互译过程中起到提纲挈领的指导作用。关于中、英旅游文本的特点,在第七章还将重点阐述。

1. 形合与意合

汉语和英语语系不同。汉语属于汉藏语系,属于"意合"语言,受东方文化重辩证逻辑的影响,注重直觉领悟,语言表达与分析重意不重形,句子与句子之间关系隐藏于上下文中,多用排比、对仗,注重隐性连贯,凭经验、语境、语感和悟性去意会和补足语句的整体内容,"以神统形"。英语属于印欧语系,属于"形合"语言。英文受西方文化重形式逻辑的影响,句子和句子中的各个成分就像树和树枝一样围绕主谓结构散开,多使用表示逻辑—语法关系的连接词语,重视形式上的衔接与连贯,"以形统意",句子之间的关系清晰,结构严谨,层次分明(连淑能,2010:83)。第七章旅游景点介绍翻译还将重点讨论。

例1. 大明湖<u>百花映日</u>,<u>万树争荣</u>,水鸟翔集,锦鳞戏泳,<u>怪石嶙峋</u>,<u>流水潺潺</u>,自然景色美不胜收。在大明湖八百多种花卉草木中,数量最多、久负盛名的是荷花和柳树。公园的湖内池中广种荷花,盛夏时节红白竞放,花光照眼,叶翻绿浪,香气袭人,湖畔岛上有垂柳千余株,浓荫覆岸,柔条拂水,临风起舞,婀娜多姿。

译文:In the dreaming lake park visitors could enjoy the bright colors of flowers, heavy shades of trees, and watch birds fly and fish swim. Lotus flowers and the willow trees form the major part of the park's 800 kinds of plants. In summer, white and red flowers glimmer among the sea of leaves, giving off delicate scents. Along the banks and on the islands the more than one thousand willow trees dance in the breeze.

分析：汉语旅游材料用词华丽，描写引人入胜，其中有很多四字格，突显汉语写作的特点，如"百花映日""万树争荣""怪石嶙峋""流水潺潺"等，是典型的意合句，符合中国人的阅读习惯；而译文删除不必要的修饰语，仅留汉语文本中的实质信息，花、树、鸟、虫、鱼都用简单、直接的英文描写。与汉语旅游文本相比，英语旅游文本重视形式上的衔接与连贯，信息集中、语言朴实、层次分明。

例2. The Golden Temple's sheer vastness and the glory of its architecture and ornamentation make for an unforgettable experience enjoyed by all visitors, whatever their spiritual beliefs, as does the warm welcome and friendliness offered by the volunteer workers on the complex.

译文：金殿规模巨大，建筑宏伟，装饰精美，令人观之难忘。无论您的信仰如何，志愿者的热情友好都会令您备感温暖。

分析：英文文本是一个逻辑严谨的长句子，语言平实客观，注意句子之间的逻辑关系，"以形统意"。考虑到汉语意合句的语言特点，译文用词凝练含蓄，行文讲究声律对仗，尽量不用连接词，"以意统形"，并使用"规模巨大""建筑宏伟""装饰精美""观之难忘""备感温暖"等四字词语增强汉语的语言气势，以吸引读者的注意和兴趣。

2. 华美与简约

中文旅游文本大多辞藻华丽，喜引经据典，善用文人墨客的诗句，使用大量的修饰性形容词；语言表达上多用比喻、夸张等修辞手法；而英文注重逻辑性，重写实，用词强调简洁朴实而自然，风格直观（蔡小玲，2011：62）。在文体风格上，英语旅游文本大多风格简略，结构严谨，行文简洁明了，注重信息的准确性，追求的是一种自然理性之美（舒娅，2014：6）。相反，中文旅游文本的文字比较"文学性"，特别是描写性旅游文本，常用四言八句、夸张的写作手法，浓墨重彩，渲染诗情画意盎然的氛围；而英语旅游文本常用口语体和大量描述性文字，力求体现艺术性和美感，使用优美和文学性较强的形容词，如"picturesque"（风景如画的），"idyllic"（田园诗般的）等（王小兵，倪娜，2013：114）。

例1. 崂山，林木苍翠，繁花似锦，到处生机盎然，春天绿芽红花，夏天浓阴蔽日，秋天遍谷金黄，严冬则玉树琼花。其中，更不乏古树名木。景区内，古树名木有近三百株，50%以上为国家一类保护植物，著名的有银杏、桧柏等。

译文：Laoshan Scenic Area is thickly covered with trees of many species, which add credit for its scenery. Among them over 300 are precious ones, half of which are plants under state-top-level protection. The most famous species include gingko and cypress.

分析：中文辞藻华丽，重"意象"而不是"具象"，追求的是一种意境美、朦胧美。英文的景物描写大多实景实写，客观、忠实再现自然。但是这种超越现实、虚实不定的朦胧美，对于讲英语的旅游者来说，是浮夸、不真实的。译文保留实用信息，将原文中语言繁复的四字词语删除不译，化繁为简，体现了英文的简约美。

例2. The sculptures cover a range of subjects: sceneries and constructions such as rivers, bridges, hills, gardens, waterfalls, pavilions, towers, temples, and pagodas; Buddhist carvings such as Bodhisattvas, Buddhists, flying Apsanas, enshrined monks; animals such as flying dragons, dancing phoenixes, lions, elephants, unicorns and oxen.

译文：雕塑中有山水桥梁、园林瀑布、亭台楼阁和殿宇宝塔等建筑物；人物有诸佛菩萨、飞天供养人；鸟兽有飞龙舞凤、狮子、麒麟、象和牛等。

分析：英文对雕塑中景物的描写，客观具体，无华丽辞藻进行修饰；译文采用增译法，运用汉语特有的连珠四字句和平行对偶结构，朗朗上口，呈现出一幅美丽图景，渲染了景点的意境和氛围，将英文的"简约美"转换为汉语的"华美"，符合中文读者的语言特点和审美观照。

3. 作者视角与读者视角

汉语是"意合"语言,"遗形写神",强调"意境两忘,物我一体",文本中可不用主语,多角度、多视点叙事,无明显表示衔接关系的连接词从而缺少连贯性的特点。英语是"意合"语言,语法规则严格,讲究句式结构的逻辑层次和有机组合,表现为一种严谨的空间搭架式立体结构,逻辑严谨,思维缜密,主语一般不可缺省。英汉互译应注意英汉不同的语言特点,以及英汉思维的差异,调整原文的主语和叙事角度。英译汉,一般可省译主语;汉译英,则可从作者视角介入(We/I approach)或读者视角介入(You approach)。语篇或段落主语应一致,避免产生歧义。

例1. 四方八景阁位于公园中心最高处(海拔40米),面积575平方米,主体三层,重檐。登上三楼,可以看到八方景色。

译文:The Viewing Pavilion is located on the highest point of the central park (40 meters above sea level), covering an area of 575 square meters. Its main building has three stories and double eaves. It enables you to enjoy the view in all directions on the third floor.

分析:原文为意合句,叙事角度不一,"八景阁""面积"以及"登上"主语不同,属于中文散点视角写法。译为英文,需使用指示代词,增加语义连贯和衔接,将句子衔接在一起,并使段内主语一致,避免读者阅读、理解障碍。

例2. 旅客必须遵守宾馆的规章制度,服从工作人员的管理,爱护公共财物。

译文:Every guest has the obligation to abide by the rules and regulations of the hotel, corporate with the personnel in carrying out their duties and take good care of the property in the hotel.

分析:原文为游客须知,采用一般现在时。"游客须知"之类的信息型文本,以提供信息为主,除了采用一般现在时,语气还应以平和的劝导式为主,采用作者视角或读者视角更有亲和力、说服力,避免居高临下,给人咄咄逼人的印象。改译文本如下:

Our guests are kindly expected to heed the rules and regulations. Your corporation will be highly appreciated in making our services effective.

三、旅游文本的语言特点

英语善于使用名词、形容词，呈静态叙述；汉语多使用动词，呈动态叙述（杨莉等，2020：133）。英语常用动词名词化、动词同源形容词表达动词意义，忌重复，常用代词或其他手段来代替需要重复的词语；汉语善用动词，动词常重复或叠加，为了获得强调效果，往往将同一意义反复表达在汉语语言中。英语为形合句，大量使用衔接词连接语篇；汉语为意合句，少用甚至不用衔接词，常用连动式或兼语式句子。在语篇构建上，汉语以归纳方式构建语篇，"先分后总"；而英语以演绎方式构建语篇，"先总后分"。旅游涉及社会、政治、经济、自然、科技等多个领域，语言不是限定在某一专业领域内使用，与其他语言有共性，也有其独特性。

1. 用词特点

词汇特点是专业文体一个十分明显、特别重要的方面。特定词语的使用可以将一种文体区别于普通语言和其他专业文体。与其他专业领域不同的是，旅游语言不是在有限的专业群体内使用的语言。通常情况下，它的促销和劝说功能使其成为一种容易被普通大众所接受的语言。旅游语言在措辞方面有其独特性，主要表现在关键词语的选择、外来词语的使用、专门词语的跨学科性以及构词等方面（丁大刚，2008：2）。

（1）关键词语

旅游文本中会出现一些常见的关键词语，是旅游文本当中的高频词汇。这些关键词通常反映了下列心理主题。3R：浪漫主义（Romanticism）、回归（Regression）、重生（Rebirth）；3H：幸福（Happiness）、享乐主义（Hedonism）、太阳中心论（Heliocentrism）；3F：娱乐（Fun）、幻想（Fantasy）、童话故事（Fairy Tales）；3S：大海（Sea）、阳光（Sun）、社交（Socialization）（丁大刚，2008：3）。这些旅游文本中的高频词汇满足了普通大众的审美期待，更能为游客所欣赏、接受，鼓励他们前往旅游。

例1. Peerless in its imagination and attention to detail, the Resort is also a hermetic bubble cocooned from the real world. Everything runs like clockwork, and nothing shatters its illusions of fantasy. Unless you're a confirmed cynic, Walt Disney World Resort will amaze you.

分析：这是一段有关迪士尼乐园的描述。我们可以看到"imagination""bubble""illusion""fantasy""amaze"等词语，文字描述很好地契合了3F心理主题。也许，人们内心对于迪士尼乐园的期待就是这样一个充满幻想的童话世界。

（2）外来词语

由于旅游景点中蕴含历史文化，旅游文本的另一大特色就是外来词语的使用，这些外来词语一般涉及的范围主要是人名、地名或者一些跨文化的意象。旅游文本中外来词语的使用，可以增强旅游者的归属感和认同感。

例1. The heart of the Spanish settlements is Plaza de la Constitution, a leafy square flanked by Government House Museum and the grand Basilica Cathedral. The splendid Flagler College started out as the Ponce de Leon Hotel, built by Henry Flagler in 1883, a year after he honeymooned in St. Augustine.

分析：本段是对圣奥古斯丁的描述，由于该地是西班牙殖民者佩德罗·梅嫩德斯·德阿维尔斯于1565年建立的美国殖民地，因此，对这一景点的描述涉及了一些西班牙语词汇，如"Plaza de la""Ponce de Leon"，体现了旅游文本当中的外来语特点。

（3）专门词语

由于旅游有综合性、复杂性等特点，涉及诸如建筑学、地理学、艺术、历史等领域，旅游文本中会出现大量的专门词语。

例1. 我们惊诧地发现，一片树林生长在海水之中。这片树林聚集了不同品种的红树科植物。它们或许是自然界最名不副实的树木，明明是绿色，却叫做红树林。其实，这些树木富含一种叫做单宁酸的特殊成分，树干或树枝断裂以后，便会氧化成红色。

分析：原文在讲到红树林的成因时，提到了一些有关化学的词汇，如单宁酸、氧化等术语。

例2. The suspended temple is spectacular from a distance. It consists of 40 cave rooms carved into limestone, fronted with wooden facades, columns, and tiled roofs, all connected by a series of catwalks and bridges perched on jutting beams and posts socketed into solid rock.

分析：在描写让人叹为观止的悬空寺时，文中使用了建筑相关的词汇，如"wooden facade""column""tiled roof""catwalk""jutting beam""post"等。

（4）缩略词与复合词

缩略词是为了表达的简洁采用缩略形式以节约篇幅。例如：

B&B=bed and breakfast; LTB=London Tourist Board; BBS=Bulletin Board System; BLD=breakfast, lunch, dinner

复合词是英文当中一种常见的构词方法，形式灵活且丰富。例如：

going-to-the-sun road; win-your-weight-in-beer competition; gold-domed Colorado State Capitol

（5）文化负载词

文化负载词是指在语言系统中，最能体现语言承载的文化信息、反映人类的社会生活的词汇。这些词汇是当地文化的积淀，最能突显语言中浓厚的民族色彩和鲜明的文化个性，是旅游文化的灵魂（金惠康，2006:103）。文化负载词又称"词汇空缺"，包含了某种特定的文化信息，在译入语中难以找到与源语词汇所含文化信息相对应的词（贾文波，2012：63）。

例1. 九斗碗

译文：Jiudouwan (It means nine dishes. Nine is a lucky number with a meaning of longevity, academic success and everlasting.)

分析：九斗碗是巴中市的风俗，凡是哪家结婚生子、建房等都要请亲朋好友来聚一聚，在坝坝宴上大吃一顿，俗称吃"九斗碗"。之所以称宴席为"九斗碗"是因为一般每席有九碗菜；另一个原因则是民间视"九"为吉数，"九"寓意九九长寿、九子登科、天长地久。"九斗碗"在英语中很难找到与中文相对应的词。因此，对于文化负载词的一种处理方法是直译加注的方法，以弥补目的语中文化现象的缺失。

例2. 广生宫中供奉的是在古代社会中很有影响的子孙娘娘，即保佑妇女多生儿女、顺利生儿女的民间神，四川也叫送子娘娘。

译文：The deity enshrined in Guangsheng Hall was the Goddess of Fertility who was very influential in ancient China and blessed women to have more and more children and give birth to sons and daughters smoothly. In Sichuan, she was also called Songzi Goddess.

分析：中国传统文化中，儒、道、佛三教流传下来诸多早期神话和后来的民间故事，而后逐渐形成了中国独特的神话体系，由此出现诸多神仙人物，子孙娘娘就是其中之一，也是具有中国传统意象的文化负载词。"子孙娘娘"采取了归化译法，译为"Goddess of Fertility"，而"送子娘娘"采取音译+直译，译为"Songzi Goddess"，这是因为前面"子孙娘娘"采取归化译法，读者已经从中轻松理解其文化意义，后面的"送子"采取异化译法，读者不仅能理解，而且有一种新奇感，有利于"中国文化走出去"。

（6）名物化

根据《现代语言学词典》的界定，名物化是指"从其他某个词类形成名词的过程或从一个底层小句得出一个名词短语的派生过程"。词性转换是构成语言多样化不可或缺的因素。英语名物化分为词汇名物化（lexical nominalization）和句项名物化（clausal nominalization）。词汇名物化指的转换，一般把动词和形容词名物化成一个新的词项，表示一般的行为时间或属性；句项名物化指任何一个小句作为一个级成分在另一个小句中充当名词的功能（胡开杰，2006：103）。

词汇名物化结构主要由名词、形容词、动词等词汇及其词组派生，如形容词"hesitant"派生为名词"hesitancy"，"precise"派生为名词"precision"；动词"perform"派生为名词"performance"，"discover"派生为"discovery"。句项名物化结构是指在小句中起名词作用的任何一个限定或非限定性小句，它包括名词性小句、不定式和动名词等，如：What I have to do is to work hard. Watching the football match was really excited.

例1. 在山环水绕、婉转曲折之间，布满亭台楼阁，分布着145处景观。有些景观直接以水为主题。圆明园内汇集天下的胜景和各名园的精华。

译文：Halls, buildings and pavilions were seen scattered among hills and winding streams, 145 landscapes in the gardens, some graced with the theme of water, were built in <u>imitation</u> of enchanting scenes from all over the country. Hence it was the screams of gardens.

分析：译者将动词imitate改为imitation，是动词名物化的用法，符合英文旅游文本词汇名物化的表达方法，使译文更简洁、顺畅。

例2. 早晨在公园里，常可见遛鸟者。

译文：<u>Taking a walk in parks with caged birds in hand</u> is a common scene in the early mornings.

分析：该句以动名词形式开头组成一小句，是句项名物化在旅游文体中的运用。句项名物化是旅游翻译常用的方法，本句项名物化的使用，使文本句式多样化，丰富了旅游文体结构。

2. 句法特点

汉语句子为意合句，注重直觉感受和整体和谐，连词成句、行为铺排不求句法形式完备（杨元刚，2008：257）；成分之间结构较为松散，短句较多，呈"曲线型"的描述方式；善用动词，以动词为中心，形成"流水型"句式结构，语言偏动态；英语句子为形合句，注重理性判断和逻辑分析，常用被动式和非人称表达法；善用名词、名物化结构；句子以主语和谓语为核心，形成"树权型"句式结构（涂靖，2016：13），语言偏静态。

（1）多主动、忌被动

旅游英语多主动、忌被动，这在旅游文本，特别是描写景物的中文旅游文本中较多出现。使用主动语态，可以最大限度地发挥动态语的优势，使文本产生更好的"呼唤""感染"功能，但是在某种语境下，例如在<u>不必说出主动者</u>、<u>不愿说出主动者</u>、<u>无从说出主动者</u>或者是为了便于连贯上下文等场合下，英文旅游文本也会使用被动语态，避免给人以主观臆断的感觉，使文本表现得更为客观、正式，语气更加委婉（叶欣，2014：14—15）。

例1. 瀑布从丛林灌木中奔腾而出，飞流直泻，被树林、岩石层层阻隔、激荡，变成千万道雪白晶亮的飞瀑，直落沟底，蔚为壮观。

译文：Cascades splash over the bushes and trees of the dykes, interrupted by rocks and trees, forming screens of galloping water, which drop straight down to the bottom of the valley.

分析：中文描写景观全部使用了主动语态。译文除了一处因语境需要用了被动语态外，主句、分句、分词结构也使用主动语态，形成连动句，一气呵成，将树正群海的瀑布描写得气势磅礴、栩栩如生。

例2. 水映山容，使山容益添秀媚，山清水秀，使水更显柔情。有诗云："岸上湖中各自奇，山觞水酌两相宜。只言游舫浑如画，身在画中原不知。"

译文：The hills overshadow the lake, and the lake reflects the hills. They are in perfect harmony, and more beautiful than a picture.

分析：即使是非人称主语，译文也使用了主动语态，如第一句"水映山容"，也可译为"The lake is overshadowed by the hills, and the hills are reflected in the lake"，但译为主动语态使文本更有气势，更有移情功能，与后文衔接更自然。

（2）形容词替换关系从句

例1.美国著名的拉什莫尔国家纪念碑位于南达科他州西南海拔1829米的布莱克山拉什莫尔峰顶。

译文一：The Rushmoore National Monument which is well-known in the United States is erected on the Rushmoore Peak, 1829 meters above sea level, of the Black Hills in the southwest of South Dakota.

译文二：The well-known Rushmoore National Monument in the United States is erected on the Rushmoore Peak, 1829 meters above sea level, of the Black Hills in the southwest of South Dakota.

分析：译文二用形容词替换关系从句，将"The Rushmoore National Monument which is well-known in the United States"改为更易理解的简单句"the well-known Rushmoore National Monument in the United States"，句式简练、文笔流畅。

例2. 高地错落的群瀑<u>高唱低吟</u>，<u>大大小小</u>的群海碧蓝澄澈，水中倒映红叶、绿树、雪峰、蓝天。

译文：The waterfalls, <u>high or low</u>, roar and hum; the lakes, <u>big or small</u>, are blue and crystal clear.

分析："高唱低吟"译为"high or low"，后置修饰"waterfalls"；"大大小小"，译为"big or small"，后置修饰"lakes"，未用关系代词"which"引导定语从句，整个句子节奏明快，句式紧凑，朗朗上口。

（3）现在分词用作后置定语替换主动定语从句

例1. 当微风停止的时候，高山湖泊静如明镜，<u>蓝天和白云将自己的身影留给这高原上的小海</u>，四面山峰栖息在湖水之中。站在方圆几十公里的大海子边，看<u>高原黄鸭在水面飞翔</u>，听<u>空山鸟语美妙的音乐</u>，让人冥想这海子的灵性。圣洁的水将洗却尘世的忧怨，让生命归于永恒。

译文：When the breeze stops, the lakes are as smooth as mirrors, <u>reflecting flawlessly the trees, the azure sky, the white clouds and the mountains nearby</u>. Birds <u>chirping in the mountains</u> and highland ducks <u>swimming on the blue water</u>, you will sense the immensity of the lakes and comprehend the profound significance of our earthly paradise.

分析：一般而言，英语旅游文体大多风格简约，结构严谨而不复杂，注重信息的准确性和语言的实用性，最忌啰嗦堆砌。译文用"reflecting flawlessly the trees"作定语修饰"mirrors"，"chirping in the mountains"修饰"birds"，"swimming on the blue water"修饰"ducks"，形成两个独立结构，均用现在分词替代定语从句，行文简洁，句型多变，结构严谨。

例2. 1月，独自一人，行走大龙菁仙人谷步道，爬坡下坎，沿途古木参天，溪流叮咚，卧龙树、仙人石景观活灵活现，包头王传说神奇美丽，2小时森林运动下来，小汗淋漓。

译文：In November, you may become sweaty after doing two-hour sports in the forest after walking alone along the footpath through Immortal Valley of Dalong Qing. The journey is filled with uphill climbs and slopes, ancient trees <u>towering to the skies,</u>

tinkling streams, crouching dragon trees, vivid Immortal Stones, and mysterious and beautiful legends of King Baotou.

分析：译文用"towering to the skies"作定语修饰"ancient trees"，替代了定语从句"which towers to the skies"，句式更加紧凑、简洁。

（4）过去分词用作后置定语替换被动定语从句

例1. 还有宋代朱熹、王十朋，明代张瑞图等历代文人骚客<u>留下的</u>摩崖石刻。

译文：In addition, there are inscriptions on the precipices <u>left by the ancient celebrities</u> such as Zhu Xi, Wang Shipeng of the Song Dynasty and Zhang Ruitu of the Ming Dynasty.

分析：此句用"left by the ancient celebrities"替代"which were left by the ancient celebrities"，使译文句式更加紧凑、明快，反映了旅游文本的一般特点。

例2. 登上玉京山，放眼四望，田畴上大小村庄星罗棋布，屋宇相连，阡陌纵横，滔浪起伏。

译文：Standing at the summit of the Yujing Hill and looking around, one will see down below level fields studded with hamlets and villages, where cottages stand in neat row, footpaths crisscross the farmland, and rice ears wave in the winds.

分析："大小村庄星罗棋布"译为"studded with hamlets and villages"，未用"which"引导定语从句；全句采用地点状语主位化和过去分词后置作定语，将5个四字格词语构成的意合句译为一句简洁明快的英文单句，有利于读者快速接受信息。

（5）名词词组作同位语

例1. 作为<u>一家专业的历史文化风貌保护开发企业</u>，衡复发展在项目开发过程中，力求最大程度遵循原真性。

译文：Hengfu, <u>a company specializing in protection and development of historic and cultural buildings</u>, tries its best to keep the original features of the valuable buildings.

分析：旅游英语常用同位语，以起到解释说明的作用。译文使用同位语而非独立句，使英文句型更加紧凑。

例2. 天安门，<u>原为明清两代皇城的正门</u>，始建于明永乐十五年（1417年），原名承天门，清顺治八年（1651年）改建后称天安门。

译文：Tian'anmen, <u>the major of the palace during the Ming and Qing dynasties</u> was first built in 1417, <u>the 15th year of Yongle reign of the Ming Dynasty</u>. Its original name of Chengtianmen (Gate of Bearing Heavens) was changed to its present in 1651, <u>the 8th year of the Qing Emperor Shunzhi's reign</u>.

分析：文中"the major of the palace during the Ming and Qing dynasties"为"Tian'anmen"的同位语；"the 15th year of Yongle reign of the Ming Dynasty"为"1417年"的同位语；"the 8th year of the Qing Emperor Shunzhi's reign"为"1651年"的同位语，后项是对前项的信息补充和说明，便于读者理解。

（6）祈使句的使用

例1. 整个桥统一和谐，人一踏上桥面，会同桥一起起伏荡漾，如泛轻舟。大家行走的时候，请走上桥中间的主走道板。<u>注意安全！请不要故意摇晃！</u>

译文：When you cross the bridge, there is an amazing experience: as soon as you set foot on bridge, you have the sensation of drifting in a small boat on calm waters. <u>Please keep to the wooden boards in the centre of the walkway and try not to sway too much.</u>

分析：祈使句有请求、命令、叮嘱、号召人们做某事的意义。译文将原文中的提示语译为："Please keep to the wooden boards in the center of the walkway and try not to sway too much."起到委婉的提示、劝告作用。

例2. <u>轻舟飞驰，顺激流而下</u>，本已神魂飘荡，岂知误入鬼谷，更见沿途两岸魅影重重，白骨森森，魔哭鬼笑不绝于耳，僵尸骷髅争起啮人，怎不令人心惊肉跳，夺命狂呼。此等百般恐吓，万端惊险，<u>非勇敢者莫行!</u>鬼谷漂流。

<u>Let the canoe rocket along with riptide</u>, which really make your mind fly over. But suddenly you will be frightened to death at the sight of scenery of ghost valley: images of ghost layer and layer along the sides, bones of the dead shining the terrible light, continuous cries and laughing of the monster and ghost, corpse and human skeleton disputing to eat human. How frightening to make living dead! Such threat by all means

and terror by all ways, without courage, please stop! Drifting in Ghost Valley.

分析：英文偏静态，汉语偏动态。为了增强英文旅游文本的呼唤功能，译文使用了两个祈使句："Let the canoe rocket along with riptide"和"please stop"，增强了文本的呼唤功能，使译文更加动态，有感染力。

3. 篇章特点

语篇结构是在特定的文化中组句成篇的方式。从语篇角度观察翻译，翻译就是由源语语篇引发的译语语篇生成过程（Neubert，1992：2）。译语语篇一旦形成，它就必须符合译语读者的思维方式和阅读习惯，而要做到这点，译者就应对源语语篇结构、信息排列、意义层次、语篇连贯及逻辑修辞等方面进行调整，以适合译文读者的思维方式和阅读习惯，否则译语语篇的可接受性就会大大降低（李运兴，2001：191）。由于汉、英旅游文本在篇章结构、语言表达、详略程度等方面存在较大差异，为了传递信息、感染受众，译者应尽可能使用译文读者熟悉的语言形式和篇章结构，以实现翻译的交际目的（祝东江，蒲轶琼：2015：83—85）。

（1）"分总"与"总分"

旅游文本的翻译应增进旅游者对旅游目的地的了解，激发他们的游览兴趣。为此，译者应选择符合译入语读者的语言传达文本的信息，实现跨文化交际意图（康宁，2005：85—89）。汉语语篇通常"先分后总"，即先描述，后分析、阐述，最后归纳总结。英语旅游文本通常"先总后分"，先用一个主题句概括全文中心思想，然后阐述或补充细节。翻译旅游文本，译者应根据译入语读者的思维习惯重构旅游文本的语篇结构。为了抓住读者的眼球，引起读者的兴趣，汉译英时可将主题提至句首，然后分条叙述，补充细节；英译汉，则反其道而行之。

例1. 金陵梅桩园位于古林公园西南角，占地4000平方米。它依原有山坡的自然地势而设，石景、铺装地、木桥、木构架亭等点缀其间，营造了自然、野趣的风格，为一座观赏梅树桩造型及梅花品种的专类园。梅树桩有一百多盆，有的生长数百年，有许多精品在全国的梅展上获得金、银等奖项。

译文：Jinling Plum Bonsai Garden <u>is a specialized garden</u> for enjoying both plum stump shapes and plum blossom varieties. It lies in the southwest corner of Gulin Park, covering an area of 4000 square meters. It is set up following the natural terrain of the original hillside, interspersed with rockscapes, pavements, wooden bridges and timber-framed pavilions, adding a natural and rustic charm. There are more than 100 plum stumps, some of which are more than 100 years old. Many quality products won gold, silver and other medals at the national plum bonsai exhibitions.

分析：通过阅读原文本，得知"……为一座观赏梅树桩造型及梅花品种的专类园"是本段的主题句。汉译英时，根据英文"先总后分"的语篇结构，应对此句的位置进行调整，将其放在句首，发挥开门见山、总揽全局、点名要旨的作用，再对主题句进行补充，描述细节，提供背景信息。这样既遵循了西方读者的思维逻辑，也符合英文的表达习惯，使译文结构严谨、重点突出、逻辑清晰，达到更好的旅游宣传效果。

例2. 天池的水从一个小缺口上溢出来，流出约1200米，从68米高的悬崖上往下泻，成为<u>著名的长白山大瀑布</u>。

译文：<u>The famous Changbai Waterfall</u> is formed by Heavenly Lake water running from an exit gently for about 1,200 meters (740 miles) and suddenly becoming churning rapids dropping from a 68-meter-high cliff.

分析：中文主旨句置于句末，采用的是"先分后总"的篇章结构。英译时应注意中、英思维的差异性和逻辑顺序，转换中、英思维，将最重要的主旨句置于句首，突出文本的重点信息，让读者先入为主，一目了然。译文遵循外国读者的思维逻辑，"先总后分"，符合英文的篇章布局和写作方式。

（2）主位与述位

主位（theme）是话语的出发点，是已知信息；述位（rheme）是话语信息的主体部分，是新信息，主位和述位共同组成主述结构（Halliday, 1970：161）。主位在句子最靠左即开头，句子围绕这个成分组成语篇，主位也是作者/译者欲突出的部分（丁大刚，2008：67）。英文旅游文本状语多"主位化"

（"thematization"），置于句首，而中文旅游文本中的"主位化"使用不多。时间、地点状语作为形式主位，有利于使无序的景点有序化，便于读者根据地点指示进行游览(刘辰诞，1999：63)。一个篇章中的主位结构是作者为达到一定的交际目的有意安排的，并不是简单的词序变化。无标记主位（unmarked theme）与有标记主位（marked theme）的交替使用能够避免篇章、句子结构的单一性，使篇章更富有变化，同时，消除由于形式单一带来的枯燥和乏味感觉，收到意想不到的文体效果（金春伟，2002：15）。

a. 时间、地点状语主位化

例1. All through the endless night, Pompeiians wandered about the streets or crouched in the ruined homes or clustered in the temples to pray.

整个不眠之夜，庞培人或在街上乱闯，或蜷缩在已毁的家里，或挤在神庙里祈祷。

分析：译文将表示时间或地点的状语前置，并不是简单地调整词序，而是提供不同的"出发点"。时间状语被主位化，强调的是事件发生的时间（"整个不眠之夜"），展现事件发生的脉络和过程。译文略有修改。

例2. Beneath the protecting shroud of ash, the city lay intact.

译文：在那层具有保护性的火山灰下，庞培城完好无损。

分析：奇怪的是，庞培这座城市竟"完好无损"。实际上也不奇怪，因为表示方位的状语"beneath the protecting shroud of ash"被主位化，作为已知信息提供给了读者，因此庞培城"完好无损"。"完好无损"是述位，是对主位给出的补充或说明。

b. 非谓语动词短语主位化

例1. 青岛坐落在山东半岛南部，依山临海，天姿秀美，气候凉爽，人称"东方瑞士"。白天，青岛宛如镶嵌在黄海边的绿宝石，夜里则像一只在大海中摆动的摇篮。难怪许多人乐意来这里疗养。

译文：Qingdao, known as the "Switzerland of the Orient", is situated on the southern tip of the Shandong Peninsula. Wedged between hills and waters, the city is endowed with a beautiful scenery and a delightful climate. By day, she looks like an emerald inlaid in the coastline of the Yellow Sea and, at night, a cradle rocking upon the sea waves. No wonder so many people would like to seek rest and relaxation here.

分析：旅游英语常将非谓语动词主位化，非谓语动词或短语置于句首，使景物的具体位置、面积、方位等在人们心中留下深刻印象，如译文为了突出青岛"依山临海"，将其译为"Wedged between hills and waters"，置于第二句的主语之前。

例2. 九寨沟的风光，因它的内涵丰富，<u>很难以一字穷述</u>，还需继续探幽发微。

译文：Jiuzhaigou is rich in natural beauty, <u>but to depict the diverse natural beauty of Jiuzhaigou in one or two words is not nearly enough</u>. So you should go and explore its beauty by yourself.

分析：译文使用动词不定式主位化，"很难以一字穷述"译为"but to depict the diverse natural beauty of Jiuzhaigou in one or two words is not nearly enough"，突出九寨沟之美，难以言表。"很难以一字穷述"与"还需继续探幽发微"两句想要表达寓意内涵近似，而"diverse"已有"内涵丰富"之意，均可省译。

四、旅游文本的体裁和类型

文本是语言的一种书面表现形式，它往往具备完整的含义，并且具有重要的指引作用，能够帮助人们去理解一项事物。也就是说，文本是一种功能性的书面文书，即不局限于长篇大论，可以是一篇结构完整的文章，可以是一段文字、一句话，甚至是一个具有完整意义的词（王菲，2015：128—129）。旅游文本是一种记叙、描写、介绍旅游活动和现象的应用型文本，体裁形式多样，包括旅游指南、旅游行程、旅游委托书、旅游广告、解说词、景点介绍、旅游推销手册、宣传手册、旅游地图、旅游宣传标语指示牌等（陈刚，2009：3）。

英国社会语言学家格雷厄姆·丹(Graham Dann)依据传播载体的差异将旅游文本分为声音、图像、书面和感觉文本，依据旅游阶段的差异将旅游文本又分为旅行前（pre-trip）、旅行中（on-trip）和旅行后（post-trip）文本（Dann，1996：

277）。旅行前文本有旅游广告、旅游宣传册、旅游宣传单、旅游合同等；旅游中文本有旅游指南、旅游景点介绍、导游词、旅游地图等；旅行后文本有旅行见闻、旅行报告、旅行评论等。但这种划分并不是固定的，比如旅行评论可以根据需要在旅行前、旅游中阅读（丁大刚，2008：14）。

从文本功能来讲，大多数旅游文本具有信息功能，也兼备"呼唤""诱导""审美""寒暄"等其他功能。需要注意的是，不同类型的旅游文本功能侧重不同，如旅游手册、指南、标示语以"信息型"为主；旅游广告以"呼唤型"为主；旅游网站、导游词、景点介绍、旅行后文本包括游记、旅行随笔则属复合型。各类旅游文本使用目的不同，语用、篇章结构也有较大差别。

1. 旅游广告

广告的特点是简明扼要、便于记忆、新颖独特。旅游广告的目的在于宣传旅游景点和推广旅游产品，刺激人们消费。因此，旅游广告往往篇幅短小精炼，表达独特，富有感情色彩和感染力。例如：

Daily Non-Stop to London 直达伦敦（维京航空公司）

A New Perspective 全新感受（芬兰航空公司）

Hada in hand, we'll be waiting for you. 手捧哈达等着您。（西藏自治区）

Breezes through Coconut Trees 椰风吹不尽（海南省）

2. 旅游网站

相比于线下旅行社，现代人更加倾向于在旅游网站查询资料、制订旅行计划。网站具有以下特点：版块明晰、信息充足、更新快速、反馈及时。旅游网站囊括旅游广告，旅行指南，旅行后文本，如游记、旅游评论等，因此，旅游网站的用语、句型、篇章结构等无法从一种类型的旅游文本中概括出来。总体来看，旅游网站篇幅庞大，架构多层，各版块既独立，又能构成一个整体。

图1.3　加拿大魁北克旅游网页

来源：https://www.quebec-cite.com/en，登录时间2021.3.3

图1.4　新加坡旅游网页

来源：http//www.visitsingapore.com/，登录时间2021.3.3

3. 旅游手册

旅游手册一般由语言文字和非语言文字两部分构成。语言文字部分通常包括标题、口号、正文、联系信息等。非语言文字部分包括标识（logo）、插图、地图等。通常情况下，旅游手册的正文会分几个部分，每个部分又有标题，分专题介绍目的地以及与旅游有关的事项。正文通常有以下内容：①旅游目的地或旅游设施的评价性断言。②旅游目的地或旅游设施简介。③以导游的形式介绍主要景点。④实用细节信息(例如地理位置、交通、联系方法、价格等）。⑤规章制度(例如禁止拍照、禁止给动物喂食等）（丁大刚，2008：59—61）。以下为两则旅游手册节选部分，供参考。

目　录

```
四川 ........................................ 1
  最佳旅行季节 ............................ 1
  艺术采风 ................................ 1
  民族风情 ................................ 2
  来去自如 ................................ 2
  吃在这里 ................................ 3
  购在这里 ................................ 3
  语言之妙 ................................ 3
  装备 .................................... 4
  预算 .................................... 5
  安全 .................................... 5
  实用信息 ................................ 5
```

图1.5　《藏羚羊自助旅行手册》

来源：《藏羚羊自助旅行手册》编写组.旅游黄金线自助游手册 四川·重庆[M].北京：中国轻工业出版社，2002.

(Depart 6 days earlier; meet the rest of the group in Lima on day 1 of the tour)

Visit the majestic islands of Galapagos, where animals roam free in their natural habitats. Live an incredible experience following Charles Darwin footsteps and sharing priceless moments with the mega diverse fauna that you will only encounter in this unique place.

Includes:
- 1 night in Guayaquil + transfers
- 4 nights accommodation at selected Hotels in Santa Cruz and Isabela
- Excursions & navigations with Naturalist English speaking guides
- Daily breakfast
- Additional economy class airfares

图1.6　《南美旅游手册》

来源：https://southamericatourism.com/brochures/，登录时间2021.3.6

旅游手册的篇章结构有以下两个特点：①篇章结构的不连续性和反复性。②地点、时间状语主位化（丁大刚，2008：65—67）。

例1. 四川又称"巴蜀",位于中国中部偏西的长江上游,东为长江三峡,西为青藏高原,北有秦岭,南有云贵高原,处于青藏高原向平原、丘陵过渡的地带,是中国古代重要的文明中心之一,战国时便有"天府之国"的美誉。魏、吴、蜀三国相争,在这片广袤大地上留下了深深的烙印。近年来成都广汉三星堆大量珍贵文物的出土,更将中华民族文明史推进到6000多年前。四川境内地貌复杂奇崛,河网密布,除川西北的白河、黑河属于黄河水系,其余均属长江水系。

四川的美食小吃让人欲罢不能,陈麻婆豆腐、夫妻肺片、赖汤圆、钟水饺、谭豆花、韩包子……连大师傅们都能跟着小吃创出名头,可想而知美味到了何种程度;更有鱼头火锅、兔火锅、鸡火锅、香菇火锅等各式各样麻辣诱人的佳肴,美不胜收。

就四川大多数风景区的自然风光而言,夏秋两季最美。夏季水量充沛,各地因水而增色不少;秋天则是绚烂多彩,观峨眉山雪景;到西岭雪山滑雪,则应冬季前往。

以感受民族风情为主要目的的朋友,应根据各民族的传统节日而选择合适的时间,譬如想看到康定跑马山"跑马溜溜"的场面,无疑要选择农历四月初八当地转山会这天。

四川著名剧种川剧以绝活"变脸"著称,流行于四川全省及云贵部分地区。木偶剧以杖头木偶最盛,其中川北大木偶乃杖头之最,流行于川北仪陇马鞍场一带,且多"人偶"(幼童扮演的)同台,以假乱真,亦真亦假。

……

进出四川以铁路和公路为主,也有飞机航班和水上交通。

分析:以上为旅游手册文字节选部分。首段介绍四川的地理位置、历史文化背景和地貌特征,下文依次介绍四川的美食、自然风光、民族风情、文化艺术及交通,各段落间相互独立,呈现篇章结构不延续的特点;手册语句围绕地点和时间展开,例如"战国时""近年来""四川境内""夏季""各地"等。旅游手册篇章结构还有反复性的特点,反复性是指各部分结构相似,内容反复。

例2. 这里有世纪曙光首照地括苍山;九台沟景色迷人;风电场雄奇宏伟;永安溪水清流翠。

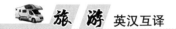

译文：In the western part of Linhai stands a towering mountain as Kuocang Mountain, atop which spreads a magnificent wind farm. On it shines the first rays of the sun at the beginning of the New Millennium in the Chinese mainland. Downhill extends a picturesque scenic range called Jiutaigou Valley. Along the foot winds the crystal clear Yong'an Stream.

分析：旅游手册还体现地点、时间状语主位化的文本特征。原文用四个分句转换表达方式，分别交代了四个景点的内容，是汉语行文各自为政的意合句。译文对原文的逻辑进行了调整，增译了"在临海西部""顶上""山顶""下山""山脚下"五个方位词，通过地点状语主位化，如"In the western part of Linhai stands...""On it shines...""Along the foot winds..."等，置于小句句首，以线性发展方式展开，亦实现了英语语法的连贯、句子结构的一致、思维的融合。

4. 旅游公示语

在旅游景区内，与旅游宣传册、地图、传单等相比，公示语更加引人注目。旅游公示语的作用在于给予游客指示和提醒。旅游公示语的篇章结构具有以下特点：

（1）短小精悍

标示语讲究简洁精确、突显醒目，因此篇幅必须短小、内容准确。例如：

Beverage Not Included 酒水另付

Passengers Only 游客止步

Staff Only 闲人免进

（2）开门见山

旅游标示语往往采用开门见山的结构，提高效率，明确意义，快速传递信息。例如：

Look Around and Then Across! 一站、二看、三通过！

Stay away from scalpers! 请勿跟随黄牛到市场外交易，以防不测。

If you see anything suspicious, call 110 for the police. 发现可疑情况，请拨110

报警。

（3）语体多样

旅游标示语篇章具有不同语体。例如：

Mind your head! 小心碰头！（口语体）

The grass so fair, needs your care. 小草青青，足下留情。（诗歌语体）

Your satisfaction is our priority. 您的满意是我们的追求。（广告语体）

For your own rights and benefits, please ask for the receipt and keep it for any claim. 为保障您的权益，索取并妥善保存发票。（法律语体）

Attention: Strike the window with this hammer for escape in case of fire.

乘客须知：发生火灾时，请用榔头击碎车窗玻璃逃生。（说明语体）

5. 旅游景点介绍

旅游景点介绍是在旅游景点使用、以说明文体介绍景点基本情况的一种文本，其功能主要在于传递信息，但也兼有教育功能、诱导功能、移情功能、审美功能等，增加旅游者的人文、历史、自然等知识，增强他们的游览兴趣。旅游景点介绍、说明词多为信息型文本，一般具有内容客观、文字简练、目的明确等特征（张姣，2013：128）。

中国人介绍景点时，篇章内容和形式上受古代骈体文影响，讲究整齐对偶、声韵和谐，大量使用排比对称、四字结构、修饰性词语和烘托性的语言，读起来朗朗上口，给人以美的享受（张正荣，黄婷，何姣姣，2009：55）；结构上以空间顺序发展，以归纳方式为主；而英文景点资料则强调自然客观，文风平实，较少使用主观色彩强烈的词汇，句式简洁，篇章开门见山，以线性顺序发展，以推论方式为主。

例1. <u>山清水秀</u>，<u>沙滩秀美</u>，<u>瀑布磅礴</u>，<u>竹林茂密</u>，村舍<u>星罗棋布</u>，构成了一幅<u>美丽</u>的山水画，游客们沉浸其中，感受舒适、安宁、和谐的惬意。

分析：这是一则桂林漓江的中文景点介绍，开篇连用5个四字词语，结构工整，音律和谐，极富画面感。该句以空间顺序描写，由远及近，由大及小，经过一系列铺垫后总结突出了漓江秀丽的景色。

例2. Watching Old Faithful Geyser erupt is a Yellowstone National Park tradition. People from all over the world have journeyed here to watch this famous geyser. The park's wildlife and scenery might be as well-known today, but it was the unique thermal features like Old Faithful Geyser that inspired the establishment of Yellowstone as the world's first national park in 1872.

分析：这是一则关于老忠实间歇泉的英文景点介绍，全段为推论式结构，首先告知游客此地为必游之地，引起重视，接下来论述该景点的客观事实，用词简朴直观，只用了几个形容词，如"famous""well-known""unique"以及"the world's first"表示最高级的表达方式，不像中文旅游文本那样极尽渲染、烘托之能事，符合英文旅游文本注重写实的特点。

例3. 胡家大院傍河而建，前有临街店铺，后有运河码头，既有北方大院的壮观沉实，又有南方住宅的灵巧秀美，体现了"顺天然，亲人和"的精神追求。

译文：Built along the riverside, with shops along the frontage street and a canal wharf in the back, Hu Family Courtyard blends the Northern and Southern architectural styles of China, both spectacular and delicate. This best represents harmony between man and nature, a spirit highly valued in Chinese culture.

分析：原文结构工整，音律和谐，四字词相互对仗。此外，原文按空间顺序描写"胡家大院"前后左右的样貌，给人一种立体的感觉。译文则并未拘泥于原文的篇章结构，而是灵活调整原文结构，地点状语主位化，置于句首，用质朴的语言描写景物。

例4. Connecticut's magnificent 105-mile-(170-kilometre-)long shoreline, is scalloped by coves, inlets, and harbors, dotted with beaches, marinas, and state parks. Historic towns and villages also lie along the coast.

译文：康涅狄格州海岸线长170千米，美丽壮观。海岸线上呈扇形排列着多个小海湾和大小港口，还点缀着众多海滩、小船坞和州立公园，海滨还有不少历史村镇。

分析：原文篇章内容十分简洁，用了大量名词，无过多花里胡哨的渲染和烘托，在结构上呈英文线性顺序发展，流畅连续。

6. 导游词

导游词是导游人员引导游客观光游览的讲解词。在篇章结构上，导游词一般分为3个部分：欢迎词、景点讲解、欢送词。在篇章内容上，导游词应该具备口语化、知识性、逻辑性、美感性和现场感等特点（丁大刚，2008：114）。无论是站立式讲解还是移动式讲解，导游词的撰写或翻译都应遵守"面中取点""点面结合""以点带面""以点拓面"的要求，做到重点突出，即景生情，双向互动，景点讲解与讲解对象应当做到时空融合，均在游客的可视范围之内（朱华，2016：29—30）。导游词的翻译既要如实介绍景点信息，又要生动形象，激发听众的兴趣和共鸣。

例1. Dear friends, there are some colored frescoes on the cliff. They're cliff paintings of men and women, flowers and animals. The red colors have not faded yet for hundreds of years. Although many mysteries of the Bo people remain unresolved, their cliff paintings clearly show us how they lived, and how they loved and hated.

译文：亲爱的朋友们，悬崖上刻有彩色壁画。<u>有男人</u>，<u>有女人</u>，<u>有花儿</u>，<u>还有动物</u>。<u>百年风雨</u>，<u>历经沧桑</u>，悬崖上的壁画仍旧光彩如新。<u>僰人之谜</u>，<u>迷雾重重</u>，但这些壁画清晰地展示了他们的生活方式，他们的<u>爱恨情仇</u>。

分析：这是一则四川僰人悬棺景点导游词。英文语言质朴，用朴实、简洁的语言描述景点的特点；而译文采用分译法，"有……有……还有……"的排比句，使译文顿时有了动感，文本有了气息。此外译文还使用了许多四字词语，朗朗上口，又极富美感，符合中文导游词的语言特点。

例2. 大家好。很高兴能和大家一起游览有着"人间天堂"美称的苏州。苏州自古以来就被人们誉为"园林之城"，有"江南园林甲天下，苏州园林甲江南"的说法。苏州以园林美景久负盛名，享誉天下。苏州古典园林历史绵延2000余年，在世界造园史上有其独特的历史地位和价值。1997年12月，联合国教科文组织遗产委员会将苏州古典园林列入世界文化遗产名录。

下面我们就进入留园去细细品味一番吧。首先，请大家回头看一下刚刚经过的这扇黑漆大门，大家一定感到非常奇怪，为什么这么别致的园林，门厅却如此不起眼呢？其实，苏州的园林很多都是辞官引退后回乡的官僚所建的私家花园。

他们由于长期在朝为官，深感身心疲惫，所以不愿应酬世俗烦事，只想去追求一种寄情山水的隐居生活。因此，苏州的私家园林均无气派显眼的高大门楼，其正门都力求淡化、简单，以求接近普通民居。

译文：Hello, My dear friends. It's my pleasure to join you while visiting this beautiful city, Suzhou, which is dubbed "the heaven on earth". Since ancient times, Suzhou has been praised as "the city of gardens", and there is an old saying "gardens in the south of Yangtze River belittle those elsewhere, and Suzhou's gardens belittle those in the south of the Yangtze River". Due to their beautiful scenery, Suzhou's gardens enjoy good reputation both at home and abroad. It has a history of more than 2,000 years which earned it unique historical status and value in world gardening history. In December of 1997, UNESCO designated Suzhou's Classical Gardens as a World Heritage Site.

Now, <u>let's go and appreciate all this beautiful scenery</u> in the Liu Garden. Firstly, <u>please turn back and look at the black gate we have just walked through.</u> <u>You must feel strange why</u> in such an unconventional garden the gate isn't conspicuous. In fact, most gardens in Suzhou were built as private gardens by officials after they resigned from their posts. After a long period of being officials, they were exhausted and no longer wanted to deal with vexing problems. They just wished to pursue a life in solitude, so none of the private gardens in Suzhou have big gates. They are very simple and similar to gates at ordinary people's houses.

分析：首先介绍苏州园林的历史地位、园林特色、艺术价值等，以"面中取点"开篇；接着取"点"留园，重点介绍留园门的艺术特点，"以点带面""点面结合"，拓展了苏州古典园林的文化内涵。导游词语言朴实但不乏修辞，如使用比喻、拟人等修辞手法；第一人称和第二人称交替使用，采用作者视角介入、读者视角介入，如"let's go and appreciate all this beautiful scenery..." "please turn back and look at the black gate we have just walked through." "You must feel strange why..."增强了文本的对话性，拉近了与游客的距离。

7. 旅行后文本

旅行后文本指的是旅行见闻、报告、评论、游记等。此类文本包括但不限于说明文、散文、记叙文等题材。旅行后文本表达的是旅游者的心声，多以第一人称的口吻叙述，记叙旅游目的地自然知识、人文知识、风俗文化等方面的内容（丁大刚，2008：216），常用夹叙夹议，对所见所闻发表个人主观性评价，作者身份的可识别性高，描写对象的地域性明显。旅行后文本不同于旅游景点介绍、导游词预制文本，具有个性化的特征，更能吸引个性化的游客，是游客喜闻乐见的一种旅游文本。

例1. ...that is to say, within a mile of the main ocean—no stranger, I say, but would expect to see its entrance into the sea at that place, and a noble harbour for ships at the mouth of it; when on a sudden, the land rising high by the seaside, crosses the head of the river, like a dam, checks the whole course of it, and it returns, bending its course west, for two miles, or thereabouts; and then turning north, through another long course of meadows...

分析：这是一段旅行后文本。文本以作者视角介入，以第一人称的口吻描写了韦弗尼河流向突变的情况，并运用拟人化的写作手法，将高高突起的陆地比作一个人，仿佛"审视"整条大河的流向，为读者带来了刺激新鲜的阅读体验。作者视角介入、夹叙夹议、主观评述、文本的地域特色都体现了旅行后文本的特征。

例2. 东西两石垒，高各有二三百尺，离江面约两里来远，东西台相去只有一二百步，但其间却夹着一条深谷。立在东台，可以看得出罗芷的人家，回头展望来路，风景似乎散漫一点儿，而一上谢氏的西台，向西望去，则幽谷里的情景，却绝对的不像是在人间了。我虽则没有到过瑞士，但到了西台，朝西一看，立时就想起了曾在照片上看见过的威廉·退尔的祠堂。这四山的幽静，这江水的青蓝，简直同在画片上的珂罗版色彩，一色也没有两样，所不同的就是在这儿的变化更多一点儿，周围的环境更芜杂不整齐一点儿而已，但这却是好处，足以代表东方民族性的颓废荒凉的美。

分析：这是一段描写"钓台山"的旅行后文本。文中以第一人称视角描写了

"钓台山"的自然风光，文中涉及诸多人文景点，如"罗芷的人家""谢氏的西台""威廉·退尔的祠堂"等。作者以清新自然的文笔渲染了景点静寂的意境，描写了萧瑟垂条之美，抒发了浓重的个人情感。

本章小结

根据雷柏尔旅游系统模型和旅游活动的特点，旅游翻译可分为游前、游中、游后翻译，即旅游者从客源地到目的地"离""经""到"的翻译过程。游前翻译包括：旅游广告、旅游网站、旅游指南、旅游手册；游中翻译包括：旅游景点介绍、景点导游词；游后翻译包括：游记、博客、旅游评论等。中文旅游文本辞藻华丽，多用四字词语，重修辞渲染，出现大量历史典故、历史人物等，善引用文人墨客的诗词、楹联，用修辞手法铺垫和营造独特意境；英文旅游文本文风朴实，重逻辑，重写实，偏向用客观理性的语言描述事实，多用名词、分词、动名词、形容词、非谓语动词。中文旅游文本人文色彩比较浓烈，主观感受融入客观事物，文本中出现大量典故、引言、历史人物等；句式松散灵活，常用对偶、排比修辞手法，使句子工整、对仗；英文旅游文本比较客观、理性，常以"旁观者"的身份描写事物；注重逻辑性，语言成分按语法严格排列，层次分明。翻译旅游文本应根据中、英旅游文本的不同特点，采取不同的翻译策略和方法，满足不同文化背景游客的审美需求。

翻译实践

一、热身练习

翻译下文，并对译文做简要分析。

1. 坐潭上，四面竹树环合，寂寥无人，凄神寒骨，悄怆幽邃。

2. Inside are strange peaks, limestone caves, rare birds and towering trees, together with spring babbling on the way and mists weathering the mountain tops.

3. 园区是一片倾斜的海岸，没有刻意的雕琢，也不震撼人心，似乎只是造物主的原作，幽静恬美。徜徉其间，但见白浪激礁，松林覆坡，红岩嶙峋，沙滩如银，景色如画如诗。

4. Welcome to breath-taking views, unforgettable moments and impressive scenery. Springtime in Interlaken debauches with blooming landscapes, natural alpine air, crystal clear rivers and rustling waterfalls. Snow-covered mountains and sunny days invite for springtime skiing in the Jungfrau region.

5. 中国历史名人曹操曾赋诗赞曰："慨当以慷，忧思难忘；何以解忧？唯有杜康。"

6. The harbor looked most beautiful in its semi-circle of hills and half-lights. The color of a pearl gray and a fairy texture...This Arctic scenery has a beauty which is the exact antithesis of the Christmas card of tradition. Soft, melting halftones. Nothing brittle or garish.

7. 这儿的峡谷又是另一番景象：谷中急水奔流，穿峡而过，两岸树木葱茏，鲜花繁茂，碧草萋萋，活脱脱一幅生机盎然的天然风景画。各种奇峰异岭，令人感受各异，遐想万千。

8. The barrier islands are unoccupied, so the coral here is healthier and the water even cleaner than in the more popular parks farther south.

9. 十八水景区位于广西贺州市北郊21公里处的路花山区。因峡内飞瀑十八处，故名"十八水"。

10. If you have an interest in experiencing the life of the local people, you might as well book a room in a resident's home and learn to cook home local dishes with what you've just bought from the water market.

二、巩固练习

翻译下文，并对译文做简要分析。

1. In the new millennium, abundant parklands, a vibrant downtown, and a number of well-known museums define this growing city. Denver is set picturesquely at the foothills of the Rocky Mountains.

2. 整个门庭冷冷清清，一脉相承的雷姓后代三百多人都搬出了故居。

3. Whether a destination or a midway stop on the way through, you'll find great opportunities to play, discover, and explore.

4. 花径公园有白居易堂、觅春园、孔雀馆等参观景点，是集山水、人文、古代、现代为一体的综合性公园。

5. The lake is one of the most beautiful in the country and offers one of the most panoramic views thanks to the many small rises in the land which allow you to admire the unspoiled and boundless countryside.

6. 北戴河，在宁静与内敛中任时光流逝，看涛走云飞，花开花谢，成就不朽的传奇，等待着懂得她的美的旅游者到来。

7. Taiwan Island is rich in more than 110 kinds of minerals with coal, oil, natural gas, gold, silver, copper and sulphur as its main resources. It is also extremely rich in terrestrial heat, a great variety of plants and forest occupies 52% of the land area of the whole island, holding the first place in all China. It is rich in water resources too and the output of Taiwan's coral occupies about 80% of the world total production, winning the fame of "The Kingdom of Coral". Taiwan is also one of the main regions which export butterflies in the world.

8. 福建山清水秀，风光旖旎，更兼有众多人文景观，民俗风景独具。惠安女、客家女的服饰与故事，畲族"三月三"，高山族丰年祭……无一不是九州奇葩、八闽一绝。

9. The city is remarkably intimate and accessible, its compact layout ripe for rambling. You never know what you'll find among the atmospheric lanes: a hidden garden, an antique book market, a 17th-century distillery—always worlds-within-worlds, where nothing ever seems the same twice.

10. 福州定光塔，俗称白塔，于唐天佑元年（904年）最早用木头搭建而成。据说在挖掘地基时发现了闪闪发光的宝珠。因此，该塔取名"定光塔"。明嘉靖十三年间（1534年）被雷火击毁。四年后在原址重建了一座砖塔，塔高只有原先的四分之三。

三、阅读翻译

阅读下文，重点翻译下画线部分。

Sentosa

Before it was known as Sentosa, this island just off Singapore's southern coast was a British military fortress. After the Japanese Occupation in World War II, Singapore returned to British rule, and the island was renamed "Sentosa" which translates to "peace and tranquility". <u>Over the course of its remarkable history, Sentosa has transformed into a beloved island resort, known for its tropical beaches, luxurious hotels and thrilling attractions.</u> Whether you're looking for an adrenaline rush or a day of bold exploration, a world of adventure awaits you at Sentosa.

Avid explorers looking to discover the island's varied charms and natural landscapes will be able to choose from a range of inspiring activities. To get your bearings, take reference from three beaches that span Sentosa's coastline. <u>Each beach holds its own unique charm: Siloso Beach is the island's most bustling stretch, and home to various restaurants and attractions; Palawan Beach's playgrounds, parks and lagoon are perfect for families, and Tanjong Beach is ideal for a tranquil gateway.</u>

Nature lovers fascinated with Southeast Asia's wealth of tropical flora and fauna can further their pursuit of knowledge with a hands-on journey at Sentosa Nature Discovery. This nature trail begins at an interactive gallery—where visitors will get the chance to brush up on their skills of scientific enquiry—followed by a showcase of Sentosa's teeming wildlife and heritage trees native to Singapore and Southeast Asia.

Drop by the S.E.A. Aquarium for a trip under the sea, one of the largest oceanariums on the planet, this attraction is home to more than 100,000 marine animals, allowing for up-close encounters with fascinating creatures from the deep. <u>A range of educational programmes makes this a perfect location for families looking to foster a love for learning and growth in their little ones.</u>

Soar high on adrenaline, as you partake in Sentosa's various thrill-seeking attractions.

<u>To live out your dreams of soaring like a superhero, drop by iFly Singapore, the world's largest wind tunnel for indoor skydiving.</u> The 18-foot-tall acrylic "glass walls"—allow you to enjoy panoramic views of the South China Sea and Siloso Beach. State-of-the-art technology will lend you wings in an experience that simulates free falls from heights of 12,000 to 3,000 feet. First timers need not fret, as trained professionals will be on hand to guide you.

For more high-octane activity, brave new heights at the Mega Adventure Park—Singapore. The park's star attraction—dubbed the MegaZip—is Southeast Asia's steepest zip wire. Those courageous enough to hop on this adrenaline-pumping ride will get to experience a whole new perspective of Sentos's lush jungles and white beaches from 450 metres in the air. Other activities include a high ropes course, rock climbing wall and a 15-metre free fall simulator.

If a day of sun, sand and surf is up your alley, spend the afternoon at Hydrodash instead. <u>Located along the waters of Palawan Beach, Singapore's first floating aquapark is an unforgettable experience for the young and the young at heart.</u> Romp with your family and loved ones as you slide, slip and splash through the zones of this massive inflatable obstacle course.

After all that fast-paced action, wind down and experience Sentosa and Faber Peak as you take a ride on the Cable Car Sky Network, and soak in a stunning bird's-eye view of Sentosa island and Mount Faber.

第二章　旅游翻译策略和方法

旅游文本蕴含着丰富的人文、历史、地理、文化信息，大部分旅游文本会涉及当地的人文地理、风土人情。旅游翻译并不是单纯的语言转换或结构性改写，也不是原文与译文在词汇、句法、语篇、文体上的"对等"，而是在功能上和交际上应具有"充分性"（adequacy）。奈达认为："对于翻译中的文化交流，不能拘泥于词汇、语法、修辞手段的对比，更重要的是让读者理解并欣赏译语的文化内涵。"（Nida，2001：78）纽马克（Peter Newmark）强调："译文对译语读者产生的效果与原文对原文读者产生的效果一致。"（Newmark, 1988:22）因此，旅游翻译必须掌握与旅游文本相适应的翻译策略和方法，在交际功能上需具有"充分性"；在交际效果上需具有"一致性"。但是由于中、英语言文化上的"不可通约性"，如何让读者理解旅游文本中的文化和民族特色，有效传递旅游信息，对译者来讲，是一个巨大的挑战。

一、功能翻译理论与旅游翻译

旅游翻译属于应用翻译的一种，翻译目的性很强。旅游的翻译目的是传播蕴含在自然和人文景观中的旅游信息，以便吸引游客旅游；而读者阅读旅游文本的目的是接收旅游信息，了解目的地的自然风光、风土人情等，以便决定是否出行以及出行的方式。译者对源语文本信息的选择、翻译策略的运用以及译文形式的确定应根据文本的功能和翻译目的做出决定，不能局限于传统译论所强调的"信""达""雅"，从而影响译文在译语文化环境中的交际功能和作用。功能翻译理论的这些主张与旅游翻译的要求契合，是指导旅游翻译的理论基础。

由此看来，翻译并不是单纯的语言转换，而是一种"交际互动"（"communicative interaction"）、"跨文化活动"（"cross culture event"）。翻译的目的和功能是译者考虑的最重要的因素,也是决定翻译策略和方法的根本出发点。在这一过程中,委托人与被委托人之间是一种互动关系。它要求译者根据委托人的翻译要求("translation brief")、文本的类型和功能以及翻译活动的目的决定源语文本信息的选择、翻译策略的运用以及译文的表现形式,以便顺利完成翻译跨文化活动的文化转换和交际目的(Snell,2001:47),而不是追求译文与原文的"忠实"和"对等"。

1. 文本功能和类型

德国翻译理论家凯瑟琳娜·赖斯(Katharina Reiss)认为:"在正常的情况下,文本类型决定译者的翻译方法;文本类型是影响译者选择适当翻译方法的首要因素"(Reiss & Vermeer, 1984:175)。旅游领域很广,文本体裁不同,涉及不同文本类型,而不同的文本类型有不同的文本功能。赖斯把文本功能主要分为内容突出型文本(content-focused texts),亦称"信息型"文本;形式突出型文本(form-focused texts),亦称"表达型"文本;感染突出型文本(appeal-focused texts),亦称"操作型"或"感染型"文本三种,译者应根据文本类型及其功能采取相应的翻译策略和翻译方法。翻译"信息功能"文本时,译文要充分传达指涉功能;翻译"表达功能"文本时,译文风格要以原文本为导向;翻译"操作功能"文本时,可采用"归化法",以便译文读者获得与原文读者相同的情感反应(刘军平,2009:375),也就是"一致性"。

2. "目的论"

翻译具有明确的目的性,是一种以原文为基础的、有目的的、人际的跨文化言语交际活动。功能翻译理论的核心是"目的论"(Skopostheorie),由德国翻译理论家赖斯和汉斯·费米尔(Hans Vermeer)提出。"目的论"认为,受译语读者文化、期待和需求的影响,译文的受众才是翻译最重要的因素,而不是传统翻译理论认为的以"忠实"为核心要素的原文和作者。旅游文本的翻译,无论是英译汉还是汉译英,都应着眼于翻译目的和译文预期的功能,结合译文读者的社会文化背景知识、对译文的期待或社会知识以及交际需要等,决定具体的翻译策略和翻译方法。为了实现文本的预期功能和翻译目的，可采用"等功能翻译"，也可能采用"异功能翻译"。

二、旅游翻译的策略

旅游翻译是一种跨语言、跨社会、跨时空、跨文化、跨心理的交际活动。同其他类型的翻译相比，它在跨文化、跨心理交际特点上表现得更为直接、突出、典型、全面（陈刚，2004：59）。由于旅游翻译的特殊性、多样性和杂合性，在处理旅游文本时，译者应重视中外语言文化差异，采取与旅游文本相适应的翻译策略，才能取得"跨语言、跨社会、跨时空、跨文化、跨心理"的不同群体读者期望的阅读期待和翻译效果。好的译文便于旅客查阅信息、了解景点的情况，还可以使没有条件或不愿旅游的人不必前往旅游目的地便能通过翻译的文字了解该目的地的自然景观和人文景观（朱梅，2017：01），而要取得好的翻译效果，必须掌握正确的翻译策略和方法。

1. 翻译策略的基本概念

语义翻译与交际翻译是两大翻译策略。语义翻译强调在译文中尽可能保留原作者的语言特色和表达方式，保留原文的结构和文体风格；交际翻译要求摆脱原文结构的束缚，发挥译语的优势，强调功能对等，更注重的是译文的整体效果，译文与原文在语言、内容、文体风格等方面可以不一致。"异化"和"归化"是偏重文化翻译的概念。"异化"要求保留原文的"异质性"；"归化"要求用译入语的表达方式获取或代替原文的语言和文化符号。"直译"和"意译"主要局限于语言层面的翻译，"异化"和"归化"则立足于文化背景下的翻译，"异化"可视为"直译"概念的延伸，而"归化"可视为"意译"概念的延伸。

（1）语义翻译与交际翻译

交际翻译与语义翻译的根本区别在于交际翻译强调信息产生的效果，语义翻译强调信息内容传递本身。语义翻译力争表现原文确切的意义，译文尽可能保留原文的结构和文体，强调再现作者的思维过程而非其意图，力求保留原作者的语言特色和独特的表达方式。因此，语义翻译追求的是译文内容的准确性，强调"对等"、客观，要求尽量保留原文词汇和句法的特色（杨士焯，1989：68），在译文中呈现源语的语言结构和特征。在翻译方法上多用"异化"，采用直译，译文直接、具体，但有可能造成"认知意义和语用意义"的丢失，出现读者感到晦涩难懂的情况。

交际翻译更多考虑的是读者的感受，更强调译文的可读性和译文读者的反应，要求"摆脱原文结构的束缚，发挥译语的优势"（廖七一，2004：48）。为此，译者可对原文进行改写、编译，有权调整原文的逻辑关系，重新组织句法，运用译语更常见的搭配方式和常用词语。由于交际翻译不拘泥于原文的内容或形式，注重的是译文的整体效果，在翻译方法上多用"归化"，采用增译、省译、合译、重构、转换、逆序等翻译方法，以弥补语义翻译中的语言和文化缺失，使译文更流畅、地道，简明易懂。但由于交际翻译或增、或减、或改，可能导致一些内容被忽略或过度阐释，偏离原文的意义。

（2）"异化"与"归化"

"异化"翻译是指在一定程度上保留原文的"异域性"或"异质性"（foreignness）、故意打破目标语言常规的一种翻译策略。"异化"（"foreignization"）以源语文化为归宿，采用作者所使用的源语表达方式传达原文的内容。在"异化"翻译中，译者向源语作者靠拢，吸纳源语的表达方式，保留外来文化的语言特点。"异化"翻译考虑民族文化的差异性，保存和反映异域民族的语言风格，让译文读者理解原文中的"异国情调"；而"归化"（"domestication"）从译文读者视角来实现源语本土化，主要考虑目的语读者的语言习惯和接受能力，运用符合译入语的文化及语言表达方式的方法来传递原文内容。"归化"翻译以目的语语言和文化为归依，遵循目标语言的规范并用目标文化材料替代源语旅游文化，采取符合目标语读者的语言习惯的方式进行翻译，让译语读者能够从译入语的表达方式获取原文的意义，理解外来文化的语言特点。

从翻译实践来看，"异化"和"归化"与语义翻译和交际翻译相对应，但更偏重文化翻译。无论使用"归化"还是"异化"，都需要在两者中进行动态选择，或两者并用，不能仅用一种翻译方法。"异化"翻译故意打破目标语言常规，追求一种不透明、不流畅的言语风格，且译本中所含源语文化信息过多，容易造成译文晦涩难懂；而"归化"翻译由于抹杀了源语文化的"异域性""异质性"，有可能不利于本土文化的对外传播，因此过度"归化"对于中国"文化走出去"亦不可取（汪宝荣，2005：13—17）。归化、异化策略的选择应结合本土文化，有利于本土文化对外传播，同时考虑译文读者的审美心理和语言习惯，多角度、多方位地实现旅游翻译的跨文化交际。

（3）"直译"与"意译"

从历史上来看，"异化"和"归化"可以被视为"直译"和"意译"的概念延伸，但又不完全等同于"直译"和"意译"。"直译"和"意译"关注的核心问题是如何在语言层面处理形式和意义，而"异化"和"归化"则突破了语言因素的局限，将视野扩展到语言、文化和美学等层面。按韦努蒂（Venuti）的说法，"归化法"是"把原作者带入译入语文化"，而"异化法"则是"接受外语文本的语言及文化差异，把读者带入外国情景"（Venuti，1995:20）。由此可见，"直译"和"意译"主要是局限于语言层面的价值取向，"异化"和"归化"则立足于文化大语境下的价值取向，两者之间的差异还是显而易见的。"异化"和"归化"通常归为翻译策略，而"直译"和"意译"归属翻译方法。

视频学习：观看视频，试分析翻译策略在解说中国传统节日春节中的运用。

词汇/翻译策略	春节	年夜饭	红包	除夕	春联	福	年糕	牛年	饺子	压岁钱	守岁
归化	Chinese New Year	New Year Feast/ reunion dinner	lucky money	New Year's Eve	New Year scrolls	blessing	rice cake	in the year of Ox	dumplings	lucky money	waiting for the New Year to arrive
异化	Spring Festival		Hongbao/ red packets			Fu					

2.语义翻译策略指导下的旅游翻译

语义翻译策略指导下的旅游翻译，常用"异化"翻译。"异化"翻译法使译文冲破目的语语言和文化的束缚，保留原文中的异国情调。就保留源语旅游文化、促进旅游消费和文化交流而言，"异化"翻译有利于在目标语中保留我国旅游文化的异国情调，增强国外游客的好奇心，激发其旅游兴趣和旅游行为，也有利于对外文化传播。但"异化"翻译也有缺陷，生僻的术语、不流畅的言语风格，以及译文中所含源语的大量文化信息可能会造成译文晦涩难懂，从而降低旅游语篇的可读性和可接受性（郭建中，1998：15），阻碍旅游者的旅游行为。

例1. 为了吸引更多的来自世界各地的游客，新疆的许多城市建设都保留了当地的文化特色。乌鲁木齐、吐鲁番、哈密、昌吉、伊犁、库尔勒、喀什、和田等城市都将古丝绸之路遗迹保存了下来……

译文：Many cities in Xinjiang have preserved their cultural characteristics in order to attract more tourists from all over the world. Some cities keep the relics of the ancient Silk Road, such as Urumqi, Turpan, Hami, Changji, Ili, Korla, Kashi, Hotan and so on.

分析：这段译文中，译者对地名的翻译采用了"异化"翻译策略，新疆地名根据当地少数民族语言的发音译出，"乌鲁木齐"译为"Urumqi"，"吐鲁番"译为"Turpan"，"伊犁"译为"Ili"，"库尔勒"译为"Korla"，"喀什"译为"Kashi"，"和田"译为"Hotan"；也有直接用汉语拼音译出的，比如"哈密"译为"Hami"，"昌吉"译为"Changji"。采用"异化"翻译，可以保留少数民族文化在目标语中文化的独特性和"异质性"。

例2. 1989年和1990年，先后在郧阳区青曲镇曲远河口的学堂梁子发现了两具人类头骨化石，属直立人类型。

译文：In 1989 and 1990, two fossils of Homo erectus skulls were discovered at Xuetang Liangzi at mouth of Quyuan River in Qingqu Town, Yunyang District.

分析：译文倾向于本族化，向源语、作者靠拢，将"郧阳区"译为"Yunyang District"，"青曲镇"译为"Qingqu Town"，"曲远河口"译为"mouth of Quyuan River"，让西方读者了解中国的语言和文化，把西方读者带入中国情景，即便是"学堂梁子"也将其译为"Xuetang Liangzi"，采用的是语义翻译策略。

"学堂"很容易让人联想到英文"school",但"学堂梁子"是一个地名,因此译文采用音译法。

3. 交际翻译策略指导下的旅游翻译

交际翻译策略指导下的旅游翻译大多使用"归化"策略,旨在尽量减少译文中的异国情调,为目的语读者提供一种自然流畅的译文。旅游文本中的历史人物、典故是一个国家或地区特有的文化色彩词,在翻译这些文化色彩浓重的词时,如果过多"异化"会增加译语读者的阅读障碍。"归化"翻译遵循目标语言规范,向目标语读者靠近,译文流畅,因而通俗易懂、雅俗共赏,可读性和可接受性都较高,比异化翻译更能吸引潜在外国游客。旅游文本中的历史人物、典故是一个国家或地区特有的文化色彩词,在翻译这些文化色彩浓重的词时,过多"异化"会增加译语读者的阅读障碍。但由于"归化"翻译过分倚重目标语言的固有表达形式和文化,在一定程度上会影响中国文化在目标语中的"显现",不利于中国文化对外传播,因此过度"归化"在旅游文本外译中也是不可取的。

例1. 位于广西壮族自治区东北部的桂林,是中国著名的历史文化名城,素有"桂林山水甲天下"之美誉。

译文:Located in the northeast of Guangxi Zhuang Autonomous Region, Guilin has always been a famous historic and cultural city in China, reputed as "East or west, Guilin landscape is the best".

分析:译文采取了交际翻译策略,套译西方文化中的俗语"East or west, home is the best",将"桂林山水甲天下"进行"归化"处理,比直译为"Guilin landscape is the best in the world"更容易吸引西方游客。

例2. 云冈石窟是在北魏中期起凿的,北魏经历了"太武灭佛""文成复法"。文成帝和平年间,云冈石窟开始大规模营建,前后计六十多年。

译文:From the mid period of Bei Wei Dynasty, the massive construction of Yungang Grottoes started and during that time, the whole nation experienced Persecution of Buddhism by Emperor Tai Wu and then Renaissance of Buddhism by Emperor Wen Cheng as well. After that, from He Ping Era of Emperor Wen Cheng (about A.D. 460—465), Yun Gang Grottoes had been under massive construction over 60 years in total.

分析：原文讲述太武帝在位期间曾两度下诏灭佛，云冈现存45座石窟、59000余尊佛像在文成帝"复法"后开始修建，持续六十余年建成。译文采取交际翻译策略，将"太武灭佛""文成复法"译为"Persecution of Buddhism by Emperor Tai Wu"和"Renaissance of Buddhism by Emperor Wen Cheng"，并增译了"文成帝和平年间"的具体时间，以便外国读者更好地了解中国这一时期的历史文化。

4. "归化"与"异化"相结合的旅游翻译

如前文所述，"归化"翻译遵循目标语言规范，向目标语读者靠近，译文流畅，因而通俗易懂、雅俗共赏，可读性和可接受性较高；"异化"翻译有利于保留旅游文化的异国情调，增强国外游客的好奇心，激发其旅游兴趣，两种翻译策略和方法各有优点，也各有缺陷。"归化"翻译过分倚重目标语言的固有表达形式和文化，抹杀了源语中的"异质性"，会影响源语文化在译语文化中的传播；而"异化"翻译能保留源语的"异质性"，但如果处理不好，生僻的文化负载词、不流畅的言语风格可能会降低旅游语篇的可读性和可接受性，从而影响旅游文本的吸引力。

因此，旅游翻译不可能只遵循一种翻译策略或采用一种翻译方法，既不可能完全以源语文化为归宿，也不可能完全以目的语文化为归宿。翻译旅游语篇时，既要考虑传播中国文化（采用"异化"翻译），尽量保留中国文化元素，尽量多地宣传中国文化；也要考虑译文读者的文化背景和阅读习惯（采用"归化"翻译），尽可能提高译文的可读性和可接受性，以便最大限度地吸引游客。"异化"和"归化"不分孰优孰劣，也不可能做到平分秋色，而应根据特定的翻译目的、文本类型及读者接受程度等不同因素对其进行现实的、具体的、动态的选择，有时"异化"，有时"归化"，更多的时候是两者并用，相得益彰。

例1. 远在两千多年前，哈密曾是汉代张骞第一次通西域开通丝绸之路的要塞。

译文：Hami had been a fortress two thousand years ago in the Han Dynasty of China, when Zhang Qian (an envoy sent by the emperor of the Han Dynasty to Darouzhi State) explored the Western Region for the first time to open up the Silk Road.

分析：译文采取了"异化"与"归化"相结合的翻译策略。张骞是历史人物，承载重要的历史信息，采用音译+释义，译为"Zhang Qian (an envoy sent by the emperor of the Han Dynasty to Darouzhi State)"；"丝绸之路"国外已有通用译法，译为"the Silk Road"。两个地名"哈密"和"西域"采用不同翻译策略，前者采用"异化"，译为"Hami"；后者采用"归化"，译为"the Western Region"，因为前者是一个地名，后者是更广阔的地理概念，如"中原"译为"the Central Plain"，而不译为"Zhongyuan"。

例2. 路左有一巨石，石上原有苏东坡手书"云外流春"四个大字。

译文：To its left is another rock formerly engraved with four big Chinese characters Yun Wai Liu Chun (beyond clouds flows spring) written by Su Dongpo (1037—1101), the most versatile poet of the Northern Song Dynasty (960—1127).

分析：译文采取"异化"与"归化"相结合的译法。原文中"云外流春"具有丰富的文化内涵和文艺色彩，但汉语水平一般的外国游客难以理解。翻译成英文时，译文采用音译"Yun Wai Liu Chun"加注"beyond clouds flows spring"的形式，"异化"与"归化"相结合，较好地传达了原文的意义。

三、旅游翻译的方法

根据功能主义翻译理论，译者应在分析原文的基础上，以译文预期功能为依归，结合外国游客的社会文化背景及其对译文的期待，选择翻译策略和方法（陈水平，2012：45）。由于中西文化背景、写作风格以及语言结构等存在差异，在处理源语信息时，译者不仅要理解原文的意图，同时也要考虑目的语读者的思维方式以及对源语文化的接受程度和意愿，因此，掌握正确的翻译策略和方法尤为重要。为了实现旅游文本传递信息、促进行动这两大功能，译者应在语义翻译和交际翻译策略的指导下，采取适合不同文本功能的翻译方法。语义翻译策略指导下的翻译方法主要有：直译、音译等。交际翻译策略指导下的翻译方法主要有：意译、增译、省译、拆译等。其中一些翻译方法的称谓不同，但手法相似，只是侧重点或视角不同。

1. 直译

所谓"直译",是一种既保持原文的内容,又保持原文形式的翻译方法。采用"直译",译文的语言与原文的语言拥有相同的表达形式,体现了相同的内容,并能产生相同的效果(冯庆华,2002:40)。由于直接翻译了语言的字面意义而实现了语言的全部转换,"原汁原味"译介了异域民族的社会、传统和文化思想,让游客更容易、更自然地体味到原文的文化风俗,更利于促进对外文化交流(张少兰,2007:139)。

例1. 和东门一样,成都人都把西门叫作老西门,因为在成都的西边后来也有了一道新西门。

译文:Just the same as the East Gate, people in Chengdu refer to the West Gate as the old West Gate because the New West Gate was built on the western end of Chengdu City.

分析:译文采取直译法,保留原文的结构和文体,在内容和语言上向源语靠拢,呈现了源语的语言结构和特征,有效、忠实地传达了原文信息。

例2. 我们明天的日程是上午去外滩观光,坐磁悬浮列车,下午去浦东陆家嘴金融贸易区参观。晚餐我们安排在国际饭店。晚餐后各位可以去南京路步行街走走,到"新天地"酒吧喝杯啤酒。

译文: Our itinerary for tomorrow is sightseeing at the Bund and a ride on the MLT in the morning and a visit to the Lujiazui Financial and Trade Zone in the afternoon. We will have dinner at the International Hotel. After that, you can take a walk on the pedestrian mall of Nanjing Road and have a beer at the New Heaven and Earth bar street.

分析:这是导游词中的一部分。在本文的翻译中,译者主要采取了直译法,顺应了源语的形式,再现了原文中的内容,对于原文中出现的地名,如"陆家嘴""国际饭店""南京路"等,译者采取了音译法与直译法,简单明了,有利于目标语读者直观地了解源语的风格特色。

例3. 孟昶鼓励全民植树。所植之树为芙蓉。几乎是家家门前有树,遍街是树。时人称成都为"芙蓉城"。

译文: Emperor Meng Chang encouraged people to plant hibiscus trees. In front of every house there were trees, also the trees all over the streets. People called Chengdu "City of Hibiscuses" or "Rongcheng".

分析：这是一则导游词，译者主要采取了直译法，顺句顺译，保留了原文的内容、结构和文体风格，仅对后蜀皇帝和成都别名采用了音译+注释的翻译方法。

例4. Melia Bali Resort is known for its serenity and charm. You can choose to golf, play tennis or squash, participate in water sports, take Balinese dance classes or have a massage. Whether you spend your holiday taking advantage of our many activities or relaxing in quiet contemplation, you will return home refreshed and renewed.

译文：梅丽亚巴厘度假村以她的宁静和美丽闻名，你可以在这里打高尔夫球、网球或壁球，做水上运动，学跳巴厘舞或者去做按摩。无论你在这儿度假，参加这里的活动，还是自己一个人安静地思考和休息，回去时你们都会感到精神饱满，焕然一新。

分析：原文属于信息类文本，介绍梅丽亚巴厘度假村基本的信息，不含特色文化词，因此译文主要采取直译法，语言清晰流畅，有效传递了目的地旅游信息。

2. 意译

意译从意义出发，将原文的主要意义表达出来，不需过分注重局部意义的真实。如不能直接采用原作的结构和表达形式，译者可改变句子结构和表达方式传达原作的内涵，再现原作的效果，实现功能对等即可。旅游翻译作为一种实用文体翻译，有较强的目的性和实用意图，主要目的是让读者、游客产生旅游行为。因此，旅游文本的译文不应固守原作的表达模式，不应追求汉、英旅游文体风格、形式与内容上的完全相同，而应使译文符合目标语读者的语言习惯（芦文辉，2008：123）。译文表达上可采用意译法，扬长避短，减少交流障碍（赵春玉，李春明，2010：51）。

例1. 遵守游览秩序，坚持五讲四美。

译文：Observe the tourist order and keep good manners.

分析：这是一则旅游公示语，以传递信息为主要目的，使用祈使句。

对于"五讲四美"这种带有浓厚中国文化色彩的表述,若直译为"Five Particulars""Four Beauties",目标语读者会不知所云。考虑到传递信息的目的以及译文的可接受性,对这类具有中国特色的表述应以意译为主,译出原文主要意义即可:"keep good manners"。

例2. Here in New Hampshire there are many opportunities to find a peaceful spot hidden among the lush forests of tall evergreens and hard woods or next to a rambling brook or pictorial lake.

译文:新罕布尔什州森林茂密,绿树常青,小溪蜿蜒曲折,湖边风景如画,到处都是宁静的好去处。

分析:此段旅游英语虽不长,但信息量较大。译文采用意译法,根据汉语意合句的特点,调整原文的语句结构,将原文中的名词性短语"the lush forests of tall evergreens""hard woods""rambling brook""pictorial lake"译成汉语的四字短语"森林茂密""绿树常青""小溪蜿蜒曲折""湖边风景如画",结构工整对称,文字优美,准确流畅,符合汉语读者的期待视野和阅读习惯。

3. 增译

增译法又名"增益"法,又称"增词"法,指根据英汉两种语言不同的思维方式、语言习惯和表达方式,遵循一定的规则,增添一些词、短句或句子的翻译方法,它包括语法性增译、目标性增译、注释性增译、修辞性增译等(朱娟辉,2009:148)。

例1."上有天堂,下有苏杭",逛湖滨路,游西湖,不要错过湖边礼品风情街。

译文:As the Chinese proverbs goes, "There is paradise in heaven, so there is Suzhou and Hangzhou on earth." You may not miss the gift while wandering around the West Lake.

分析:通过对比原文和译文,可以看出译文在原文基础上增加了一些连接词,属于语法性增译。原文是典型的汉语意合的句子,如果直接按照中文的表达习惯进行翻译,外国读者读起来就感到一头雾水。考虑到目的语读者的思维方式和语言习惯,译者增加了一些衔接成分,如"As the Chinese proverbs goes" "while"，将汉语隐性衔接部分用英文衔接方式衔接起来，语意连贯，符合英文"形合"的表达方式。

例2. 7月份就到增城去参加荔枝节。吃荔枝可以满足口腹之欲，在此期间举办的歌舞表演、美术摄影展览等更使人大饱眼福。

译文：July is the perfect time for you to visit the Lich Festival in Zengcheng, where you can feed yourself with the delicious Lichi, enjoy fabulous entertainment shows and artistic photograph exhibition at the same time.

分析：原文中并未涉及具体主语，属于无主句，是中文意合句的表达方式，翻译成英语时应添加主语，尤其是在旅游文本中，添加第二人称会让游客感到亲切，增加人际功能（phatic function）。译文增添了两个第二人称"you"，让读者感受到的不仅仅是平淡的文字描述，更是一份人文气息和关怀。

例3. 三官殿里有一株茶花树，在寒冬腊月开出一树鲜花，璀璨如锦，因此又名"耐冬"。

译文：There is a camellia tree in the Sanguan Palace blooming fully in midwinter, so it is called Naidong, meaning it can stand bitter cold winters.

分析：将山茶别名"耐冬"的含义"经受严寒"进一步阐释，采用了音译与增译的翻译方法，便于目标语读者理解原文含义，也利于目标语读者了解原文的文化意象。

例4. 绍兴是越瓷的产地。

译文：Shaoxing is the home of Yue Porcelains. Yue is a state name used to refer to the Shaoxing region in ancient China.

分析：原文提到"越瓷"，但一般外国读者不一定熟悉"越国""越瓷"。出于对历史文化理解的需要，译文增译了"越国"的历史信息，对其进行解释，减少了读者在理解译文时遇到的障碍，达到较好的语境效果；也给描述的对象添加一些神秘感，激发了外国游客的游览欲望。

4. 省译

旅游英语大多语言质朴，忌讳同义重复，描写客观，行文干净利落；而汉语旅游文本倾向连用四字词语，辞藻华丽；句式多平行对仗，力求行文工整、声律对仗、文意对比。因此，汉译英应遵循英语语言的特征，把原文中一些不太重要的信息或语义重复的信息省译掉（夏康明，范先明，2013：115），突出文本的交际功能。

例1. 交通便利，区位优越，风景秀丽，地貌独特，生态资源丰富，植被青翠，潭地密布，溪流纵横，群岭对峙形成幽谷，松柏苍劲，气象万千，众多的山峰拟人尚物，惟妙惟肖。

译文：It has convenient transportation and superior location. It is beautiful natural scenery with unique geomorphic structure and diversified vegetation environment.

分析：原文景点介绍颇具中国语言特色，短语繁多，语义重复，大量使用四字词语"交通便利""区位优越""风景秀丽""地貌独特"等，形成平行对仗句式；而英语重"形合"，更习惯用长句表达完整的意群。因此，译文采用"it has …""it is …"句式，将汉语13个四字词语整合为两个英语形合句，省译了多余的修饰语，突出了原文的重点信息、实用信息。

例2. 在我国最早的典籍中，即有有关这条河的记载。"漆沮既从，沣水攸同"（《尚书·禹贡》），"沣水东注，维禹之绩"（《诗经·大雅》），说明沣水在远古就是一条著名的河流。

译文：Records about this river can be found even in the earliest Chinese classics, which proves that the Fenghe River has been well-known since ancient times.

分析：《尚书》《诗经》是中国古籍，文中引用了沣水、漆水、沮水以及大禹治水的典故。对于英语读者来说，这些背景知识非常陌生，读者很难理解；如果用注释法，译文又会变得冗长，不符合英文简洁性的特点。综合考虑，特别是考虑译文的可读性，译文省译原文的引言，用总结式的语言"Records about this river can be found even in the earliest Chinese classics"，进行高度概括，帮助外国读者理解原文承载的文化信息。

例3."烟水苍茫月色迷，渔舟晚泊栈桥西。乘凉每至黄昏后，人倚栏杆水拍堤。"这是古人赞美青岛海滨的诗句。青岛是一座风光秀丽的海滨城市，夏无酷暑，冬无严寒。西起胶州湾入海处的团岛，东至崂山风景区的下清宫，绵延八十多华里的海滨组成了一幅绚烂多彩的长轴画卷。

译文：Qingdao is a beautiful coastal city. It is not hot in summer and not cold in winter. The 40-km-long scenic line begins from Tuan Island at the west end to Xiaqing Gong of Mount Lao at the east end.

分析：中国人在写景状物时喜欢引用名人名言或古诗词，读了会加深景观印象，并从中得到艺术享受，但在外国读者看来，这些似乎都是画蛇添足，可有可无。首句译为"Qingdao is a beautiful coastal city"，"先总后分"，符合英文旅游文本的构建，也是对前面古诗最简洁的概括，因此可省译用于渲染文本的诗歌，并不影响表达原文主要意思和译文读者对原文其他部分的理解，反而使英译文本更加干净利落，符合信息功能为主的旅游文本的特点。

例4. 黄山怪石，千奇百怪，令人叫绝。似人似物，似鸟似兽，情态各异，形象逼真。黄山怪石从不同的位置，在不同的天气观看情趣迥异，可谓"横看成岭侧成峰，远近高低各不同"。其分布可谓遍及峰壑巅坡，或兀立峰顶，或戏逗坡缘，或与松结伴，构成一幅幅天然山石画卷。

译文：Spectacular rocky peaks will inspire your imagination. Some look like human beings, birds or animals or many other objects. Something that makes the stones even more fascinating is that they assume varied shapes when seen from different angles. Every stone has its own fantastic legend.

分析：原文文辞优美，大量使用四字词语和平行对偶结构，如"千奇百怪""令人叫绝""情态各异""形象逼真"，并引用诗句，意在工整对仗，渲染一种诗情画意，体现了汉语旅游文本的特点。若采用相同的形式和结构，逐字译出，译文势必臃肿堆砌、结构松散、言之无物、华而不实，会严重破坏英文的美感。译文摆脱原文形式的束缚，省译了诗歌，仅用了一些感染性强的形容词，如"spectacular""varied""fantastic"等去修饰实实在在的景物，符合英文用词以及英文旅游文本重写实的特点，同样产生了文本的移情功能、审美功能。

5. 音译

音译（Transliteration），顾名思义，是一种译音代义的方法（刘祥清，

2008：38）。"音译也称转写，即用一种文字符号（如拉丁字母）来表示另一文字系统的文字符号（如汉字）的过程或结果"（方梦之，2004：96）。国际标准化组织（ISO）在1982年通过了将《汉语拼音方案》作为汉语罗马字母拼写法的决定。在翻译中国人名、地名和其他一些专用名词时统一使用汉语拼音，如Li Bai（李白）、Beijing（北京）、Shanghai（上海）、Baozi（包子）等都是直接用汉语拼音翻译。音译可以避免文化曲解，但它并不能解决文化缺省的问题，译者还必须对文化缺省部分给予积极补偿，否则仍然无法达到跨文化交际的目的，因此音译法通常与其他翻译方法结合起来使用（杨贤玉、乔传代，2014：61），如音译加直译。北京故宫的"太和殿"可译为"*Taihe Dian* (Hall of Supreme Harmony)"或"*Taihe Dian* or Hall of Supreme Harmony"。这种音译与直译相结合的方法是目前国内较流行的翻译方法，能让国外读者更直观地感受到中国语言文化的独特风采，在传播中国文化的同时达到吸引游客的翻译目的。

（1）音译+增译

例1. 林则徐。

译文：Lin Zexu, government official of the Qing Dynasty (1636—1912) and key figure in the Opium War.

分析：英译中国人名通常采用音译，但考虑到目标读者对中国的历史人物形象知之甚少，因此在音译人名时可对人物基本信息进行补充，如对"林则徐"的译法就采取了音译+增译的方法。

（2）音译+注释

中国的历史文化博大精深，源远流长，悠悠华夏历史涌现了大量特有的文化符号，主要体现在历史典故、民俗风貌、节气习俗等方面，而对这些独特文化符号和历史现象的翻译，除了音译保持其原风貌，还应增加相应的注释，以便更全面、准确地阐释中国文化的内涵，让外国游客更好地理解、吸纳中国文化。

例1. 三月三节。

译文：San Yue San Festival (a festival that usually takes place on the third day of the lunar third month, when minority people, especially the young get together for folk song contest or making friends with each other).

分析：如果只把"三月三节"音译成"San Yue San Festival"，外国人对这一特有的中国民俗会感到迷惑不解；通过音译+注释，将"阴历三月初三，少数民族，特别是青年男女欢聚一堂举行民歌大赛，并借此交友"之意译出，便能增进外国读者对中国这一少数民族传统节日的了解。

例2. 京剧中的角色有四种类型：<u>生</u>、<u>旦</u>、<u>净</u>、<u>丑</u>。

译文：There are four types of role in Peking Opera today, namely, <u>the sheng (male role)</u>, <u>dan (female role)</u>, <u>jing (painted face)</u>, and <u>chou (clown)</u>.

分析：考虑到目标语读者的文化背景，译者采取音译+注释的方法，简明扼要地向目标语读者介绍了京剧角色生、旦、净、丑的基本意义，有利于目标语读者对京剧角色形成直观的认识。

（3）音译+类比

例1. <u>郑和</u>7次下西洋都是在<u>福州马尾</u>扬帆出海的。

译文：<u>Zheng He (Eastern Marco Polo)</u> went to the west for 7 times and every time he took <u>Mawei, a famous harbor in Fuzhou</u>, as the starting point to set sail.

分析：从译语读者接受能力的角度出发，译者将郑和这一中国人非常熟悉的历史人物与西方游客所熟悉的人物马可·波罗进行类比，拉近了文本人物与游客之间的距离，使游客能较为容易地理解郑和这一中国历史人物；译者还对马尾港口进行了释义，以利于读者了解马尾港口的历史地位和意义。但是采取类比法，需注意类比事物两者之间的关联性，让目标语读者产生联想。

6. 改译

改译是指在不影响原文基本意义，不损害原文文化内涵的基础上对原文的语序、结构、文体等进行必要的调整，以达到宣传目的，尤其是对中国诗词及文言文等的翻译（袁翠，廖娟，2012：152）。改译实际上也是增译、省译、重构、逆序等在翻译中的综合运用。

例1. 刘备<u>章武三年病死于白帝城永安宫</u>，五月运回成都，八月葬于惠陵。

译文：Liu Bei died of illness in <u>223</u> at present <u>Fengjie County</u>, <u>Sichuan Province</u>, and was buried here in the same year.

分析：这句话传达的是中国三国时期的历史事实，但是直接翻译成英语，外国读者很难理解。首先，年号"章武"外国人就难以理解，"白帝城永安宫"更不知在何处，这些极具中国特色的历史文化信息很难用短短几句话阐释清楚。原文共三句，却包含了四个古地名与时间，"绝对"忠实原文的翻译不仅会增加读者的阅读负担，还会使不谙中国历史的外国人一头雾水。因此，译文采取了改译的方式，增加了解释；删除次要信息"五月运回成都"，减少了文化干扰；置换一些信息，换用公元纪年和今天的地名，便于外国游客理解、接受。

例2. 嵩阳书院的将军柏，是中国现存的原始古柏。诗人李观兴诗谓："<u>翠盖摩天回</u>，<u>盘根拔地雄</u>。<u>赐封来汉代</u>，<u>结种在鸿蒙</u>。"据传说，西汉元封元年（公元前110年），汉武帝游中岳时，把三株高大茂盛的古柏分别封为"<u>大将军</u>""<u>二将军</u>""<u>三将军</u>"。现在还成活的只有大将军和二将军两株。

译文：In the Songyang Academy, there are two great cypresses, which are the oldest in China. <u>As the legend goes</u>, in the year 110 B.C., when Emperor Wudi of the Han Dynasty visited the central mountain, he was greatly surprised to see such big cypresses there, so he conferred them the title of "<u>the Great General</u>" "<u>the Second General</u>" and "<u>the Third General</u>". "The Third General" died many years ago. Now, only the other two generals still stand there vibrantly.

分析：文章介绍了将军柏高大茂密以及古老的历史。译者省译了用于渲染文本的诗句，保留传说中的实质信息，并增译"As the legend goes"提示，删、减、改并用。译文语言简单明白，浅显易懂，避免了译文的重复，又展示了原文诗词的意境，使之更接近英语读者的阅读习惯。

7. 拆译

拆译法也叫"分句法"，是指为了符合译入语的表达习惯，改变原文结构，把原文的某个成分从原来的结构中分离出来，译成一个独立成分、从句或并列分句。英语重"形合"，长句较多；汉语重"意合"，短句较多。英语的后置修饰语有时会很长；而汉语修饰语一般前置，不宜过长。因此，汉译英可采用拆译法，将中文的若干四字格按意群拆分，缩译为一个英文句子；而英译汉则相反，可将英语句子的某些成分，如形容词、副词、独立结构单独分译成汉语短句或汉语四字格。

例1. City of Diverse Cultures, The Garden City, The Fun City, City for the Arts and Gateway City—these are some of the names given to Singapore to show visitors what this exciting destination can offer to visitors who want to indulge their senses on a holiday as well as those who have a wish to stay in Singapore.

译文："多元文化之城""花园之城""乐趣之城""艺术之城""通道之城"——这些都是人们赋予新加坡的美名。无论是对前来度假、尽享其美的游客，还是对希望在新加坡居留的人们，这些美名都意味着新加坡是一个令人向往的目的地。

分析：原文使用了几个定语从句将整个段落串成一句。英译汉时，考虑到中国读者的阅读习惯，译者对英文中的复杂句进行了拆分，单独成句，不仅传达了原文的意义，也符合词语意合句的特点。

例2. 牛羊肉泡馍的特点是肉嫩汤浓，香醇味美，食后再饮一小碗高汤，更觉余香满口，回味悠长，是一种高蛋白质、高碳水化合物、高能量的食品。一年四季均可食用，冬季更佳。

译文：Diced pancakes in mutton or beef broth (Yangroupaomo or Niuroupaomo) better known as Pita Bread Soaked in Lamb Soup, is characterized by tender meat and delicious broth. If you drink a bowl of thin soup after taking it, you'll get a lingering flavor in the mouth. Rich in protein and carbon dioxide, it is a special food of high-energy that can be taken all the year round, winter being the best season.

分析：译文将原文两句话的结构进行了调整，将其拆分成三个句子，分别介绍了牛羊肉泡馍的特点、顾客的品尝体验、牛羊肉泡馍的食用季节。拆分译出后，语义层次更清晰。此外，译文还增译了"if you..." "you'll..."，补充了拆分句子的主语，符合英文形合句的特点。

8. 类比

类比法是指由一类事物所具有的某种属性，可以推测与其类似的事物也应具有这种属性的推理方法。为了使旅游信息在英语读者中产生最佳反响,译者可以有的放矢地对旅游资料进行"加工",把源语中的有关内容转化为译入语读者熟悉的内容,用"以此比彼"的方法拉近读者与中国文化的距离,使他们产生亲近感,激发他们的游兴(姚宝荣等,1998:28)。

例1. 现在的大雁塔共有7层,高64米,呈方形角锥状。

译文:The present Dayan Pagoda has seven storeys and is 64 metres high in the shape of a square pyramid.

分析:这是有关西安大雁塔外观的介绍,描述了大雁塔呈方形角锥状的景观。若用英语直译"方形角锥状",外国读者无法理解大雁塔的造型,也难以在他们心中形成大雁塔直观生动的形象。此处译者借用举世闻名的金字塔与大雁塔进行类比,有利于读者形成对大雁塔直观的认识和具体印象。

例2. 济公劫富济贫,深受人民爱戴。

译文:Jigong, Robin Hood in China, who robbed the rich and helped the poor are loved by the people.

分析:译文将济公比作西方人所熟知的罗宾汉。通过音译与类比,让外国读者理解中国人为何如此爱戴济公。但是,罗宾汉(一个英国民间传说中的侠盗式英雄人物)、济公(一个举止癫狂、不受戒律约束的中国和尚),他们的文化身份和形象是否相同,如此关联、类比是否恰当,值得深思。

9. 套译

套译是借用译入语中某些惯用结构来进行翻译的一种方法。被借用的结构可以是成语、谚语、一句诗或者本身就是广告标题或口号。总而言之,这个被借用的结构必须是人们喜闻乐见、家喻户晓的语料(刘季春,1997:44)。

例1. 中原之行哪里去?郑州亚细亚。(郑州亚细亚超级商场广告)

译文:While in Zhengzhou, do as the Zhengzhounese do.—Go shopping in the Asian Supermarket.

分析:这句广告的英译套用了英语谚语"While in Rome, do as the Romans do."这则谚语意思是,身处罗马,要像罗马人那样行事,也就是中国人所说的

"入乡随俗"。外宾来到郑州,看了这则地道的英译广告,会有宾至如归的感受,前去购物。

例2. 食在广州。

译文: East or west, the Guangzhou cuisine is the best.

分析:译文套用英语谚语 "East or west, home is the best." 翻译广州美食,译为 "East or west, the Guangzhou cuisine is the best." 不仅传神达意,人情味十足,也给人宾至如归的感受,容易在目标语读者中产生共鸣。

10. 合译

合译,亦称"缩译",即把原文中两个或两个以上的简单句、主从复合句或并列复合句等译成一个单句的翻译方法;或指把英语长句译成汉语时,把英语后置成分按照汉语的正常语序放在中心词前,使修饰成分在汉语句中形成前置。合译法的句子修饰成分不宜过长,否则会形成拖沓,或造成汉语句子成分在连接上的纠葛(纪俊超,2014:394)。

例1. 到九寨沟旅游,沿途及景区内有高、中、低档的食宿服务设施。九寨沟主要由九寨沟宾馆、九寨沟管理局招待所、诺日朗宾馆、九寨山庄等提供食宿服务。

译文:Tourist facilities of different classes are available on the way to and inside Jiuzhaigou Valley, in which accommodations are provided mainly in the Jiuzhaigou Hotel, the Jiuzhaigou Administration Hostel, the Nuorilang Hotel, Jiuzhai Villa, etc.

分析:译者通过定语从句 "in which accommodations are provided mainly in the Jiuzhaigou Hotel..." 将原文两个句子合并,译为英文一个单句,句子的逻辑关系更清晰,语序更连贯,结构更完整,也符合目标语读者的用语习惯。

例2. 飞水潭是鼎湖山空气含负离子最高的地方之一,飞瀑、绿树、幽潭组成了一个清凉世界。

译文:The Flying Water Pool, known as one of the iron-richest places in Dinghu Mountain, presents a cool world with its flying waterfall, green trees and deep pool.

分析:译成英文时,译者调整了句子结构,将汉语两个句子整合成英文

一个句子，主谓分别为："The Flying Water Pool... presents..."，再用"known as..." "with"等衔接其他英文句子成分。合译后的译文句式简洁、逻辑清晰、层次分明，充分体现了英语特有的句法结构和语言特征。

本章小结

旅游翻译属于应用性翻译。旅游文本的翻译，无论是英译汉还是汉译英，都应着眼于原作者的交际意图与译文预期实现的功能，结合译文读者的社会文化背景知识、对译文的期待或社会知识以及交际需要，选择正确的翻译策略和方法，可采用语义翻译，也可采用交际翻译，功能翻译理论对指导旅游翻译具有重要的理论意义。在功能翻译理论指导下旅游翻译还需处理好"异化""归化"的理解和应用。过多"异化"，源语文化信息过多，容易造成译文晦涩难懂，影响译文读者阅读理解；过多"归化"，不利于本土文化的对外传播，影响中国"文化走出去"。功能翻译理论指导下的旅游策略分两大类：语义翻译和交际翻译，主要方法有：直译、意译、增译、省译、音译、改译、合译、拆译、类比、套译等，需要根据文本类型和翻译目的合理运用。

翻译实践

一、热身练习

翻译下文，并对译文做简要分析。

1. Look into the distance and you will have a nice view of the White Swan Pond in the Pearl River and boats up and down the river with the bright moon and twinkling stars in the sky.

2. 白洋淀的荷花，历史悠久，别具一格，每个生长阶段都留下不同的美感。春天"小荷才露尖尖角"，盛夏"接天莲叶无穷碧，映日荷花别样红"，金秋"留得残荷听雨声"。

3. Tiny islands are strung around the edge of peninsula like a pearl necklace. Hunk

of coral reef, coconut palms and fine white sand.

4. 与现代化的上海博物馆不同，南京博物馆古色古香，以辽代建筑风格为特色，巍巍松树，四周环抱。

5. Tolkien's Middle-earth—that's what photographer Frans Lanting calls Fiordland, New Zealand's largest national park. Webs of cascading water, veils of cloud, and stands of silver beech lend mystery to this secluded southwestern edge of the South Island.

6. 豫园设计独特，布局精致，融南北方建筑于一体，既荟萃了明代的建筑艺术精华，又开创了清朝古典园林的建筑风格，小中见大，以有限的空间创造出无限的意境，完美地展示了宏伟秀丽的豫园景色。

7. The hub of public life is the "Piazza San Marco" (St. Mark's Square) where tourists and citizens sit on the terraces of the famous Florian and Quadri cafes to listen to the music, dream and see the mosaics of St. Mark's glow under the rays of the setting sun. The Quadri is more popular but the Florian is the best-known café： founded in 1720, it has received Byron, Goethe, Musset and Wagner within its mirrored and allegory-painted walls.

8. "湖甸烟雨"指的是尚湖，位于常熟西南郊，虞山脚下，所以又名山前湖、西湖。这里湖面宽广，碧波荡漾，芦苇丛丛，飞禽喊喊，颇具天然野趣，现已建为湖滨公园。

9. Or relax in al fresco cafés that edge Market Square (the main square) and enjoy the hypnotic clops of horses' hooves and the regular quarterly chimes of the carillon from the square's belfry as it plays out Green Sleeves.

10. 登阁则西山如黛，湖光似镜，跃然眼帘；俯视则亭馆扑地，长廊萦带，景色全囿于一园之内，其所以得无尽之趣，在于借景。

二、巩固练习

翻译下文，并对译文做简要分析。

1. Badwater, a salt water pool, is about 280 feet below sea level and the lowest point in the United States.

2. 园以水池为主体,廊桥亭榭,布置得宜。园外莘峰叠翠,举目在望。水光山色,浑然一体。

3. Here nature created a series of amazing, almost lunar landscapes, ever-changing as the constant wind moves the sand about, revealing the most incredible colors.

4. 华清池,著名皇家园林,坐落于骊山脚下,位于西安市城东30公里处。华清池内有自然造化的天然温泉,所以远近闻名。提及骊山这一名称的来历,我们都知道"骊"在古代指代深黑色的马,而远远望去,骊山形如一匹飞奔而过的黑色的骏马,故该名称由此而来。

5. The desert is a place where man feels his own impotence and inferiority, where it is most difficult to make nature submit to this will...

6. 泰宁的大金湖,享有"百里湖山,灵冠天下"的美誉。大自然的鬼斧神工锻造了这里的形态万千和神奇灵秀。峡谷、山峰、岩穴、丹崖,实在引人入胜;青山、绿水、鸟语、花香,可谓万物生长。

7. In fact, the desert reminds one again and again that nature is superior to man, asking the passerby eternally to respect what has been created by nature and inviting him to consider the future in the light of his past mistakes.

8. 桂林的山,平地拔起,百媚千娇,像高耸云霄的奇花巨葩,盛开在锦绣江南;漓江的澄水,澄明清澈,晶莹碧绿,恰似翡翠玉带,逶迤在奇峰秀山之间。

9. Danya Hill is rising from the sea. It is reddish brown on the whole. The hill is reflected in the boundless blue sea. Sometimes, the hill is draped in a veil of mist. The hill with Penglai Pavilion on its top forms an admirable picture.

10. 福建土楼是世界上独一无二的山区大型夯土民居建筑,依山就势,布局合理,吸收了中国传统建筑规划的"风水"理念,适应聚族而居的生活和防御要求,巧妙地利用了山间狭小的平地和当地的生土、木材、鹅卵石等建筑材料,具有节约性、坚固性、防御性强的特点,是极富美感的生土高层建筑模式,冬暖夏凉,可抗台风地震。

三、阅读翻译

阅读下文，重点翻译下画线部分。

<u>有人说：改革开放以来，成都的文化成果在中华大地传播最快、最广的有两种，一是势如燎原、红遍九州的火锅；一是震耳欲聋、响彻大地的"雄起"！</u>

成都的足球队在全国不算最好的，但是成都的球迷在全国算是最有名的。他们的有名，不仅在于他们的狂热，他们的风度，更重要的是，他们在全国率先发出了"雄起"的呐喊。<u>这一呐喊已经响彻了我国足球赛场，传遍了大江南北。它远比"LAIAOLAIAO"的呼声更有气势，更有力度，更有内涵。</u>

在震耳欲聋的"雄起"呐喊中，不仅是对足球的企望。正如一个球迷在成都体育中心所说的："我不是哪个队的忠实球迷，成都的冠城和五牛两个队这两年的成绩也都不好。我就是想来看球，想来大声武气地大喊雄起。心头想喊，平时找不到地方可以尽情地喊，就只有在这里喊。<u>我想成都的足球要雄起，成都的其他方面也要雄起，单位效益要雄起，全家身体要雄起，大人的收入要雄起，娃娃的成绩要雄起，成都的所有都应当雄起！</u>"

成都人喊"雄起"，想"雄起"，这是一种强烈的企盼，在强烈的企盼背后，是一种精神、一股力量。

第二篇

游前文本翻译

第三章 旅游广告翻译

广告,顾名思义就是"广而告之"。广告是一种劝说性或支配性的交际活动,目的非常明确,即在有限的篇幅里吸引顾客的注意力,激起他们的兴趣和购买欲望并促使他们采取行动(吴朋,2007:58)。广告的主要功能是打动读者,诱发游客的消费行为。广告翻译亦然,它强调的是译文的效果,不仅要提供明白易懂的信息,而且还要具有原文"切肤之感"的感染力,让译文读者也能获得同样的感受,因此译文的效果和读者的感受应是广告翻译最重要的标准,这种侧重于读者感受的等效标准是由广告的功能所决定的。它不仅是衡量译文优劣的尺度,更是语际转换中调整改动的准绳(苏淑惠,1996:51—56)。

中、英旅游广告的语言有相同之处,也有差异。中文旅游广告善于托物寄情,寓情于景,注重旅游产品和服务的形象描述,语言生动、形象;英文旅游广告语言简洁、精练,最突出的特点是"对话性",广告语言亲切、自然,没有强迫感,易于游客理解、记忆(撒忠清,2007:108)。由于旅游广告是一种独特的语类,旅游广告的翻译既要考虑克服因中西方思维方式不同所导致的语言文化差异,又要顾及目标语读者的审美和心理需求,根据不同的广告风格题材,从内容到形式进行适当的改写、调整、再创造,以保证旅游广告的"关注价值"和"记忆价值"。

一、旅游广告概论

1. 旅游广告的定义

旅游广告借助媒介传播,塑造明确的旅游地形象,吸引旅游者前往旅游目的地游览、消费。从大众传播学角度来看,旅游广告传播是传播信息的行为或过程(张国良,1999:6);从广告学角度看,旅游广告是通过有偿取得的、可控的宣传媒介和形式,对商品、服务和观念进行社会化、群体化的传播,从而影响公众促成整体营销计划的推介管理活动（何修猛，2008：4）。旅游广告内容极广，包含"吃""住""行""游""购""娱"旅游六要素。根据旅游广告的功能和作用，可将旅游广告定义为：由旅游目的地国家、地区、旅游组织或旅游企业以付费的方式将旅游产品方面的有关信息通过非人员媒介传播出去，以扩大影响和知名度，树立旅游产品和企业的形象，达到促销目的的一种形式（徐德宽，王平，1998：169）。

（1）广告AIDAM过程

一般来讲，受众从注意广告到采取购买行为经历五个阶段，即AIDAM过程：1. 引起注目（attention）；2. 提起兴趣（interest）；3. 激起欲望（desire）；4. 引起行动（action）；5. 加深记忆（memory）。在前四个阶段中，受众的注意力一直是诱发购买行为的催化剂（何敏，李延林，2006：99—102）。因此，旅游广告的翻译须注意广告对受众产生作用的过程和机理，引起注意、提起兴趣、激起欲望、加深记忆，才能诱发旅游者的消费行为，达到旅游广告效果。

（2）广告的风格题材

旅游广告可分为直述式、叙述式、描述式三种不同风格题材。翻译旅游广告，首先要确定旅游广告属于哪一种风格题材，然后再确定翻译策略。直述式广告以传递信息为侧重点，其特点是用直接、精练的语言将广告产品的特点客观地表述出来。对于此类广告翻译，应用平实的语言准确地传达原文的信息；对于叙述式的旅游广告，要采用汉语中叙事性语言，把故事娓娓道来，但要保留原文的实用信息，不能随意添加和删除这些信息；对于描述式广告，则尽可能发挥汉语描写语言的优势，语言尽可能生动形象，语气夸张，给消费者描绘一个鲜明的形象，从而使其对所描述对象产生深刻的印象（丁大刚，2008：45—46）。对于广告中的修辞格，能保留则通过直译进行保留；不能保留则进行修辞转换或意译，应尽可能实现译文与原文功能的对等。

（3）旅游广告的特点

旅游广告的作用在于吸引潜在的消费者去认识商品，产生兴趣，然后采取行动。因此，旅游广告的语言必须有强烈的鼓动性和说服力，带有"半文学体"的色彩，其语言一般有两个特点：一是关注价值，广告的语言形式生动形象，别出心裁，引人注目，使潜在消费者偶一接触，即生探奇之心；二是记忆价值，广告中的文字既简单明了，又朗朗上口，给潜在消费者以深刻印象。通常，旅游广告能捕捉消费者心理，运用各种修辞手段，形象而又令人信服地宣传所要表达的内容，以实现广告词的关注价值和记忆价值（齐放，2009：208—210）。

因此，旅游广告翻译一定要有"切肤之感"的感染力，只有有感染力的广告翻译作品才会实现旅游广告的"关注价值"；旅游广告翻译需朗朗上口，在消费者心中产生深刻印象，才能实现旅游广告的"记忆价值"。为了实现旅游广告的"关注价值"和"记忆价值"，旅游广告的翻译应简短易记，节奏鲜明；使用比喻，借物传情；使用双关，一举两得；使用转喻，形象生动；使用对比，突显特色；使用排比重复，语句畅达、节奏明快；使用祈使句，有说服力、有敦促力；使用时尚语言，脍炙人口。

二、旅游广告的用词特点

一个精彩的旅游广告口号可使整个广告神韵飞扬，使旅游者一见钟情（文珍，荣菲，2000：70）。语言是思维和文化的反映。词汇作为旅游广告的基本元素之一，对旅游广告的创作和翻译尤为重要。新颖独特、准确易记的词汇有助于体现旅游产品的与众不同，使其在激烈的同行竞争中脱颖而出。中西方文化背景和思维方式存在差异，中、英文旅游广告的用词有相似之处，也有不同之处。掌握中、英旅游广告用词的特点，译出中、英广告的特色，才能实现旅游广告的"关注价值"和"记忆价值"。

1. 中文广告的用词特点

中国人重形象思维，故汉语重意境的描述，善用描述性语言，多用华丽辞藻以增强其语言的感染力和渲染力，该特点在旅游广告的用词上亦深有体现，如大量使用渲染性的动词、形容词和四字结构。中文旅游广告会使用一些描述性很强的动词或形容词，偏爱使用汉语独有的成语以及四字结构，使广告简洁易记，朗朗上口，节奏鲜明，有现场感，传物传情，语言时尚，脍炙人口（金惠康，2006：414）。故中文旅游广告多运用渲染性的形容词、四字结构等，以增强广告的艺术感,强化广告的宣传效果。

2. 英文广告的用词特点

英文旅游广告善用动词和形容词。动词给人活力之感,广告中动词的使用可使旅游者的思想活跃起来,并促使他们采取行动,以达到鼓励游客消费和预定的效果;英文旅游广告善用形容词,但与中文旅游广告不同,英文旅游广告不会使用华丽的书面化形容词,而代之以简单的口语化形容词,如"new""good/better/best""great""beautiful"等。这些形容词带有诱导性,偏口语化,容易打动消费者,达到广告宣传目的。

英文旅游广告也使用变异拼写。广告英语中的变异拼写主要是将一个词素与一个不合语法的词素或与一个创造出来的假词素进行组合(丁大刚,2008:37)。英文旅游广告中的拼写变异,词趣洋溢,新意溢出,无不给人以眼前一亮的感觉,既真实纯朴又个性鲜明、寓意深长,能产生意想不到的"广告效应"(赵爱萍,2008:2901),如"TWOGETHER"就是"TWO"和"TOGETHER"组合而成的变异拼写词汇。

英文旅游广告多用人称代词。旅游运营商常以第一人称自居,"I"和"we"等人称代词的使用给顾客一种承诺,让他们觉得这是一个可信任的机构;还可以给游客带来亲切感,缩短两者之间的距离,有助于实现人际功能(杨雁,2002:117)。第二人称"you"的使用给游客一种平等对话的感觉,使游客感到旅游经营机构促销或提供服务的针对性,引起旅游者对特定广告下意识的反应和注意,增强广告的解释、说明和劝导功效(撒忠清,2007:108)。

例1. 观音故里,吉祥圣地。

译文:The Hometown of Kwan-yin, a Holy and Blessed Land.

分析:这是一则遂宁市旅游广告。该广告采用四字词语结构,符合汉语旅游广告的用词特点。英文则使用两个词组,对等译出,简洁易记,指向准确,点明了遂宁是中国观音文化之乡。

例2. What it's like to be small but good.

译文:<u>麻雀虽小</u>,<u>五脏俱全</u>。

分析:这是一则经济型酒店的英文广告,用词简洁,均为日常生活用语,符合英语广告重写实的特点;译文采用四字成语,且运用比喻修辞手法,将"酒店"比作"麻雀"。"麻雀"嘈杂,"五脏"恐怖,将酒店比作"麻雀""五脏",恐有不妥,给游客一种不好的印象,不利于酒店宣传。不妨改译为:酒店虽小,设施齐全。

例3. 宜山宜水更宜宾——宜宾!

译文:Beautiful Yibin Brings You as Much Happiness as You Can Bear.

分析:这是一则宜宾市的旅游广告,该广告中文用词简洁,但三个"宜"字使得广告朗朗上口,颇具音韵和感染力,突出了宜宾山清水秀、适宜旅游的特点;英文则使用了常见的渲染形容词"beautiful",并使用第二人称"you",体现广告对顾客的承诺,拉近了与游客的距离。

例4. Fresh up with seven-up—Seven-up.

译文:七喜——清新好感受。

分析:广告措辞简洁明快,用词巧妙,重复使用三个"up",语言具有音律感,读起来朗朗上口。译文虽然没有重复修辞手法,但遣词造句同样简洁明快,具有节律上的动感和美感。

例5. Our hotel is now 100% smoke-free for your added comfort.

译文:百分之百无烟,百分之百舒适。

分析:这是一则美国纽约喜来登酒店的广告,致力于缔造一个百分之百无烟的酒店环境,让游客更感舒适。广告使用第一人称,给顾客一种被承诺的感觉;使用第二人称,则体现顾客第一的理念,增加了酒店的亲切感和吸引力。

例6. Visit Malaysia.

译文:到马来西亚一游。

分析:这是一则马来西亚国家旅游局的广告,使用祈使句,具有劝导、祈使功能,鼓励游客预订、消费。根据中文广告的语言特点,本则广告可改译为:"马来西亚欢迎你!"能更好地体现原文的劝导、祈使功能。

例7. Discover our True Nature.

译文:发现加拿大最真的一面。

分析:这是一则加拿大旅游局的广告,用动词"discover"开头,具有劝导、祈使功能，劝导游客采取行动。本则英文广告还可改译为："开启加拿大自然探索之旅"；或译为："发现最真实的一面，快来加拿大一见！"

例8. In just few drops, this man's skin is going to feel better.

译文：只需要几滴，皮肤即刻舒适。

分析：这是一则化妆品广告，使用形容词比较级，有比较性质，迎合了消费者购买商品比较选择的心理。译文质量不高，未能体现中文广告对称工整的特点，可改译为："只需滴几滴，皮肤水灵灵。"

例9. The view in Singapore from the world's tallest hotel.

译文：从世界最高的酒店里鸟瞰新加坡。

分析：这是一则威斯汀酒店的广告，使用了形容词最高级，感染力很强，但译为"从世界最高的酒店里鸟瞰新加坡"没有体现广告语的特点，可改译为："从这里，俯瞰新加坡"；或译为："会当凌绝顶，一览新加坡！"

例10. The orangemostest drink in the world.

译文：世界上最浓的橘汁饮料。

分析：这是一则关于橘汁的商品广告，广告中的"orangemostest"是由"orange+most+est"构成的，为变异拼写词。该变异拼写词不仅有效传播了广告信息，更增添了广告新意，赋予广告极大的语言魅力。根据汉语对称、意合的特点，中文广告词可改译为："橘之极，非'常橘'"；或译为："橘之极，非常'橘'"，效果更好。

三、旅游广告的句法特点

句子的语法特征是研究旅游广告文本极其重要的一个层面。中国人偏螺旋形综合式思维，汉语词汇无词形变化，词汇、词组有很大的灵活性，句子结构较为松散，语法和逻辑关系主要依靠词意表达（沈云，2006：144）。汉语重意合，注重意境的营造，这一特点在中文旅游广告文本中得到了充分的体现；西方人士偏直线型分析式思维，重理性思维，句子层次分明，逻辑关联严谨（熊力游，2004：37），句子有明显的词形变化，该特点在英文旅游广告中亦有体现。翻译旅游广告应注意中、英两种不同的思维方式并把握英汉语言的差异，准确理解广告所要传达的内容和意境,力求在目标语广告读者中发挥同等效果(李丽萍,2018:80)。虽然中、英旅游广告有差异,但也有以下共同点:

1. 使用主动语态。旅游广告一般使用主动语态,慎用被动语态,除取得特殊促销效果外,广告使用被动语态不会有其他更加令人信服的解释(文珍,荣菲,2000:74)。广告使用主动语态,句子干脆利落,劲健爽快,更容易记忆。

2. 使用省略句。省略句结构紧凑,表意突出,具有精练扼要之感,能使广告在有限的时间、空间和费用内达到最佳的宣传效果。使用省略句,能使广告起到突出重点和点明主题的功效,发挥快速传播的作用。广告省略句可省略主语、谓语,也可省略其他成分,甚至仅仅以一个词作为一个句子,达到言简意赅的效果(杨雁,2002:119)。

3. 使用祈使句。旅游广告的目的是劝说旅游者接受某种旅游产品或服务,或者接受某些观点。祈使句是实现目标的一个有效句式,本身包含请求、命令、号召旅游者去做一些旅游经营机构所期待的旅游行为的意义,具有说服力和感染力,能够打动消费者的心扉(撒忠清,2007:109),因此旅游广告常用祈使句。

4. 使用疑问句。疑问句根据旅游产品的特点和旅游者的心理设问作答,重点突出,针对性强,具有选择消费者的定位作用(曾咪,2009:79)。疑问句一般与游客的某种需求有关,能直接刺激游客了解更多相关的服务,从而促进游客消费。疑问句让游客直接参与到对话之中,因此更容易引起读者的共鸣。

例1. Go with the flow. Soft, swaying shapes, so right for summer.

译文:紧随潮流,柔软、摇曳的姿态,夏天穿着是如此舒适。

分析:这是一则服装广告,使用了祈使句,有直接规劝和诱导消费行为的功能。为了让译文押韵,产生更好的广告效果,广告译文可改为:"紧随潮流,柔软、摇曳的姿态;夏天穿着,那是如此自在!"以便更好地实现广告的"记忆价值"。

例2. Traveling abroad? Use Visa. All you need.

译文:要出国旅游吗?请用维萨卡。满足一切所需。

分析:这是一则维萨卡公司的广告。广告采用问句形式,自然而然地引出推销的产品,重点突出,针对性强,是一则典型的对话性英文广告。"请用维萨卡"就已经隐含了"满足一切所需",因此没有必要将此句译出。该广告可改译为:"出国旅游吗?就用维萨卡。"

例3. A Great Way to Fly.

译文:非凡之旅。

分析:这是一则新加坡航空公司的旅游广告。广告采取省略句形式,省略了主语和谓语;译文则直接用一个四字词语作广告。对比广告原文,译文虽仅有四个字,但表意突出,感染力很强,体现了广告的"记忆价值"。

例4. 穿上"双星"鞋,潇洒走世界。

译文:Double Star Takes You Afar.

分析:这是一则"双星"鞋的广告,使用现在时态和主动语态。一般现在时表示现行状态,主动语态则发出动作,催人产生行为。

例5. Don't Leave Home Without It!

译文:出门在外,随身携带。

分析:这是一则美国运通卡的广告,使用祈使句,增强了广告的说服力和感染力,诱导消费者产生购买行为。

例6. Walk in Britain in Style

Enjoy a relaxed, escorted walking tour

through idyllic village and countryside.

Stay at character country hotels.

See the real Britain close-up.

译文:风度翩翩英国行

享受轻松的有人陪伴的徒步旅行,

穿越民风淳朴、风景宜人的乡村。

住宿在富有特色的乡下旅馆。

目睹真正的英国田园风光。

分析:这是一则英国旅游广告。原文、译文均采用无主句(省略主语),并使用了祈使句、主动语态。广告结构紧凑,表意突出,语言形式极具艺术感,营造出英国田园意境之美。但译文稍有不足,翻译广告应在忠实原文的基础上,尽

可能接近原广告的艺术风格,试译如下:

风度翩翩英国行

导游伴我慢步行。

过乡村,越田野,看田园风光。

住乡下特色旅馆,

近民风,观民情,享英伦风情。

四、旅游广告对话性的特点

中、英旅游广告都具有对话性的特点,对话性是旅游广告最突出的特点之一。所谓"对话性",是指广告发起者和消费者之间文本上或心理上的对话,是一种心理暗示或交流,并不一定是你来我往的对话,具有对话性的广告语言亲切自然、没有强迫感(李艳,2012:45)。带有对话性质的广告可以带给旅游者一种亲切、自然的感觉,令人心情放松和舒畅,而这正好能满足旅游者的心理诉求,同时能实现旅游广告的目的(陈莉,2018:209—210)。英文旅游广告的对话性体现在语言的大众化、口语化;中文旅游广告的对话性则体现在四字词语的使用以及语言的韵律感、节奏感。中、英旅游广告所呈现的对话性,使广告更具有感召力和亲和力,产生更好的传播效果。

例1. 一册在手,纵览全球。(《全球杂志》)

译文:With a single copy of *The Globe* in hand

You can enjoy a wide view of the world.

分析:这是一则《全球杂志》广告。原文采用四字对仗结构,朗朗上口,便于读者理解记忆;译文则用两个短句译出,采用第二人称"you",像是在与游客直接对话,向他们承诺针对性的服务,体现了英文旅游广告的特点。

例2. You'll Love Every Place of Victoria.

译文:你会热恋维多利亚的一草一木。

分析:这是一则关于维多利亚的广告。广告采用第二人称"you",给人平等对话的感觉,增加了广告的亲和力。中文将"Every Place"译为"一草一木",不仅符合中文广告常用四字结构的特点,而且准确表达了原文的语意。

例3. Your Kind of Fun.

译文:随心所欲。

分析:这是一则卡尼维尔游轮的广告,中、英文本都很简练。英文广告中的"kind""fun"都是大众化、口语化的词汇,而使用第二人称"your",则使广告具有对话性;中文广告采用四字词结构,听起来朗朗上口,行文简短,容易记忆。

例4. Britain, It's Time!

译文:英国之游,正是时候!

分析:这是一则英国旅游广告,具有明显的口语化特点。"It's Time"具有对话性和广告的劝导功能,像是广告发起者在面对面号召游客前往英国旅游。

五、旅游广告的修辞特点

修辞手法是人类语言中共有的比较积极活跃的因素。在旅游广告翻译中,修辞手法的运用会给旅游文本增添文化元素和风格特点(曾咪,2009:78—80)。无论是中文还是英文旅游广告,都大量使用各种修辞手法。英文旅游广告常用比喻、双关、转喻、仿拟等修辞手段以及幽默风趣的语句给读者强烈的感官刺激,赢得消费者对其产品或服务的认可和青睐;中文旅游广告倾向使用比喻、拟人、对比、排比、夸张等修辞方法,并用四字结构,辅之其他修饰手法加强语气,如海口城市广告语"椰风海韵,南海明珠"使用比喻的修辞方法;"一步跨进历史,一日畅游中国"宣传语使用夸张的修辞方法(李丽萍,2018:79—80)。

翻译与修辞的最大契合之处在于两者都是运用语言象征为主、面向受众的交际活动,且与现实社会紧密相关,最基本的共同特性都是交际(林菲,2015:77)。英语中大部分修辞可以在汉语中找到对应或类似的修辞手法,反之亦然。但是由于不同民族审美、认知差异,修辞蕴含的文化意义不同,若将这些修辞格如实译出,没有相应知识储备的外国游客并不能理解;而中、英文都有一词多义,特别是文化负载衍生的双关修辞格往往在目标语中难以还原。因此,译者应以实现功能对等为要旨，以实现广告"关注价值""记忆价值"为目的，发挥译入语的优势，并不一定非要对等译出修辞格。

1. 明喻（Simile）

明喻是把至少具有一种共同属性或特征的两种不同事物进行对比的一种修辞手段，典型表达方法是：A像B，通常用"如同""像……似的""好像""像"等词来表明两者之间的共同属性，标志词常用like，as，seem，as if，as though，similar to，such as等。广告运用明喻，能渲染语言的具体性和形象性，增添广告感染力。

例1. 红梅相机新奉献。

译文：My love is like a Red Rose. (Red Rose Camera)

分析：这则英文广告的翻译灵感来自罗伯特·彭斯（Robert Burns）的名诗"A Red, Red Rose"中的第一句，"O, my love is like a red, red rose."译文使用明喻修辞格，拉近了广告与目标语消费者的距离，较好地提升了产品形象。

例2. 广州又称"羊城""穗城"，是祖国的南大门，早在秦汉时期就是繁华的都会。

译文一：Guangzhou, also called "Goat City" or "Spike City", is the South Gate of our motherland. It became a prosperous metropolis in the Qin and the Han dynasties.

译文二：Guangzhou, also called "Goat City" or "City of Rice Ears", is the South Gate of our motherland. It became a prosperous metropolis during the Qin and Han dynasties.

分析：这是一则广州城市广告。译文使用明喻修辞格，把广州比作"羊城""穗城"，增加了广告的"关注价值"，激发外国游客游览广州的兴趣。

例3. 欲把西湖比西子，淡妆浓抹总相宜。

译文：The West Lake looks like the fair lady at her best. Whether she is richly adorned or plainly dressed.

分析：这是一则引用中国诗歌的旅游广告。译文使用明喻修辞格，不仅赋予西湖之美以生命,而且喻体新奇别致,情味隽永,衬托出西湖的隽永灵秀之美,也体现了广告的"记忆价值"。

2. 暗喻(Metaphor)

暗喻本体和喻体同时出现,它们之间在形式上是相合的关系。暗喻蕴涵丰富,立意新颖,表达委婉贴切。喻词常用"是""就是""成了""成为""变成"等判断词语充当。暗喻的典型表达方法是:"甲是乙",但不是所有由"是"连接的语句都是暗喻。

例1. 在亚洲展开您的双翅,同我们一起高飞望远。

译文:To spread your wings in Asia. Share our vantage point.

分析:广告使用了暗喻修辞格。"高飞望远"一词出自《临江仙》:"梦里高飞望远,酒香飘送红颜。"译文采用直译法,译出喻体"您的双翅"("your wings"),表达了游客可以如同鸟儿一样在亚洲轻畅旅游,增加游玩的乐趣。译文还考虑到两国语言差异,将广告后一句译为"Share our vantage point"(vantage point意为"优势""有利位置"),使广告的语言文化内涵达到了统一。

例2. You're better off under the Umbrella.

译文:在"伞"的保护下,你会更加安全。

分析:这是一家旅行保险公司的广告,广告不长,但比喻生动、贴切。广告形象地把保险比喻成"保护伞",游客购买保险后犹如置身于"保护伞"下,时刻被保护着,感受到一股温馨和暖意。译文采用直译法,将保险译为"伞",让顾客觉得保险值得信赖。

例3. ...Blessed by year round good weather, Spain is a magnet for sun worshippers and holidaymakers...

译文:……天公作美,四季如春。西班牙就像一块磁铁,吸引着酷爱阳光、爱好度假的人们……

分析:英文中的暗喻译成中文时变成了明喻,巧妙、生动地宣传、推广了西班牙旅游胜地。

例4. 中国河南——功夫的摇篮。

译文:Henan in China—the cradle of Chinese Kungfu.

分析：这是一则河南旅游广告。该句属于判断式隐喻，判断词"是"被破折号取代，隐喻河南是中国功夫的摇篮，激发游客到河南的旅游兴趣，突显了广告的"关注价值"。

3. 夸张（Hyberbole）

夸张是指有意识地把事实夸大或故意言过其实，以达到强调或突出目的的一种修辞手法。夸张从主观出发，通过渲染，表达深切的情感，以达到感人的效果。

例1. Hilton Is Giving Away More than 13,000,000 Airline miles. That's Kind of Like Having Your Own Private Jet.

译文：希尔顿酒店度假集团派送了1300多万英里（2000多万公里）的免费飞行旅程，为您提供私人包机，免费！

分析："……为您提供私人包机，免费！"，极尽夸张之能事。广告以非常明确、针对个人的口吻，运用夸张修辞格刺激游客消费。

例2. ...It's no wonder the Philippines has some of the finest beach resorts in the world.

译文：难怪菲律宾群岛有世界上最美的海滨度假胜地。

分析：这则广告运用夸张修辞格，用形容词最高级"世界上最美"来表现菲律宾群岛的自然风光，体现了广告的"关注价值"，吸引游客前往菲律宾游览。

4. 排比（Parallelism）

排比是一种把结构相同或相似、意思密切相关、语气一致的词语或句子成串排列的一种修辞方法。排比句把意义相关或相近、结构相同或相似、语气相同的词组或句子排列起来，排比项意义范畴相同，排比项诽迭而出，语气一贯，节律强劲，带有列举和强化、拓展文意的性质，其修辞功能可以概括为："增文势""广文义"。

例1. One of the greatest pleasures in life is simple to be respected by an individual.

To speak and be heard.

To ask and be helped.

译文：人生最大的快乐就是受人尊重，

说话时有人聆听，

求助时有人帮忙。

分析：原广告运用了排比句式。译文则保留了原文中的排比结构，顺畅达意，节奏感很强，广告有很强的感染力，用排比句式体现了广告的"记忆价值"。

例2. 你会享受这阳光明媚的轻松日子。

欣赏明亮的蓝天、壮丽的日落，

感受到异样的芬芳、幽静的海滩、轻柔的海风。

还有品尝到那绝妙的食物。

译文：You'll enjoy relaxed sunny days.

Bright blue skies. Breathtaking sunsets.

Exotic scents. Secluded beaches.

Soft evening breezes. And food that simply out.

分析：原文运用了排比句式，"享受""欣赏""感受""品尝"构成中文排比句，感染力强。译文在"You'll enjoy..."后罗列名词短语，用英文短句代替原文的排比结构，节奏明快，同样起到了广告宣传作用。

5. 押韵（Rhyming）

押韵，又作"压韵"，是指在韵文的创作中，在某些句子的最后一个字，都使用韵母相同或相近的字或者平仄统一，使朗诵或咏唱时，产生铿锵和谐之感。使用同一韵母的地方称为"韵脚"。押韵运用语言的声音规律，音韵和谐，生动悦耳，能使广告产生声情并茂的效果。

例1. Be good to yourself. Fly Emirates. —Emirates 纵爱自己，纵横万里（阿联酋航空）

都是他乡客，去时故人心。（中心大酒店）When you come, you are a guest of ours; when you leave, we are the friends of yours. —Central Hotel

分析：第一句英译汉，押头韵，加强节奏感；第二句使用了平行结构，押尾韵，朗朗上口。英汉互译应尽可能保持原文的语言特色，翻译出旅游广告的风格，能翻译出韵体更好。

例2．"城市，让生活更美好" Better city, Better life

"诗画江南，山水浙江" Poetic Jiangnan, Picturesque Zhejiang

"上海，精彩每一天" 7 Wonders of the world, 7 Days in Shanghai

分析：旅游广告翻译时应遵循简短易记、节奏鲜明、合乎韵律、符合大众审美特点的原则。译文押头韵，节奏紧凑，给人视觉、听觉融合的美感，充分体现了广告的"记忆价值"。

例3. More sun and air for your son and heir.

译文：这里有充足的阳光、清新的空气，一切为了您的子孙后代。

分析：作者巧妙运用了两对谐音字：sun—son，air—heir，韵律十足，读起来朗朗上口，亦增添了原文的幽默感。

6. 反复（Repetition）

反复是特意重复使用某些词语、句子或段落的修辞手法，有增强语气或语势、表达强烈情感的作用。反复修辞格能加强语气，表达强烈的情感，使文本产生音乐感、节律感。

例1. Yes, the Philippines. Now! —Ministry of Tourism of the Philippines

译文：是的，菲律宾群岛。现在！——菲律宾国家旅游局

分析：广告两次重复"Philippines"，以加深游客对菲律宾的印象。反复强调广告关键词，能使文本产生强烈的呼唤功能，广告效果更好。

例2. Premiere airplane for a premiere airline.

译文：一流的飞机供给一流的航空公司。

分析："Premiere"译为一流，突出其在众多航空公司中出类拔萃。这个词在原广告和译文广告中都被反复使用，强调一流航空公司，增强了文本的语气。

例3. Double delicious. Double your pleasure.

译文：双份美味，双份愉快。

分析：广告重复"双份""double"，突出美味，加强了语气，渲染了美味带来的愉悦效果。

例4. Travel in style—dine in style. The MGBahn is more than just a railway, and offers numerous special excursions in winter: fine food or going on a special outing all make the trip unforgettable.

译文：优雅地旅行——优雅地用餐：马特宏圣哥达不仅仅是一条铁路，还为游客提供许多冬季特殊短途旅行项目：精美的食物，或是特别的短途观光，都会让您流连忘返。

分析：本例中"in style"与"special"出现了两次，属于反复修辞格。译文采用直译法，重复使用"优雅"二字，使译文具有与原文同等程度的感染力。译文略有修改。

7. 双关（Pun）

双关指的是在一定的语言环境中，利用词的多义或同音的条件，使语句产生双重意义。双关言在此而意在彼，是一种富于文字情趣的修辞手法，被誉为"语言的精灵"（the genius of the language）。双关的运用使广告语言幽默风趣，诙谐机智，一箭双雕，达到言已尽而意无穷的艺术效果。

例1. The driver is safe when the road is dry; the road is safer when the driver is dry.

译文一：路面干燥、司机安全；司机清醒、路面安全。

译文二：路面无泥泞，司机较安全；司机不饮酒，途中险情少。

分析：广告利用"dry"一词构成双关语。"dry"在不同语境下，意义不一样。广告中的"dry"告诫司机"开车不饮酒，饮酒不开车"，一语双关，对司机起警示作用。

例2. Butlin's—the right choice.

Don't labor the point, or be conservative in your choice, or liberal with your money. Come to Butlin's for the real party.

Great Party Ahead.

译文一：布特林旅游公司——你明智的选择。

不要唠叨讲个没完，

不要保守，也别犹豫，

不要放任自由地乱花钱。

到布特林旅游公司，参加实实在在的聚会吧。

盛大的聚会正等着你！

译文二：旅游就来布特林！

不必事必躬亲，

不用过于拘谨，

不需挥霍重金，

来吧，派对之旅。

盛大聚会等着您！

分析："labor" "conservative" "liberal" 分别指英国三个政党：工党、保守党和自由民主党。"labor the point" 是"详尽说明、事必躬亲"之意，"be conservative in your choice" 为"选择时态度保守"之意，"liberal with money" 指"大手大脚地花钱"；而"party"一语双关，有两层含义：政党或聚会。相比而言，虽然译文二由于"文化缺省"没有做到一语双关，但更好地体现了译语广告的"关注价值"和"记忆价值"。

8. 拟人（Personification）

拟人是一种修辞手法，将生物或无生物当作人，给它们以人的思想情感，具有人一样的声情笑貌。拟人就是事物"人格化"，用写人的词句去写物。旅游广告中运用拟人，可以把静态的旅游广告描写得极富动态，赋予事物以生命，从而达到宣传、推广的目的。

例1. A wide range of land and sea recreational facilities awaits you.

译文：广阔的陆地和海洋娱乐设施在等着您。

分析：本例中"await"的施动者通常是人，这里用了拟人修辞手法，使文字变得生动活泼，吸引游客前往旅游、消费。

例2. Last but not least, Beatenberg beckons from high above Lake Thun, a sun terrace par excellence and also the longest village in Europe.

译文：位于图恩湖上方的比登堡正在向您招手，游客在这里的阳光露台上可以欣赏四周美丽的景致，比登堡还是欧洲最狭长的村庄。

分析：广告将比登堡"人格化"，向游客招手，形象生动。使用拟人修辞，增加了旅游外宣文本的立体感，提高了宣传效果。

六、旅游广告的翻译策略和方法

由于语言文化上的差异，一则优秀的广告对其他民族来说未必就是好的广告。如果依样画葫芦、一字不动地译成另一种语言就不一定能达到原有的效果，有时甚至可能适得其反。旅游广告中包含各种信息，从人文历史到自然风光都具有"关注价值""记忆价值"。翻译旅游广告，应尽可能地保留原广告中的文化，将源语中蕴含的文化信息尽量完备地传达到译语中去，即"文化传真"，实现其"关注价值""记忆价值"。语义翻译策略能让游客领略到源语中异域文化的风采，在旅游广告外宣翻译中可以起到"本土文化传真"的作用。语义翻译策略指导下的旅游广告翻译方法主要有："直译法""音译法"以及"音译+直译"等形式。

广告翻译侧重的是广告效果，译者首先考虑的是使广告如何产生"关注价值""记忆价值"。为了保证译文具有原文同等的表现力与感染力，甚至优于原文，广告翻译允许因语言文化的差异而对原文所涉及的有关语篇结构方面的词句、修辞手法，尤其是非信息成分进行"有意识的语义变动"（金隄，1989：53），这正是交际翻译策略提倡的翻译方法。交际翻译策略指导下的旅游广告翻译方法主要有：意译法、删减法、增补法和套译法等。更多的时候，为了产生广告的"关注价值""记忆价值"，旅游广告的翻译是语义翻译策略与交际翻译策略的结合。

例1. 美女话西施，美酒推灵芝。

译文：Xi Shi is the most beautiful of woman, so is Lingzhi Medicated Liquor the most beautiful liquor.

分析：该广告词以美酒喻美女，创意新颖，意境优美，具有强烈的美学功能和移情功能。译文采用意译法，巧妙地概括出广告的信息功能；又通过"the most beautiful of woman"和"the most beautiful liquor"对比，"Lingzhi Medicated Liquor"与"the most beautiful liquor"押尾韵，在强调产品特点的同时，突出了广告的美感功能，是交际翻译策略在旅游广告翻译中的运用。美中不足的是，译文在结构上未能体现原广告的文体风格。

例2. 开汤审评，清香四溢，滋味鲜醇，回味甘甜，余香犹存，经常泡饮，明目清心，止渴益神，减肥健美，堪称茶中佳品。

译文一：After you infuse it, the tea is full of delicate fragrance, if you taste it carefully, the flavor is mellow with a sweet and lasting fragrance. To drink often cannot only quench your thirst, benefit your mind but also make you slim, strong and handsome and clear your eyesight. <u>So it is regarded as the best quality tea among all kinds of teas.</u>

译文二：Being fragrant, refreshing and mellow, your tea presents a lingering aftertaste of mild mellowness. Drinking it often cannot only quench your thirst, repose your mind, but can sharpen your eyes and beautify your figures. <u>No wonder tea is the best in China</u>!

分析：译文一采取直译法，全文翻译中文广告，强调对等，反而不如译文二在对原文高度概括的基础上删繁就简的意译法。可见广告翻译并不提倡字、词、句、篇章的对等翻译。英文广告倾向具体，简洁凝练，在无法达到语言、结构对等的情况下，广告翻译允许采取交际翻译策略，对原文所涉及的有关语篇结构方面的词、句、修辞手法，尤其是非信息成分进行"有意识的语义变动"。

例3. 旅游城市广告

原文	译文
1. 财富之城，成功之都	Chengdu, Can Do！
2. 成渝之心，天府之源，灵秀资阳	Witty Ziyang, Heart of Chengdu-Chongqing Region, Land of Abundance
3. 宜山宜水更宜宾——宜宾！	Beautiful Yibin Brings You as Much Happiness as You Can Bear
4. 中国酒城，醉美泸州	A City of Chinese Liquor, the Intoxicating City of Luzhou

分析：广告1采用意译+音译，押尾韵，朗朗上口，用"can do"便概括了成都成为"财富之都""成功之都"的原因；广告2采用直译法，通过同位语结构，再现资阳在成都重庆地区的重要性；广告3采用意译法，并使用英文比较级，达到了与原文一样的宣传效果；广告4采用直译法，"醉美"通"最美"，一语双关，译文保留了原文平行结构。从以上译例可以看出，旅游广告的翻译以交际翻译策略为主，重视的是文本的"功能对等"，而不是语言和形式上的对等。

例4.

原文	译文
1. 携程票务，尽享里程	Earn mileage from your favorite airlines when you book with Ctrip.
2. 境内自由行，包便宜！	Domestic escapes. Book now!
3. 苏州同里水乡行	Explore the Venice of the East. Suzhou & Tongli Water Town Tour.
4. 包价游，超便宜！	SACE on Packages!

分析：广告1采用意译法，将原文的内涵表达出来，但未能做到在结构上与原文保持一致，没有突显广告的记忆价值；广告2采取意译法，将原文"包便宜"译为"Book now"，虽然与原文不太吻合，但使广告产生了更强的劝导功能、呼唤功能；广告3采用类比法，把苏州、同里比作东方威尼斯，但篇幅过长，效果不如原文；广告4简短有力，保持了原文的语言风格，达到了推广效果。从以上中、英文广告可以看出，中文旅游广告体现了均衡对称、整齐和谐的语言风格；英文广告删繁就简，简明扼要，多使用时间指示词、祈使句，便于记忆。

本章小结

旅游广告是一种独特的语类，它利用语言艺术的一切可能，从语音、词汇、语法、修辞、形式、语篇等多方面体现了广告语言的艺术特点。从功能角度讲，旅游广告应该归属于纽马克所说的"呼唤型"文本。在用词上，中文旅游广告多用形容词和四字词语；英文旅游广告多用代词、动词、形容词及变异拼写。在语法上，中文旅游广告多用省略句，力求实现广告言简意赅的效果；而英文旅游广告多用祈使句、省略句及问句，以增加广告的感情色彩和感染力。在整体风格上，中、英文旅游广告都具有对话性特点，对话性特点使得广告便于读者理解和记忆，且增加广告的渲染度和感染力。翻译旅游广告应根据广告的类型、体裁，在目的语中尽可能选择与原广告相应的语言和风格，但最重要的是突出广告的文本功能，引起游客对广告的关注，提高他们对旅游产品、旅游服务和旅游目的地的兴趣，触发广告AIDAM过程，诱发他们的消费行为，产生旅游广告的"关注价值""记忆价值"。

翻译实践

一、热身练习

翻译下文，并对译文做简要分析。

1. 新北京，新奥运。（城市广告）

2. Big thrills, small bills.（出租车广告）

3. 醉在贵州（城市广告）

4. Good to the last drop（雀巢咖啡广告）

5. 随时为您服务。（旅行社广告）

6. Around the corner, around the world, we are around to help.（旅行社广告）

7. 喝一杯即饮柠檬茶令你怡神醒脑!（柠檬茶广告）

8. 体积虽小，颇具功效。（旅行箱广告）

9. 许多人来到四姑娘山一睹芳容后，惊叹不已：太美了，太美了！简直像仙境一样！（景区广告）

例10. 高楼摩天，星光灿烂，火树银花，瑰丽绝伦，上海的夜色多么迷人。（城市广告）

二、巩固练习

翻译下文，并对译文做简要分析。

1. Savor the Past, Seize the Moment.（旅游局广告）

2. The Ritz-Carlton evidence that treasures can still be found on the beach.（酒店广告）

3. Going East, Staying Western.（宾馆广告）

4. Flowers by Interflora speaks from the heart.（花店广告）

5. No caffeine. Virtually no calories.（饮料广告）

6. Come to New York and See the World.（城市广告）

7. Every time a good time—McDonald（美食广告）

8. One man's sushi is another man's steak.（美食广告）

9. 阿坝之旅，让心灵回归自然。（城市广告）

10. 忙碌了一天？有时差反应吗？打电话请按摩师放松一下吧！（休闲广告）

三、阅读翻译

阅读下文，重点翻译下画线部分。

山海和鸣

<u>在中国东南，有一片浸润在山风海涛间的神奇之地，福建</u>。山海交辉，孕育着独特、绮丽的福建文明：十八万年前的人居洞穴，三万年前的人工石铺地面，五千年前的陶灯，三千多年前的悬棺葬，两千年前的闽越王城，千年前的洛阳桥，百年前的船政学堂……今天，福建自然生态优良，森林覆盖率已连续43年保持全国第一；亚热带季风气候下的生物多样性及丰富度，位居全国前列。1985年，中国成为《保护世界文化和自然遗产公约》缔约国。今天，福建已有4项基于大自然造化和前人创造的自然与文化珍宝，被列入《世界遗产名录》。一个绿色生态的福建，一个文明璀璨的福建，从历史走向未来。

福建的故事来自山。福建世界遗产保护传承，从"山"里走出第一步。1999年武夷山被正式列入《世界遗产名录》，成为福建第一个、中国第四个文化与自然遗产。"东周出孔丘，南宋有朱熹"，孔孟之后最伟大的思想家朱子成长、传道的足迹，遍布武夷山。在南宋至清代的七百多年间，朱子理学是官方正统哲学思想。朱熹学说、著述的广泛传播，塑造了后世中国人的家国理想、伦理价值和

精神世界；朱子学传播到东亚、东南亚，成为东亚文明的重要组成部分。从西晋开始，北方移民大规模的入闽迁徙持续不断。不同时期的"福建人"在这里开拓新家园。

"世界上独一无二的山区大型夯土民居建筑"——福建土楼，在福建西南部，演绎着一代代更新的宏大故事。这些圆形、方形、半圆形、弧形的土楼，适宜山地生活的聚族而居，抵御外袭。2008年，福建土楼因其"东方血缘伦理关系和聚族而居的传统文化的历史见证"及普遍价值，被正式列入《世界遗产名录》。从闽东到浙西，木拱廊桥飞跨山壑溪河，便利百姓风雨跋涉。桥梁承载的是信息传递，是商业贸易。而廊桥上的一木一瓦，更传递着中国传统乡村社会的信仰、道德与温情。廊桥的飞檐，跨越的是丹山，映照的是碧水。福建泰宁，拥有中国丹霞地貌组成中最完好的古夷平面、最密集的网状谷地、发育最好的崖壁洞穴和最宏大的水上丹霞。2010年"中国丹霞"（泰宁），作为世界自然遗产被列入《世界遗产名录》。

福建的故事，来自海。福建的世界遗产保护传承，必然激荡着海洋的波涛。从一千年前的唐朝起，福州、泉州、漳州、厦门轮替成为不同历史时期中国的重要港口。借助季风和洋流，从福建港口出发的货物，和神秘的东方传说一道，被带到了遥远的西亚、东非和欧洲。19世纪中期到20世纪中期这一百年间，在厦门的鼓浪屿上，闽南本土居民、外来多国侨民和华侨群体在共同营建一个"历史国际社区"。九百多座不同风格的历史建筑、自然景观，勾勒出1.88平方公里内中国、东南亚和欧洲建筑及其文化价值的融合脉络。

在2017年第41届世界遗产大会上，"鼓浪屿：历史国际社区"成为福建第4处世界遗产。福州是福建的省会城市，她已有两千两百多年的建城史。位于福州城市中心区的三坊七巷，城市中心居住区的历史已延续了千年，街巷格局被称为"中国城市里坊制度活化石"。个性丰满而独特的建筑、装饰，强烈传递着传统福州士人精英阶层的影响力和艺术趣味、家国理想和道德追求。在19世纪后半期的航海图中，这座伫立在闽江下游马限山上的航标塔，被称作"中国塔"。山下曾诞生了中国近代第一个造船厂，中国第一座学习西方航海与船舶技术的学校——福建船政学堂。今天的福建，是中国21世纪海上丝绸之路的核心区和互联

互通的重要枢纽。这里是中国最早提出建设数字化的省份，是中国首批国家生态文明试验区。这里有先进的制造业、发达的远洋渔业、丰富的物产和多彩的文化生活，持续提升着人们对幸福的感知。

<u>五千年的福建文明，正在上演新的史诗</u>！

第四章　旅游网站翻译

随着全球经济、交通飞速发展，人们的出行方式发生了巨大的变化。互联网、云计算、云储存技术日新月异，人们可以通过网站查询旅游信息、网上预订、网上支付，这些改变了人们的出行方式。在全球化和大数据时代，互联网技术为全球旅游业开展线上线下旅游业务提供了条件。游前，游客不仅能24小时查询吃、住、行、游、购、娱等相关旅游信息，还能通过网站了解旅游目的地的风景名胜、历史文化、民俗、美食等，出发前可在线上预订机票、酒店等；游中，游客可以参考旅游网站上推荐的餐厅、购物中心、游乐场所，或选择旅游交通，也可以根据自己的需求重新规划旅游线路；游后，网站作为一个反馈平台，游客可以发布自己的游记、感想、评论，与其他游客在线互动，为后来的游客提供更多的游览信息，提供建议，促进旅游企业健康发展。

案例研究

爱尔兰旅游网站翻译

从爱尔兰旅游网站以下几个界面可以看出，该网站呈现典型的英文网站界面设计的特点。首页顶端与各个页面链接，从左到右是"Destinations""Things to do""Plan your trip""Help and advice"；打开网站链接，第二页出现"Amazing landscapes""The great outdoors""A taste of Ireland"等栏目。网站整体布局呈"倒金字塔"结构，重要内容位于第一页，依重要程度排列。此外，网站首页中心位置特别设计了一个短视频，以读者的视角讲解爱尔兰各地的旅游风光，画面生动，音乐动人，给人一种身临其境之感。

Amazing landscapes

We like our landscapes just the way nature made them – rugged, weathered and with plenty of attitude.

3 min read
10 reasons why Ireland is always in season

No matter the time of year, you'll find a warm welcome.

The great outdoors

Looking for adventure? You've come to the right place. One day you're golfing at the edge of the Atlantic, the next you're ziplining through a forest or hiking through the hills.

3 min read
7 gorgeous spots for wild swimming

Take a dip in the crystal clear lakes and rivers on the island of Ireland.

第四章　旅游网站翻译

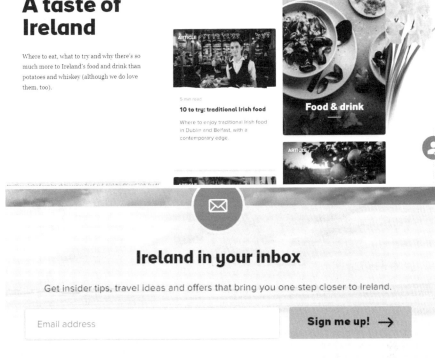

图4.1　爱尔兰旅游网站截图

来源：https://www.ireland.com/en-gb/#，登录时间2021.4.5

从语言上看，爱尔兰旅游网站大量使用褒义形容词，如"amazing""incredible" "gorgeous"，渲染景色，吸引旅客；从叙事角度上讲，使用第一人称和第二人称，如"We like our landscapes…""One day you're golfing…""the next you're ziplining…"给人一种老朋友在聊天的感觉；语言通俗化、口语化，以拉近与浏览用户的距离，如"Looking for adventure? You've come to the right place."使用短语、短句或句项名物化，代替复杂句式，创造一种读者容易理解的语言结构，如"On the road""10 to try""Where to enjoy?"大量使用祈使句、主动语态，如"Take a dip in the crystal clear lakes…""Sign me up"等，带有较强的诱导功能和劝导功能。

一、旅游网站的结构和内容

旅游网站囊括旅游广告、旅游指南、旅游目的地介绍等文本，因此旅游网站的篇章结构无法从一种类型的旅游文本概括出来。总体看来，旅游网站架构层次多、信息充足、更新快速。虽然各版块独立，但又能构成一个整体，由文本、图像、动画、声音、视频、表格、导航栏等七个部分组成。因此，网站的翻译是一种包括文本和非文本的转换过程，其目的是使读者自如高效地把握相关旅游资讯，从而激发旅游动机和旅游行为（林菲，2015：76）。旅游网站的翻译无论涉及哪一种旅游文本，都应以译语读者为中心，在传递旅游信息的同时，激发旅游者的旅游动机或旅游消费行为。

1. 旅游网站结构

旅游网站每一个网页都有一个主题，根据主题布置页面内容、板块和其他辅助内容。通常情况下，旅游网站的页面分为三个或四个栏目，中间一栏为主要内容，左边一栏为导航信息，有时导航信息在顶端，右边常常为与主要内容有关但不太重要的附加信息。网页用户的浏览习惯一般是从左上方浏览至右下方，网页的字体设计需要考虑用户的浏览习惯。为了突显广告，网站对一些核心字体可进行艺术化的处理，以便吸引游客的注意。一些旅游网站还包括旅游地图导航等内容。

旅游网站的空间组成部分由链接（主要是独立的名词结构)和散布在主要文本周围的导航按钮、菜单、广告、搜索框等构成。网站没有起点，也没有终点，具有流动性。与固定的、静止的印刷页面不同，网页上的文件是动态的，可以随时改变和升级。网页语篇以一种流动的、开放的形式在电脑显示器上出现，又很快消失，从来不是稳定的。网页上的内容具有协作性，读者可以参与他们所阅读的文本的建设，读者和作者可以共享电子空间，这样，他们之间的界线消失了。

网站文本没有中心，也没有边缘，没有内部或外部。当一个电子文本与另一个文本链接以后，或一个文本被复制出来传给另一人之后，各文本之间的间隔或区别也消失了。网站的超文本是"多层次的"，"无限地重新确定中心"，因此网页上的超级链接、网页的交互性以及网页的多功能性会影响网站文本的语篇特点（丁大刚：2008：91）。网站文本的语篇与图像还具有互文性，翻译旅游网站页面，无论是格式还是语篇，需注意网站超文本功能这一特点。

下面以香港旅游发展局网站为例，简要分析旅游网站的结构和内容，为旅游网站的本地化和翻译做铺垫和准备。

图4.2　香港旅游发展局官网首页

来源：https://www.discoverhongkong.com/eng/index.html, 登录时间2021.4.14

图4.2为香港旅游发展局官网首页。从排版上看网站分为三栏，上面一栏为导航信息，中间一栏为重要信息，右上一栏为网站的个性化服务，方便旅客通过搜索引擎进行相关操作。"Staycation"是一个拼缀词，意为"宅家度假"，作为网站的主题，字体放大，进行了艺术化的处理，翻译时需做相应的"前景化"（"foregrounding"）处理。

图4.3　香港旅游发展局官网WHAT'S NEW菜单栏的内容

来源：https://www.discoverhongkong.com/eng/index.html, 登录时间2021.4.14

点击第一个"WHAT'S NEW"下拉菜单栏下的内容，可以看到中间栏的图片和文字非常直观地展示了关于三个方面的内容，分别是游客在香港必游十大项目、香港旅游出行方式、香港周末游推荐线路，该栏目强调香港"新旅游"体验。

图4.4　香港旅游发展局官网EXPLORE菜单栏的内容

来源：https://www.discoverhongkong.com/eng/index.html，登录时间2021.4.14

点击第二个"EXPLORE"下拉菜单栏的内容，可以了解到关于香港旅游景点、饮食、购物、户外活动、文化、艺术、巡游等方面的信息，文字简洁、一目了然。

从以上网站页面可以看出，旅游网站是动态化的页面，不同于旅游指南、旅游手册，它可以根据最新的时事更新内容和界面。该网站设计合理，采用英、法、日、韩等多种语言，具有简洁、美观、人性化的特点，符合旅游网站的总体设计要求，对香港的旅游宣传和促销起到了良好的作用，也为旅游网站翻译提供了很好的借鉴。

2. 旅游网站的内容

旅游网站载体很多，如旅游广告、旅游手册、旅游指南、旅游景点介绍、旅游日志、旅游评论等，内容也很丰富，提供机票、酒店、旅游线路等，涉及吃、住、行、游、购、娱等方面的综合咨询与预订服务，向游客介绍目的地的风景名胜、风土人情、历史文化等。旅游网站的这些内容主要依靠文字和图像呈现，也少量使用音乐、视频等。旅游网站文字简明扼要，但需有感染力；图像直观生动，但需配说明文字；常用美化语言的修辞手法，如明喻、隐喻、排比、夸张等。

下面就旅游网站涉及的吃、住、行、游、购、娱六个方面的内容，结合旅游网站的语言特点和翻译方法举例说明。

一、吃

例：品尝地道点心

上酒楼"饮茶"，点一壶好茶，选几样点心，看看报纸，与朋友聊聊天……想体验这种极富当地特色的饮食文化，你可以去<u>平民路线的莲香楼</u>、<u>洋溢文人雅士风的陆羽茶室</u>，或是<u>坐拥维港美景、头顶米其林三星光环的龙景轩</u>。

译文：Devouring dim sum your way, any time of day

Dim sum: not only Hong Kong's breakfast staple, but a peek at our many societal rungs. Join the crack-of-dawn crowd and eat alongside the working classes at Lin Heung Tea Room, rub shoulders with the all-day crowds at Luk Yu Teahouse or enjoy these delicious bites dished up tycoon-style at Lung King Heen.

来源：https://www.discoverhongkong.com/eng/index.html，登录时间2021.4.14

分析：这段网文是香港旅游发展局官网饮食方面的内容。网站除了介绍香港美食、茶饮、点心外，还向游客推荐了几家香港具有代表性的港式茶餐厅：莲香楼、陆羽茶室、龙景轩等，介绍了这些茶餐厅的消费群体以及特色，供游客选择。英文网页首句采用标题式写作方法，接着连用两个祈使句，文字非常简洁，起到了鼓励消费的劝导作用，对中文网站的翻译有很好的借鉴意义。

二、住

例：Apartment accommodation is ideal for New Zealand travellers who want the quality of a hotel stay combined with the flexibility of self-catering facilities.

Apartments are a great option when you're staying in a major city or resort town. You can cook your own meals, do your own laundry and enjoy the feeling of having your own space while on holiday.

Many are similar in price to a high quality hotel suite with daily or regular servicing and they're perfect for couples, groups or families. Some even have access to gymnasiums and swimming pools.

译文：既渴望享受酒店的优质服务，又希望拥有自助式的自由自在，酒店式公寓可谓到新西兰旅游最佳的下榻之选。

如果想要待在大城市或度假胜地，入住公寓式酒店是个绝好的选择。你可以自己做饭，自己洗衣服，享受度假时拥有自己的空间给你带来的自由自在。

不少公寓的房价与高档的酒店套房相当，可为客人提供每日或定期的客房服务，是情侣、团体或家庭游客的完美之选。有的公寓甚至还拥有健身房和游泳池。

来源：https://www.newzealand.com/int/buscoach-transport/，登录时间2021.4.14

分析：这段文本是新西兰旅游网站中住宿方面的内容，为游客提供了多种住宿选择，既有酒店，又有酒店式公寓，并且分别介绍了住酒店和公寓的优势，非常人性化。由于此段网文是信息型文本，译文采用了直译法，在传达网站信息的同时，再现了原网站的语言风格；在叙事角度方面使用了第二人称，使文本产生了友好亲切的"对话性"，也体现了一定的诱导功能。

三、行

例：Bus travel and coach transport is ideal if you prefer to make your way around New Zealand without the hassle of self-driving. Sit back, relax and enjoy the ride.

Coach bus travel is flexible and easy. A cost-effective alternative to air travel with daily scheduled passenger services available throughout the country. There's also a multitude of coach companies serving the main tourist routes.

Hop on, hop off travellers' networks, where you buy a pass for unlimited travel, can move you around New Zealand's major destinations very effectively. In Auckland there are buses that circulate around key attractions, allowing you unlimited travel for a fixed price.

译文：想省下自驾的麻烦，又想环游新西兰，那么巴士与长途客车将是你的理想之选。悠然坐定，从容观光，旅行原来可以如此简单！

搭乘长途汽车是比飞机旅行更实惠的环游新西兰的旅行方式。新西兰很多长途客运公司开辟了主要的旅游线路。

"随上随下"旅客网允许你购买无限搭乘的通程票，带你实惠玩转新西兰的主要旅游景点。奥克兰（Auckland）有往返于主要景区的巴士，允许你在支付一定费用之后，无限搭乘。

来源：https://www.newzealand.com/int/buscoach-transport/，登录时间2021.4.14

分析：这段网文介绍了新西兰旅游交通方面的内容。旅游网站为游客提供交通服务咨询和预订服务，无论是自驾、巴士还是长途客车，网站都为游客提供了出行选择。网文为信息型文本，兼有呼唤功能、劝导功能，以读者视角"you"介入，使用祈使句"Sit back, relax and enjoy the ride""Hop on, hop off travellers' networks"。译文直译与意译相结合，既传达了旅游交通信息，又起到了旅游网站文本的呼唤、诱导作用，"悠然坐定，从容观光，旅行原来可以如此简单！"就是一例。

四、游

例：Welcome to the Guggenheim, where you can immerse yourself in video, film, and performance by some of today's most exciting artists inside our spiraling rotunda. Safety measures and requirements are in place for your well-being.

译文：欢迎来到古根海姆博物馆！在这里，您可以沉浸在视频、电影中。在我们旋转的圆形大厅里，您可以欣赏到当今最激动人心的艺术家们的表演。安全措施和要求已就位，保障您的健康。

来源：https://www.guggenheim.org，登录时间2021.4.14

分析：这是古根海姆博物馆网站向游客介绍博物馆游览方面的内容。游客在古根海姆博物馆可以进行各种游览活动。译文根据文本的功能，使用第一人称（作者视角）和第二人称（读者视角），拉近与参观者的距离，产生了亲切友好的互动；同时采用拆分法，将原文长句分解为若干短句，语气诚挚、文字简明扼要。

五、购

例：在露天市集、购物街血拼

香港有不少露天市集，各有特色，各具个性。摩罗上街和庙街夜市是挖掘古董和旧物的绝佳去处；女人街和赤柱市集则以售卖服装饰物、旅游纪念品为主。

译文：Haggling at the city's street markets

Hit the streets and shops at <u>our</u> many outdoor markets. Cat Street (Antiques) and Temple Street Night Market are antique and vintage favorites, while Ladies' Market, Stanley Market all sell everything from branded clothing to bric-a-brac.

来源：https://www.discoverhongkong.com/eng/index.html, 登录时间2021.4.14

分析：这是香港旅游发展局官网购物方面的内容。购物是香港最具吸引力的特色之一，网站介绍了香港著名的购物中心：摩罗上街和庙街夜市、女人街和赤柱市集，供游客选择。译文在传达原文的实质性信息的同时，将原文的陈述句改为祈使句："Hit the streets and shops at our many outdoor markets"，并使用了第一人称"our"，使译文具有较强的呼唤功能、诱导功能，达到了旅游宣传、劝导的目的。

六、娱

例：Chimelong Safari Park's shows are well-known both at home and abroad. The funny elephants and Apes of Huaguoshan Theater are not only eye-openers, but also draw convulsive laughters.

译文：长隆野生动物世界的动物表演驰名国内外。滑稽搞笑的大象表演、<u>明"猩"云集</u>的花果山剧场表演都令人<u>忍俊不禁</u>、<u>大开眼界</u>！

来源：https://www.chimelong.com/gz/safaripark/, 登录时间2021.4.14

分析：这段网文向游客介绍了长隆野生动物世界游玩方面的内容。译文将花果山剧场中的"Apes"译为"明'猩'云集"，使用了双关修辞手法，暗指野生动物园中的动物明星大猩猩，巧妙风趣，吸引了游客的注意。另外，采用汉语四字格词语，如"忍俊不禁""大开眼界"，并将该段末句的句号改译为感叹号，增强了网站的诱导功能、呼唤功能。

二、旅游网站的文本功能

文本是网页上最重要的信息载体，网页中的主要信息一般都以文本形式呈现；而图像在网页中具有提供信息并展示直观形象的作用；动画在网页中能有效地吸引访问者更多的注意力；声音使网页动听悦耳，能用音频调动潜在旅游者的感受；视频文件使网页效果更加精彩且富有动感；表格在网页中用来控制页面信息的布局方式，让网页用户阅读文字、数据一目了然；导航栏在网页中是一组超链接，通过导航栏，网页用户可以获取更多的旅游咨询。网页中的文本、图像、动画、声音、视频、表格、导航栏等七个元素，在旅游网站建设中都发挥着不同的功能和作用。显然，网站的翻译主要是对网站文本的翻译，对图像、动画、声音、视频等的翻译比重较小，因此，本节主要探讨旅游网站文本的功能和翻译，从宏观层面为旅游网站翻译提供翻译思路和方法。

1. 旅游网站的信息功能

旅游网站具有信息性，但呈现的信息必须实时、准确、有效。旅游网站在视觉组织上允许把具有不同功能和不同交际目的的多种文本、信息包含在一个文件中。一个网页上的空间可以分为几个不同的部分，通过一些链接和散布在主要文本周围的导航按钮、菜单、广告、搜索框等组织在一起发布信息。网站的搜索引擎为用户提供了人性化的设计，方便浏览者根据自己的要求搜寻旅游信息，也促成了用户和商家的交互模式，例如搜索框（search），发布旅游日志、评论等。因此，旅游网站的翻译要注意旅游网站文本的这些特点，译文应体现网站的信息功能，不能因"诱导"而失真，因追求语言美而损失实质信息。

例1.

Morning and Night Markets Gathering Food and Souvenir Stands

Talad Nampu or Nampu Market is another market that has been around in Chanthaburi's city center for many years, providing from food, local products, clothing, dried preserved products, fruits, fresh seafood, souvenirs for both locals and visitors to Chanthaburi from morning to night time. If you are even lacking anything for your trip, we promise you will find what you need here.

译文：

早市、夜市——食品、纪念品摊汇集地

南浦市场是泰国的另一个市场，多年来一直在尖竹汶府（Chanthaburi）的市中心，为当地人和游客提供24小时的商品供应，包括当地物产、服装、干腌制产品、水果、新鲜海鲜、纪念品。如果你在旅途中缺任何东西，我们保证你会在这里找到你需要的东西。

来源：http://amazingthailand.org.cn，登录时间2021.4.14

分析：南浦市场是一家位于尖竹汶府市中心的夜市，24小时为游客提供各种商品，网站介绍了泰国尖竹汶府市旅游购物方面的内容。本段是信息型文本，译文根据原文的功能，注重信息的实时、准确、有效，采用"等功能翻译"（"equifunctional translation"）。网页用"等功能翻译"还是"异功能翻译"（"heterofunctional translation"），取决于网站经营者的目的。

例2. Clear water and a rich underwater world make the shallow waters of Kemi an ideal place for snorkeling. On the way, simple equipment is needed to jump into the water. The instructor will use bread or fruit to attract a school of colorful fish, so that you can experience the wonderful feeling of swimming with the fish. The night market on Aonan Beach brings together more than 100 seafood restaurants and bars, offering the best variety and freshness of seafood. Try Kemi's authentic cooking, accompanied by gentle sea breezes and the romantic singing of the bar singer.

译文：清澈的海水，丰富的水下世界，让甲米浅海成为理想的浮潜之地。跳岛途中，只需简单的设备就可以跃入水中。教练会用面包或者水果引来色彩斑斓的鱼群，让你体验与鱼群共游的奇妙感觉。也可以在夜市吃一次海鲜大排档，澳南海滩的夜市汇集了百余家海鲜餐厅和酒吧，提供的海鲜种类和新鲜度都首屈一指。尝尝甲米原汁原味的烹饪美食，身边还有温柔海风以及酒吧歌手的浪漫歌声。

来源：http://amazingthailand.org.cn/Content/Index/shows/catid/115/id/1.html，登录时间2021.4.14

分析：这是另一则信息型网站文本，从美食、游览、娱乐三个方面介绍了泰国旅游胜地甲米。译文仍然采用信息型文本的一般翻译方法，但不是平铺直叙，而是采用了对偶修辞格（"清澈的海水，丰富的水下世界"）、使用祈使句（"尝尝……"）、汉语四字格（"色彩斑斓""首屈一指"）、第二人称代词（让你……）等，在传递原文信息的同时使文本产生了网站经营者所希望的诱导功能，但译文没有因"诱导"而失真，没有因语言美而损失实质信息。

2. 旅游网站的诱导功能

旅游网站文本的另一个特点是诱导性，诱导性是旅游网站文本最重要的特点之一。旅游网站的语言设计可用新奇诱导、名人诱导、利益诱导等方法刺激旅游者的消费欲望，引发消费行为，还可以采取竞赛诱导、对比诱导、悬念诱导等激发他们的游兴，吸引游客，提高旅游服务质量，增强服务效率。因此，旅游网站文本常用夸张、拟人、排比、反问、设问、对偶、比喻等修辞手法，以提高网站文本的表达效果和语言张力。翻译旅游网站应注意这些特点，增加译文的诱导、祈使功能。旅游网站的翻译不能因过分平实而失去其诱导功能，影响旅游网站的宣传、促销功能和作用。

例1. A stunning confluence of scenery, culture and cuisine, Busan packs an eclectic offering of activities to suit all travelers: hike hills to Buddhist temples, settle into sizzling hot springs and feast on seafood at the country's largest fish market.

译文：釜山荟萃了风景、文化和美食的精华，这里五花八门的活动足以让所有旅行者心满意足：登山游寺，泡热乎乎的温泉，或是在韩国最大的鱼市大嚼肥美的海鲜。

来源：http://chinese.visitkorea.or.kr/chs/index.kto，登录时间2021.4.3

分析：从诱导性功能上看，网文文字优美，形象生动。译文使用了名物化结构，将"confluence"转译为动词"荟萃"，将同位语"A stunning confluence of scenery, culture and cuisine"置于句首，突显旅游目的地的景点、文化、美食，吸引游客前往釜山旅行，增强了网站文本的诱导功能。此外，译文还使用一系列带有祈使性质的动词，如"登""泡""嚼"等，以及带有渲染的词汇，如"荟萃""精华""肥美""热乎乎的"等,让游客有一种身临其境的感觉,仿佛能感受到温泉烟雾缭绕的热气,置身于海鲜市场,闻到鱼腥,感受到了鱼肉的肥美。

例2.Compared with Phuket, which is also on the Andaman Sea, Kemi is more low-key, private, introverted and simple, like a piece of uncut jade, just a little bit of brilliance has been detected.

译文:相比于同在安达曼海的普吉,甲米更加低调、私密,也更加内敛和淳朴,仿佛一块璞玉,刚有些许的光华,就被人觉察到了。

来源:http://amazingthailand.org.cn/Content/Index/shows/catid/115/id/1.html,登录时间2021.4.3

分析:从诱导性功能上看,这段网文采用了排比、比喻的修辞手法,突出了甲米旅游景点的优点:低调、私密、内敛、淳朴,让游客有一种宁静致远的感觉。译文采用"等功能翻译"方法,使译文同样带有原文强烈的诱导功能:想要远离喧嚣、感受淳朴自然,到甲米旅游吧。译文略有改动。

三、旅游网站的语言特点

旅游网站是一种新的语篇体裁,有以下特点:大量使用形容词和强调性语言,特别是大量使用褒义形容词,以吸引潜在旅游者的眼球,感受景色之美(尚路平,2014:110);使用第一、二人称,给人一种老朋友在聊天的感觉,使语篇具有对话式特点;使用通俗、口语化的词语,拉近与旅游者的距离(周红,2015:60);主动语态比重高于被动语态,表达更加顺畅,拉近网站与浏览者的距离(丁大刚,2008:92);使用简单句,用词简洁,常用拼缀词,在有限的网页空间给读者提供更多的信息;少用从句,多用短语、短句或句项名物化,创造一种可以被读者理解的句式代替复杂的句式结构;多用祈使句或感叹句,使文本带有诱导功能和劝导功能。

由此可见,虽然旅游网站是以信息功能为主的旅游文本,但大量使用形容词和强调性语言,多用祈使句和感叹句,主动语态多于被动语态,语篇具有对话式特点，因此旅游网站也有诱导、呼唤等功能，而不是"承载旧信息的新媒介"。帕翠西亚·皮奇尼尼（Partrizia Pierini）认为，旅游网站篇章呈现"可用性"的特点，而影响"可用性"的因素有网站设计、网站导航、网页搜索等（Pierini, 2007: 113）。因此，旅游网站文本普遍采用倒金字塔式结构，即先叙述结果，再展开论述，这与英美读者的阅读习惯是相呼应的（景兴润，2015: 49）。这也是旅游网站的特点。

例1. In a fast-paced city like Hong Kong, there's always something new happening. From new attractions to upcoming events, there's never a dull day in Hong Kong.

译文：在香港这样一个快节奏城市，总有<u>新</u>鲜事儿发生。<u>新</u>的景点、<u>新</u>的活动，香港从未闲下来过。

分析：这句话是香港旅游发展局官网"WHAT'S NEW"菜单栏下的文本，引出香港"新"旅游"新"在何处。中文网站重复使用三个"新"字，语言简洁有力，使文本具有强烈的诱导功能、呼唤功能、感染功能。

例2. Hong Kong of China is ready to welcome our friends from the world with the air travel bubble relaunching in May! And it's all thanks to pioneering innovations and effective health policies. Check out five things that Hong Kong is doing to protect the health and safety of its visitors as they explore around the city.

译文：中国香港"航空旅游气泡"将于5月重启。凭借创新科技配合有效的卫生政策，香港已经准备就绪，欢迎世界各地朋友来港！看五大卫生防疫和安全措施，让你来港备感安心、放心。

来源：https://www.discoverhongkong.com/eng/index.html，登录时间2021.4.14

分析：这段话是香港旅游网站"EXPLORE"菜单栏下的文本，反映了新冠肺炎疫情背景下香港最新的旅游政策以及游客最关心的安全问题。译文使用多个动词，并将英文的陈述句改为祈使句："欢迎……"最后一句"看……""让……"更是体现了汉语"动态性"语言的特征。动态性的网页加上动态性的语言：绝配！

例3. In a city as vibrant as Hong Kong, all the best experiences are here—from cultures ancient and modern, to vistas natural and urban, and flavors local and international. With such diverse choices, we know that you might need some help. So, here's a list of the top experiences not to miss when you're in Hong Kong.

译文：香港好玩的地方实在是太多了，不晓得怎么选？十大必玩推荐：<u>品</u>香港古今文脉、<u>赏</u>香港中外时尚、<u>玩</u>香港城乡胜景、疯狂血<u>拼</u>……——都要放到口袋清单。<u>出发吧！</u>

分析：这是香港旅游发展局官网十大旅游景点推荐。译文没有根据原文亦步亦趋，而是根据中文广告话语的特点，对篇章进行了重构。开头使用了一个设问句，使网站文本具有"对话性"；接着使用了祈使句"品""赏""玩""拼"，一连串动词并用，最后还增译了一个颇具呼唤功能的话语："出发吧！"这种本地化的翻译方法对原文内容进行编译、改写，以满足中文游客的旅游期待，使网站有更强的呼唤功能、诱导功能，体现了中文网站功能性语言的特点。译文有改动。

例4. Hike up the Morning Trail to the Peak Galleria, where refreshments await—along with classic picture-postcard skyline views across both sides of Victoria Harbour. Alternatively, the Peak Tram offers a scenic sprint up to the top with stellar views along the way. For a different view, come at sunset when the sky erupts into brilliant reds before blinking back to life with a million lights below.

译文：想拥有一个神清气爽的早晨？不妨早起，健行上太平山顶吧！晨运径是登上山顶的理想路径，到达山顶广场欣赏维多利亚港两岸的景色，风光优美如明信片一般，让人心旷神怡。除了健行，山顶缆车是不少人游览山顶的方法之一，坐上这个历史悠久的交通工具，在美景陪伴下，不一会儿便到达山顶站。而日落时分到访又是另一番景象，这时候的天空渐渐变色，是不可错过的梦幻时刻，城市中万家灯火的景致，定能让你深深感受夜香港的美。

分析：这句话是香港旅游发展局官网健行登山旅游的推荐文字。译文没有根据网站原文亦步亦趋，而是根据中文广告话语的特点，对篇章进行了重构。开头使用了一个设问句，使网站文本具有"对话性"："想拥有一个神清气爽的早晨？"接着使用了祈使句"不妨早起，健行上太平山顶吧！"增强了文本的呼唤功能。此外，还根据情景有意识地增译了主观感受，寓情于景，如"让人心旷神怡""在美景陪伴下""定能让你深深感受夜香港的美",以满足中文游客的审美旅游期待,体现了中文网站功能性语言的特点。

例5. Home to the country's <u>largest</u> national park, a <u>dramatically imposing</u> coastline and of course the city itself, there is so much to explore in Aberdeen City and Shire. Fusing <u>striking</u> granite architecture, a <u>rich</u> and <u>inspiring</u> history, a <u>dynamic</u> modern arts scene and perhaps Scotland's <u>strongest</u> industrial heritage; the country's <u>third largest</u> city offers a host of treasures, just waiting to be explored again and again.

译文：拥有全国最大的国家公园，海岸线亦令人叹为观止，阿伯丁市和夏尔有很多值得探索的地方。风格鲜明的花岗岩建筑，极其深厚的历史底蕴，富有生机活力的现代艺术风貌，还有苏格兰最强大的工业遗产。作为全国第三大城市，阿伯丁市和夏尔坐享无数珍宝，值得您前来"淘宝"。

来源：https://www.visitabdn.com/，登录时间2021.5.4

分析：原文用了8个不同的褒义形容词，如"imposing""strongest"以及形容词最高级"largest""strongest"描写该地的自然风光和历史遗迹；句首采用独立结构"Home to the country's largest national park, a dramatically imposing coastline and of course the city itself..."，创造一种读者容易理解的句式代替复杂的结构；尽量用短语、短句代替从句，如"Fusing striking granite architecture, a rich and inspiring history, a dynamic modern arts scene..."，语言简练、句式灵活，富有呼唤功能、诱导功能，吸引游客前往观光。

例6. <u>We</u> have 14 scenic railways in Wales. They were built years ago to transport Welsh slate and people and share a common charm of old time steam trains with plenty of paintwork and polished brass. Most of them are pretty old which is why they go so slow but at least it means <u>you</u> can enjoy the magnificent scenery.

译文：威尔士有14条风景秀丽的铁路。它们是几年前建造的，用于运输威尔士石板和人员。与那些涂有油漆和抛光黄铜的老式蒸汽火车一样，极具怀旧复古之风情。大多数蒸汽火车都相当古老，速度缓慢，但正因如此，您可以慢悠悠地享受壮美风景。

来源：https://www.visitwales.com/，登录时间2021.5.4

分析：这段语言朴实，多为陈述句，但叙事角度采用第一人称和第二人称。开篇的"we"好像是威尔士人向全球游客发出邀请，邀请大家去做客；结尾的"you"语气平易近人，拉近了与游客的距离，是一种对话式风格的旅游宣传文字，虽然语言质朴，同样使文本产生了良好的劝导功能和诱导功能。整个网站语言没有生僻词汇，用词偏口语化，十分接地气，适合各个年龄层的游客阅读。

四、旅游网站的本地化翻译

本地化行业标准协会（Localization Industry Standards Association，简称LISA）将本地化定义为对产品或服务进行修改以满足不同市场需求的过程。从翻译角度讲，本地化是将一个产品按特定国家或地区语言市场的需要进行加工，使之满足特定市场的用户对语言和文化的特殊要求的活动（中国翻译协会，2011）。翻译只是本地化活动中的一部分，除了翻译之外，本地化项目还包括项目管理、软件工程、测试等。本地化翻译与一般的翻译不同，不仅要翻译，还要使语言的外观适应产品图标、页面排版习惯等要求（张莹，柴明颎，2011：77—80）。旅游网站的本地化翻译还涉及超语言成分，对原文中的标记、图表、出版信息等超语言方面也要进行本地化处理。由于语言维度和文化维度的影响，本地化翻译较一般意义上的翻译难度更大。

1. 语言、文化维度与本地化翻译

本地化翻译受文化维度和语言维度两个方面的制约和影响。从语言维度看，旅游网站的本地化主要涉及词、句、篇章三个层面的翻译。在文化迁移方面，本地化翻译将文化维度理论，即运用五项价值维度——个人主义与集体主义、权力距离、不确定性规避、男性主义和女性主义以及长远观念与短期观念作为本地化翻译指导，处理文本中的文化差异（肖卫国，刘跃斌，2011：15）。文化维度考虑的是内容的取舍，语言维度考虑的是如何翻译。以下是中外两个旅游网站首页截图。

第四章　旅游网站翻译

图4.5　四川省文化和旅游厅官网

来源：http://wlt.sc.gov.cn/，登录时间2021.5.7

图4.6　新西兰国家旅游官网

图4.6　新西兰国家旅游官网（续）

来源：https://www.newzealand.com/，登录时间2021.5.7

从版块设置上看，四川文旅厅网站采用"政治文旅二合一"的网站结构，首页设有"政务版块"，如政务公开、政民服务等内容，"旅游版块"在整个页面布局中占比较小；新西兰旅游网站没有政务板块，内容均与旅游咨询相关。

从关键词来看，四川文旅厅网站没有关键词；而新西兰旅游网站关键词非常醒目，并使用了中文"你好，欢迎来到新西兰"，很显然，是为了吸引中国游客，带有强烈的呼唤性色彩，吸引中国和世界各地游客到新西兰游玩。

从页面设计上看，四川省文旅厅页面线条流畅、框架板正，首页有国徽，没有旅游logo，营造出一种庄重严肃的氛围；新西兰旅游网站的页面主要以图片为主，首页有旅游logo——银蕨（新西兰国树）。

对比以上两个网站可以看出，由于受文化维度和语言维度的影响，中英旅游网站差异较大，版块、页面、文本等有所不同，语言差异更明显。中文旅游网站更具有集体主义的特征，而英文旅游网站更具有个人主义特征。此外，受政治因素、宣传重心、语言习惯、意识偏差等因素影响，中英旅游网站，特别是旅游官网在内容、结构、功能等方面也存在较大差异，掌握这些差异对处理好旅游网站中的两个维度，有效地实现旅游网站本地化的翻译至关重要。

2. 旅游网站本地化翻译的要求

网站的本地化，就是将现有的网站变得能被目标读者所接受、使用和在文化上认同的过程，它包括针对产品的使用和销售地对产品进行语言、技术与文化的同化(丁大刚,2008:95)。因此,本地化翻译将产品信息从一种语言翻译为另一种语言的同时,必须对产品携带的文化内容做一些修改,尊重并迎合目标市场用户的审美和习惯,目的是克服产品本身的文化障碍,从而吸引更多的本地用户,在目标市场推广和销售。因此,本地化的过程就是翻译产品"入乡随俗"的过程。

处在本地化环境中的翻译过程更具"干涉性",在内容与形式的取舍方面会与传统的翻译不同,这是因为文化维度不同所致。此外,本地化翻译对于形式和内容同等看重。对于传统的翻译而言,内容与形式基本上是固定不变的,而在本地化背景中,由于数字媒体环境下的翻译需要,也有可能对形式进行大的改动,可以对文本、背景、图像及声音改到满意为止。例如,网站本地化的语言支持会涉及对主页的总体规划、字体、颜色表、图像设计等所有传递信息的非文本因素(马文丽,王利明,2005:15—18)。

3. 旅游网站本地化翻译的方法

基于旅游网站本地化的翻译,译者有很大的话语权。在不影响原文思想表达的前提下,旅游网站文本的翻译可采取创造性的翻译策略,对原文进行有针对性的整合,如改写或改编、编译等。编译在很大程度上可以消除语言文化障碍,采用大众所熟知的源语言文化元素代替原文中不被大众所熟知的文化元素(董踩,2021:186),弥补原文与译文在社会文化、体裁风格和修辞等方面存在的差异;而创译在广告翻译、旅游翻译、网站翻译等领域被广泛应用,这是因为这些领域的文本含有因文化差异而不能在目标语文化中进行表述的源文化因素,通过"文化过滤"("cultural filter"),使译文符合译入语的文化背景(高士等,2016:123)。

因此,旅游网站文本的本地化翻译过程实际上就是根据客户的认知、意愿以及网站组织者的目的将网站文本进行编译、创译,并使其符合旅游目标市场形象宣传、推广营销的过程。按照功能翻译理论,成功的网站文本翻译主要取决于是否能实现公司组织预先设定的目标和功能。译文文本的功能是网站文本翻译的重中之重,译文与源语在语言、体裁、篇章上是否对等是次要的,而要实现公司组织预先设定的文本功能,离不开符合文本目的的创造性改写,既可以采取"等功能翻译"策略，也可以采取"异功能翻译"策略，以实现旅游网站预设的功能和翻译目的。不同于其他文本的翻译，旅游网站本地化的翻译在内容取舍、篇章重构等方面，可能会完全颠覆你的想象。

（1）等功能翻译

在很多情况下，旅游网站文本既有信息功能，也带有诱导功能，无论是吃、住、行，还是游、购、娱，信息型旅游文本都带有或多或少的诱导功能，鼓励旅游消费行为。旅游网站的翻译可采用"等功能翻译"，也就是说将原文本的功能移植到目标语文本，以实现原文与译文的"功能对等"。如果网站文本是信息功能文本，译文就呈现原文的信息；如果网站文本是呼唤性功能文本，译文就呈现其呼唤功能。

例1.

The Off Season

Valid from 23/4/2021—23/7/2021

A warm and contemporary haven in the heart of Hobart. Your Getaway is Our Giveaway this Off Season. Experience a 3-night stay including a full breakfast and welcome drinks for two, $100 F&B dining credit, free valet parking and 1 p.m. checkout.

译文：

淡季

有效期：2021年4月23日——2021年7月23日

<u>我们酒店位于霍巴特中心，为您提供温暖、现代的避风港</u>。淡季，<u>您的短假由我们承包</u>。体验3晚(含全套早餐和双人欢迎饮料)，100美元餐饮积分，免费代客泊车，下午1点退房。

来源：https://www.australia.com/en，登录时间2021.4.14

分析：这段网文介绍了旅游住宿的优惠条件，包括餐饮积分、免费代客泊车等，说明了退房时间，使用典型的英文旅游网站语言，是典型的网站住宿推荐文体，属于信息型文本。网文使用第一人称；名词词组替代长句；祈使句替换陈述句；使用并列结构和独立结构。译文采用"等功能翻译"，在再现原文信息功能的同时，也通过中文的语言形式使网站产生一定诱导功能，如："我们酒店位于……""为您提供温暖、现代的避风港""您的短假由我们承包"。但总体上讲,译文体现的是原文本的信息功能。

例2. From conquering mountain trails to exploring neon-lit streetscapes, Hong Kong is a city that offers myriad possibilities and experiences. Go from ancient temples to glistening skyscrapers, then dip into bustling city markets before decamping to seaside villages. The only question is — where to start? Read on for a list of unmissable experiences to tick off your Hong Kong wish list.

译文:香港拥有无穷无尽的旅游体验,你可以踏足登山步道,亲近大自然;亦可漫步霓虹灯点缀的街道,感受大都市的繁华。从古老的庙宇到极富现代感的摩天大楼,从热闹市集到海边渔村,感受不一样的风情,其乐无穷。选择太多不知如何取舍?以下为你推荐香港十大必玩景点,这座城市最精彩的好去处,马上带你走个遍!

来源:https://www.discoverhongkong.com/eng/index.html,登录时间2021.4.14

分析:这段网文是香港旅游景点的推荐,属于旅游网站中的呼唤型文本。网站使用带有强烈感情色彩的形容词,以第二人称视觉介入("your Hong Kong wish list"),采用祈使句、设问句,如"Go…""Read…""where to start?",并将传统的英文静态语言改为活力四射的动态语言。译文采用"等功能翻译",也使用祈使句、设问句,如"选择太多不知如何取舍?""马上带你走个遍!";大量使用四字词语,如"摩天大楼""海边渔村""其乐无穷"等;多处使用第二人称代词"你可以……""为你推荐……""马上带你走……",是劝导口语体,不仅呈现了原文本的呼唤功能,而且还增强了文本的诱导功能。

(2)异功能翻译

旅游网站的翻译也可以根据旅游宣传、促销的目的,采用工具性翻译中的"异功能翻译"方法。"异功能翻译"就是转换原文功能,使目的语文本的功能优先于原文本的功能。例如,译者可根据译语读者的文化背景、认知能力和对回译文本的期待视野,不受原文本类型和功能的约束,将信息型文本转变为诱导型文本,以触发网站用户的旅游动机和旅游行为,起到比信息型文本更好的旅游宣传效果。

例1.This is a world of rich culture, fantastic wonders and endless fun. What are you waiting for！Just come and have fun with us in the Window of the World！

译文：<u>一个蕴涵深厚文化底蕴的世界！一个包罗精彩万象的世界！一个令人乐而忘返的世界！还等什么？</u>365天，世界与您共欢乐！

来源：http://www.szwwco.com/en/，登录时间2021.5.7

分析：英文旅游网站采用疑问句、反问句、祈使句以及渲染性极强的形容词为游客勾勒出该主题公园的独特之处，并用第一人称和第二人称增强文本的互动性。中文网站采用了原文的句式和修辞手法，并用"异功能翻译"，将原文第一句的陈述句改译为排比句，从而大大增强了文本的渲染性和诱导性，将原来的信息型文本转化为呼唤型文本，达到更好地吸引游客的目的。

例2. Comprising more than 100 shops and stalls that stretch across a full kilometre, the Ladies' Market is one of the most iconic street bazaars in town. While the market is most famous for its bargain womenswear (hence its name), you'll also find accessories, jewellery, toys and quirky souvenirs. Bargaining is the norm here so never accept the seller's first offer. If you prove yourself to be a steely haggler, you may even find yourself walking away with your objects of desire at 20 or 30 per cent of their original prices.

译文：女人街只有女人才会逛吗？不不不！女人街之所以得名，是因为早期这里的摊位多贩售女性服装与用品。可是现在除了女装，这里还可以找到男装、箱包、首饰、玩具、化妆品，以及家居用品等，款式多样，价格便宜。女人街汇集超过一百个摊位，布满长长一公里的街道，人群熙来攘往，是香港最有代表性的露天市集之一，很多精明消费族都爱到这里挑选廉价物品与旅游纪念品。这里的东西大多可以还价，要货比三家才不会吃亏！

来源：https://discoverhongkong.com/eng/explore/shopping/iconic-street-market.html，登录时间2021.7.30

分析：从英文网站来看，这是一个典型的信息型网站文本，以传达旅游购物信息为主，语言朴实无华，没有过多的渲染成分。中文网站为了适应旅游本地化的要求，采用了"异功能翻译"方法，把原文的部分信息功能转换为呼唤功能。中文网站彻底重构了原文，将中国游客最感兴趣的女人街街名的来历置于句首,并采用设问句,使用重复修辞格,增译了"女人街只有女人才会逛吗?不不不!"极大地增强了文本的诱导功能;在中文网站中,译文又将原文末句的句号改译为感叹号,大大增强了旅游网站文本的诱导功能。

案例研究一

方特欢乐世界本地化翻译

旅游网站文本的翻译重点在于使源语的语言文化框架和话语世界在译文文本中得到再现,保证网站本地化后的文本内容相对于目标读者和搜索引擎的最优化。成功的网站翻译必须满足公司组织预先设定的目标,译文文本的功能是网站文本翻译首先考虑的因素,与源语文本在其他任何层面上保持一致都是次要的(丁大刚,2008:97)。方特欢乐世界根据公司组织预先设定的目标,遵循译入语的语言和文化维度,采用异功能翻译方法,大胆地对原文进行了重构,是网站中旅游景点介绍文本本地化翻译的成功范例。

1. 原文

方特欢乐世界

方特欢乐世界坐落在安徽省芜湖市长江大桥经济技术开发区,占地125万平方米,其中水域面积为72万平方米,陆地面积为53万平方米,现为中国规模最大的第四代主题公园。方特采用当今最先进的理念和技术精心打造,全球500强企业深圳华强集团投资建成,由恐龙半岛、西部传奇、维苏威火山、失落帝国、火流星等15个主题项目区构成,堪称"国际一流",是国家5A级旅游景区。方特于2007年对外营业,娱乐项目老少皆宜,每年吸引世界各地游客,畅游欢乐世界!

2. 译文

Fanta Adventure Land

Looking for an ideal place to enjoy yourself?

Change lanes. Come to Fanta Adventure Land! Enter a fantastic and exotic wonderland where you can meet with dinosaurs, explore the magical outer space, tangle in a fierce and heart-pounding battle between blaze and flood, scream in the middle of Vesuvius volcano—all these dreams come true in the same day and at the same place! Located in Wuhu, our Adventure Land is a beloved destination for visitors all around the world. Opened in 2007, the Land is divided into 15 extravagantly themed land—Dino-Rampage, Mysterious West, Lost Empire, Vesuvius, Flare Meteor and so on.

3. 平行文本

平行文本1: Enter a magical kingdom where you can sail with pirates, explore exotic jungles, meet fairy-tale princesses, dive under the ocean and rocket through the stars-all in the same day! Disneyland Park is a beloved Southern California destination where generations of families have made their Disney dreams come true. Opened in 1955, Walt Disney's original theme park is divided into 8 extravagantly themed lands—Main Street, U.S.A., Tomorrowland, Fantasyland, Mickey's Toontown, Frontierland, Critter Country, New Orleans Square and Adventureland.

平行文本2: Need to slow down and take a break? Change lanes. Come to New Zealand.

The land of the long white cloud is a country of stunning, diverse natural beauty with mountains, rivers, lakes and scenic beaches. It is blessed to be home to one of Earth's richest flora zones, which include unique fauna such as the kiwi bird, the national symbol. Our three warm islands have what you need to relax. The distances in New Zealand are large and it can easily take up to three or four weeks on each island to properly explore it, but the highlights can be seen in several days. We will offer you a casual lifestyle and many comfortable accommodations.

资料来源：王婷，翟红梅.旅游平行文本对比分析研究——以芜湖方特与加州迪斯尼乐园为例[J].山西农业大学学报（社会科学版），2014(04)：392—396.

分析：平行文本1是加州迪斯尼乐园的英文简介，语言平实、客观真实，向读者或游客传达关于加州迪斯尼乐园的主要信息，即"一个历史悠久、充满奇幻、人心向往的主题公园"。由于西方的文化维度与中国的文化维度不一样，迪斯尼乐园简介开篇不像中文简介那样介绍迪斯尼乐园的地理位置、占地面积、重要地位等，而是用一系列动词，如"enter""sail""explore""meet""dive""rocket through"等，以时间和空间顺序，对迪斯尼乐园游乐项目进行描绘，让游客实实在在地感受游乐项目本身，以吸引游客。其他信息也非常客观，在整体传达基本信息的基础上,达到了诱导、呼唤游客前往游览的预期功能。

平行文本2是对新西兰旅游目的地的介绍。在这段英语介绍中,第一句话以设问的形式开始,给人新奇的感觉:"Need to slow down and take a break?"(想放慢生活节奏来休息一下吗?)一句日常生活中的问话,轻松、随意、自然,然后向游客直接发出邀请:"Come to New Zealand",这种一问一答对话式的开篇形式,反应的是苏格拉底式的思维方式,具有启发性和个性化的色彩,更能够引起游客的旅游兴趣,诱导功能、呼唤功能都很强;使用第一人称介入,"our three warm islands..." "we will offer you..."友好热情,增进了亲和感、与游客的互动,也是个人主义价值在西方文化维度的体现。

方特欢乐世界中文简介详细地介绍了其地理位置、占地面积等信息,但它是一个游玩乐园,这些信息对外国游客到此一游并没有实质意义。中文简介许多都与游乐设施无关,如"全球500强企业深圳华强集团投资建成""方特采用当今最先进的理念和技术精心打造""堪称'国际一流'"等,反应的是中国的文化维度,体现的是集体主义精神、对权威的尊重、长远观念。如果译成英文,属于冗余信息,不符合外国游客对旅游景点的期待,会让人感到文不对题,不胜其烦。

方特欢乐世界本地化翻译舍弃了原文冗杂的介绍占地面积、地理位置等的信息,对原文进行了重构,重点信息放在游玩项目上。篇章布局借鉴平行文本2,开篇使用设问,以引起游客的关注:"Looking for an ideal place to enjoy yourself?"随后直接向游客发出邀请:"Come to Fanta Adventure Land!"接着借鉴平行文本1中的一系列动词"enter" "explore" "tangle" "scream",以时空顺序对游玩项目做具体描述,并且注意从属结构的逻辑层次,用"where"连接从句。译文还借鉴两个英文平行文本,以个人视觉和读者视觉介入,交替使用"You approach"和"We approach",如"you can..." "our Adventure Land..."等,增强了文本的诱导功能、呼唤功能。译文无论从语言维度还是文化维度,都是本地化翻译成功的译例。

案例研究二

《重庆大酒店》本地化翻译

对比以下两个译例,原译亦步亦趋,篇章照旧,全文照译,不敢根据旅游网站的预设功能对原文进行创造性的改写和重构，未对原文的信息进行取舍，违背了旅游网站本地化翻译的方法，而改译本根据译入语的文化和语言维度，对原文进行了符合本地化要求的改写和编译。本地化的翻译不追求与源语文本在体裁、语域、语言/语篇上保持一致，而是以文化维度的五个价值作为本地化翻译指导，参考目标语平行文本，对旅游网站的中文文本进行创造性的改写、编译。因此，改译本语言更简洁，句式更紧凑，风格更接近广告语体，使网站文本更有呼唤功能、诱导功能、祈使功能。

1. 原文

重庆大酒店

重庆大酒店是三星级旅游酒店，位于重庆市沙坪坝区繁华地段，地理位置优越，交通便利，距沙坪坝三峡广场、商业步行街仅举步之遥。酒店拥有较为完备的商务设施和综合齐全的配套服务，现有各类客房225间，不同大小的会议室共6个，拥有中式、西式餐厅，宴会厅3个，可同时容纳600人就餐，酒店还设有桑拿洗浴会所、酒吧、棋牌室等休闲娱乐设施，是商务、旅行的理想下榻之处和各类宴会、会议的上佳选择之所。我们愿以"诚信第一、用心服务、不断进步"的承诺为您的事业发展助上一臂之力！重庆大酒店热诚欢迎您的光临！

2. 原译

Chongqing Grand Hotel, located in the bustling area of Sha Pingba section, Chongqing's science and technology and culture center. It is a hotel opened in 1988 with a long history golden brand, is a core enterprise of Chongqing Tourism Holdings Limited, co-capitalized by Hong Kong Kwoon Bus Holdings Limited. It is a business hotel in new concept with complete facilities. Redecorated in 2002, with investment in total 8 million yuan, now we have 225 guestrooms, 6 traditional Chinese-style and Western-style conference rooms in different sizes, 3 Chinese-style and Western-style dining rooms, banquet halls and favor rooms that can accommodate 600 people at the same time. Meanwhile, we provide complete facilities and comprehensive services. We will bring you heart to heart business service of personalization, humanitarianism and digitalization to give you a hand on your way to success. Welcome to Chongqing Grand

Hotel!

3. 改译

Welcome to Chongqing Grand Hotel

Looking for an ideal hotel?

If you want to feel the prosperity of the city and need extremely convenient transportation, you've just found what you want!

Located in the heart of Sha Pingba district, this 3-star hotel is very close to Three Gorges Square and the pedestrian street. Our hotel is renowned for complete commercial facilities and responsive service. We have 225 guest rooms, 6 conference rooms, 3 Chinese-style & western-style restaurants and 1 banquet hall, all of which can accommodate 600 people at the same time. After coming back from a tiring business meeting or shopping with many bags, you can choose to take sauna, have a few drinks or enjoy music in our bar to relax yourself; if you don't feel like going out, playing bridge with your friends in our card room will also give you much fun. You will never regret choosing our hotel to stay or hold parties or meetings!

Enjoy the first class service offered by one of the "top ten hotels" in Chongqing!

4. 平行文本

平行文本1：Welcome to Royal Lancaster London, Hyde Park's proud mid-century architectural icon, with breathtaking views of the famous London skyline. In 2017, we celebrated 50 happy years and our treasured reputation for truly charming hospitality.

LOCATION：Our coveted location affords us spectacular views over Hyde Park and London's famous skyline. A short stroll West will take you to quaint and cultured Notting Hill and Holland Park. Walk East to Marble Arch and the vibrancy of Oxford Street or amble South through the park and find yourself in Kensington or Knightsbridge. Of course the rest of London is within easy reach, with Lancaster Gate tube station next door and Heathrow Airport a mere 20 minutes from nearby Paddington Station.

来源：https://www.royallancaster.com/, 登录时间2021.1.6

平行文本2：Our Ritz team are thrilled to welcome you back to The Ritz.

With the Summer fast approaching and London starting to come alive, it is the ideal time for a city break or an unforgettable dining experience either inside or al fresco in our new Italian Garden.

The wellbeing of our guests and colleagues remains paramount and so your visit to The Ritz will now look and feel slightly different, with our enhanced set of hygiene and safety measures.Rest assured our dedicated team will provide you with a warm welcome and world class service, that The Ritz is renowned for, leaving you with long lasting memories.

来源：https://www.booking.com/hotel/gb/the-ritz-london.en-gb.html, 登录时间2021.1.6

平行文本3： Stay in the heart of London–Excellent location

Overlooking London's Green Park is the world-famous The Ritz London. This stunning Neoclassical building offers the height of opulence with luxurious bedrooms, exquisite British cuisine, and classic afternoon teas.

来源：https://www.theritzlondon.com/staysafe/, 登录时间2021.1.6

平行文本4： You can't get closer to London!

Just step out of the hotel's door and you're right in the liveliest part of London: Piccadilly Circus. The most famous theatres, restaurants and shops are all within a few minutes walk of the hotel. The choice of entertainment within a few hundred yards is absolutely unbeatable—you'll feel the pulse of Piccadilly from the Regent Palace: it's right at the heart of London. (The Regent Palace Hotel, London)

来源：https://www.regentpalacehotel.co.uk/default.htm, 登录时间2021.4.6

资料来源：覃海晶.平行文本比较及其对中文酒店文宣英译的启示[J].考试与评价(大学英语教研版)，2014(01)：51—56.

分析：从重庆大酒店中文文本来看，除最后一句外，整篇都是围绕介绍酒店基本功能进行的，文中"位于……""距离……""现有""拥有……""容纳……""设有"之类的表达，均是重庆大酒店语篇功能的体现。全篇皆以局外人，即第三人称的视角对酒店情况进行客观描述，译者隐性、客观陈述。中文文本以酒店或酒店名作主位，酒店具体信息作叙位，反复用"酒店"一词主导介绍，以实现文本的衔接、连贯以及主题扩展。很显然，由于受宣传重心、语言习惯、意识偏差等因素影响，重庆大酒店的中文网站文本具有明显的集体主义的特征（酒店是集体的，不是我个人的）。网站中的"我们愿以'诚信第一、用心服务、不断进步'的承诺为您的事业发展助上一臂之力！"更是体现了中国文化的价值取向。

从4个平行文本来看，英文酒店外宣从明显的个人视角介入，体现了西方个人主义特征，如平行文本1和平行文本4中的"take you to..." "find yourself in..." "Just step out of..."；运用大量最高级及褒义词汇或短语，如平行文本1中的"breathtaking" "truly charming" "coveted"等，语言节奏明快；使用比喻修辞，如平行文本3和平行文本4中的"the pulse of..." "the heart of London"等。在英文酒店文宣中，非谓语动词短语主位化明显，比如平行文本1中的"Walk East to Marble Arch"等，采用前景化的语言风格，使酒店的位置、面积和方位等在人们心中留下先入为主的深刻印象。凡此种种，使英文酒店文宣带有明显的"广告语言"特点，无论是语言维度还是文化维度，与中文网站都大不相同。

因此，重庆大酒店的本地化翻译必须按照公司组织预先设定的目标和功能，采取符合文本目的的创造性编译、创译或改写，而译文与源语在语言、体裁、篇章上是否对等是次要的。在内容取舍、篇章重构等方面，本地化翻译不能以原文为归依，而应当"入乡随俗"，使译文符合目标市场用户的审美和习惯。为了公司组织预先设定的目标和功能，甚至可以采取"异功能翻译"，将重庆大酒店的中文信息型功能文本改译为符合其公司目的的英文呼唤型文本。

1. 从文化维度的角度，改译本采用西方常用的个人视角介入，使用"We approach"和读者视角"You approach"构建整个译文语篇；省译了类似"我们愿以'诚信第一、用心服务、不断进步'的承诺为您的事业发展助上一臂之力！"的话语。

2. 借鉴平行文本1，重构了原网站的文本，将中文归纳式的篇章结构改为英文演绎式结构，连网站的标题都改写了："Welcome to Chongqing Grand Hotel"，起到类似广告英语中标题语(tag line)或口号(slogan)的作用。

3. 对文本结构做调整，在首句增译了句子，并独立成段："Looking for an

ideal hotel?"具有平行文本4"You can't get closer to London!"同样的语言功能。用设问或双重否定表示肯定更能吸引读者的注意力。

4. 根据平行文本2和平行文本4大量使用对话性语言,改变了原文平铺直叙式的新闻报道风格,引入读者视角"you",并采用第一人称替换"酒店",如"If you want to feel..." "you can choose to take sauna..." "Our hotel is renowned for..." "in our bar to relax yourself..."等,使译文具有对话性。

5. 在句首增译一设问句:"If you want to feel the prosperity of the city..."并根据平行文本3和平行文本4中的比喻修辞手法,增译了"in the heart of..."根据平行文本中大量使用最高级和褒义的词语,改译本增译了"...is renowned for..." "the first class"等,是符合文本目的的增译,这在旅游网站本地化翻译中是允许的,不要大惊小怪。

6. 末尾使用祈使句,如"Enjoy the first class service..."并增译了"one of the 'top ten hotels' in Chongqing",提高了重庆大酒店的品位和档次,增强了文本的诱导功能、劝导功能。为了实现文本的预设功能,此种符合公司组织预设功能和目的的创译可能会颠覆一般读者的想象。

以上两个案例的重要启示是:本地化翻译不能将传统的译论"信""达""雅"视为金科玉律,而应根据文本的预设功能、目标语读者的阅读习惯,采取增、删、改、重组等翻译方法,适当运用祈使句和修辞手法;也可使用块状化语言,或将某个(些)句子单独成段译出;既可采取"等功能翻译",也可采取"异功能翻译",以满足公司组织或用户预先设定的目标,激发旅游者的动机和行为。

本章小结

本章从旅游网站的内容、结构、语言特点、本地化等方面介绍了旅游网站的翻译方法。旅游网站载体很多,如旅游广告、旅游手册、旅游指南、旅游景点介绍、旅游日志、旅游评论等,关键词高度集中、用语高度简洁,具有信息性和诱导性。旅游网站文本与普通印刷文本不同,不仅要确保网站核心信息的转换,而且还要保证网站本地化后的文本内容相对于目标读者和搜索引擎的最优化。旅游网站本地化的翻译必须考虑两个维度：一个是文化维度，一个是语言维度。文化维度考虑的是内容的取舍，语言维度考虑的是如何翻译。既可采取"等功能翻译"策略，也可采取"异功能翻译"策略。在功能、体裁、语域、语言/语篇四个层面中，旅游网站的译文与源语在语言、体裁、篇章上保持一致并非译者优先考虑的事项。由于政治因素、宣传重心、语言习惯、意识偏差等原因，中外旅游网站所呈现的页面存在诸多差异，这给旅游网站本地化带来诸多挑战。成功的旅游网站本地化翻译应当满足公司组织或用户预先设定的目标，激发旅游者的旅游动机和行为，在内容取舍、篇章重构等方面，旅游网站的翻译可能会颠覆一般读者的想象。

翻译实践

一、热身练习

翻译下图，并对译文做简要分析。

1.

2. A favourite amongst residents with kids, the Peak Lookout is housed in a 19th-century Grade II historical building and offers families options of indoor and outdoor dining. The view of the South China Sea is perfect from the back patio. There are highchairs available and a kids' menu offering both Western and Eastern delights. It is a great option to pair with the Victoria Peak Circle Walk and your visit to The Peak!

3. 上善若水，水养万物。曾文通经常去造访他家附近的一处山泉瀑布，从而让心灵得到水的洗礼、滋养。清洌山泉，激流撞石，声似颂钵之音，清明悦耳；深山涧水，飞珠滚玉，琮琮急流奔去，终化涓涓。

4. "I always enjoy taking the Star Ferry, it's somewhere I take guests who are new to Hong Kong," says Dautresme. "It offers an amazing, unrivalled viewpoint from which to experience the drama of the harbour. There's nothing like it; it's one of the only harbours where you have such density and urbanism so close to the water," he adds. "The Star Ferry allows you to absorb that."

5.
世界最大的皇家宫苑——避暑山庄景区

形貌如中华成一统，名胜集全国于一园，文化融华夏五千年。

承德避暑山庄始建于1703年（康熙四十二年），占地564万平方米，是世界现存最大的皇家园林。避暑山庄按中国地理形貌选址设计，以西北山区、东南湖区、北部平原区之形状地貌构成中国版图的缩影。园内亭、阁、轩、榭、庙宇等120余组景观，融南秀北雄为一体，集全国名胜为一园，可谓山庄咫尺间，直作万里观。

二、巩固练习

翻译下文，并对译文做简要分析。

1. I love the perspective it offers me as I photograph the city below. It is layer after layer of district, mountain, district, mountain.

2.

Tsing Yi Nature Trails

These trails take you up many steps, but it's worth the climb for the sweeping views of the waters, bridges and lands surrounding Tsing Yi Island. There are many sitting-out areas along the way. Be sure not to overlook the wild flowers, such as Bougainvillea in vibrant fuchsia shades, and Trailing Lantana with small purple flowers.

3. Location, location, location — Hong Kong has it good! Within easy reach of the city are some of China's most fascinating destinations. Hong Kong is part of the Greater Bay Area, along with Macao and nine municipalities in southern China's Guangdong Province, namely Guangzhou, Shenzhen, Zhuhai, Foshan, Huizhou, Dongguan, Zhongshan, Jiangmen and Zhaoqing. The area possesses the most extensive cluster of ports and airports in the world and Hong Kong, together with the other Greater Bay Area cities, can jointly offer diversified travel experiences.

4. After stepping off the ship, take in Hong Kong's stunning skyline as you stroll along the Tsim Sha Tsui Promenade, passing the Hong Hong Clock Tower and continuing to the Avenue of Stars. This promenade that juts out over the water is where you will find Hollywood style handprints of Hong Kong's biggest stars, including Bruce Lee, who has his own statue, and Michelle Yeoh Choo Kheng, who played the formidable matriarch in Crazy Rich Asians. Make use of AR technology to interact with your favourite stars.

5. Check out after breakfast and be at the Emu Bay Boat Ramp at 9 a.m. for a three-hour marine adventure. Join fifth-generation islander Andrew Neighbour on his high-powered jet boat to swim with dolphins and visit a colony of long-nosed fur seals. Feel free to try a bit of fishing before driving five kilometres (three miles) west towards Cygnet River, stopping for lunch at the quirky Frogs & Roses café, a rustic timber shed set inside a plant nursery that serves pizzas topped with ingredients from the owner's veggie patch.

三、阅读翻译

阅读下文，重点翻译下画线部分。

Gardens by the Bay

Located by the Marina Bay Waterfront in the heart of Singapore, Gardens by the Bay is a sanctuary for nature lovers and budding horticulturalists alike.

Comprising three distinct spaces over 101 hectares–Bay South Garden, Bay East Garden and Bay Central Garden, this oasis of lush greenery has won multiple accolades since it first opened in 2012.

These include the "Landscape Award" from *World Architecture* News in 2013, the "Best Attraction in Asia Pacific" from *Travel Weekly* in 2015 and the "Best Attraction Experience" at the 2019 Singapore Tourism Awards.

Here's a rundown of what to see and do at Gardens by The Bay.

Flower Dome

The beauty of nature beckons visitors to the Flower Dome in Bay South Gardens. Covering 1.28 hectares, this verdant space is the larger of three cooled conservatories, and broke the Guinness World Record as the World's Largest Glass Greenhouse in 2015. It is home to plants and flowers from five continents, from thousand-year old olive trees to magnolias and orchids.

While certainly one of Gardens by the Bay's most spectacular attractions, the Flower Dome is far from the only floral paradise that awaits visitors.

Floral Fantasy

As you explore Gardens by the Bay at your leisure, be sure to keep an eye out for Floral Fantasy.

The second of the Gardens' three indoor conservatories delves into realms of both history and fantasy. Each of its four distinct zones taking inspiration from fairy tales and the storied Hanging Gardens of Babylon, with cavernous spaces, dramatic driftwood sculptures and works of floral art.

Cloud Forest

Gardens by the Bay's third conservatory—the aptly named Cloud Forest—is a mist-filled landscape of rare vegetation and dramatic vistas.

Towering above the conservatories' ferns and pitcher plants is Cloud Mountain, a 35-metre tall structure veiled in mist and covered in lush vegetation. Your imagination is bound to soar as you scale its heights, and discover plant life from the tropical highlands.

Super Tree Grove

As you exit the conservatory, you're likely to notice a grove of soaring, surreal structures, known as the super trees. These vertical gardens span 25 to 50 metres in height, with two of the towering structures connected by the dramatic arch of the OCBC Skyway. When dusk falls, the grove lights up with the Garden Rhapsody, a spectacle of light and sound. For an unforgettable view of Singapore, ascend to the top of the Super Tree Observatory, a 50-metre-high observation deck, which boasts an unobstructed vista of the beautiful Marina Bay district.

Round off your visit to Gardens by the Bay with an unforgettable sunset at Bay East Garden. The lush open lawns and beautiful waterfront will give you an unobscured view of Singapore's skyline.

第五章 旅游指南翻译

"指南"一词来源于"指南针",是指提供有关目的地信息的出版物。旅游指南类型很多,既有像《孤独星球》(*Lonely Planet*)那样包括旅游线路、景点、吃住等信息的旅游指南,也有像关注吃、喝、玩、乐的《吃游玩乐指南》,还有介绍特色手工产品的旅游指南;旅游网站上的指南通常被称为"旅游攻略"。旅游指南的优点是态度客观中立,信息准确翔实,内容丰富多元;不足之处是内容庞杂,涉及吃、住、行、游、购、娱等各个方面,如果没有自己明确的想法和偏好,容易迷失在海量的指南信息中。

旅游指南是游客获得旅游目的地相关信息的重要渠道之一,在结构和内容上有许多雷同。大多数旅游指南都包含文化信息和实用信息。在历史、文化、地理、自然等概览之后常常是有关景点活动、交通货币、住宿、餐饮、联系方法等的一些实用信息和建议(林莉,2011:207)。旅游指南通常以信息型为主,也有促销型、诱导型旅游指南。盖茨(Getz)和赛勒(Sailor)就将旅游指南分为三种类型:信息类型,如描述性的旅游目录和行程指南;促销类型,如为旅游景点做宣传的促销指南;诱导类型,如旅游目的地营销手册(Getz & Sailor, 1993: 329—353)。总体来讲,旅游指南以传递信息为主,这是旅游指南与旅游手册的主要区别。关于旅游指南与旅游手册的异同,详见第六章论述。

一、旅游指南文本的特点

旅游指南除了介绍旅游景区、景点外,还包括衣、食、住、行、民俗风情等旅游资讯,为旅游者提供旅游活动信息(任孝珍,2010:85)。旅游指南既包含吃、住、行、游、购、娱等实用性旅游信息,也包含目的地的旅游形象和文化信息。旅游指南能够增进读者对目的地人文历史、自然景观、民族文化的了解,并通过他们在旅游目的地的旅游行为，拉动旅游目的地的经济和人文交流。下面是 *EYEWITNESS TRAVEL USA* 和《意大利》旅游指南目录。

图5.1　*EYEWITNESS TRAVEL USA* 目录　　　　图5.2　《意大利》目录

在互联网和大数据时代，除了纸质版旅游指南外，多数旅游官方网站也提供旅游指南，方便游客查询相关信息。以下是香港旅游发展局官网旅游指南截图。

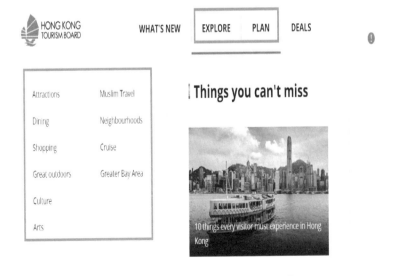

图5.3　香港旅游发展局官网旅游指南

图5.3　香港旅游发展局官网旅游指南（续）

当陈述客观事实时，旅游指南多用陈述句，动词多为一般现在时；对于旅游目的地的评价，常使用主观描述性语言；而提供建议时，多使用情态动词，且使用一些口语化的语言（丁大刚，2008：173）。对于描述性信息，旅游指南也会使用具有感染力的形容词，使文本暗含诱导、祈使功能。中、英文旅游指南语言差异较大，英文注重写实，中文辞藻华丽，翻译时应坚持游客第一，以读者为中心的原则（陈刚，2014：32），设法化解英汉两种语言在逻辑、语体风格、文化等方面的差异引起的理解困难，减少译文读者在摄取信息的过程中遇到的障碍（袁晓宁，2013：93）。

1. 中文旅游指南文本的特点

总体来讲，中文旅游指南语言朴实，以传达旅游信息为要旨，但受古代骈体文影响，语言也会出现整齐对偶、声韵和谐、辞藻华丽的特点。在遣词造句方面，中文旅游指南一些文段会采用四字结构、修饰性词语和短语、烘托性语言等来强调意境美，也可能会使用大量的历史典故、诗词歌赋等让读者身临其境（王才英，2014：42），这与英文指南大不相同。汉语重意合，行文不需要英文那样的连接词，因此中文旅游指南文本的逻辑不如英文那么严密，译为英文时，需通过上下文厘清句子的逻辑和语意的层次关系。

例1. 北京在历史上曾是五朝古都，从金朝至今的800多年里，建造的帝王宫殿、园林和陵墓数目众多。从紫禁城开始，城市有一条自南而北长达7.8公里的中轴线，从永定门、天安门、神武门向地安门伸展，最后到钟鼓楼……整座城围绕着位于中心的紫禁城环形分布，<u>方正庄严</u>。从高俯瞰，城中<u>红墙黄瓦</u>，<u>碧波涟漪</u>，<u>城外环绕的大马路笔直宽阔</u>，<u>处处都带着一种别样的"大气"</u>……一提北京，人们就能感觉到那种雍容华贵的气场，<u>崇敬之情油然而生</u>，或者小有嫉妒地评价一下它"大得不实诚"……

分析：这是《中国自助游》旅游指南中关于北京的介绍，提供北京城市布局和悠久历史等实用信息。指南多处用四字词语，如"方正庄严""红墙黄瓦""碧波涟漪"等；使用描述性和评价性语言，如"城外环绕的大马路笔直宽阔""人们就能感受到那种雍容华贵的气场，崇敬之情油然而生……"展示北京的城市魅力。

例2. 武汉素有"九省通衢"之称。这里自然风光独特，<u>四季气候分明</u>，拥有大都市罕有的众多湖泊。这里<u>人文景观丰富</u>，<u>素有"历史文化名城"之美誉</u>，<u>浓郁的楚文化特色、深邃的人文气质</u>诱人前往。代表性景点有黄鹤楼、东湖风景区……城市建设进程中的新旧风貌杂糅，是这个城市给人的基本印象。<u>热闹的街区</u>、喧腾的工地、精明的商贩、纳凉的市民一起涌动在城市的洪流中，使武汉被公认为"最具平民化特色的城市"。

分析：这是《经典中国游》旅游指南关于武汉的介绍，用描述性和评价性语言概括了武汉的自然风光、文化底蕴和城市特点，如"自然风光独特，四季气候分明"；"浓郁的楚文化特色、深邃的人文气质……"等。指南结构比较松散，多为意合句，鲜用连接词衔接句子，如"热闹的街区、喧腾的工地、精明的商贩、纳凉的市民……"与前一句联系并不紧密。

2. 英文旅游指南文本特点

英文旅游指南语言平实，虽然也有渲染成分，但相对于中文旅游指南，语言和内容比较客观。在词语选择上，英文旅游指南简练质朴，仅用形容词来描述事物的本质特征，没有给人浮夸的感觉，力求给读者最为真实的感觉（崔娟，2017：51）。在篇章结构上，英文旅游指南一般将最重要、最生动和吸引眼球的信息放在首段，然后具体描述，各个成分用连词、介词等衔接，行文逻辑严密，条理清楚。

例1. With its skyscrapers and bright lights, this is a city of superlatives. It covers an area of 304.8 sq miles (789 sq km), and comprises the five distinct boroughs of Manhattan, the Bronx, Queens, Brooklyn, and Staten Island. Most of the major sights lie within Manhattan, the southern tip of which was the target of the September 11, 2001 terrorist attack. Glittering shops, museum, and theaters are located in Midtown and along Central Park.

分析：这是 *EYEWITNESS TRAVEL USA* 旅游指南中介绍纽约的一段文字，主要介绍纽约的面积大小、行政区和主要景点分布，也有一些描述性语言，如 "skyscrapers" "bright lights" "Glittering" 等，但总体上文风淳朴，语言简练，以突出实用信息为主。在逻辑上，第一个句子使用with复合结构，采用情境化语言作独立主格。

例2. Chicago, a city almost 3 million people, covers 237 sq miles (614 sq km) of the US's Midwest. Situated at the southwest edge of the vast Lake Michigan, the city claims 26 miles (42 km) of lakefront. Despite burning to the ground in 1871 and witnessing terrible social unrest, the city was soon rebuilt and emerged as the financial capital of the Midwest. Today, this third-largest city in the US is world-famous for its innovative institutions, and for its colorful and turbulent political history. It is also home to US President Barack Obama.

分析：这是 *EYEWITNESS TRAVEL USA* 一段关于芝加哥的介绍。指南开头介绍了城市的基本情况，包括人口、面积、地理位置等实用信息，语言客观，无过多渲染；指南文段后面介绍了城市特色，仅用了少许形容词 "world-famous" "colorful" "innovative" 等；在语篇逻辑层面上，a city almost 3 million people作Chicago的同位语，situated at the southwest edge of the vast Lake Michigan地点状语主位化，突出重要信息。

例3. Getting Around:

Bicycle

Bath's hills make getting around by bike challenging, but the canal paths along the Kennet and Avon Canal and the 13-mile Bristol & Bath Railway Path (www.

brisrlbathrailwaypath.org.uk) offer great cycling.

Bus

Bus 18 runs from the bus station, High St. and Great Pulteney St. up Bathwick Hill past the YHA to the university every 10 minutes. Bus 4 runs every 20 minutes to Bathampton from the same places.

Car& Motorcycle

Bath has serious traffic problems (especially at rush hour). Park & Ride services operate from Lansdown to the north, Newbridge to the west and Odd Town to the south. It takes about 10 minutes to the center; buses leave every 10 to 15 minutes.

分析：这是*Great Britain*旅游指南的一段文字，向读者提供关于交通方面的实用信息，诸如在英国旅行常用的交通工具、开车线路、发车间隔时间，包括旅游咨询网站等，全是陈述事实，没有主观评论或建议。

值得一提的是，虽然中、英旅游指南在行文风格上存在这样或那样的差异，但是在同一语言的旅游指南中，语言、风格也可能大不相同。一些旅游指南以非常客观的形式陈述有关旅游目的地的事实和数据，让旅游者自行决定它是否值得游览；而一些旅游指南则非常主观地描述旅游目的地，使用大量评论性语言（形容词、情态标记等），甚至告诉读者应该做些什么、看些什么、去哪儿等（丁大刚，2008：174）。

二、旅游指南信息分类

鉴于旅游指南由不同部分组成，不同部分又各有特点，可以根据其性质和功能分为一级主题（first-level）、二级主题（second-level）和三级主题(third-level)。一级主题是指南首页概括性介绍，力求简洁，突出重点信息；二级主题列出一级主题中的重点，介绍特色信息，唤起游客潜在兴趣；三级主题是一些小型特定项目，倾向更为具体的描写，让游客了解当地风情。在三级主题下，旅游指南文本又包含了不同的文本信息，具有不同性质和功能。鉴于此，曾利沙将旅游指南信息分为八大类，其中事实性信息、评价性信息、描述性信息、文化信息是旅游指南最基本的信息。不同的指南信息附带不同的文本功能，应采取不同的翻译策略和方法（曾利沙，2005：19—23）。

第一类 事实性信息（Factive information）

基本性质：文本基本信息，有关旅游地及其项目特色、条件和环境等方面的介绍。

信息功能：客观介绍旅游目的地及其项目的综合知识。事实性信息又分历时性和现时性两种。前者是关于旅游地及主题项目相关历史事件以及对现在的影响；后者则是对其现时发展状况的介绍。

信息特征：客观性

翻译要求：应该对原文信息进行甄别，把握实质信息，删除冗余信息。

例1. 南京夫子庙是供奉和祭祀我国古代著名的大思想家、教育家孔子的庙宇，其全称是"大成至圣先师文宣王庙"，简称"文庙"。夫子庙始建于宋景祐元年，由东晋学宫扩建而成。

译文：The Confucius Temple is a place to worship and consecrate Confucius, the great thinker and educator in ancient China. The Temple, also known as Wenmiao in Chinese, was first set up in 1034, on the basis of an extended study hall in the Eastern Jin Dynasty (317—420).

分析：原文是南京旅游指南中对南京夫子庙的介绍，属于事实性信息。原文中"大成至圣先师文宣王庙"和"夫子庙始建于宋景祐元年"是有关夫子庙的历史称谓和年代，对于一般外国读者无实质意义，属于冗余信息，翻译时删去。

例2. 杭州历史悠久，自秦时设县治以来，已有2000多年历史。杭州是华夏文明的发祥地之一。早在4700多年前，就有人类在此繁衍生息，并产生了被称为文明曙光的良渚文化。杭州曾是五代吴越国和南宋王朝两代建都地，是我国七大古都之一。

译文：Hangzhou has enjoyed a history of over 2,000 years since the county administration was established in the Qin Dynasty. It is one of the cradles of Huaxia (China) civilization. As early as about 4,700 years ago, there were human beings living in the Hangzhou area. Hang zhou, one of the seven ancient capitals of China, was the capital in Wuyue State of the Five Dynasties and the Southern Song Dynasty.

分析：这是杭州旅游指南对杭州城市的介绍，整个文段属于事实性信息，介绍了杭州的历史。画线处"并产生了被称为文明曙光的良渚文化"与原文内容关联性不大，且与前文出现的"杭州是华夏文明的发祥地之一"意义重复，故删去。

第二类 评价性信息（Evaluative/appraisal information）

信息性质：附加信息——对旅游目的地及其项目的评价。

信息功能：加深游客对旅游目的地及项目的认识和信任。

信息特征：具有暗示性或诱导性，带有原作者个人的情感，主观性较强。

翻译要求：对过度渲染、夸张或累赘的文字、内容进行审读、甄别，删除不实信息。

例1. 杭州是中国著名风景旅游城市，以秀丽迷人的西湖自然风光闻名于世。意大利著名旅行家马可波罗曾这样叙述他印象中的杭州："这是世界上最美丽迷人的城市，它使人觉得自己是在天堂。"在中国，也流传着这样的话："上有天堂，下有苏杭。"

译文：Hangzhou is a tourist city renowned for its natural scenery and particularly for the charming West Lake. A famous ancient Italian traveler, Marco Polo, once described his impressions of Hangzhou like this: "This is the most charming city in the world. It makes one feel as if he /she were in paradise." In China there is a similar saying: "In heaven there is a paradise, while on earth there are Suzhou and Hangzhou."

分析：该文选自杭州旅游指南，主要介绍杭州的美景，其中评价性信息"以秀丽迷人的西湖自然风光闻名于世"，突显了西湖的品位。后文引用马可波罗对杭州的评价："这是世界上最美丽迷人的城市，它使人觉得自己是在天堂"，以及中国广为流传的一句话："上有天堂，下有苏杭"来印证指南的主题：杭州——"人间天堂"。翻译时可保留这些评价信息，加深主题。

例2. 香港地方虽小，却多姿多彩。她那与众不同的气质，是多么独一无二……中国人的传统，加上百年西方的影响，香港俨如一个多元的万花筒，眼见耳闻，千姿百态，难怪号称"动感之都"。

译文：Hong Kong is a small place that lives large. A living fusion of East and West, it presents visitors with an ever-changing kaleidoscope of color and culture. Combining around 150 years of Western influence and 5,000 years of Chinese traditions, Hong Kong has its own special brand of magic and mystique.

分析：原文是《香港旅游锦囊》中一段对香港的介绍，文字信息既有描述性信息，也有评价性信息。译文中评价性信息"她那与众不同的气质，是多么独一无二"被弱化，因为与原文中香港"多元文化"信息相冲突，故未译出；另一处评价信息"难怪号称'动感之都'"与文中"large"的内涵没有多少关系，未体现香港多元文化和"万花筒"的特征，故也略去不译。由此可见，旅游指南的评价信息在翻译时需审读和甄别，译与不译取决于是否有助于突出指南的主题信息。

第三类 描述性信息（Descriptive information）

信息性质：兼具基本信息和附加信息——对旅游目的地及其项目进行描述。

信息功能：让游客更好地了解旅游目的地及项目的性质和特征。

信息特征：兼具客观性和主观性，主观性的文字可能有夸大事实的倾向。

翻译要求：中、英描写景物方法不一，汉语寓情于景，辞藻华丽；英文客观写实，语言质朴，描述性信息的取舍不同。因此，汉译英应当化"华美"为"简约"，省略冗余和华而不实的语言；英译汉应当化"平淡"为"神奇"，多渲染。

例1. 水韵天堂，真真切切，穿梭在绿色的丛林中呼吸着清新的茶香，听着凄美动人的爱情故事，仿佛置身于天堂梦境，感动又欣喜。

译文：You may enjoy all the excitement and joy by taking a walk along the West Lake.

分析：这是杭州旅游指南对西湖景点的描写，其中有一些过度渲染、夸张的成分。原文本的主题信息是"漫步西湖"，那些描述性信息，如"水韵天堂，真真切切""呼吸着清新的茶香，听着凄美动人的爱情故事"等是中文常用的渲染景色的手法，在英文中属于华而不实、过渡渲染的信息。若将其译出，不仅文字累赘，也不利于指南主题信息的传递。因此，译文省略了这些描述性信息，将原文本的主要信息——"漫步西湖"译出即可。

例2. 中国广西一大片<u>古老深远、壮美的国土</u>。<u>十万大山峰峦叠嶂，古木参天，流水潺潺</u>。十万大山，一个响亮的名字；<u>十万大山系列食品是广西山水哺育出来的品牌</u>；"十万大山"是广西农垦人的共同名字。

译文：<u>Great Mountain, a brand dealing with farming produces of Shiwandashan in Guangxi, China, is a famous brand of Guangxi State Farms Group Co. Ltd.</u>

分析："一大片古老深远、壮美的国土""十万大山峰峦叠嶂，古木参天，流水潺潺"，这些充满诗情画意的描述是出于渲染情感或顺应汉语行文习惯的语言，对产品介绍和企业宣传无多大实际意义；"十万大山，一个响亮的名字""'十万大山'是广西农垦人的共同名字"，也是口号式宣传语和励志语，并无实质性内容，对于外国读者是冗余信息。本指南的主要信息是"十万大山系列食品是广西农垦集团有限责任公司的品牌"，其余皆为出于渲染目的的附加信息，汉译英可删除，保留基本信息即可。

第四类 文化信息（Cultural information）

信息性质：兼具基本信息和附加信息——阐述旅游目的地及其项目的文化特色。

信息功能：加深游客对旅游目的地文化的了解。

信息特征：有可能文化过载、跨文化交际障碍。

翻译要求：译者应注意中外文化差异，把握国外游客对当地文化的感知能力和接受能力，消除跨文化交际障碍。

例1. During the "<u>Hunger Winter</u>", Zuiderker served as a morgue.

译文：在"饥饿之冬"时期，南教堂充当了陈尸所。（注："饥饿之冬"：1944—1945年冬季，在德国占领的荷兰地区爆发了一场饥荒，人们将第二次世界大战期间的这段时间称为"饥饿之冬"。

分析：这则旅游指南来自《孤独星球·荷兰》。"Hunger Winter"是一个文化负载词，如果不具体解释其含义，会让游客产生文化隔膜，导致文化过载。译文根据译文读者的感知能力和接受能力，采用释译法，文中加了注释，帮助读者理解。

例2. 南宋淳熙年间，王益祥官至江东提刑，退隐后居坊内，改名衣锦坊，沿用至今。

译文：When Wang Yixiang, a chief justice of the south of Yangtze River region, retired and lived here during the Chunxi period of the Southern Song Dynasty (1127—1279), it was given the present name, which implies that someone has "returned to his hometown in full glory".

分析：本文出自福州《三坊七巷旅游指南》，介绍了当地的特色建筑——衣锦坊。"衣锦"是指华丽的衣裳，"衣锦坊"有"衣锦还乡，荣归故里"之意，译文释译为"returned to his hometown in full glory"，让外国游客更好地理解"衣锦坊"之意。如果只音译而不加释义，会影响译文跨文化交际的效果。

第五类 召唤性信息（Vocative information）

信息性质：附加信息——就特定项目向游客发出带有召唤性特征的语言信息，一般置于有关事实信息之后。

信息功能：激发或唤起游客的旅游热情或兴趣，诱发旅游行为。

信息特征：带有劝导、祈使、鼓励的特点。

翻译要求：译文需具有诱导功能，视情况可采用"异功能翻译"，将原文中的信息功能转换为召唤性、诱导性功能。

例1. 游兰州必游城隍庙，文化购物，收藏必去城隍庙。

译文：The City God Temple of Lanzhou has become one of the must-see sights for one-day tour in Lanzhou. He who has never been to the Temple is not a real collector.

分析：这是关于游兰州城隍庙的旅游指南。中文指南虽属信息型文本，但也带有少许呼唤性功能，如句中"必游……""必去……"两个祈使、劝导性的话语，引发游客游览隍庙的兴趣。译文第一句使用"must-see sights"合成词，带有较强的劝导、诱导功能；第二句采用套译法，套用"不到长城非好汉（He who has never been to the Great Wall is not a real man）"译为"He who has never been to the Temple is not a real collector"，采用双重否定表示肯定的形式，增强了指南的劝导功能、呼唤功能。

例2. From intangible culture to world-class theme parks. From mouth-watering street food, to breathtaking natural vistas and beyond, Hong Kong has it all!

译文：想体验独特文化，又想品尝让人垂涎欲滴的街头小吃？想去世界级主题乐园，又想享受郊外野趣？在香港，一个旅程，轻松玩个透！

分析：原文选自香港旅游发展局官网，属于玩乐指南。英文网站两个"from...to..."介词短语形成排比句，语气强烈，吸引游客眼球；又用渲染性形容词"mouth-watering"，唤起游客的美食欲望；最后画龙点睛，"Hong Kong has it all!"召唤游客前往香港旅游。译文延续了原文的风格，但比原文更具呼唤功能。具体译法是：将原文的陈述句改成三个疑问句，如此一来，译文连发三问，形成排比句，且制造出一个悬念，产生了更强烈的呼唤功能。译文最后一句采用述译法给出答案："在香港，一个旅程，轻松玩个透！"使文本产生了强烈的诱导功能。

第六类 提示性信息（Information of tips）

信息性质：基本信息兼具附加信息——依附于二三级主题信息后的有关注意事项。

信息功能：向游客提供项目开放时间、交通乘车、购物须知及民俗禁忌等信息。

翻译要求：注意使用提示语、劝导语，突出文本信息本身为要旨，可适当增加一些提示、劝导功能。

例1. Getting There & Away

Fua'amotu International Airport (tel: 35415, www.yongaairport.com) is 21km southeast and a 30-minute drive from downtown Nuku'alofa. Air New Zealand, Fiji Airways and Virgin Australia all fly into Fua'amotu from overseas. In addition to local offices, all are also bookable via Jones Travel.

译文：福阿穆图国际机场（Fua'amotu International Airport）（电话35415，网址：www.yongaairport.com）位于首都努库阿洛法的东南方向，距市中心21公里，约30分钟车程。国际航线方面，可搭乘新西兰航空、斐济航空和维珍澳洲航空抵达。旅客除了在上述航空公司的汤加办事处订票外，还可以通过琼斯旅行社

（Jones Travel）订票。

分析：原文选自《孤独星球：拉罗汤加、萨摩亚和汤加》旅游指南，是最为常见的交通提示性信息。指南采用陈述句，无过多描述性语言，以突出交通信息为要旨。译文在处理原文语言时，保持与原文一样的风格，准确、有效地传递了原文有关时间、方位、距离等实用信息。

例2. 自驾从福州出发，在长途北站坐车往霞浦三沙镇，然后转乘客船到嵛山马祖村。

译文：Drive from Fuzhou to North Bus Station, take a bus there to Sansha Town, Xiapu City, then take a boat to Mazu Village which is at the foot of Yushan Mountain.

分析：原文属于交通提示类信息。原文通过"从""在""往""然后"等连接词，提示游客如何使用交通工具；译文保留了中文指南以上全部信息，但将陈述句改为祈使句，一方面起到了建议作用，另一方面增加了文本的劝导作用。最后译文用"then"这一连接词，将游客使用交通工具的前后顺序、逻辑关系梳理得更加清楚。

第七类 美学信息（Aesthetic information）

信息性质：附加信息——语言具有鲜明的修辞、意象、节奏等美学特征。

信息功能：具有民族语言审美感，增强相关信息接受的效度。

信息特征：带有民族文化的审美，一般难以在另一种语言中有效地体现出来。

翻译要求：正确处理源语与目标语文字、修辞等差异，译文需符合目标语读者的审美心理和阅读期待。

例1. 一年四季，花海变幻：春天，桃李吐红，野花怒放；盛夏，乔灌葱郁，清爽宜人；深秋，枫叶烧红，五彩缤纷；隆冬，满山松柏，银装素裹。

译文：Seas of flowers are changing along with seasons of the year. In spring, peach trees and plums are in full blooms; in summer, green bushes are verdant and fresh; in fall, leaves of maple trees turn red; in winter, pine trees everywhere are covered with snow.

分析：这是《中国烟台旅游指南》中一段关于烟台昆嵛山的描写，使用了华丽的辞藻和工整的对仗句式，如画线处所示。译成英文时，译文舍弃了原文的夸张修辞和过度渲染的词语,只是将每组四字词的实质信息传递出来,如将"桃李吐红,野花怒放"译为"peach trees and plums are in full blooms",但保留了原文的排比句式,意象、结构、节奏均体现了文本的美学功能,传达了原文的美学信息。

例2. With pride, we protect and present this heritage—the world's heritage. Help us ensure that while we enjoy this wonderful area, we do not destroy it; please look then leave without a trace.

译文:我们保护和展现着这一世界遗产,并为之自豪。请尽情地欣赏,除了照片什么都不要带走,除了脚印什么也别留下。

分析:原文是《黄金海岸官方旅游指南》某处世界遗产的描写,类似于景区告示牌的内容,文风质朴,体现了英文的审美观照。中文的审美观照不一样,讲究辞藻华丽,句式对仗工整,若是将指南的后半段译成"请帮助我们……确保……当我们享受这片领域……",则不符合中文的审美。故译文使用排比句,双重否定句式:"除了照片什么都不要带走,除了脚印什么也别留下。"体现中文旅游指南的语言特色和中文读者的审美观照。

第八类 风格信息(Stylistic information)

信息性质:附加信息——主要指个人文字风格。

信息功能:增强或影响基本信息接受的效度。

信息特征:具有原作者个性特征,如文字运用或简明轻快,或典雅圆润。

翻译要求:译文应尽可能体现原文的文体风格,但由于两种语言的"不可通约性",如果译文无法体现原文的风格,应舍弃风格对等,做到功能对等。

例1. My first glimpse of the massive city wall of Xi'an transfixed me. This earth and brick structure stands restored to grandeur, 40 feet high, 8 miles round, its old archers' towers still intact. ...You can make an uninterrupted circuit of Xi'an atop the city wall by foot. This is the ideal way to survey Xi'an upon arrival. An admission fee of RMB 10 ($1.20) is collected at entrances inside the wall.

译文:当我第一次见到西安城墙时,便被它的雄伟所折服。这是一座土砖结构的建筑,墙高12米,周长13.74千米,内部的塔保存完整,展现出往日的雄风……你可以在城墙上走一圈，一览西安，这算是了解西安的最佳方式。景区收费处设在城墙入口，门票10元人民币。

例2. 甘熙故居俗称"九十九间半"，始建于清嘉庆年间，现共有四组五进穿堂式建筑群，占地面积9500多平方米，建筑面积5400余平方米，是南京现存面积最大、保存最完整的清代私人住宅。建筑群在平面布局上为坐南朝北，中轴线由北向南建有门厅、轿厅、大厅、后厅和后堂等房屋，各进建筑多以墙垣隔成院落，整个故居内共有大小天井35个。

译文：Initially built in the Qing Dynasty, the former Residence of Ganxi, popularly known as "Ninety Nine and a Half Rooms", is the largest and best preserved private residence of the Qing Dynasty in Nanjing. With an area of 9,500㎡ and a floorage of 5,400㎡, the Residence is made up of four south-facing integrated clusters of houses, with entrance halls, sedan chair porches, front living rooms, rear living rooms built from south to north along an axis running through the houses. The Residence contains as many as 35 walled-up courtyards with one such yard in each of the clusters.

分析：以上都是城市景点介绍，但文体风格不尽相同。英文指南以第一人称的视角"我"，介绍了西安城墙。这种以个人叙事的方法介绍旅游景点，有较强的劝导作用，增强了信息接受的效度，是外国作者景点介绍的写作风格。中文指南则以第三人称介绍了甘熙故居，文字朴实、不带个人感情色彩，是一般中国作者或译者的写作风格、翻译风格。

三、旅游指南信息处理

信息布局理论（information grounding theory）认为，前景信息是语篇中的核心信息、关键信息；背景信息起辅助、解释或强化作用。语言线索和非语言线索在语篇的构建中都发挥作用，但非语言线索的语言形式是对传递的信息进行前景信息与背景信息的调配，更能影响句子的信息组合和篇章结构。在句式选择及信息分布上，应分清信息的语义、层次，确定主要信息和次要信息，让文中的前景信息突显，使其在整个语篇中起关键作用，以便顺利完成言语交际（李明，李思伊，2017:32—33）。英汉逻辑思维不一样，对于信息处理的方法也不同，前者总是以一个核心结构为中心，其他成分（信息）围绕中心展开；后者信息主次不均匀，呈多点分布态，多为流水句、连动句，靠读者整体理解意义，因此英汉互译需正确处理前景信息与背景信息之间的关系。对于文化信息的处理，还需考虑中西文化差异和译语读者的接受能力。

1. 语义辨析

中文旅游文本信息分布点比较均匀，轻重主次不太分明；辞藻华丽，常用四字成语、平行结构，"以意统形"，给人一种朦胧的诗意美。读者读后往往能感受到意境优美，但语义不是太清晰，印象比较模糊，对于外国读者更是如此；多数情况下，英语旅游文本注重实质信息，语言简洁明了、通达流畅，采用显性衔接，用连词、介词、关系代词等衔接句子，语言线索明显，语义清晰、层次分明，句子结构紧凑且富有逻辑性。

例1. 长白山谷底林海，古木参天，遮天蔽日，有数不尽的珍禽异兽，是我国野生动植物资源的宝库。

译文：With boundless ancient tall trees and rare animals, Changbai Mountain underground forest is a treasure trove of wildlife resources.

分析：汉语旅游文本主观性较强，讲究意境和谐，情景交融，虚实相生，在描写景物自然美的同时传递内在情感美，但语义不太清晰，读者需整体感悟意义。英文删繁就简，向读者阐明主要信息，准确传递关键信息，前景信息在句中起关键作用："Changbai Mountain underground forest is a treasure trove of wildlife resources"，突出了文本的核心信息、重点信息和实用信息。

例2. 乘坐缆车缓缓飘行在林海之上，绝美的原始空中花园风景尽收眼底，白云袅袅，满目苍翠，时有飞鸟在脚下掠过，时有树梢花朵似探手可及，如在碧波上荡舟滑行，悠然惬意。

译文：You will have the panoramic view of the spectacular natural hanging garden with up-curling clouds and verdant plants on the car above the forest sea. Sometimes, birds would flit through beneath the car and it always seems that treetops and flowers are within your reach. It is like rowing in blue waves.

分析：英文重写实，注重实用信息，审美重点为客观景物本身，而非其前面的"华而不实"的修饰语，这些修饰语有可能造成语义模糊。"白云袅袅""满目苍翠"的主要信息即为"白云"与"苍翠"，用"苍翠"之名指"植被"之实；译文剥离语言外壳，将中心意象首先译出，另用简约的修饰语，将其译为"up-curling clouds""verdant plants"。旅游文本的英译应提炼中文中的主要语义信息，分清虚实、厘清主次。如果一味死守原文，译文就会增加读者的阅读负担，破坏流畅的审美体验，甚至让原文与游客之间在理解上出现更深的鸿沟。

2. 层次梳理

英汉互译应梳理不同句子成分，通过调整原文的句法结构厘清语义层次。汉译英，应先找到语义中心（前景信息），将其放在最重要的位置，将次要的语义（背景信息）围绕语义中心，根据其与语义中心之间的关系处理句子的主次关系；英译汉，则应根据汉语的语言特点和逻辑将次要的语义信息前置，进行语义铺垫，语义中心则置于句末，先分后总，前因后果，使句子易于理解。

例1. 祈年殿是皇帝祈谷的地方，殿高38米（包括6米高石座），直径30余米，砖木结构，中间没有横梁。

译文：Used as a place for the emperors to pray for good harvest, the Hall of Prayer for Good Harvests, 38 meters high (including 6 meters of stone terrace) and over 30 meters in diameter, is built of wood and brick, with no beam in the center.

分析：祈年殿是"砖木结构"是语义的重点，也是最重要、最核心的信息——前景信息，其余均为背景信息。译者将"皇帝祈谷的地方"状语主位化，置于句首，而将"殿高38米（包括6米高石座），直径30余米"处理为后置定语，修饰中心词"祈年殿"，再将"中间没有横梁"用"with"组成介词短语，处理成状语。这样一来，原文的汉语数个小短句变成一个英文长句，表达了多个不同的语义层次，逻辑严明、层次清晰、重点突出。

例2. 纵览全市，火树银花，千簇万重；层层叠叠，倒映水中；毗连天际，衔接繁星，如凌太空。身临其境，顿觉心旷神怡，虚幻缥缈，浮想联翩，城市灯光呈现出高挂星空的景象。

译文：A panoramic view of the city lights, either like fireworks in clusters or reflected in water, presents a real tapestry of lights merging with stars high up in the sky. Upon seeing all this, one cannot help feeling his mind roaming and imagination soaring on wings.

分析："城市灯光的全景呈现出一片高挂星空的灯火的景象"是前景信息，其余为背景信息，不是译文的重点，可省译或缩译。译文将"火树银花，千簇万重；层层叠叠，倒映水中"这几个四字格按照其内部语义关系缩译为一个精炼的修饰成分，因为"in clusters"就包含了"千簇万重、层层叠叠"的语义；另将"毗连天际""如凌太空"两个四字格作省译处理，因为其语义已包含在"merging with stars high up in the sky"之中。第二句，译文"one cannot help feeling his mind roaming and imagination soaring on wings"已有"身临其境，顿觉心旷神怡，浮想联翩"这一基本语义，故将原文中渲染重复性的词语"虚幻缥缈"亦省略不译。译文信息取舍合理，重点信息前景化，语义清晰、层次分明。

3. 文化过滤

"译者处理的是两种文字，面对的却是两大片文化。"（王佐良，1989:19）英语和汉语属于不同体系，因地理环境和社会习俗不同，语言表达方式不同，两者词汇出现非对应或者非重合的现象，它们之间缺少文化共鸣，如"饺子"译为"dumplings"，却失去了辛苦做饺子的过程和其乐融融地围在一起吃饺子的场景联想；"夫妻肺片"译为"*fuqi feipian*"，不如译为"sliced lungs sold by husband and wife"或"sliced beef and ox tongue in chili sauce"更能促进跨文化交流。对于旅游指南中的文化信息，译文需进行"文化过滤"，或补充背景信息，或省略不译；可"异化"翻译，也可"归化"翻译。

例1. 七月初七之所以被称为乞巧，是因为民间俗信这天牛郎、织女会天河，女儿家们就在晚上以瓜果朝天拜，向女神乞巧，希望能心灵手巧，婚姻美满。

译文：The day is called a day of "Qi Qiao" because traditionally people believe on the day Niu Lang and Zhi Nv, characters from Chinese fairy tales, will meet again above a river in the sky. Therefore, girls worship them with fruits at night and prey to the goddess Zhi Nv for "Qiao", meaning skillful hands and a good match and luck in marriage.

分析："天河""乞巧""牛郎、织女"等文化负载词都采用了释译法。在西方文化中，"天河"是"milky way"，是古希腊神话中赫拉的乳汁洒在了天空中，像一条银河在天空中闪烁着；而中国文化中的"天河"就是一条河，喜鹊搭起一座桥让牛郎、织女相见，因此可将"天河"直译为"a river in the sky"，而不一定译为"milky way"，更能传达中国的文化信息。"乞巧"采取释译法，适当补充文化信息，是因为这一文化负载词信息更复杂，比"天河"更难理解，故进行了文化补偿："Qiao"，meaning skillful hands and a good match and luck in marriage.

例2. 金童山：亦称"金童玉女"，位于诺水河镇西北角，前临玉皇坝，后依凤凰岭，双峰依偎，脉脉含情，卓然玉立，高耸入云。民间传说，早年玉皇大帝的御印失落于玉皇坝，遂派身边的玉童下界镇守，玉女不耐寂寞，偷偷下界幽会，玉皇震怒，谪为"石笋"。

译文：Mount Jintong, also named "Gold and Jasper" which means boy and girl attendants of fairies, is also located in the northwest of Luoshui River Town, back to Yuhuangba and in front of Fenghuangling. The two mountains cling dependently as if they are full of affections. They sit quietly and toweringly as if clouds can kiss them easily. Accordingly to the legend, in the ancient time of Jade Emperor, the royal seal was lost into Yuhuangba, and then the Golden boy and Jade girl were dispatched for the garrison. However, the Jade girl could not endure the loneliness but was indulged into secret rendezvous, which enraged Jade Emperor. Soon, the Jade girl was banished here as a stalagmite.

分析：原文"金童玉女""玉皇大帝""玉皇""御印"是中国独特的悠久历史文化衍生出的用语和形象，是语用学文献中最能反映社交与语言选择的关系成分。旅游翻译的目的是让译语读者读懂看懂，获取相关的文化知识，并让其喜闻乐见，对于原文中出现的、译文读者不易理解的文化信息需进行适当说明，以消除跨文化交际障碍。译文使用定语从句"which means boy and girl attendants of fairies",对"金童玉女"进行了意义增补,使原文"金童玉女"所表达的意义更为明确,有利于外国游客朋友更好地理解和接受原文的文化信息。

四、旅游指南翻译原则

旅游指南为游客提供吃、住、行、游、购、娱等旅游信息,虽然具有公益性,但编写指南的目的还是吸引游客前往旅游目的地旅游,带动当地旅游、社会、经济发展。因此,旅游指南的翻译应以旅游指南出版的目的为导向,提供相关信息,引导游客尊重当地民风、民俗,促进人文交流,理性消费,快乐旅游。为此,旅游翻译应遵守以下原则:读者为中心原则、有效传达信息原则、主观描述忠实原文原则。

1. 读者为中心原则

旅游指南文本的翻译应以译入语为归依,在功能、体裁、语域、语言/语篇四个层面上,向指南的目标语靠拢,为此可采用各种变译手法,使译文被读者理解、接受。因此,翻译旅游指南文本,一方面应充分考虑目标语读者的文化背景、认知思维、语言表达、情感态度和信息接受能力,减少文化理解障碍;另一方面应对信息合理取舍,不以信息等量交换作为信息传送质量标准;此外,还应以译语读者喜闻乐见的语言方式传递指南中的信息,以实现旅游文本的信息功能。

例1. 公元1398年在此设所建城,设"狼烟墩台"。

译文:In the year of 1398, a garrison post was set up here together with "smoky towers" to warn of pirates.

分析:指南中的"狼烟墩台",是明朝为防倭寇侵扰,当地军民在临海北山上设置的,也称"烽火台"。军民发现敌情后,昼升烟,夜举火,以此为报警信号,因此简称"烟台"。但西方并无此类军事设施,如果不增译相关信息,外国读者可能无法理解,故译文考虑到外国读者的文化背景和认知能力,补译了"to warn of pirates",以增进其对"狼烟墩台"的理解。

例2. 鲤鱼门以海鲜美食驰名，最适宜三五知己晚饭共聚。在这里，顾客<u>可到海鲜摊子亲自挑选鲜活的海产</u>，<u>然后亲自交给菜馆炮制</u>，<u>客人更可指定烹调的方式</u>。当然，在点菜前宜先查询价钱。

译文：This fishing village is popular for its seafood and ideal <u>for a night out with friends</u>. You can choose your own fresh fish (<u>so fresh it's still swimming in a tank!</u>) and decide how you'd like it prepared. Make sure you ask the price before ordering.

分析：译文总体忠实原文，突显鲤鱼门海鲜不容错过，但形式、内容与原文却不尽相同。考虑到读者的文化背景、语言表达和信息接受能力，译文化繁为简，采取缩译法，删除了中文不必要的信息，如原文中的"可到海鲜摊子……""然后亲自交给菜馆炮制"等，保证了译文的简洁性；但为了增强指南的劝导、感染功能，译文又增译了"so fresh it's still swimming in a tank!"此句的翻译取决于是以作者为中心还是以游客为中心。如果以作者为中心，则照文直译，不必增译。

2. 有效传达信息原则

旅游指南提供吃、住、行、游、购、娱等旅游信息，多为信息型文本，译文必须首先保证信息内容准确、无误，才能有效地实现旅游指南在译入语中发挥正确的指南作用，如发现指南中的信息有疑问或有误，应查询资料甄别、勘误。但是旅游指南内容的准确性不应以译文对原作者"忠实"来判断，而应以传递的信息不被译文读者误解作为判断（Nida，2001：129）。译文的"有效性"固然是建立在"准确性"基础上的，但"准确性"应利于读者理解、欣赏。

例1. Juneau is possibly the most spectacularly located capital city in the US. It is also the most remote, with no road access to the outside world or even to the rest of Alaska. With its large resident population, as well as <u>over one million visitors</u> who arrive during the short summer (late May—early Sept), Juneau is the busy hub of the Inside Passage. Sandwiched between steep-sided forested peaks and the Gastineau Channel, the heart of the city is an intriguing mix of modern high-rise buildings and historic gems such as the <u>Red Dog Saloon</u>, and the Alaskan Hotel.

译文：朱诺大概是美国所有州府中周围环境最壮美的一个。它也是最偏远的州府，没有公路与外界相通，甚至没有公路与阿拉斯加其他地区相通。城中的大量居住人口，再加上每年在短暂的夏季（5月下旬至9月上旬）来旅游的<u>70万游客</u>，使朱诺成为内海航道上的繁华枢纽。市中心夹在森林覆盖的陡峭山峰与加斯蒂诺海峡之间，市内建筑风采迷人，既有现代高层建筑又有<u>红狗沙龙</u>和<u>阿拉斯加人宾馆</u>类的历史明珠。

分析：判断传递信息的有效性是通过译文能否被正确理解。原文主要为事实性信息指南，翻译需准确、无误，但译文将"over one million"译为"70万"，导致信息失真，误导读者。此外，"Red Dog Saloon"被译为"红狗沙龙"，游客会感到一头雾水；"Alaskan Hotel"被译为"阿拉斯加人宾馆"，更是让读者一脸茫然。查询维基百科，红狗沙龙为朱诺淘金时期供淘金者交流信息的酒吧，也是朱诺最早的人工旅游景点；而阿拉斯加宾馆建于1913年，是该地最早的宾馆。因此"Red Dog Saloon"可译为"红狗沙龙酒吧"；"Alaskan Hotel"则译为"阿拉斯加宾馆"，改译如下："既有现代高层建筑，又有红狗沙龙酒吧、阿拉斯加宾馆这类宝贵的历史建筑"。

例2. On the Annapurna Circuit, the Annapurna Conservation Area Project (with New Zealand government assistance) has introduced the Safe Water Drinking Scheme—a chain of 16 outlets selling purified water to trekkers. Its aim is to minimize the demand for plastic mineral-water bottles. An estimated one million plastic bottles are brought into the Annapurna Conservation Area each year, creating a serious litter problem.

译文：安纳布尔纳峰保护区项目（在新西兰政府的帮助下）在安纳布尔纳峰环路上引进了安全饮水计划(Safe Water Drinking Scheme)——设立了16个分销机构向徒步旅游者出售纯净水。其目的在于减少对塑料瓶装矿泉水的需求。每年大约有100万个塑料瓶被带入安纳布尔纳峰保护区，造成了严重的垃圾隐患。

分析：指南源于《孤独地球：尼泊尔》，介绍安纳布尔峰保护区项目的相关情况，是典型的信息型文本。译文遵循信息有效传达原则，采用直译法，完整地传递了原文的信息。如"the demand for plastic mineral-water bottles"直译为"对塑料瓶装矿泉水的需求"，"等量"传递了原文的信息，但略显生硬。建议以中文读者更能接受的方式翻译，省译为"瓶装矿泉水"，而不必一字不漏，译为"塑料瓶装矿泉水"。译文的准确性、有效性应以"传递的信息不被译文读者误解作为判断"，同时兼顾读者的阅读体验，有利于译文读者对原文的理解，"等效"传递原文信息比"等量"传递原文信息更符合翻译的总体原则。

3. 主观描述忠实原文原则

旅游指南中的某些内容是根据作者个人旅行体验所写的主观感受，具有较强的个人感情色彩。旅游指南中的评价性信息、描述性信息、召唤性信息、美学信息等主观性较强，也带有个人偏好。翻译这些主观描述，首先应甄别信息的真实性；其次由于中外语言、审美的差异，对于主观描述的翻译应把握"忠实"原文的分寸。一般来讲，英译汉可适当增译，包括信息性增译和语法增译；汉译英则应删繁就简，不能"过译"。

例1. Most Everest trekkers opt to fly one way to avoid having to repeat the difficult initial Jiri to Lukla leg. This introduces its own problems, as fights to Lukla are notorious <u>for cancellations, waiting lists and short-tempered trekkers</u>, although things have improved in recent years.

译文：多数前往珠穆朗玛峰的徒步旅行者都选择乘机抵达或离开，以避免重复走颇为艰苦的吉里到鲁克拉路段。但这样做也有麻烦，尽管近年来情况有所好转，<u>但飞往鲁克拉的班机还是经常出现取消、延误等情况</u>，而且乘客中不乏坏脾气者。

分析：作者以个人的旅行经验，告诉游客在尼泊尔乘机的旅行经历。译文并未将"notorious"照本宣科地译为"臭名昭著的"，因为这个词带有太强的个人情感倾向，需甄别、过滤相关信息，把握分寸，毕竟太强烈的负面评价有悖于旅游指南提倡的客观性。翻译旅游指南需遵循主观描述忠实原文的原则，但也需甄别信息的客观性、可靠性。

例2. 满觉陇自明代开始就是杭州桂花最盛的地方，每当金秋季节，珠英琼树，人行桂树丛中，沐"雨"披香，别有一番趣意。

译文：Manjuelong Village has been regarded as a place where sweet osmanthus blooms most beautifully since the Ming Dynasty. Every autumn, flowers of osmanthus trees are in full bloom. A stroll in the osmanthus forests and fragrance will offer you a rare enjoyment.

分析:"沐'雨'披香,别有一番趣意"属于评价性信息,是作者的个人感受。"沐'雨'批香",仿佛游客沐浴于桂花香气之中,有夸大之嫌,译文将其译为"A stroll in the osmanthus forests and fragrance will offer you a rare enjoyment",同样表达了个人感受,但更为客观,符合西方人士的审美和主观评价,亦符合英文简洁的表达方法。

五、旅游指南翻译方法

旅游指南为游客提供各类信息,主要有事实性信息、评价性信息、描述性信息、文化信息、召唤性信息、提示性信息、美学信息、风格信息八个类型,是旅游者游前、游中重要的参考资料,也是旅游者旅游决策、出行、购买行为的重要依据。因此,翻译旅游指南应在信息准确的基础上翻译,并通过旅游指南中的评价、描述、提示呈现旅游指南文本的语言、美学、风格等,为游客提供吃、住、行、游、购、娱等参考,实现指南中的信息功能、召唤功能。

1. 以读者为中心原则下的调整

旅游指南除了信息功能,也具备一定的外宣或召唤等功能,在表达形式和诉求手段上应遵循以读者为中心的原则,让受众感觉自然亲切,对可能让受众感觉别扭的内容、表达方式和诉求手段则应进行必要的调整(陈小慰,2013:95—100)。由于指南中的文化信息带有源语民族的思维和文化特征,译文考虑译入语读者的心理需求,可直译,也可意译,或两者并用,提高旅游指南译文的可读性和接受性。

例1. 紫云屏是寺门前的"照墙"。

译文:The Ziyun Screen is "Zhao Qiang" (a short screen wall facing the gate of mansion) in front of the temple.

分析:"紫云屏"是国家级保护文物,建于明万历四年(公元1576年),位于泉州开元寺,为寺门对面的一堵高大照墙。照墙是风水影响下的特色建筑形式,为避免气冲,于房屋大门前建一堵墙。如果音译"照墙",由于"文化空缺",外国游客会不知所云。译文以读者为中心,采取音译加注的翻译方法,不仅阐述了"照墙"为何物,而且说明了"照墙"设置的具体方位,便于英文读者理解。

例2. 全县532个岛屿,星罗棋布,犹如朵朵荷花,散落在碧波万顷的东海之中。

译文:Consisting of 532 islands, Daishan County looks like lotus flowers spreading all over the vast expanse of the blue water in the East China Sea.

分析:指南为景物描写,属于描写性信息。中文景物描写常常不是为了写景本身,而是激发游客对景点的美好遐想,辞藻堆砌,极尽渲染之能事,如用"星罗棋布"重复表达"散落"之意。英文语言质朴、相对客观,重在表达实质信息。因此,以读者为中心原则下的调整,一是以读者为中心的语言调整,将汉语意合句、四字语言调整为英文形合句,状语主谓化;二是以读者为中心的内容调整,删除中文的繁复冗余,如省译"星罗棋布"。

2. 有效传达信息原则下的直译

在有效传达信息原则指导下,旅游指南中的事实性信息、提示性信息以及风格信息翻译一般采用直译,以便快捷、有效地传达原文信息。直译的优点是直接呈现原文的句式和内容,并能体现原文的风格特征,因此旅游指南的翻译应采取"直译优先"的原则。但由于中、英语言文化上的差异,直译并非语言上、形式上逐字逐句翻译,而应用地道的目的语语言表达原文的内容和意义,以实现信息传递的"有效性"。译文是否有效,在于信息能否被译语读者正确理解。对于指南中的文化信息,则可直译与意译相结合,以弥补"文化空缺"。

例1. Make sure you are in good health before departing, as there is very little medical attention along the trails and rescue helicopters are not only very expensive but must be cleared for payment in advance.

译文:在出发之前一定要确保自己的身体处于最佳状态,因为沿途几乎没有设施,救援直升机不仅费用高昂而且必须提前付费。

分析:指南提示游客沿途无任何医用设施,救援直升机需提前支付高额费用,以此警戒游客身体状况良好才能开始徒步。这些提示性信息对游客至关重要,甚至关乎性命安危,必须准确、可靠。译文采取直译法,顺句顺译,信息等量交换,完整、准确地传达了原文信息。

例2. You will be sharing the trail with man and beasts, usually carrying large burdens— not for fun but to scrape a living, so show respect. If a mule or yak train approaches, move to the high side of the trail. If you move to the outside you are at risk of being knocked over the edge. Buffalo will happily trample all over you, especially when they are moving downhill— give them a wide berth.

译文:一路上可能会有许多人或牲畜从你身边经过,他们通常都背负着沉重的负担,不是为了消遣而是以此维持生计,所以你应该表现出尊重。如果有骡子或牦牛长队向你走来,最好在地势较高的地方暂避一时,如果你在道路外侧的话,就有被撞倒的危险。水牛有可能会踩伤你,尤其在它们下山的时候一定要远远地躲开。

分析:译文总体上采取直译法,呈现了原文的信息内容和风格。考虑到译文的可接受性,译文个别地方也采用了意译法和其他译法,如"sharing the trail with man and beasts"译为"有许多人或牲畜从你身边经过";而"happily trample all over you"省译了"happily"。如果直译为"高兴地",对于游客来说,显然是荒诞不经;译文在"move to the high side of the trail"之后增译了"暂避一时"。全文内容和结构以直译为主,用地道的语言有效地呈现了原文的内容和意义。

3. 主观描述忠实原文下的变译

旅游指南中作者的主观感受或建议旨在通过个人的旅行经历对旅游者施加影响,或给予建议指导。翻译主观描述应基于事实,不能随心所欲,影响指南信息传递的准确性。主观描述多为描写性或美学信息,文本或多或少具有祈使、劝导、渲染功能,翻译这些主观描述,可在忠实原文基础上采用变译,如增译、省译、释译、编译等翻译方法,以还原作者的感情色彩,提高译文的可读性,但应注意英汉语言、审美的差异，把握分寸，做到增词不增意，减词不减意。

例1. Besides the fish that comes in steamed, brown stew or escoveitch form, there is delicious conch soup (lunchtimes only) and breakfast specials such as ackee and saltfish. Great, if occasionally grungy.

译文：除了美味可口的蒸鱼、浓汤炖鱼或腌鱼，还有一道香喷喷的海螺汤（仅午餐供应）。早餐有特色的西非荔枝果和鳕鱼。除个别时候口感欠佳，总的来说味道还是很棒的。

分析："除个别时候口感欠佳，总的来说味道还是很棒的"为作者主观评价。"grungy"，牛津词典解释为"dirty in an unpleasant way"，指"脏的、低劣的、龌龊的"之意。如果将"grungy"这个带有强烈个人主观感受的词直译为"低劣的""龌龊的"，游客恐怕会再也没有吃饭的欲望，与整个语境"总的来说味道还是很棒的"也不相符。译文译为"口感欠佳"，既保留了作者的态度，也呈现了原文的诱导功能："总的来说味道还是很棒的。"

例2. 清晨日出，傍晚日落，彩霞满天飞，映照在湖中，水天一色，中间不时有鸟飞过，有早出晚归的渔民唱着歌划着小舟驶过，远远望去，恍若仙境。

译文：During sunrise and sunset, the horizon is carpeted with rosy clouds, reflecting in the lake. There are birds flying across the sky, and songs from fishermen who are rowing boats on the lake. Seen from a distance, it seems like a fairyland.

分析：这段文字是作者主观印象中对日出日落的描写：满天彩霞、水天一色、唱歌划舟、恍若仙境。翻译指南中的主观描述，应考虑中、英语言、审美的差异，在忠实原文的基础上，采用变译方法，着重翻译有效信息；如"彩霞满天飞，映照在湖中，水天一色"译为"the horizon is carpeted with rosy clouds, reflecting in the lake"；"渔民唱着歌划着小船驶过"译为"songs from fishermen who are rowing boats on the lake"，声画结合，突显"恍若仙境"的意境，增词不增意，减词不减意，既呈现了原文的美学信息，又不露痕迹地使文本产生祈使、渲染之功效。

本章小结

旅游指南的使用贯穿于游前和游中，涉及吃、住、行、游、购、娱各个方面，兼具信息功能和呼唤功能。一方面，旅游指南给游客提供旅游的基本信息；另一方面吸引游客前往目的地旅游，具有指南针的引领作用。总的来讲，旅游指南分为客观信息类文本和主观描述类文本两大类，其中客观信息类文本主要包含事实性信息、提示性信息、文化性信息；主观描述类文本则包括评价性信息、描述性信息、召唤性信息、美学信息、风格信息等，不同文本应遵循不同的翻译原则和方法。旅游指南中事实性信息、提示性信息的翻译应遵循有效传达信息原则，可采用直译法；描述性信息、文化性信息、美学信息、风格信息则应遵循读者为中心原则，可采用增减、重构、编译等变译方法。对于主观描述信息的翻译应注意把握分寸，可直译，也可意译，最重要的不是与原文的形式对等，而是与原文功能上的对等。

翻译实践

一、热身练习

翻译下文，并对译文做简要分析。

1. 山上有"九宫八观七十二庵"。

2. Accommodation on Eua is budget all the way, baby.

3. 西溪自古就是隐逸之地，集"梵、隐、俗、闲、野"于一身。

4. Generally not needed for stays of up to six months. Not a member of the Schengen Zone.

5. 云南自古就被视为蛮夷之地，事实上云南是一片丰饶而富足的土地。

6. Tucked away in a fold of the hills in the heart of the Cowal peninsula, this Victorian garden is a riot of colour in spring and early autumn.

7. 杭州，中国八大古都之一，距今已经有2200多年的历史。五代吴越和南宋王朝曾在这里定都，使此地成为历史文化名城。

8. Grass grows around the domed bell tower, and the arched doorways were bricked up long ago, but the shell of this ruined church (1812) defiantly remains.

9. 这里，既有老城区别具韵味的欧陆风情，又有新城区大气磅礴的都市风貌；既有传统的名胜古迹，又有新开发的特色旅游产品；既有醉人的青岛啤酒，又有好客的青岛市民……

10. Traveling around the largest state in the US requires a great deal of advance planning. From endless snowfields, towering mountains, majestic rainforests, sweeping tundra, active volcanoes, and the spectacular northern lights to some of the world's most abundant wildlife preserves, Alaska has much to offer its visitors.

二、巩固练习

翻译下文，并对译文做简要分析。

1. Smooth like rum and hot like a spicy plate of jerk, Jamaica ensnared me instantly.

2. Glowing like beacons as their gilded windows commandeer the sunset, the twin forty-storey sentinels of Mandalay Bay soar above the southern limits of the Strip.

3. This temple is the oldest Zen temple in Kyoto. It was built in 1202 by the Priest Eisai, who introduced tea to Japan.

4. The distinctive Newar pagoda temples are a major feature of the Kathmandu Valley skyline, echoing, and possibly inspired by, the horizon's pyramid-shaped mountain peaks.

5. Amsterdam works its magic in many ways: via gabled Golden Age buildings, the boat-filled canals, and especially the cozy brown cafe, where candles burn low and beer froth high.

6. 鉴于洞庭湖的独特生态环境，每年9月至翌年3月都是观鸟的理想时间，以12月上旬最热闹，当局会举办盛大的观鸟节。

7. 三台山环水绕，建筑飞檐仿古，亭阁宛然秀美，环境十分幽静。这里的茶楼也不错，不妨喝上一壶。

8. 变幻莫测的海象、海市蜃楼的奇观、八仙过海的神话、徐福东渡的故事、秦始皇射鲛的传说为烟台的山山水水增添了许多神秘的色彩。

9. 怀化，作为张家界——凤凰——怀化——桂林名山名水古城古村黄金旅游线上的一颗璀璨明珠，正以更加开放的姿态诚迎四方来客、笑待八方嘉宾！

10. 昔日的九龙城寨是一个"三不管"的地方，可以说是龙蛇混杂之地。其后，城寨全面清拆，并于1995年于原址建成今日的九龙寨公园。九龙寨公园曾获颁荣誉奖状，它具有江南园林风格，并刻意保留了现今难得一见的中国南方"衙门"建筑，以及历史遗迹如南门古迹、石匾、大炮、柱基、清朝官府的碑铭等。

三、阅读翻译

阅读下文，重点翻译下画线部分。

Vermont

Vermont's varied attractions are scattered throughout the state. Historic villages and the natural splendors of the Green Mountain National Forest grace the south, while in the northwest Lake Champlain provides a backdrop for the lively college town of Burlington. Famous ski resorts such as Stowe are perched amid the mountains that run the length of the state. In fall, Vermont's display of leaf colors is spectacular.

This huge spine of greenery and mountains runs for 550 sq miles (1,400 sq km)—almost the entire length of Vermont—along two-thirds of the Green Mountain Range. The mountains, many of them over 4,000 ft (1,200 m) high, have some of the best ski centers in the US, including Sugarbush and Mount Snow.

The National Forest is divided into northern and southern sectors, and encompasses six wilderness areas, many of them with no roads, electricity, or clearly marked trails. Less primitive areas of the forest, however, have picnic sites, camping grounds, and more than 500 miles (805 km) of hiking paths, including the famous Long and Appalachian Trails. The area's lakes, rivers, and reservoirs offer excellent boating and fishing, and there are designated paths for horseback riders as well as bikers.

In the southwest corner of the Green Mountain National Forest is Bennington, Vermont's third-largest city. An important manufacturing center, Bennington is also home

to the small but prestigious Bennington College. Three 19th-century wooden covered bridges (just off Route 67) herald the approach to the town, which was established in 1749. A few decades later, Ethan Allen arrived on the scene to lead the Green Mountain Boys, a citizen's militia that scored several decisive victories against British forces during the Revolutionary War.

The town's most prominent landmark is the 306-ft-(93-m-) high Bennington Battle Monument, a granite obelisk commemorating a 1777 battle, when Colonial forces defeated the British. The monument looms over the Old Bennington Historic District ringed by Federal-style brick buildings. The 1806 First Congregational Church is particularly striking, with its vaulted plaster and wood ceilings. Next to the church is the Old Burying Ground where one of America's most loved poets, Robert Frost, is buried.

A major attraction for visitors is the Bennington Museum and Grandma Moses Gallery. Apart from an impressive collection of Americana, the museum has a gallery devoted to folk artist Anna Mary (Grandma Moses) (1860—1961), who lived in the Bennington area. A farmer's wife with no formal art training, Grandma Moses started painting landscapes as a hobby when she was in her mid-seventies. "Discovered" by critics in 1940, her distinctive primitive paintings soon won international renown.

第六章　旅游手册翻译

旅游手册提供的信息是旅游者想从旅游经营商或旅游代理商那里获得的信息。从这个角度来说，旅游手册具有促销作用，在一定程度上减少了销售人员的工作量，降低了销售成本。旅游手册还有象征作用，当旅游者购买产品前无法亲眼见到或检查产品时，旅游手册便可以成为旅游产品的替代品。旅游者提前阅读产品描述，旅游过程中参考旅游手册，事后回忆旅游经历时再次翻阅旅游手册，这时的旅游手册充当的是社会学家所指的"意符"、指代产品或真实旅游的经历（霍洛韦，2006：290）。

随着互联网的发展，电子旅游手册应运而生，为游客了解旅游景点提供了另一种选择。互联网能提供旅游手册中的大多数信息，电子旅游手册的补充作用越来越明显，但还没有迹象表明传统旅游手册将被电子旅游手册取代。此外，旅游手册在旅游代理、旅行社的店面，在各地游客中心随处可见，其充当社会学家所指的"意符"、指代产品或真实旅游经历的作用是网站上那些电子旅游手册无法取代的。本章讨论的旅游手册是指旅游经营商用来宣传旅游景点、吸引游客前往旅游目的地的宣传手册。

一、旅游手册与指南对比

旅游手册是一本小册子，提供旅游目的地和旅行途中吃、住、行、游、购、娱等信息。从形式上看，旅游手册有精美彩印，也有黑白印刷；有的使用大量文字介绍，有的则提供精美的图片；有的被印刷装订成书或小册子，有的被印刷成传单放在旅行社或酒店柜台上，供旅游者取阅或邮寄给客户（林莉，2011：121）。不同的旅游手册作用也不同，有的主要为游客提供信息（如航空公司时间表）；有的既提供信息，也诱导消费者购买产品（如介绍旅游产品）；有的是为了吸引潜在游客。

旅游指南属于商业广告性应用文本，有约定俗成的编写体例，其信息结构一般包括"旅游地景区/观/点+观赏项目特色+主题活动+营业时间+门票价格+可乘交通工具+注意事项+民俗禁忌"等。形式可分为折叠式或手册式，由当地旅游部门或旅行社或景区提供或摆放在酒店或公开发行。国内旅游指南习惯采用中、英文对照加附图形式，文字受篇幅限制，一般要求简明扼要，突出景观/点主题的关联性（曾利沙，2009：15—17）。

旅游手册与旅游指南相比较，两者在内容上有许多相同之处，从文本功能上看，二者都为旅游目的地提供相关信息；从内容上看，都包括对旅游目的地吃、住、行、游、购、娱等的相关介绍；从语言上看，基本上都由语言文字和非语言文字两部分组成；从形式上看，旅游手册更正式，包含封面、标题、口号、正文、封底等，多为印刷体；而旅游指南形式更多，除了纸质版外，许多国家和地区的旅游官网也提供旅游指南，网上的旅游指南通常也被称作"旅游攻略"。

但是旅游手册与旅游指南也有区别：第一，旅游指南属于应用文本，主要为语言内容，图片是附加信息；而旅游手册是由语言文字和非语言文字两部分构成，没有语言和非语言的侧重。第二，旅游指南内容更翔实，信息量更大；而旅游手册注重形象展示，图片等信息比重更大，文字信息相对较少。从字面上理解，旅游手册是一种便于浏览、翻阅的小册子，重在展示形象；而旅游指南让潜在游客对旅游地有一个比较全面的了解，发挥的是"指南针"的作用，内容更详细。从某种意义上讲，旅游手册是旅游指南呈现的一种形式；而旅游指南是旅游手册的具体内容。

此外，旅游手册有较强的促销功能，而旅游指南一般不以广告、促销为目的。《孤独星球》就明确指出：《孤独星球》系列丛书提供独立、客观的建议。我们的指南不刊登广告，不收费推荐景点或为企业代言。我们的作者也拒绝通过付费或以折扣的方式换取任何形式的正面报道（转引自丁大刚，2008：169）。旅游手册示例如下：

例1.

分析：这是一本马来西亚旅游手册的部分截图。从形式上看，它主要以图片为主，配合少量文字介绍；从中间有订书机痕迹可看出，它是一本小册子，而不只是一张传单；从目的来看，这本旅游手册主要介绍马来西亚旅游景点、地图以及马来西亚旅游特色。结合图片和文字，游客能够大概获取马来西亚的旅游信息。

例2.

分析：这是越南旅游手册的截图。从形式上看，手册主要展示图片，少量文字提供旅行社的联系电话、官方网址等。从目的来看，手册主要为游客提供越南旅游信息。游客通过查看手册，便能大致了解酒店信息，不用一一打电话询问，既方便了游客，也减少了相关工作人员的工作量。

二、旅游手册的文本结构

旅游手册一般由语言文字和非语言文字两部分构成。语言文字部分，通常包括标题、口号、正文、联系方式等；而非语言文字部分包括标识、插图、地图等（林莉，2011：205）。语言文字和非语言文字共同构成一本旅游手册，从而使旅游手册提供的信息更加形象生动。旅游手册文字和视图的混合使用，易于激发游客采取行动，购买旅游产品，游客是从旅游手册的文字和视图两方面获取旅游信息的。

1. 标题

旅游手册最吸引人的是标题。在每本手册的开头，撰稿人利用标题明确告诉读者国家、城市或景点。成功的手册要以醒目的标题打动人心，吸引读者。标题是赢得游客注意力的第一要素，只要吸引了读者的注意，读者就会拿起旅游小册子阅读更详细的内容（许琰，2007：192）。旅游机构宣传目的不同或者旅游内容不同，旅游手册的标题也不同。有的标题就是该旅游景点，有的标题由描述性词语和旅游景点共同构成，还有的标题以旅游活动命名等。

例1. The J. PAUL GETTY MUSEUM

译文：保罗盖蒂博物馆旅游手册

例2. LAKE ARROWHEAD VILLAGE

译文：箭头湖村旅游手册

例3. Gleneagles Golf Course Brochure 2014

译文：2014格伦伊格尔斯高尔夫球场简介

例4. EAT & DRINK

译文：餐饮

例5. DON'T MISS LOS ANGELES

译文：不要错过洛杉矶

分析：以上旅游手册标题有的直接以旅游景点命名，有的由描述性词语和旅游景点共同构成，在第一时间吸引游客的注意；有的标题以旅游活动命名，让读者对旅游内容一目了然。在表达方法上，有的运用祈使句，使文本产生呼唤性作用。

2. 口号

旅游手册的口号和广告语类似，通常文字简练，直接准确，具有宣传性、鼓动性，以提炼旅游目的地的整体形象，扩大旅游地的知名度和影响力。

例1. Chase the excitement, enjoy the thrills.

译文：追逐刺激，纵享激情。

例2. Come for the atmosphere, stay for the company.

译文：为体验氛围而来，为与同好相聚而留。

例3. Savour the art of slow travel.

译文：品味漫游艺术。

例4. Experience the rich tapestry of arts and culture.

译文：体验丰富多彩的艺术和文化。

例5. Taste every cuisine in our food-obsessed nation.

译文：在这片热爱美食的国土上品尝每一道料理。

例6. Find the extraordinary.

译文：寻找非凡。

分析：以上五个旅游口号与广告语相似，直奔主题，简洁有力，具有强烈的鼓动性、诱导性，激发游客前来消费体验的欲望，宣传旅游景点或旅游促销活动，一定程度上提炼了旅游目的地形象。

3. 正文

通常，旅游手册的正文会分几个部分，每个部分又有标题，分专题介绍目的地以及与旅游有关的事项。正文内容的撰写通常遵循以下几个语步，每一语步都有其交际目的，通过一系列的语言特点来实现（林莉，2011：205）。

（1）有关旅游目的地或旅游设施的评价性断言

（2）旅游目的地或旅游设施的历史简介

（3）以导游的形式介绍主要景点

（4）介绍实用细节信息，如地理位置、交通、联系方法、价格等

（5）介绍旅游注意事项

例1.　　　　　　　　　Centro Vasco da Gama

Welcome to Vasco da Gama, a Shopping Center with unique architectural features that brings at your disposal 170 stores, including 33 restaurants, 6 cinema screens, a Health Club and various Customer Service options.

Vasco da Gama is easily reachable. It is serviced by an efficient transport network with direct access to the Shopping Centre via the Oriente Station. 10 minutes away from Lisbon city centre and 5 minutes away from Lisbon International Airport, Vasco da Gama has indoor parking with a capacity of around 2,700 parking spaces.

Besides the wide commercial offer, including brands with international awareness, this Shopping Centre has beautiful balconies with a panoramic view to the Tejo River. This Shopping Centre is the perfect place for a walk, for shopping or to enjoy a drink at the end of the day.

Vasco da Gama Shopping Centre is located in one of the most recent Lisbon areas—Parque das Nações (Park of Nations), where Expo 98 was held. It opened in 1999, offering 170 stores, including 33 restaurants, as well as a hypermarket.

Opening hours: Every day, 09h00 — 00h00

Address: Avenida Dom João Ⅱ Lotel.05.02 1990-094 Lisboa, Portugal

译文：　　　　　　　　　达伽马购物中心

欢迎光临达伽马购物中心，本建筑构造独特，中心内共有170余个店铺随时为

您服务，其中包括33间餐厅、6间影院、1个健身俱乐部，还有各种客户服务供您选择。

达伽马购物中心地理位置优越，从里斯本东方火车站（Oriente Station）可直达购物中心，方便快捷。购物中心距里斯本市中心约10分钟车程，距里斯本国际机场约5分钟车程，商场内设有室内停车场，共有2700个车位。

购物中心所售商品琳琅满目，涵盖众多国际知名品牌，中心阳台造型美丽，您可在此一览特茹河的全貌。此外，购物中心还是闲逛漫步的不二之选，您可以在一天的辛劳之余来此购物或是小酌。

达伽马购物中心坐落在里斯本的最新区——万国公园，这里曾举办过1998年世界博览会。公园于1999年开业，共有170余家商店，包括33家餐厅，以及一家特大型超市。

营业时间：每天9点到24点

地址：里斯本Avenida Dom Joio Ⅱ街道Lote1.05.02号 邮编：1990-094

分析：这是一本购物中心旅游手册的语言文字部分，包含标题、正文和联系信息。手册的标题是Centro Vasco da Gama（达伽马购物中心），以游览目的地作为旅游手册标题。手册的正文即是文本的第一至第四段，介绍该购物中心的内部设施、景点特色、交通位置、地理位置等。手册的联系信息包含购物中心的营业时间、地址和邮箱。

例2.　　　　　　　　HAREWOOD

—THE IDEAL DAY OUT FOR EVERY MEMBER OF THE FAMILY

Bin Garden & Adventure Playground

Home to many exotic and entertaining species, Harewood's Bird Garden works closely with UK and overseas collections in captive breeding some of the world's rarest creatures. See those beautiful birds including penguins, flamingos owls and parrots at close quarters in their lovely lakeside setting.

The ever popular Penguin Feeding takes place daily at 2 p.m.

Bird Adoption Scheme: for those who like to actively help in important conservation work —details from the information centre (telephone 0113 218 1001).

Visit our website www.harewood.org.

译文：　　　　　　　　　　哈伍德庄园
　　　　　　　　——每一位家庭成员的理想游地

百鸟园和冒险乐园

哈伍德的百鸟园里聚集着许多异国鸟类，它们品种繁多，引人入胜。该百鸟园同英国以及一些海外的鸟禽饲养机构密切合作，哺育着一些全世界最为珍稀的鸟类。您可以站在周围美丽的湖畔，近距离地观看企鹅、火烈鸟、猫头鹰、鹦鹉以及别的鸟儿。

人气很旺的企鹅吃食表演在每天下午2点举行。

鸟禽领养计划：想积极参与动植物保护工作的朋友们，可以从信息中心了解详细信息（咨询电话：0113 218 1001）。

更多有关信息，请浏览我们的网站：www.harewood.org。

分析：这是一本哈伍德庄园旅游手册的语言文字部分，包含标题、口号、正文和联系信息四个部分。手册的主标题是HAREWOOD（哈伍德庄园），以旅游目的地作为旅游手册的标题。手册的正文即文本的第一段，介绍了哈伍德的百鸟园丰富多样的鸟类、动物表演。手册有联系电话和官方网站。

以下为两个国外英文旅游手册截图，从中可以直观了解旅游手册的构成和主要内容。

Outside

Inside

图6.1　法国旅游手册

分析：这是一本法国旅游手册。语言文字部分包括标题、口号、正文、联系方式等。标题以目的地法国为名，简洁明了；口号简短有力，具有号召力和感染力：See a world that is both Old and New；正文部分主要介绍了旅游景点，并使用了评判性语言，如"world class""breathtaking"等形容词，还含有注意事项和细节的实用信息；联系方式包括电话、邮箱、官网以及地址信息。非语言文字部分包括标识、插图、地图等，图片主要选取的是著名景区，如埃菲尔铁塔、勃朗山等以吸引游客，同时起到宣传作用。

图6.2 天空旅游公司手册

分析：这是天空（Sky Tour）旅游公司手册。语言文字部分包括标题、口号、正文、联系方式等，印刷在手册外页。标题直接使用公司名称Sky Tour，并使用副标题Life in the clouds，简洁明了；口号动感，极具感染力；正文主要介绍了三个旅游项目，其中包含目的地相关的评价性，如"majestic""intelligent"等；联系方式含有电话、邮箱以及网址。非语言文字部分包括标识、插图、地图等。

三、旅游手册的文本功能

旅游手册受众主要是潜在的旅游者。这类旅游者一般有心仪的旅游地，同时希望进一步了解该地更多的信息。因此，旅游手册的主要作用是通过向这些潜在旅游者提供实用的旅游信息，以达到吸引游客到该地旅游的目的，其最主要的文本功能是信息功能，也有一些文本兼有呼唤功能、美学功能、人际功能等。英国翻译理论家纽马克在《翻译教程》（*A Textbook of Translation*）一书中将文本功能划分为六类，其中信息功能、呼唤功能、美学功能和人际功能为主要类型。

1. 信息功能，指文本对客观事实的描述以及对客观信息的传达。信息功能的目的在于传达信息，让读者了解事物。旅游手册最重要的功能是信息功能，旨在向旅游者提供各种实用的旅游信息。

2. 呼唤功能，指文本对读者内心已有的经历、知识、感情等个人意念的呼唤、诱导、启发（平洪，2002：22）。旅游手册借助描述性句子"发出指令或诱导性信息"（丁大刚，2008：71），使读者做出一定反应。

3. 美学功能，指文字具有感染力，能调动旅游者的审美情趣。一些旅游手册通过生动形象、感染力强的文字取悦、吸引潜在的旅游者，调动他们的旅游情绪和行为，满足他们的审美需求。

4. 人际功能，指促进友好交流的功能。人际功能的目的是保持文本发出者与读者之间的友好交流。旅游手册的人际功能主要体现在以作者视角和读者视角介入，使用第一和第二人称，拉近与目标读者的距离，保持友好互动。

下面以《香港旅游手册》关于南丫岛的介绍为例，简要分析旅游手册中体现的文本功能及其翻译策略和方法。

南丫岛

南丫岛位于香港的南部，是香港第三大岛屿，由于岛的形状和树丫十分相似，因此便称为南丫岛。南丫岛安静祥宁，吸引了许多年轻一辈和居港外籍人士到榕树湾一带聚居，无论星期一还是星期日，南丫岛都给人一种悠闲的感觉，弥漫着一种异国浪漫风情，没有市区的烦嚣。沿着榕树湾走，一路上都是精致的小店铺，有卖手工艺品的、有卖绿色生活用品等的，似乎这儿的人都在乎生活品质和品位。

饮食：岛上有传统的西餐厅，更有印度餐、地中海餐等特色菜馆。中餐则以海鲜为主，都是岛上渔民现捕的，最有名的是"龙华海鲜"和"天虹海鲜"这两家。

交通：在香港岛的中环四号码头，每天各有十多班"港九小轮"公司的渡轮到南丫岛的索罚湾和榕树湾，从早上7点营业到晚上11点。

译文：　　　　　　　　　　　Lamma Island

(1) Located in the south of Hong Kong, Lamma Island is the third largest island in

Hong Kong which is named from its branch-like shape. (2) Lamma Island is quiet and peaceful, attracting many young people and foreigners living in Hong Kong to live in the vicinity of Yung Shue Wan. Different from the hustle and bustle of downtown area, Lamma Island gives you a leisurely feeling with a diffused exotic romance.

(3) Walking along the road of Yung Shue Wan, you could find that there are delicate small shops filling in the road such as those who sell handicraft or those who sells green living products. It seems that the people here all care about improving their taste and quality of life.

Food: There are traditional western restaurants on the island, as well as special restaurants such as Indian food and Mediterranean food. The Chinese food is mainly seafood, which are caught by fishermen on the island. Longhua Seafood and Tianhong Seafood are the most famous Chinese restaurants there.

(4) Traffic: At the Central Pier Fourth on Hong Kong Island, there are over ten rounds of ferries of the Hong Kong & Kowloon Ferry heading to Sok Kwu Wan and Yung Shue Wan from 7am to 11 pm.

这段材料是《香港旅游手册》中关于南丫岛的介绍。译文（1）（4）向游客介绍南丫岛的地理环境和交通信息，体现的是文本的信息功能，主要采取的是直译法，语言客观朴实；译文(2)使用"quiet and peaceful""hustle and bustle""leisurely""exotic romance"等描述性较强的形容词和名词，刻画了南丫岛安静美好的景致，营造了南丫岛的旅游环境，使译文具有信息兼美学功能，主要采用的是重构法；译文（3）增译了第二人称"you"，拉近了与游客的距离，增进了文本的人际功能，其目的是与游客建立良好的人际关系。

四、旅游手册的语言特点

旅游手册与旅游广告都属于旅行前文本，在文本结构、用词特点等方面有相似性，也有不同。旅游手册是"提供有关某一地点或其他方面信息的小册子"（霍洛韦，2006：290），提供旅游目的地的游览景点、交通、住宿、餐饮、购物等信息，语言相对客观，但旅游手册也有一定的诱导功能，吸引旅游者到目的地旅游，或说服旅游者选择旅游产品，有呼唤型文本（广告文体）的特点。前面几个例子中，达伽马购物中心、哈伍德庄园、南丫岛都是信息型文本，但在用词、句型结构方面也体现了一些广告文体的特征，如使用短句、独立结构、祈使句等，以便吸引顾客注意，前往参观、旅游、消费。

1. 旅游手册的用词特点

（1）形容词

英语旅游手册在介绍旅游目的地、旅游活动项目或旅游景点时，特别是在描述性文本中，会使用富有积极意义的形容词来加强语气，带有广告语的渲染性色彩，许多形容词体现了浪漫主义、享乐主义、幸福快乐、梦幻奇想、回归重生以及追求阳光、大海、沙滩（sun, sea, sand）的3S旅游情结。

例1. With careful planning, many of the city's most famous sites and unique experiences can be enjoyed during a two-day visit.

译文：我们会为您提供详细的旅程规划，您在这两天的旅程中，可观赏到纽约多处最著名的景点，获得与众不同的旅游体验。

分析：这是一段关于"纽约两日游"手册的引入语介绍，句中使用了三个正面积极的形容词"careful""famous"和"unique"。"careful"修饰"planning"，表明本次旅行规划细致，游客可放心；"famous"修饰"sites"，表明旅游景点有名，很受游客青睐，让游客感觉物有所值；"unique"修饰"experiences"，表明所观光的景点独特，游客旅行行程丰富，体验良好。三个形容词都是富有积极意义的词语，具有很好的宣传和推广作用。

例2. With its exceptional location in Lisbon's famous district where it occupies the top floors of the historical building Armazéns do Chiado, the 4 star Hotel Lisboa Regency Chiado (now renamed Hotel do Chiado) is one of Lisbon's finest hotels, and part of Portugal's heritage.

译文：Lisboa Regency Chiado，现名希亚多酒店（Hotel do Chiado），位于里斯本著名的希亚多城区，是四星级酒店，坐落于历史性建筑物希亚多仓库

（Armazéns do Chiado）顶层，地理位置优越，是一家四星级酒店，也属于葡萄牙文化遗产。

分析：这是一本酒店旅游手册的正文，介绍酒店的地理位置和历史，句中使用了三个形容词"exceptional""famous"以及"finest"。"exceptional"修饰"location"，"famous"修饰"district"，表明酒店地理位置优越，住在酒店生活便利，鼓励游客前来居住；"finest"修饰"hotels"，表明该酒店高级，宣传性和诱导性都较强，以满足游客的美好期待。

例3. Outstanding views over Lisbon and luxurious furnishings in both public areas and guestrooms combined with an excellent service help to make the Regency Chiado Hotel the ideal environment for a very relaxing holiday—or working holiday.

译文：在这里可以眺望整个里斯本的风景：内部公共区域及客房内奢华的家具设计，再加上优质的客服体验，使得Regency Chiado酒店成为休闲度假、工作旅行的最佳选择。

分析：这是一本酒店旅游手册的正文，介绍酒店的设施和优势，句中使用了五个形容词"outstanding""luxurious""excellent""ideal"和"relaxing"。"outstanding"修饰"view"，表明酒店地理位置优越，视线好；"luxurious"修饰"furnishings"，表明酒店设施华丽、舒适；"excellent service"表明酒店服务周到。这些形容词都具有积极意义，让人觉得酒店舒适怡人、服务周到，给人一种是"顾客不二选择"的感觉，具有很强的宣传效果。

例4. This is the place to come to indulge in the country's fantastic seafood—glass cabinets display fabulous tiger prawns, huge red scarlet shrimp, spikey shellfish (known as spiny dye-murex), crab, lobster, oysters, and of course, the classics in every Portuguese restaurant: clams and *percebes* (barnacles).

译文：想要体验葡萄牙最鲜美的海鲜盛宴？这里绝对是最佳选择——玻璃陈设柜摆设着令人难以置信的斑节对虾、硕大鲜美的龙虾、尖矛棱角的贝类海鲜（即带刺染科骨螺）、螃蟹、龙虾、牡蛎，当然还有所有葡萄牙餐厅的经典海鲜：蛤蚌和狗爪螺（藤壶）。

分析：这是一本餐厅旅游手册的正文，介绍餐厅美食，句中使用了形容词

"fantastic""fabulous"和"huge",用于修饰美味佳肴,体现了餐厅原料丰富、品质上乘、品种多样,吸引游客注意,起到了很好的宣传作用。

例5. Pacific Coast Highway (Highway 1) was named California's first scenic highway in 1966. One of the world's most stunning drives, its most beautiful stretch is through Big Sur.

译文:1966年,太平洋海岸公路(1号公路)被命名为"加州第一风景公路"。它是世界上最令人惊叹的车道之一,其中大苏尔这段车道最美。

分析:这是一本介绍美国海岸线风景的旅游手册的正文,描述太平洋海岸的高速公路,句中使用了形容词"stunning"和"beautiful",都是积极正面的词,给公路的描写增色不少,让公路风景更有层次感,内容更丰富,渲染性强。

(2)名词

旅游手册是以信息功能为主的文本,因此大量使用名词或形容词+名词,组成名词短语,直截了当,简明扼要,客观忠实地传达了相关旅游信息。

例1. With its lantern-bedecked streets, cheerful street vendors and traditional boutiques, Chinatown is truly a feast for all senses.

译文:街道挂满灯笼、摊贩不停地吆喝、传统风格的精品店鳞次栉比,为游客呈现出唐人街真正的感官盛宴。

分析:这个句子介绍新加坡步行街,"lantern-bedecked streets""cheerful street vendors""traditional boutiques"三个名词+感染性的形容词组成名词短语,将步行街的景点一一呈现出来,直截了当。

例2. The treatment includes: Round trip transportation from your accommodation, Use of the Sauna, Jacuzzi, Hammam, Kneipp, Chromotherapy showers, Relaxation Room/ Chaise-lounge and complimentary herbal teas, Essential oil treatments or facial treatments available upon request.

译文:疗养服务内容:全程接送、桑拿浴、极可意水流按摩浴、土耳其浴、克奈普水疗、色光疗淋浴、休闲室(有躺椅和凉茶免费供应)、精油按摩和面部护理,可根据客户的需求提供。

分析:这个句子介绍疗养服务的内容,全用名词或名词短语表达,主题明确，顾客一眼便能了解服务内容。

例3. Wooded hills, gray valleys, rippling rivers and waterfalls have long attracted visitors to this western corner of Massachusetts.

译文：长期以来，树木繁茂的山丘、灰色的山谷、潺潺的河流和瀑布一直吸引着游客来到马萨诸塞州的这个西角。

分析："wooded hills""gray valleys""rippling rivers"和"waterfalls"全为名词+形容词组成的名词短语，把马萨诸塞州的主要景点一一呈现，游客一目了然。

例4. Within easy reach of the capital, the four states of Virginia, West Virginia, Maryland, and Delaware are equally rewarding to explore, offering a varied area of mountains, plains, beaches and historic towns.

译文：弗吉尼亚、西弗吉尼亚、马里兰和特拉华四州都与首都距离不远，四州的高山、平原、海滩和历史城镇，应有尽有，值得一游。

分析：手册介绍美国四个州的旅游景点，使用四个地理名词，简洁清晰，说明四州地理环境丰富多样，旅游资源丰富，主题突出，宣传性强。

例5. There's something for everyone—world-class theme parks, iconic waterfront attractions, the world's first night safari, hidden gems to explore in charming neighbourhoods, lush greenery.

译文：无论是世界级的主题公园、标志性的海滨胜地、全世界首家夜间动物园、隐藏于迷人社区中的特色景点，或是茂盛的绿色景观，这里应有尽有，必能满足每个人的不同喜好。

分析：手册使用五个名词短语，将旅游景点一一罗列出来，并用不同的形容词修饰景观，以吸引游客注意。

（3）文学词语

旅游手册用词既要适用于大众群体，即通俗易懂；也要兼顾宣传，即稍显正式，但又不能像政论文和法律公文那样正式。因此，旅游宣传手册通常使用稍显正式而又能让游客眼前一亮的文学性词汇，增强旅游地的文学色彩和人文氛围，以满足来自四面八方、不同层次游客的文化需求。中、英旅游手册的文学性词汇主要体现在形容词和名词以及修辞格的运用。

例1. The pirate-themed aquarium takes you on a journey deep beneath the waves, where kids and adults alike will marvel at the weird and wonderful creatures on display.

译文：本水族馆以海盗为主题，我们将带给你一段海底之旅，在这里，动物种类繁多，神奇又可爱，孩子和大人都将感到叹为观止。

分析：本句中，"marvel at the weird and wonderful creatures（动物种类繁多，神奇又可爱，孩子和大人都将感到叹为观止）"中的动词"marvel"和形容词"weird"以及"wonderful"的运用，突显了海盗主题的水族馆的特色——奇妙而漂亮，带有较强的文学性描写色彩，起到了吸引儿童和成年人的作用。

例2. Embrace all types of winter fun at the snow resorts dotted across the Alps.

译文：拥抱冬天，享受快乐。在星罗棋布的阿尔卑斯山滑雪场，享受各种各样的冬季乐趣。

分析：本句中，"embrace all types of winter fun（拥抱冬天，享受快乐）"使用了拟人的修辞方法。"snow resorts dotted across the Alps（星罗棋布的阿尔卑斯山滑雪场）"等描写让游客耳目一新，一幅美丽的冬天画卷清晰地展现在游客面前，让游客感到其乐无穷。译文略有改动。

例3. The breathtaking views and forest-clad valleys of Belmont Regional Park make it a favourite open space for walking, running, mountain biking and horse riding.

译文：贝尔蒙特地区公园景色壮丽，山谷森林覆盖，是散步、跑步、骑山地自行车和骑马的最佳露天场所。

分析：本句中，"breathtaking（壮观的）"一词用来形容"view（新西兰贝尔蒙特地区公园的景色）"再贴切不过了；"forest-clad（森林覆盖的）"也比"having a lot of forests"更书面化，简洁且优美。

例4. Yellowstone! The name alone conjures visions of free-roaming herds of buffalo, wandering bears and towering jets of water spouting from the ground.

译文：黄石！单是这个名字就能让人遐想不已：野牛成群悠闲游走，大熊四处闲逛，地上射出的汩汩水流形成了水塔。

分析：本句中，"free-roaming herds of buffalo, wandering bears and towering jets of water spouting from the ground（野牛成群悠闲游走，大熊四处闲逛，地上射

出的泪泪水流形成了水塔）"不仅用词贴切，而且形象地勾勒出了美国黄石国家公园野生自然环境的画面，文学色彩十分浓厚，让都市的人们通过文字就能感受到大自然的气息。

例5. Its <u>distinctive</u> red doors and the unique layout <u>add the charming touch</u>; guests and visitors have come to appreciate.

译文：酒店<u>与众不同的</u>红色大门和独一无二的布局<u>有着独特的魅力</u>，吸引了众多宾客和游人前来观赏。

分析：本句中，"distinctive（与众不同的）"比"different"更具有文学色彩，"add the charming touch（有着独特的魅力）"措辞也更加书面化，更正式，但又不失文学的优美性。

2. 旅游手册的篇章特点

（1）篇章结构的同一性

旅游手册通常包括几个栏目，每个栏目都有标题，分专题介绍目的地以及旅游有关事项，每个专题篇章结构具有同一性。从内容来看，手册主要包含标题、口号、正文和联系方式。在介绍山岳风景时，介绍名称、地理位置、历史沿革、观光景点等。从结构上看，英文旅游手册的篇章结构受英语思维逻辑的影响，"先总后分"，篇章开门见山，以线性发展方式展开，以推论方式为主，评价性语言一般放在篇章之首，有提纲挈领之功效；中文旅游手册受中国人的逻辑思维影响，"先分后总"，篇章递进式演绎，以空间顺序发展，归纳方式为主，评价性语言一般放在篇章最后，有画龙点睛的作用。

a. 手册内容

例1. THE ROSE GARDEN (THAI CULTURAL SHOWS)

<u>Located 32km from the city of Bangkok</u>, the Rose Garden is <u>a huge park</u> built in the midst of rural scenery along the Nakorn Chaisn River. One of the park's major attraction is the Thai Village, which shows a Thai garland making together with vegetable carving and special shows that include Thai boxing, Thai martial arts, Thai dances especially the <u>spectacular</u> bamboo dance and some other Thai traditional shows together with the 15

minutes elephant show.

译文：玫瑰花园（泰国文化秀）

玫瑰花园距离曼谷32公里，是一座沿着那空猜西河田园风光而建的大型公园、泰国村庄是公园的主要景点之一，该景点展示了泰国花环制作与蔬菜雕刻技艺以及其他特别表演，包括泰拳、泰国武术、泰国舞蹈、摄人心魂的竹舞和一些泰国传统演出以及15分钟的大象表演。

例2. AYUTTHAYA AND BANG-PA-IN SUMMER PALACE

<u>The city is located 86km north of Bangkok. Ayutthaya was Thailand's second capital</u> from 1350 to 1767. Upon arrival, to explore the ruins of once <u>magnificent</u> temples that stood prosperously before the Burmese invasion. Then to visit the Bang-Pa-In, the Summer Palace of King V, with the mixture of Thai, Chinese and Gothic architecture. This tour will take you into a lime and place once known as Siam.

译文：大城府和邦芭茵夏宫

大城府距离曼谷北部86公里，1350—1767年间曾是泰国首府。抵达后，我们将探索缅甸入侵前繁荣昌盛的家伟寺商遗址。接下来参规邦芭茵，这里曾是第五王朝的夏口行宫，融合了泰式、中式和哥特式建筑。这段旅程将带您进入暹罗时代。

分析：例1和例2为两个旅游手册，旅游目的地不同，但文本的结构相似，开头介绍了旅游目的地的地理位置，然后是对目的地的定性描写（a huge park/Thailand's second capital）。两个手册在用词上也有许多雷同：例1使用了形容词"spectacular"来形容泰国竹舞，例2使用了形容词"magnificent"描述寺庙的宏伟，都是渲染性强、积极正面的形容词；描写景点的地理方位时，两个手册都用"located"表示地理位置。译文略有改动。

b. 篇章结构

例1. 南京的旅游景点很多，东郊有中山陵、明孝陵、灵古寺；城南有夫子庙、中华门、雨花台；城西有莫愁湖、朝天宫；城东有梅园新村、总统府旧址；城北有玄武湖、鸡鸣寺，<u>形成了南京独特的旅游观光胜地</u>。

译文：<u>The plentiful attractions in Nanjing form her unique and famous tourist</u>

resorts. Situated on the eastern outskirts of the city are Dr. Sun Yat-sen's Mausoleum, Xiaoling Mausoleum of the Ming Dynasty, and the Spirit Valley; in the southern part of the city lie the Confucius Temple, Zhonghua City Gate, the Rain Flower Terrace (Yuhuatai); in the western part Mochou Lake, and Chao Tien Temple; in the eastern part Meiyuan New Village, and Presidential Palace; in the northern part Xuanwu Lake, and Jiming Temple.

分析：原文"先分后总"，篇章递进式演绎，以归纳方式构建语篇，评价性语言"形成了南京独特的旅游观光胜地"放在篇章最后，有画龙点睛之功效；译文"先总后分"，将原文的主题句放在语篇开头，译为"The plentiful attractions in Nanjing form her unique and famous tourist resorts"，然后罗列自然景观，有提纲挈领的作用。译文开门见山，直击主题，符合英文的语篇构建，层次分明，结构严谨。

例2. This building is the country's largest museum and earliest archaeological site. It shows off the intricate designs inspired by early English Gothic architecture, featuring high steeples, wide stained-glass windows and a grand nave.

译文：该建筑拥有高高的尖塔、宽大的彩色玻璃窗和宏大的中殿，展现了早期英国哥特式建筑的精致设计。这是该国最大的博物馆，也是最古老的考古现场。

分析：英语语篇的构建习惯开门见山，先给出评价性语言，并置于句首，起提纲挈领的作用："This building is the country's largest museum and earliest archaeological site"，但汉语讲究含蓄迂回，层层递进，多采取"先分后总"的叙述方式。因此译文根据汉语的语篇特点，重构原文的语篇，将英文中评价性、归纳性的语言置于句末，译为"这是该国最大的博物馆，也是最古老的考古现场。"正好与英文篇章结构相反，符合中文旅游的篇章结构，起到画龙点睛的功效。

（2）时间、地点状语主位化

韩礼德的功能语法观认为，一句话从交际功能出发可分为主位和述位。主位是指话语的已知信息，通常位于句首，它既可能是功能性的，也可能是结构性的；述位是指话语的未知信息，是对主位的陈述。在英语旅游手册中，作者常常将地点、时间状语作主位成分，以达到一定的交际目的。

例1. Arriving at St. Peter's Square, the visitor is immediately impressed by the size of the memorable square facing St. Peter's, surrounded by the magnificent four-row colonnade masterpiece of Gian Lorenzo Bemini.

译文：置身于圣彼得广场，映入眼帘的是由杰安·劳伦佐·贝尼尼设计的四根壮丽精美的柱廊环绕中的圣彼得教堂。对面的纪念广场规模宏大，吸引着来自世界各地的游人。

分析：例句中的地点状语"Arriving at St. Peter's Square"被主位化，让读者一看到文本就知道下面要讲的内容就是"置身于圣彼得广场"后看到的景色，主位化使文本的逻辑性更强。

例2. 太清宫又称下清宫，在崂山东南蟠桃峰下、崂山湾畔。宋太祖为华盖真人刘若拙建道场于此。

译文：Situated at the foot of Pangtao Peak, beside Laoshan Bay, Taiqing Temple which is also called Xiaqing Temple was built by the first emperor of Song Dynasty for Huagai Taoist Liu Ruozhuo to deliver Taoism.

分析：这个句子的主位部分是太清宫，其余的是述位部分。"在崂山东南蟠桃峰下、崂山湾畔"是述位中的地点状语，英语译文将其前置，译成主位部分，突出太清宫的地理位置。

例3. For more than 15,000 years, the region was inhabited by Native Americans, but by the 20th century Anglo-American traditions had mingled with those of the Hispanic and Native peoples to create the regions multicultural heritage.

译文：一万五千多年来，该地区居住着美洲原住民，但到了20世纪，英裔美国人的传统与西班牙裔和土著民族的传统融合在一起，创造了该地区的多元文化遗产。

分析：此句中的时间状语"For more than 15,000 years"放在了句首，时间状语主位化，表达美洲原住民在该地区居住时间久远，突出该地区历史悠久，引导读者从时间变化这条线索解读该景点的历史变迁。

例4. 八大关是一个建于20世纪30年代的别墅居住区,<u>西邻汇泉湾,南邻太平湾</u>。

译文：<u>With Huiquan Bay on the west and Taiping Bay on the south</u>, Badaguan (Eight Passes, it was named after the famous eight passes in China.) is a villa residential area build in the 30s of 20th century.

分析：这个句子的主位部分是"八大关"，其余的是述位部分。在译文中，原文中述位部分的地点状语"西邻汇泉湾，南邻太平湾"做了主位化处理，放在句首，将无序的景点有序化，便于游客根据地点提示进行游览。

五、旅游手册的体裁

旅游手册作为宣传旅游景点信息的媒介，向游客介绍和说明旅游资源，如游览线路、食宿、购物和交通等资讯，是整合景区各方面资源向游客提供有效导向信息的载体，也是旅游景区推广、促销的重要手段，体裁多样。根据旅游手册不同板块的信息特点以及旅游手册主要的文本功能，可以将旅游手册体裁分为以下三种。

1. 信息型体裁

信息型体裁的文本主要向游客介绍旅游信息，包括景点的开放时间、门票价格、餐饮、交通、禁忌、注意事项、酒店推荐等。

例1. Most motels provide overnight accommodations. Usually located along the highways, they offer parking for your car right next to your room. Motels tend to have fewer amenities than hotels, and are less expensive. Services may include swimming pools and children's play areas as well as a restaurant. The rooms typically have one large or two smaller beds, a bathroom, a TV, and a phone. Many motels are run as part of national franchises, but some of the more pleasant ones are locally owned. The most popular motel chains include Holiday Inn and Motel 6.

译文：汽车旅馆通常都会通宵营业，随时欢迎客人入住。这些旅馆大都开在主要公路两旁，他们会把你的车停在你的房间隔壁。汽车旅馆虽然没有酒店那样舒服，但价钱上比较实惠，而且也有游泳池、供儿童游玩的场所以及餐厅，十分便捷。这里的房间通常有一张大床或者两张小床、一间浴室、一台电视机和一部电话。许多汽车旅馆都是经过国家批准才经营的，但也有很多是私人开的。最受欢迎的连锁汽车旅馆是假期旅馆和6号旅馆。

分析：以上文本属于旅游手册信息型文本，提供的信息包括：汽车旅馆的特色、地理位置、主要设施、经营性质等。

例2. Rules of the Road

All traffic drives on the right.

All distances are measured in kilometers.

Seat belts are compulsory, and children under the age of 4 are required to have special car seats.

At traffic signals, green lights mean you can proceed safely; amber lights mean prepare to stop; and red lights mean stop. A flashing red light means stop before proceeding; and a flashing yellow light means proceed with caution.

At a red octagonal stop sign, traffic must come to a complete halt before proceeding. When two or more cars reach a stop sign simultaneously from different sides of the intersection, drivers must yield to traffic on the right.

A yellow triangular yield sign directs you to give way to other traffic.

译文：道路规章制度

车辆右行。

以公里测量距离。

必须系安全带，4岁以下的儿童需要特殊的座椅。

交通信号灯：红灯停，绿灯行，黄灯等。红灯闪烁意味着行进前停车，黄灯闪烁意味着需要提起注意。

当看到红色八角形的停牌，车辆在行进前必须完全停止。当两辆或者多辆汽车从十字路口的不同方向同时遇到了停牌，司机必须遵守右侧行驶的规章制度。

黄色三角形的让路标志表示你必须给其他机动车让路。

分析：例句摘自旅游手册交通制度部分，属于信息型文本，告诉游客遵守交通规章制度，安全旅行。

2. 描写型体裁

旅游手册描写型体裁文本通过描写景物，向游客传达旅游信息。英语在景物描写方面偏重于客观景物的完美再现，感情的抒发以不妨碍再现的真实性为限，其运用主要是增加再现的形象性；汉语景物描写重在写意、传神而不重在形似逼真，努力做到情景交融，意境相谐，充满诗情画意（丁大刚，2008:153）。

例1. A fascinating city between sea and sky, like Venus, Naples attracts visitors from all over the world to enjoy her water ripples, wave clarity, sea breeze to erase your annoyance and worry. She also provides masterpieces which mark the meeting of East and West, and also gives you a spiritual shock.

译文：那不勒斯小城海天相接，如同威尼斯一样，吸引着世界各地的游客。她水色涟漪，波光澄清，清风拂面，带走你心中的烦恼，而小城中那些集东西方艺术大成的艺术杰作，更给你带来精神上的震撼。

分析：本文属于描写型文本。英文手册在景物描写时，使用了许多具有积极意义的形容词和名词词组，并采用了拟人的修辞手法。译为中文时，使用了大量的四字格和描述性极强的语句，体现了中文旅游手册的语言风格。译文使用以第二人称"你"视角介入，与游客产生了良好的互动。

例2. On the road leading from central Europe to the Adriatic coast lies a small Slovenian town of Postojna. Its subterranean world holds some of Europe's most magnificent underground galleries. Time loses all meanings in the formation of these underground wonders. The dripstone-stalactites, columns, pillars and translucent curtains, conjure up unforgettable images.

译文：从中欧通往亚德里亚海滨的途中，有一座斯洛文尼亚小镇——普斯托伊纳，这里的溶洞景观美如画廊，恢宏壮阔堪称欧洲之冠。洞中的奇观异景，其形成过程之漫长，使时光在这里也失去了意义：各种钟乳石形态各异——有的如玉柱浑圆；有的如栋梁擎天；有的如瀑布飞帘，晶莹剔透——大自然鬼斧神工，妙景天成，令人难忘。

分析：例句属于描写型文本。英语原文景物描写使用了一些具有积极意义的形容词和名词词组，采用了拟人的修辞手法，在最后一句中还用到了暗喻的修辞手法，将钟乳石比作柱子、窗帘等，为读者带来刺激、新鲜的体验。翻译时，使用了大量生动形象的四字格，运用排比句，并将原文的暗喻改译为明喻，符合中文旅游手册的语言风格。

3. 程序型体裁

程序型体裁的文本通过清楚明晰的语言，使用步骤性与程序性的文字，向游客介绍"怎样做"，如介绍交通线路、兑换货币等信息。

例1. 缆车上山顶：由中环地铁站J2出口，沿花园道步行至缆车总站。朝中银大厦的方向走，过马路，走中银大厦旁边的那条街道，走走就是上坡了，大概走10分钟，可以看见美国领事馆，缆车站入口就在旁边。

译文：Going uphill by the cable car: you could go out of the J2 exit of Central Station and walk along the Garden Road in the direction of Bank of China Tower. Then you should cross the road and step into the street beside the Bank of China Tower. After near 10mins' uphill road, you would see the U.S. Consulate and the entrance of the cable car station is near it.

分析：例句属于程序型文本，使用步骤性文字，多使用祈使句向游客介绍乘坐缆车的交通线路，步骤清晰明了，具体实用。

例2. 赴港旅客务必注意，如携带大相机、摄像机、手提电脑自中国内地关口出境，请务必向海关申明，填写登记表，并保存好申报单。

译文：But you must make declaration to the Customs, fill registration form and keep the declaration form when you carry equipment into the custom such as big camera, video camera or laptop.

分析：此例属于程序型文本，按照步骤说明，告知了旅客携带大型电子设备时的申报过程，语言简单明了，言简意赅。译文风格与原文保持一致，主体采用由三个祈使句构成的复合句，较好地传递了文本的信息功能。

六、旅游手册的翻译

旅游手册属于应用型文本，旅游手册的翻译应采取与文本相适应的翻译策略，不仅是表意，更应发挥手册的文本功能，达到旅游手册的交际目的。旅游手册文本功能不同，其翻译方法也不同。翻译旅游手册时，体现文本功能或文本功能对等是翻译第一要务。翻译旅游手册中的信息，重在传递信息。翻译旅游手册中的呼唤信息，重在诱发行动；翻译旅游手册中的表达信息，重在再现原文的语言特点和风格；翻译旅游手册中的美学信息，重在表现文本的美感（中文"意象美"，英文"简约美"）；翻译旅游手册中的人际交往信息，重在体现文本的人际功能，保持文本的"对话性"和"友好性"。

1. 信息型文本的翻译

旅游手册的信息功能文本旨在提供实用的信息，而旅游手册中的信息既有交通线路、联系方式等详尽的信息，又有介绍旅游目的地的描述性信息。旅游手册的信息功能，重在传递信息，可采用语义翻译策略，直译优先；如果不能，则可采用交际翻译策略，也可两者并用。使用语义翻译可采用直译法；交际翻译则可采用重构法、省译法、增译法等。

例1. 太平宫位于崂山东部的上苑山北麓，初名太平兴国院，是赵匡胤为华盖真人刘若拙建的道场之一。

译文：Taiping Temple is located at the northern foot of Mount Shangyuan, east of Laoshan Mountain. Its original name was "Garden of Taiping Xingguo", serving as a Taoist temple. Under the grant of Zhao Kuangyin, the founder of the Song Dynasty (960—1279), it was built for Liu Ruozhuo, a famous Taoist priest of the time.

分析：例句是一则信息型文本，但含有文化信息。译文主要采取直译法，顺句顺译。但是例句中的"赵匡胤""刘若拙"和"道场"对于国外游客都是较为陌生的人名和文化负载词，若直译出来，会造成理解障碍。因此，译文采用交际翻译策略，增译了相关的背景信息，帮助国外游客理解。

例2. Harewood is located: 7 miles from Leeds and Harrogate on the A61; 10 miles from Leeds/Bradford Airport; 22 miles from York; 5 miles from the Al and 8 miles from the A1/M1 links. Ample free parking.

译文：

地址：哈伍德位于A61公路，距离利兹和哈罗盖特分别为7英里（约11公里）；距离利兹/布拉德福德国际机场10英里（约16公里）；距离约克22英里（约35公里）；距离A1公路5英里（约8公里）；距离Al和M1的连接路段8英里（约13公里）。另外，哈伍德庄园提供大量的免费停车场。

分析：例句属于信息型文本，主要介绍哈伍德庄园的地理位置，突出便捷的交通环境。译文主要采取直译法，顺句顺译，但增译了"另外，哈伍德庄园……"属于语法增译，以便前后文衔接紧密。

2. 呼唤型文本的翻译

呼唤功能的作用在于感染读者，使读者产生亲切感，拉近与读者的距离，使读者产生共鸣，做出相应的反应和行动。旅游手册的翻译需要注重发挥其呼唤功能，增强文本的呼唤性，引起读者足够的反应。汉译英，可以通过增译第二人称、词性转换、改译等方法拉近与游客的距离，增强文本的呼唤功能。

例1. Harewood's hills are alive with this extraordinary outdoor cinematic sing along. Come along as your favorite character, and let rip!

译文：哈伍德的山上因为有了这种与众不同的、如同电影般的户外自娱歌咏会而充满生机活力。快来扮演你最喜欢的人物吧，你可以尽情发挥!

分析：译文进行了词性转换，将原文的介词转译为动词，增加了语言的动态性。译文以读者视角介入，增译了第二人称，促进了文本与读者之间的互动，人际功能良好，达到了吸引读者前往旅游目的地旅游的目的。

例2. Welcome to the Gold Coast! On the Gold Coast, a Farm Stay is a genuine "Aussie experience" where the natural environment, animals and traditional culture of the land all become the most memorable part of your visit.

译文：欢迎来到黄金海岸! 在黄金海岸，农场住宿是真正意义上的"澳式"体验，自然环境、动物和当地传统文化都将成为您整个旅程中最难忘的回忆。

分析：首句是一个英文祈使句，带有祈使功能、呼唤功能，热情友好，就像见到远方的客人一样，好客之情跃然纸上。接着介绍了最具"澳式"体验的"Farm Stay"，使用了形容词最高级"the most memorable"，增强了文本的渲染性，并以读者视角介入，使用第二人称"your visit"，像是在招呼客人，代入感很强。译文采用直译法，呈现了原文的祈使功能、呼唤功能。

3. 审美型文本的翻译

审美型的文本借用生动具体、优美而有吸引力的文字，对旅游景点进行描写。中、英文旅游手册的特点不同。中文旅游手册常通过华丽的辞藻、使用四字格来增强描述性和画面感；而英文的旅游手册偏重再现景物之美，因此在语言上相对中文旅游手册而言较为平实。在翻译审美型的旅游手册时，需要充分考虑中外旅游手册和游客不同的特点。汉译英，化抽象为具体，化"意象"为"具象"，化"华美"为"简约"，通过增译描述性语言、重构、拆分等方法来满足潜在游客的审美；英译汉，化具体为抽象，化"具象"为"意象"，化"简约"为"华美"。

例1. The Glacier Express cuts a cross-section through stunning Switzerland—pure train-travel pleasure. You are our honored guest, so prepare to be pampered in the Glacier Express. Savour meals specially prepared by our chef served in our stylish dining car. Or relax in your comfortable seat and enjoy coffee, snacks and drinks served from our mini-bar. The Glacier Express is superb in all four seasons: shimmering peaks in summer, snow-covered, fairy-tale scenery in winter, fabulous Alpine flowers in spring and a kaleidoscope of color in autumn.

译文：冰川快车横穿魅力无穷的瑞士——让您尽享火车旅行的乐趣。作为我们尊贵的客人，您可以在冰川快车享受到尽善尽美的服务：在风格别致的餐车享用我们的厨师为您精心烹制的风味美食，或轻松舒适地坐在座位上品尝迷你酒吧为您精心准备的香浓咖啡、各色小吃和饮料。一年四季，冰川快车都带给您无与伦比的旅行体验：春季，阿尔卑斯鲜花娇艳动人；夏季，千山万壑熠熠发光；秋季，各种色彩缤纷绚丽；冬季，整个世界粉妆玉砌。

分析：中文旅游手册常使用描写性强的形容词、四字格和动词，因此译成中文时，手册增译了相应动词"尽享""带给"；增译了形容词"香浓""各色"以及四字格"尽善尽美""无与伦比""熠熠发光"等。增译这些词语使译文更符合汉语的语言特征，体现了中文的"意象美"。此外，译文最后一句的翻译对原句进行了重构，按照"春夏秋冬"的顺序翻译，符合中国人的逻辑思维。

例2. 鲁迅公园园址是一片倾斜的海岸，没有刻意雕琢，也不震撼人心，似乎只是造物主的原作，<u>幽静恬美</u>。徜徉其间，但见白浪激礁，<u>松林覆坡</u>，<u>红岩嶙峋</u>，<u>沙滩如银</u>，<u>景色如画如诗</u>。

译文：Sitting on the rocky, sloping side of the coast, the park shows little signs of man's refinement, appearing as an original work of nature. <u>Strolling in the park, you can enjoy a scene full of poetic and artistic conception: waves, rocks, white sands and pines-covered slopes.</u>

分析：原句摘自中文的旅游手册，使用了大量四字词语，描写性较强。原文生动形象的描绘使汉语读者很容易感受到波涛轻拍、浪花朵朵的恬美意境，然而对于英语读者来说则过于抽象。汉译英，应注重传达实质信息，化"抽象"为"具体"，化"意象"为"具象"，以符合西方游客"简约美"的审美情趣。

4. 人际型文本的翻译

旅游手册的人际功能主要是为了和读者保持一种友好的交际关系，在翻译时可采用交际翻译策略，通过增译第二人称、改译、变换语态等方法来达到交际目的。

例1. The spectacular view of the highest hill in town, Egg Castle, is <u>to amaze you</u> with its panoramic view of Santa Lucia port.

译文：圣蛋城堡是小镇最高峰的壮观景象，在这里你会被圣塔露西亚港口的全貌所倾倒。

分析：原文是信息型文本，但文中使用"to amaze you..."，也体现了文本的人际功能。译文也采用了第二人称"你"，使文本具有对话性，拉近了与游客之间的距离，保持了原文良好的人际功能。

例2. Trails leaflets and details of tours and talks available from Information Centre.

译文：欢迎您在我们的信息中心领取观光线路的小册子或了解游览的详细信息。

分析：在翻译该例句时，译者改译了句子语态，并增译第二人称，拉近了与旅游者之间的距离，使旅游者感到亲切，增强了文本的人际功能。

本章小结

旅游手册属于以信息型为主的文本，但也有一定的劝导功能、诱导功能，信息性描写和描述性描写兼有，主要介绍旅游目的地的游览景点、交通、住宿、餐饮、购物等信息。信息型文本以提供信息为主，语言相对客观；描述型文本带有主观因素，使用一些渲染性词语，以便宣传旅游景点或旅游产品，但主观性没有旅游广告那么强。旅游手册的体裁较为复杂，同一个旅游手册文本可能包含多种体裁，也体现了不同的文本功能。旅游手册的翻译应从不同的文本功能入手。对于表达型的文本，可运用语义翻译的策略，采用直译法，重现原文内容和风格。对于信息型、呼唤型、审美型和人际型的旅游手册文本，可采用交际翻译的策略，通过重构、拆分、增译、转换语态等方法，传递手册信息，表现旅游手册的功能。

翻译实践

一、热身练习

翻译下文，并对译文做简要分析。

1. Harewood's gardens are among the most beautiful in the country. Plants from all over the world thrive in these wonderful historic settings.

2. This is a must to see Emerald Buddha or Wat Phra Karw which is unquestionably one of the most exotic Buddhist temples and at the heart of the temple itself is the most fabulous Buddha image carving from one piece of imperial green jade,

it is the religious objects in Thailand today.

3. 苏州文庙是一座与府学合二为一的建筑群，其规模之宏大，在中国仅次于曲阜孔庙。

4. From its thunderous ocean breakers crashing against rocky headlands and expansive sand beaches to its open grasslands, brushy hillsides, and forested ridges, Point Reyes offers visitors over 1,500 species of plants and animals to discover.

5. Lush boreal forests frame shimmering lakes, powerful rapids, and rugged canyons. Central parklands embrace scenic valleys and rolling hills. The panoramic southern plains stretch across colorful grasslands, fertile farmland, forested plateaus and ethereal badlands.

6. 除了观赏美丽可爱的白鹭和迷人的风景外，还可参与垂钓、棋牌、摄影、农家乐等活动，品尝荷叶系列菜品。

7. Capri gorge is a different story: trees, flowers and grass showing a picture of natural vitality.

8. In addition, St. Peter's church, Milan Cathedral and Florence Cathedral are not only the holy land of devout Catholicism, but also the world's most magnificent art boutique.

9. Egg Castle presents the spectacular view of the highest hill in the town. You will be amazed by the panoramic view of Santa Lucia.

10. 阿霸桥风光秀丽，山河壮美。座座雪峰耸入云霄，原始森林遮天盖地，茫茫草原花团锦簇，跌溪遗迹神秘奥妙，瀑布溪流蜿蜒跌宕，高山湖泊灿若明珠，藏羌村寨别具一格，肥沃河谷瓜果飘香。

二、巩固练习

翻译下文，并对译文做简要分析。

1. Shopping on the Gold Coast reflects the city's relaxed coastal lifestyle with electric boulevard boutiques, dazzling shopping centres and lively markets dotting the coastline.

2. In addition, St Peter's Church, Milan Cathedral and Florence Cathedral are not only the holy land of devout Catholicism, but also the world's most magnificent art boutique.

3. In a 1km radius there are six major themed attractions including Dream World, White Water, Wet'n'Wild Water World, Paradise Country, Warner Bros Movie World and the Australian Outback Spectacular.

4. Visiting the popular weekend market and interesting walk along the banks of Amphawa canals can see different Thai handicrafts and try some local food and desserts. Along the way to enjoy a relaxing and peaceful boat riding along Amphawa canals by private long-tailed speed boat, experience the nightlife style of the village people, and watch the sparkling fireflies along the canal side.

5. The Gold Coast Broadwater is a great expanse of easily accessible calm water with plenty of room to sail, fish, jet ski, parasail, scuba, cruise, kite surf, jet boat, kayak, swim, paddle board, snorkel, windsurf, picnic... you get the idea!

6. Capri is far away from the hustle and bustle, pleasant, vigorous. And Augustus Garden is located in the northern part of Capri including fertile wetlands, crystalline lakes, sandy beaches. deep canyons.

7. With this care, the light can be preserved for future generations—to teach visitors of maritime history and of the people who worked the light, day in and day out, rain or shine, for so many years.

8. The Lazio channel is the longest waterway in Italy. Here is a paradise for nature lovers, those who prefer the quiet life because of its rich in wonderful scenery, filled with prolific wildlife and dotted with pretty villages.

9. The tranquil Lakeside Walk meanders through enchanting woodland, past the 20 ft cascade as it plunges into a plants man's paradise of unusual Himalayan plants, before arriving at the Walled Garden, with its Spiral Meadow and world heritage plants.

10. As you unzip the boot, you'll find epic art d'architecture that leaves you speechless everywhere: the soaring dome of the Vatican's St Peter's Basilica, epitome

of Renaissance splendor, Michelangelo's frescoes waltzing across the Sistine Chapel, Caravaggios demanding attention in Rome's Galleria, da Vinci's Last Supper in Milan and the baroque feast that is Lecce in Puglia.

三、阅读翻译

阅读下文，重点翻译下画线部分。

Chube de Fado

Owned by a Fado guitarist, <u>this is one of the most atmospheric Fado clubs.</u>

<u>Located close to Sé de Lisboa (Lisbon Cathedral)</u> the cathedral in Alfama, the food and the performers are traditional, although younger stars also perform.

Its architecture tells us stories of ancient existence. <u>Solid walls, columns, arches, ogival ceiling combined with a tasteful and discret style built upon tradition.</u> The ambience that surrounds you from the Bar to the Gallery invites you to enjoy our magical atmosphere. We invite you to enjoy the fabulous dining room with the warmth of a personal welcome and the magnificence of its architecture.

<u>Refined ambience and exquisite cuisine with the varied and delicious portuguese gastronomy.</u> During your dinner or evening meal you will listen to well-known artists. Participate: sing or play an instrument and you will contribute to the "friendly atmosphere" of our Restaurant "Clube de Fado".

After making this tour through the Restaurant "Fado Club", draw your attention to the original corner where you can find the "Moorish Well". Admire it and make a wish!

Address: Rua de São João da Praça, 92—94, Alfama

Phone: 21 888 2694

第三篇

游中文本翻译

第七章 旅游景点介绍翻译

旅游景点介绍是一种文本，涵盖旅游景点的历史背景、自然地理、风格特色、景观价值等内容，目的是让游客了解景区的人文、历史和自然景观方面的知识，激发游览兴趣（马国志，2011：64）。旅游景点介绍可以分为两类，一类是置于景区内以标牌的形式对景点自然、方位、历史等的简要的说明文本，另一类是散见于各种旅游资料中对景区景物进行描写的文本（丁大刚，2008：136）如网站、指南、手册、旅游著作等。因此，旅游网站、旅游手册、旅游指南中都包含旅游景点介绍文本。

但是，旅游景点介绍文本与旅游手册、旅游指南、旅游网站等旅游资料又有区别。从形式上看，旅游景点介绍组成部分比较单一，主要由语言文字构成，一般不包括非语言文字部分，而旅游网站、旅游手册、旅游指南中既包括语言文字，又包括非语言文字部分。从内容上看，旅游景点介绍侧重于景点介绍本身，没有吃、住、行、游、购、娱等实用性旅游信息的介绍。此外，旅游景点介绍文本也没有固定的结构要求。

旅游景点介绍分为景物说明型文本和景物描写型文本。景物说明介绍旅游景点的历史文化、风土人情、科学知识、背景知识等，增加旅游者对旅游景点的了解，属于信息型文本；景物描写让旅游者在了解旅游目的地的信息的同时，引导游客欣赏旅游景观、陶冶情操、提升旅游体验，多为诱导型、呼唤型文本。由于受中西不同文化和思维的影响，中、英旅游景点介绍文本在内容上、语言上有所不同，呈现出不同的风格特征。

一、中西思维与旅游景物描写

中、英文化、历史背景不同。汉语的哲学背景是儒、道、佛的悟性，重心理意念，不重形式结构；注重话题，常常采用非演绎式的思维模式；喜欢激扬文字，抒发情感，常把情感体验与客体描述合而为一。英语的哲学背景是亚里士多德的形式逻辑和16—18世纪欧洲的理性主义，主体作为"旁观者"对客体进行描写，以客观、求实、冷静的表达方式叙述客观事物（连淑能，2010：272—275）。英语偏"静态"，汉语偏"动态"；英语重"形合"，汉语重"意合"；英语"简约"，汉语"华美"。中西思维的差异导致两种语言产生差异，对景物描写的翻译策略和方法产生影响。

中国人对景物描写主观性强，客观融入主观，借物抒情，常用渲染、夸张的词汇描写景物，如中国的水墨画讲究笔墨意趣、气韵生动、传神写照、虚实相生、无话处皆成妙境之说，烘托的是景点的"意象"；英语民族对景物的描写主观性不如中国人那么强，大多简约，结构严谨而不复杂，用字简洁明了，表达直观通俗，注重信息的准确性和语言的实用性，常常将客观的具象罗列出来，力求忠实再现景点可感的"形象"，让读者有一个明确具体的印象(丁大刚，2008：150)。中、英旅游景物描写的翻译过程实际上就是"形象"与"意象"、"动态"与"静态"、"简约"与"华美"之间的转换过程。

1. 形象与意象

形象是事物本身具有的具体形状或姿态，是事物的客观存在，包括人物、景物、场面、环境和一切有形物体（吴廷玉，2006：77）。形象之外的就是意象，是指用来表达某种抽象的观念和哲理的艺术形象（童庆炳，1998：288）。形象是具体的、直观的；意象是朦胧的、模糊的。英语描写景物以景观再现为主要目的，抒发感情为次要目的。景物描写多平铺直叙，实景实写，常用名词、形容词罗列景物的形象，追求的是景物具体、可感的"形象"，而非汉语追求的"意象"；汉语描写景物从主观角度出发，重在抒发感情，追求的是景物内在的"意"，而非景物外在的"景"，营造出一种"意境美""朦胧美"，意在托物言志，借景抒情。

例1. In spring, the Rocky Mountains are fresh, tender and full of wild flowers, as well as sprouting plants. The sound of birdsong is also pleasant in the solitude, enchanting with a great show of vitality.

译文：春天里，落基山脉展露出清新温柔的一面，漫山的野花，植物抽芽，初染新绿。莺歌燕语，婉转悦耳，令人沉醉于这生机勃勃的静谧美景中。

分析：原文形象生动地描绘了落基山脉春天的景色，具象罗列，传达的是实实在在的景观、景物；译文在遣词造句方面有所变化，使用汉语四字格、排比句来烘托、渲染意境，把形象的描述性词语转化为意象性的描述，以意传情，符合中文的审美和情趣。

例2. In the Roman twilight, nature's great dancers flock to the stage. The acrobatic twirls like wisps of smoke, a synchronised spectacle of breathtaking beauty.

译文：在罗马的暮色中，大自然的杰出舞者们涌向舞台。它们在空中矫捷地回旋，好似缕缕青烟。群鸟齐飞，蔚为壮观。

分析：译文形象生动地把英文中的名词、名词短语译成了中文四字格，并增译了渲染画面感的词汇，化英文中的形象为汉语中具体的意象，增强了景点的意境，是中文常用的表达方式。由此可以看出，英、汉对景物的描写在用词造句方面有很大不同，审美取向也不同。

例3. 峡谷中溪水时缓时急，缓时从容自在，如闲庭信步；急时飞珠溅玉，从山石上倾泻而下，形成美丽的叠瀑。峡谷两岸，林木苍翠，花草美丽。

译文：The streams at the bottom of the valley flow sometimes leisurely and sometimes quickly. When leisurely, they flow with confidence and composure; when in a hurry, they give rise to waves and rapids, jumping down from rocks and forming beautiful terraced falls. The slope of the valley is covered with the grass, flowers and trees.

分析：原文是对杜鹃峡的介绍描述，"时缓时急""缓时从容自在""急时飞珠溅玉"，以意写景，以意传情，通过意象描写峡谷溪水的变化，呈现出一幅富有动态感的画面。译文照实写景，使用名词、形容词、副词等单一词汇，把原文中的景象一一列出，意在呈现景物外在的"景"，而非景物内在的"意"。

例4. 沿湖四周，花木繁茂；群山之中，泉流竞流；亭台楼阁，交相辉映；湖光山色，千古风情，令多少人流连忘返。

译文：The causeways, bridges, pavilions, springs, trees and flowers in and around the West Lake make it a paradise on earth, where one cannot tear himself away.

分析：原文连用四字词语描写景点，重在言情、写意，不在写景。这些具有超越现实、虚实不定的朦胧美，对于许多英国国家的旅游者来讲，给人一种飘浮不定的印象，显得夸张不实；英文重写实，常用客观的具象来传达实实在在的景物之美，原文中带有情感抒发意味的描述性语言在译文中消失不见了，体现了英文的写实风格和审美。

2. 静态与动态

英语多用名词，呈静态。名词化是英语常见的现象，主要指用名词表达动词所表达的信息，如用抽象名词来表达动作、行为、变化、状态等。汉语动词没有相应的形态变化和句法限制，因此多用动词，常出现大量兼动式和连动式（连淑能，2010：133）。描写景物时，英文常使用"be"动词或动名词，给人一种静态的感觉；汉语多用动词，动态表述多于静态表述，语言生动活泼。

例1. The tide of the Yellow and Bohai Seas pours from both sides of Laotie Hill, <u>forming</u> several deep and turbulent whirlpools which bang loudly and make other shocking sounds.

译文：黄海潮和渤海潮从老铁山的两边涌来，在此处<u>卷起</u>几米深的急流旋涡，发出轰轰巨响，惊心动魄，煞是壮观。

分析：原文中"forming"是现在分词，与动词相比，偏静态，动感较弱；译文则使用动词"卷起"，形象生动地描绘了水流急湍的画面，给人一种动态感，符合中文描写动态景物的表达方式。

例2. On sunny days, the sky and river <u>are</u> a vast bright green world with no bounds between them; the thousand peaks and hills will provide a visual feast for your eyes. And on foggy days, the water <u>is</u> wreathed in mist, <u>with</u> the fog constantly disappearing and reappearing.

译文：晴朗天时，上下天光一碧万顷，千峦百嶂，尽收眼底。烟雨之日，岚雾缭绕，若隐若现，若断若续。明月之夜，群峰如洗，江波如练。

分析：原文中使用"be"动词"are""is"和介词"with"来描写景物，呈现出一种静态的画面，给人一种静态之美；译文使用大量的动态四字词语来描写景物，描绘出了桂林山水在不同天气所呈现的不同风景，画面感、动态感十足，文本的感染力极强。

例3. 每当晨雾散尽，晨光初照时，深蓝色的湖水犹如燃烧的片片火花，在湖面闪耀。

译文：With the morning mist dispersing and the sun rising, the crystal droplets of water in the lake look like sparks flashing, twinkling and dancing on the lake surface.

分析：原文是对火花海的描写，采用大量动词，传达出景物的动态感；译文将中文中的动词静态化，用静态语代替动态词汇，如"with...dispersing...rising"；使用现在分词，如"flashing""twinkling""dancing"代替动词。化动为静是英文景观描写常用的描写方式。

例4. 从梯状湖泊群奔流直泻的溪水，变成千万道飞瀑共同构成了树正瀑布。带着巨大的冲力，瀑布直落沟底，发出震耳欲聋的响声。

译文：The flowing water from the terrace-like lakes creates many splashing falls, which fall into the bottom of the valley below, with great force and deafening resonance.

分析：原文是对树正瀑布的景观描写，采用多个动词，形象生动，画面感强。译文则采用偏静态的英文语言描述，将"奔流直泻的溪水"译为"flowing water"；用介词短语替代动词，将"带着巨大的冲力……发出震耳欲聋的响声"极具动感的汉语语言译为"with great force and deafening resonance"，化动为静。

3. 简约与华美

汉语在描绘和展示自然美景时，往往更多地借助生动的言语表达一种"诗情画意"，侧重于对主观心理的描写，以抒发主观情感为主，大量使用四字格、叠词，同义反复，语言华美；英文描写景观侧重于对自然形式的描写，客观具体、用词简洁、行文明快，文风质朴，直观可感，呈现简约之美。因此，景物描写英译汉，可用汉语四字词语，使用对仗、对偶句式，通过重复、陈设、烘托，渲染景物的意境；汉译英，则应调整句子结构，删除汉语重复意义的词语和修饰成分，呈现自然、客观、可感的景物。

例1. Now, we've arrived at the observation tower to appreciate the panorama of Sand Lake. Sand Lake is similar in shape to a golden shoe; hence the name "Shoe-shaped Gold Lake". Looking over to the south, we can see the rolling sand dune; to the north, we can see green water with reeds.

译文：首先我们到瞭望塔观看沙湖的全景。在塔上，我们可以看到沙湖的形状很像一个元宝，因此当地人又称沙湖为"元宝湖"。请大家向南看，远处起伏的黄色沙山，似金波逐浪，北面碧水绿海，似翡翠镶嵌，湖平如镜，巍巍贺兰与深绿的芦苇丛倒映水中，宛如苍龙戏绿水，绿水浮苍龙。

分析：原文是对沙湖风景的描写，用词简洁，无渲染词汇，符合英文景物描写客观、写实的特点；中文则运用大量四字词语以及明喻修辞手法描写景物，如"碧水绿海""似翡翠镶嵌"以及叠词，如"巍巍"等，以增强景物的氛围感和气势，化英文之简约为中文之华美，符合中文的表达方式。

例2. When viewed from above, the pine forest undulates like sea waves under the force of winds, and sound of the wind rushing through the trees is like the sound made by the surging ocean waves. As you go deeper into the woods, you will be enchanted by the trees natural canopy, which blocks out the sun. In spring Jindalai flowers are in full bloom all over the mountain and bathe in it a scarlet red color. During summer the mountain is a green sea of swaying pines, clouds, and fog. During autumn the mountain is once again ablaze with brilliant colors, as the maple tree leaves turn red. And in winter, it is covered with white snow and become a winter wonderland.

译文：当你站在高处，风撼松林，涛声阵阵，宛如海浪一般。当你走进密林深处，就会感受到什么是古木参天、遮天蔽日了。春天，满山盛开的金达莱，殷红一片；夏天，松涛云雾，满眼是绿色的海洋；秋天，枫树红叶，苍松翠柏，五色斑斓；冬天，银装素裹，好比广寒仙境。

分析：原文是对长白山风景的描写，没有华丽的辞藻，几近"白描"，符合英文简洁性的表达习惯；中文运用了大量的四字词语来描绘长白山景色，如"风撼松林""涛声阵阵""古木参天""遮天蔽日""殷红一片""松涛云雾""苍松翠柏""五色斑斓""银装素裹"来描绘长白山景色,并使用比喻、对比、并列,反复渲染春、夏、秋、冬景色,化"简约"为"华美",增强了景观的意境。

例3.有的飞泻而下,震耳欲聋,飞花溅雾,映出彩虹;有的潺潺流淌,似珍珠翻滚。清代诗人梁春华目睹八节洞时提诗说:"绝壑飞泉流暗壁,奇峰嶂日逗寒烟。雪消洞口云开处,信是人间别有天。"

译文:Some waterfalls are roaring, filling the air with a silvery mist and displaying many brilliant rainbows in the sunlight while others are murmuring in feathery foams like pearls. Liang Chunhua, a poet of the Qing Dynasty, wrote a poem in praise of the beauty at sight of the falls, "Off the cliff water flies, over the peak mist floats; the snowy cave emerges with clouds, that is a place of unique beauty." The poem vividly depicts the elegant landscape of this waterfall.

分析:原文是对黄荆老林八节洞瀑布的描写,使用大量的四字词组,语言华美;句式对仗工整,通过重复、排比渲染美景;译文没有使用四字词语,而是用简洁的名词、形容词、动词描写景物,诗句翻译也用释译法,化华美为简约,体现了英文描写景物的特点。

例4. 蒙顶山由上清、玉女、井泉、甘露、菱角等五峰组成。诸峰相对,形状似莲花,山势巍峨,峻峭挺拔。前山,绝壁飞泉,茶畦披绿,红宇古刹,浓荫蔽日;后山,怪石嶙峋,藤萝蔓绕,杂花生树,曲径通幽。

译文:Mount Mengding consists of five peaks: Shangqing, Yunv, Jingquan, Ganlu and Lingjiao, which stand opposite each other in the shape of a lotus flower. Steep and towering, they are often shrouded in rain and fog. On the front slope of Mount Mengding you will be impressed by green tea trees, hanging cliffs and splashing springs and ancient temples tucked away in the trees. Behind, on the back slope, you will be delighted at rocks, flowers, rattans, woods as well as the winding paths.

分析:原文是对蒙顶山的描述,采用多组四字词汇,使用对偶句,对仗工整,符合中文的表达方式;译文并未按照原文译出,而是选用个别单词对景物进行罗列,用词简洁、客观具体,文风质朴,呈现出可感的简约之美。

二、中西语言差异与旅游景物描写

中西思维差异导致中、英语言差异。英文"以形统意",造句常用各种形式的连接词、分句或从句,注重结构完整、句子形式,使用显性衔接;中文"以意统形""遗形写神",重意不重形,较少使用表示逻辑—语法关系的连接词语(logic-grammatical connector),注重隐性连贯,很少用甚至不用形式连接手段,让人思而得知,凭经验、语境和悟性从整体上去领会意义,体现了中国哲学重悟性不重形式论证的特点(连淑能,2010:74—84)。

汉、英在景物描写的时间顺序和空间顺序上也存在差异。英语时间状语位置比较灵活,汉语时间状语位置相对比较固定。英文空间方式以线性顺序为主;中文则以空间顺序为主,不定点的观察通过地点的转移和特定的视角进行。英文视线观察由远及近或由内而外,汉语逻辑顺序由浅入深、由表入里、由表象到本质(方宜庆,1998:126—127)。与汉语不同,英语时间、地点状语通常被作为形式主语,以突出景点的时间和地点。

汉、英旅游文本的差异还体现在篇章布局上。受"天人合一"哲学思想的影响,汉语一般不强调主客体的区分,往往是主客体相互融合,呈隐含式语态(朱全明,2009:4)。因此,汉语的主题往往不是直截了当地进行表达,而是采用曲折、隐喻、含蓄、间接的方式展开、阐述,属于"螺旋式"的篇章结构,多为"先分后总";受逻辑分析思维的影响,英文语篇往往是先抽象、后具体,先综合、后分析,开门见山点出主题,再围绕中心句扩展,往往"先总后分",属于"直线型"语篇结构。西方还有"个人主义"的传统,特别强调个人意见的表达,通常在语篇的开头就表明观点,结语点题(董晓波,2013:54)。

1. 形合与意合

英语是"形合"语言,汉语是"意合"语言,属于两种不同的语系。英语"以形统意""以形显意",这种重形式的特点体现在多用关系词、连词、介词和其他的连接手段;而汉语描写景物时从主观角度出发,"以意统形",注重实践和事理顺序、功能和意义,隐性连贯,少用甚至不用形式连接手段。英语逻辑严谨、思维清晰，重视语句间的逻辑关系；汉语句子比较松散，主要通过语篇意义连接篇章，句与句之间的逻辑关系通常通过上下文揣摩（翟晓慧，2010:121—123）。

例1. 在空中怒吼，声音凄厉，跟雪地上的脚步声混合在一起，成了一种古怪的音乐，这音乐刺痛行人的耳朵，好像在警告他们：风雪会长久地管治着世界，明媚的春天不会回来。

译文：Howling mournfully, the wind joined with the sound of footsteps in the snow to form a strange, irritating music. This snowstorm will rule the world a long, long time.

分析：译文将"空中怒吼"和"声音凄厉"翻译成副词"mournfully"和动词非谓语形式"howling"，采用现在分词作伴随状语，仅用两个英文单词就将中文四字词语传神地译出；译文还采用动词不定式，将"成了一种古怪的音乐，这音乐刺痛行人的耳朵"译为"to form a strange, irritating music"，体现了英文形合句的语言特点。

例2. 尤其是胜似庐山瀑布的龙马潭瀑布，涨水季节，瀑布飞泻，轰鸣之声几里之外可闻，真可谓"飞流直下三千尺，疑是银河落九天"。枯水季节，泉水如丝，似轻纱垂帘，却又是另一番美景。

译文：The Longmatan Waterfall (Waterfall of Dragon Horse Pool) could match the Lushan Waterfall in its beauty. In the rainy season, water cascades down the precipitous cliffs, roaring like thunder, which can be heard several miles away. As a poem describes, "The waterfall tumbles down for three thousand feet as if the Milky Way were spilling from the heaven." In dry season, the flow of water is scanty and looks like a silver curtain, another image of beauty.

分析：原文是对龙马潭瀑布的景点介绍，大量使用四字词语，语句之间没有明显衔接，反映了中文意合语言的特点，大量使用四字词语，语句之间没有明显衔接。译文以主谓结构为主干，以谓语动词为中心，如"water cascades down…"，通过反映形式关系的代词、连词等连接句子，如"which""as if"等，并使用分词结构，如"roaring like thunder"代替谓语动词，将句子各部分分层搭架，呈现出由中心向外拓展的树形的空间结构，句末还用了一个同位语"...another image of beauty"，句子结构丰富，体现出英文形合语言的特征。

例3.自古以来，"十里秦淮"有"六朝金粉"之称。明清之际，这里曾盛极一时，河厅河房，绿窗朱户，夹岸而居。每至盛日，灯船蜿蜒似火龙，素有"秦淮灯船，天下第一"之美称。

译文：The "10-*Li* Qinhuai River" has always been known as the "Golden Powders and Perfumes of the Six Dynasties" since ancient times. During the Ming and Qing dynasties, it had been a flourishing place for amusement and appreciation. The rooms and inns with vermillion doors and green windows are lined along the river banks. Whenever in a festival day, the lantern boats, one following the other, looked very much like a fiery dragon playing in the river and so it has always been known as the "Lantern boats along River Qinhuai in spring, the best under heaven".

分析：原文是对秦淮景点的描述，以流水句为主要形式构成语篇。译文以主谓结构为主干，每个长句都只有一个谓语动词，并使用连词、介词、现在分词、独立结构、同位语等形式连接句子各部分，前后逻辑关系严密，体现出英文意合句的特点，尤其以最后一句译文最为明显。该句以"The lantern boats looked very much like..."为主干句，其余部分化实为虚，尽量避免汉语动词形成流水句，如"Whenever in a festival day..." "one following the other" "a fiery dragon playing in the river" "so it has always been known as..." "...the best under heaven"，符合英文形合句的表达方法。

例4.湖石之美，可用"瘦""皱""透""漏"四字概括。孤峙无依、袅娜玉立谓之"瘦"；千摺百叠谓之"皱"；此通于彼，彼通于此，若有道路可行为"透"；四面有眼为"漏"。

译文：Beautiful and charming, the Taihu Lake stone can be put succinctly in the following four words: "slim, creasy, hollowed and perforated" for its description. Standing solitarily without anything to back on, it looks fair and elegantly charming, and this means what we call "slim". "Creasy" suggests that the piece of stone is full of creases while through from one place to another and with paths or clefts inside to go by means "hollowed" and having pores on all sides means that the stone is "perforated".

分析：原文是对湖石的景点介绍，原文按照逻辑顺序介绍景物，呈现出线性的排调式结构，句式比较闲散，无主次之分，体现出中文意合语言的特点。译文对原文四字词语进行拆分，使用主谓方式进行重构，并采用分词、介词、连词以及从句、现在分词等将句子和各部分分层搭架，呈现出由中心向外拓展的树形空间结构，从而体现出句子之间的逻辑关系，符合英文形合的语言特点。

2. 时间与空间

时间顺序是指年、月、日的推进，季节的更替和日暮的轮换。中文旅游景物描写时间限制副句多放在主句之前；英文则可放在之前，也可放在之后。空间顺序是指通过地点转移和特定的视角展现所观察到的景物。英文重形合，旅游景物描写以线性顺序发展方式为主；中文重意合，旅游景物描写以空间顺序发展方式为主。英文信息安排往往采用"突显"语序：由近及远，由内向外，小到大，由微观到宏观，由个别到整体，由具体到抽象；中文信息安排常常按照"自然"语序：由远及近，由外向内，由大到小，由宏观到微观，由整体到个别，由抽象到具体（辜正坤，2003：358）。

（1）时间顺序

在同一个地方不同的时间里，其景物是有变化的。因此把一个景物按一定的时段依次写出来，可以表现出景物的丰富多彩，使人产生美的感受（张惠华：2008:206）。以时间为序的变化有：四季顺序（春、夏、秋、冬）；早中晚顺序（早、中、晚、夜）；前中后顺序（雨中、风中、雾中、雪中……）。翻译时一般采用顺译法，但由于英文为形合句，故汉译英时，英文的时间状语位置灵活，可放在句首，也可放在句中或句尾。

例1. 每当早春来临，梅花怒放；中秋佳节，桂子飘香，沁人心脾。

译文：In every early spring, the plum-blossoms are in a full bloom while in mid-autumn here smells whiffs of fragrant Osmanthus flowers in the air, heartening the hearts and minds of visitors in the garden.

分析：原文以时间顺序简写景色，呈现春天、秋天两幅不同景象：早春梅花怒放；中秋桂子飘香。由于中、英语言差异，汉语意合，常用对仗句式，语义多隐性衔接；英文形合，多用介词短语或连接词衔接语义。译文注意到中、英文的差别，翻译时采用介词"In every early spring" "in mid-autumn"表现不同时间的景色，用连词"while"将两个中文分句合二为一译出，对比"早春"和"中秋"，使整个句子的时间顺序更加连贯，两个时间的景色对比更加强烈。

例2. 马王堆的汉墓位于长沙市东郊。清嘉庆年间的《长沙县志》认为，马王堆与唐末、五代时期的楚国皇帝马殷父子有一定关系，故称马王堆。1972年至1974年，通过对王墓的发掘，该墓共出土了3000多件珍贵文物和一具保存完好的女尸。

译文：The Han tomb at Mawangdui is located in the eastern suburb of Changsha city. The *Annals of Changsha County* written during the reign of Emperor Jiaqing in the Qing Dynasty holds that Mawangdui has some connections with Emperor Chu—Ma Yin and his sons in the late Tang and Five Dynasties, so it was called Mawangdui. From 1972 to 1974, through the excavation of the tomb, more than 3,000 pieces of precious cultural relics and a well-preserved female corpse were excavated in this tomb.

分析：这是一则信息型文本。原文按照时间顺序对马王堆进行有序的介绍，如"清嘉庆年间……""唐末、五代时期……""1972年至1974年……"，译文采用顺译法，也按照时间顺序进行描述，如"during the reign of Emperor Jiaqing in the Qing Dynasty...""in the late Tang and Five Dynasties...""From 1972 to 1974..."，时间表达准确，信息清晰明了。

例3. 这里是"中华民国"第一任总理熊希龄的故居。1870年，熊希龄出生在这里，15岁考取秀才，22岁考取举人，25岁考取进士，熊希龄成名后，积极推动戊戌变法。1913年，他被推举为"中华民国"第一任总理。当时，这批内阁成员被称为"人才内阁"。1937年，熊先生在香港去世，享年67岁。

译文：This is the former residence of Xiong Xiling who was the first prime minister of the Republic of China. In 1870, Xiong Xiling was born here. He was admitted to the scholar named "Xiucai" at the age of 15, the first-degree scholar named "Juren" at the age of 22, and the imperial scholar named "Jinshi" at the age of 25. When Mr.

Xiong became famous, he was active to promote the reformation movement. In 1913, he was assumed to be the first Prime Minister of the Republic of China. At that time, this group of cabinet members were named "Talents Cabinet". In 1937, Mr. Xiong passed away in Hong Kong at the age of 67.

分析：这是熊希龄故居介绍，原文按照时间顺序介绍历史人物，如"1870年，熊希龄出生在这里，15岁考取秀才，22岁考取举人，25岁考取进士……""1913年，他被推举为'中华民国'第一任总理。""1937年，熊先生在香港去世，享年67岁。"译文采用顺译法，按原文中的时间顺序翻译，如"In 1870, Xiong Xiling was born here.""He was admitted to the scholar named 'Xiucai' at the age of 15...""the first-degree scholar named 'Juren' at the age of 22...""and the imperial scholar named 'Jinshi' at the age of 25..."通过不同历史阶段的描写，介绍了熊希龄先生的一生。

例4．网师园初建于宋代，原为南宋史正志的万卷堂故址。清乾隆年间（1736—1795）重建，同治年间（1862—1875）又重建，形成了今天的规模。园子占地不广，但是人处其境，会感到赏心悦目，宛转多姿，可坐可留，足堪盘桓竟夕，确实有其迷人之处，能达到"淡语皆有味，浅语皆有致"的境界。

译文：First constructed in the Song Dynasty, Wangshi Garden was originally the site for Wanjuan Hall of Mr. Shi Zhengzhi, a high-ranking official in the Southern Song Dynasty. It expanded to its present size after being rebuilt during the Qianlong reign (1736—1795) and rebuilt again during the Tongzhi reign (1862—1875). Despite its miniature size, the garden's compact layout and changeable scenes are so attractive to a visitor that he feels absorbed by its vibrant beauty. Its alluring charm can always be appropriately reflected no matter whether it is described with plain language or stated in simple words.

分析：该段是网师园的景观介绍，按照时间顺序依次讲解了网师园的历史沿革，解释了网师园因曾在北宋、南宋和清乾隆、同治年间经历了四次大规模的修建和整改，才颇具今日之规模。译文也按照原文的时间顺序逐一翻译。由于英文是形合语言，中文是意合语言，英文在处理原文中的年代顺序时，将"宋代"置于句首，时间状语主位化，译为"First constructed in the Song Dynasty"；另将"清乾隆年间""同治年间"处理为平行结构。

（2）空间顺序

空间顺序，即是按事物空间结构的顺序来说明，或从外到内，或从上到下，或从近到远，或从整体到局部来加以介绍。一般来说，描写某一静态实体或具体写景时，常用这种顺序（韩志孝，2008：60）。空间顺序是描写功能的语篇结构框架，译者理清空间顺序的关键点有两个：一是视角的辨认；二是跟踪这一视角出发的空间轨迹。对空间的语言表达，汉语有更明显的临摹性，更倚重于自然空间顺序；英语更偏重逻辑空间顺序，状语位置更灵活，常采取地点状语主位化。译好句群的空间在于译"图"，而不在于译"字"（李运兴，2001：73）。英、汉对于空间的描写，有时也会采用相同的空间顺序。

例1. <u>从诺日朗瀑布向西南行，就到了日则沟景区</u>，区内景观繁多。这些令人惊叹的景致包括：镜海、珍珠滩、五花海、熊猫海、箭竹海、剑岩等。

译文：<u>Southwest of the Nuorilang Waterfall is the Rize Gully</u>, where lie many extraordinary tourist sites, including: the Mirror Lake, the Pearl Shoal, the Five-flower Lake, the Panda Lake, the Arrow Bamboo Lake and the Sword Cliff.

分析：原文是对诺日朗瀑布的空间描述。按照英文常见的空间叙事方法，采用地点状语主位化。"Southwest of the Nuorilang Waterfall is the Rize Gully…"（"从诺日朗瀑布向西南行，就到了日则沟景区……"），句式倒装，重点信息置后，符合英文景点描写采用的句型方式。

例2. <u>藏经阁位于西北部</u>，是整个拉卜楞景区最高的建筑，有着强烈的尼泊尔风格。藏经阁共六层，顶部用金铜色的砖瓦封顶。

译文：<u>Located in the northwest of the Grand Sutra Hall</u>, the Grand Golden Tile Hall is the highest building in the Labrang Monastery and is strongly tinged with a Nepalese flavor. It is six-storied and the roof is covered with bronze bricks that are washed by gold.

分析：原文是对藏经阁地理位置的描述，主位在前，述位在后，是中文常见的描述景物空间顺序的方式。译文改变了原文对景物描述的空间顺序，把方位词置于句首,采用了地点状语主位化的方式:"Located in the northwest of the Grand Sutra Hall...",强调景点的地理位置,是英文常用的空间描写方式。

例3. 走过厨房,跨过几个门槛,打开一扇古老的小台门,眼前郁郁葱葱,一片亮堂。一个清新的园子展现在我们面前,原来,精致的篱笆把园子围了一圈,中间是一片碧绿的菜畦,旁边一棵参天的皂荚树格外显眼,角落里一段连接紧密的矮泥墙,上面长满了郁郁葱葱的各种植物。

译文:<u>Out of kitchen, over some thresholds, through an old door</u>, we came to a grassy, bright and fresh yard. Elaborate fence circles the yard. <u>In the yard</u>, there are green vegetables fields. <u>Nearby</u> a tall honey locust is well-marked. <u>At the corner</u> there is a compact connection of mud walls that lush plants cover.

分析:原文通过地点转移和特定的视角来展现所观察到的事物。首先由里到外描写,"走过厨房→跨过几个门槛→打开一扇小台门→一个园子展现在面前",接着空间描写从厨房转移到园内,由近及远描写园内景物:"中间是一片碧绿的菜畦→旁边是一棵参天大树→角落里一段连接紧密的矮泥墙→上面长满了郁郁葱葱的各种植物"。译文从近到远、从内到外的空间顺序基本不变,但方位词发生了变化,通过地点的变化展现空间的变化。具体来讲,就是采用地点状语主位化的方式描写景物,如"Out of kitchen...""over some thresholds...""through an old door...""In the yard...""Nearby...""At the corner..."通过景物空间顺序的变化全面呈现出园内景物的特色。

例4. 园林划分为<u>东西南北中部</u>,<u>中部</u>以水为主,环绕山石楼阁,贯以长廊小桥。<u>东部</u>以建筑为主,列大型厅堂,参置轩斋,间列立峰斧劈,在平面上曲折多变。<u>西部</u>以大假山为主,漫山枫林,亭榭一二。<u>南面</u>环以曲水,仿晋人武陵桃源,该区与中部以云墙相隔,红叶出粉墙之上,望之若云霞,为中部最好的借景。北部旧构已毁,今又重辟,平淡无足观,从略。

译文:This garden is divided into five parts, i.e. <u>center, east, west, south and north</u> in light of their respective locations. The <u>center section</u> consists of a large pond surrounded by hills, rockeries, and buildings, which are stringed together by a series of verandas and bridges. The <u>east section</u> features its variety of buildings. In this part large and magnificent halls are accentuated by small studies and lined by rugged rockeries, resulting in a layout full of variation. The <u>west section</u> is mainly a man-made hill covered by a maple tree grove and dotted with a few pavilions. The <u>south side</u> of the hill is ringed by water to imitate Tao Yuan of Wu Ling of the Jin Dynasty. This section is partitioned from the center section by an undulating wall. The red leaves poking above the pale white walls look like red clouds sailing from distant sky. It forms the best borrowing scene in the center section. The structures currently found in the <u>north part</u> are all recent reconstruction. These buildings lack character in design. This section will not be discussed in detail.

分析：该段采取了空间顺序法来描述留园，以"东西南北中"五个视点，由中心向外围，依次介绍留园。以中部为起点，按照东、西、北空间顺序依次介绍，对留园内部设置进行了详细描写。由于中、英思维差异，中、英文对方位词的排序位置有所不同。汉语的方位词不仅可以表示具体的方位，还蕴含着非常丰富的文化气息，自古以来就有"东尊西卑"或"南尊北卑"的说法，所以汉语习惯将方位词顺序列为"东西南北中"。译文按照汉语空间逻辑进行翻译，也是从中心向外围扩散，依次描写景观，整个篇章空间逻辑与中文一致，因为英、汉空间逻辑思维也有一致性。

（3）篇章结构

英文篇章开门见山，通常头短尾长，先点出主要的或重要的判断、结论，再追叙有关的背景、情况等；中文则头长尾短，逐层深入，先叙述背景、历史、条件等，再点出主要的或重要的判断、结论（连淑能，2010：272—275）。汉语常用"前偏后正"的句式，若用"前正后偏"的句式，则表示强调；英语复句中，语序以"主前从后"为主，在语篇上体现的是线性思维（施志贤，陈德民，2006：89）。因此，英语篇章结构开门见山，"先总后分"；汉语正好相反，迂回曲折，"先分后总"。

例1. 仙寓洞因自然景观和人文景观极佳<u>被誉为"竹海明珠"</u>。

译文：<u>It is praised as "a bright pearl of bamboo forest"</u> for its excellent natural landscape and man-made attractions.

分析：原文是蜀南竹海仙寓洞简介，先描述景点地理位置，再对景物进行概括总结，解释仙寓洞成为"竹海明珠"的原因，采用的是"前偏后正"的句式；与中文的语序不同，英文把重要的信息放在前面，"主前从后"。译文按英文"前正后偏"的句式译出，逻辑清晰、结构严谨。

例2. <u>Face to face, two eras speak to each other</u>, because here you can find Manu's inn, a building screening the entrance to the Old Town.

译文：在这里你可以看到摩奴的旅馆，该建筑直指老城区的入口。两两相对的建筑，似乎是两个时代在对话。

分析：原文句首指出两个时代对话，之后再解释其原因，采取"先总后分"构架语篇。译成中文，译文句子顺序做了改变，"先分后总"，且将因果关系隐藏起来，用抒情化的语句使建筑景色跃然纸上，体现了汉语意合句的特点。

例3. 在四川西部，有一美妙去处。它背依岷山主峰雪宝顶，树木苍翠，花香袭人，鸟声婉转，流水潺潺。<u>它就是松潘县的黄龙</u>。

译文：One of Sichuan's finest attractions in western Sichuan is <u>Huanglong (Yellow Dragon)</u>, which lies in Songpan County just beneath Xuebao, the main peak of the Minshan Mountain. Its lush green forests, filled with fragrant flowers, bubbling streams and songbirds, are rich in historical interest as well as natural beauty.

分析：原文为风景名胜黄龙的景点介绍，先描述该景点的迷人风光，然后介绍该景点的名称和地理位置，符合中国人的思维方式，采用的是"分总结构"，与英文开门见山的行文方式截然不同。英文往往采用演绎法，即开门见山摆出结论，然后再进行推演。译文采用"突显"语序，将最重要的信息作为英文主题句置于句首，译为"One of Sichuan's finest attractions in western Sichuan is Huanglong (Yellow Dragon)"，符合英文的逻辑顺序，取得了先声夺人、吸引读者的翻译效果。

例4. <u>平遥素有龟城之称</u>。六道城门南北各一为头和尾，东西各二为四足。平遥城市布局巧妙，大街小巷组成一幅庞大的八卦图案，如同龟背上的花纹。

译文：Pingyao has long been called tortoise city, symbolizing its longevity. The southern and northern gates are the tortoise's head and tail, the other four gates: two on the eastern side and two on the west are the tortoise's legs. With its avenues, streets and lanes, the pattern of the whole town resembles a Bagua (a combination of eight of the 64 Trigrams of *the Book of Changes*, traditionally used in divination), which is similar to the pattern on tortoise shell.

分析：原文采用"总分结构"。首句"平遥素有龟城之称"起到了总领全文的作用，再叙述"六道城门"组成"龟"的大致形状，再叙述"龟背上的花纹"。译文根据原文的逻辑顺序，主要采用直译法，并释译了文中的文化意象"龟"和文化负载"八卦图"，便于外国游客理解。中文多采用"分总结构"，英文多采用"总分结构"，但不是绝对的，故译文按原文篇章结构，没有调整原文的逻辑顺序。

综上所述，中西文化传统、思维逻辑不同，语言存在较大差异。从内容来看，汉语旅游景点介绍注重文化表达，侧重介绍旅游资料的社会身份特征，如社会影响、历史沿革等，将旅游资源的自然风光和人文特色结合，倾向于引用俗语、名人名言或古诗歌赋等增加旅游景点的人文特色或烘托意境；英语旅游景点介绍侧重介绍地理环境、人文历史、服务设施等，对于自然风光的描述性篇幅着笔不多（孙红梅，2010：125），即使有，也会语言质朴，注重写实。

从语言形式看，汉语旅游景点介绍大量使用四字词、叠词，同义反复，讲究声律对仗，运用比喻、夸张、排比等修辞来强化表达效果，但整体行文结构较为松散。相比之下，英语旅游景点介绍使用名词、形容词、非谓语动词，以叙述说明的方式提供实在、有效的信息，多采用提供细节的方式，整体行文结构较为紧凑。

从语言风格看，由于文化背景、思维方式不同，汉语旅游景点介绍呈现华丽溢美的风格；英文旅游景点介绍呈现直观明快的风格，两者形成鲜明的对比。中文旅游文本在传递信息时用字凝练含蓄，描写景点辞藻华丽；渲染旅游景点时，对景物刻画较为笼统，呈现意境之美。英文旅游景点介绍文本则用词简洁、逻辑严谨、行文明快、文风质朴、描写客观具体，呈现直观可感之美。英语景点说明词一般具有内容客观、文字简练、目的明确等特征（丁大刚，2008：136）。

总之，英语重形式，强调主谓结构协调一致，大量使用常用关联词语，句子呈"树状"形态，主从分明，结构完整。英语词语和结构长短交错、替代变换；状语位置灵活，可置于句首，也可置于句尾；汉语重意境、顿悟，通过整体性领悟语篇意义，句子可断可连，主谓难分，主从难辨，松句、散句、紧缩句、无主句、省略句、并列式复句交替使用，流泻铺排。受"阴阳"二元论影响，汉语词语和结构整体匀称、成双成对、对偶排比、同义反复（连淑能，2010：272—276）。

三、景物描写性文本的翻译

中文的写作美学强调景物描写"意与境混"的上乘境界，追求客观景物与主观情感高度和谐、融为一体的浑然之美。人们常将景物的内在意蕴依附于其外在的表象，使具象的景物获得抽象的人格和情感，从而做到情与景相融、虚与实相生，所谓"一切景语皆情语"，几乎成了汉语景物描写的常式（贾文波，2003：21）。汉语通过物象表现情理，强调客观融入主观；用词大多华丽缥缈，表达华丽妍美，溢于言表，主观色彩浓厚；用字宜双不宜单，讲究四六骈体，声律对仗（马松梅，2003：109）。

英语景物描写则比较理性、客观，表现为主客分明，甚至对立。描写景物时主体是"旁观者"，主张"模仿"或"再现"自然，少用或不用主观性修饰语，慎用或选用形容词或副词（连淑能，2010：274），不刻意在言辞上做过多的情景、意象渲染，具有真实自然的理性之美，与汉语写景手法形成鲜明对比。在景物描写方面，侧重完美再现客观事物；在感情方面，以不妨碍真实再现事实为限。中、英文景物描写存在审美差异，语言结构不同，直接影响旅游景观的翻译方法。

中、英旅游景物描写的翻译，实际上是两种审美方式之间的转换。译者在翻译此类材料时，首先应从审美方式转换的高度来把握（高金岭，2003：102）。景物描写性文本的翻译应以目标语读者为中心，考虑英、汉景物描写的不同审美心理，以目标语读者的审美和阅读习惯遣词造句、构建语篇。译者应当从字里行间读出原文所描述的意境，综合考虑文化、审美、心理等各种语境因素，力求实现从原文到译文在形象与意象、具体与抽象、实与虚、动与静之间的有效转换（夏瑛，2015：79）。景物描写文本的翻译方法如下：

1. 形象与意象的转换

英语在景物描写上由于偏重客观再现，追求在三维空间中再现景物的形象，景物描写多平铺直叙，实景实写，其追求的效果是具体的形象。汉语偏重借景抒情，追求在时间中的情感流动，用词华丽铺张，音韵谐美，但由于追求的是景物内在的"意"而非外在的"景"，其达到的效果是抽象的意象（高金岭，2003：101）。翻译旅游景物描写文本时，应把握英语的"形象"和汉语的"意象"，相互转化，观照不同读者的审美需求。

例1. The youngest of the Rocky Mountains, the Teton Range is a spectacular sight. Enhanced by glaciers, deep canyon, snowfields, and lakes, the range shoots up suddenly, with no foothills around it.

译文：特顿山只能算作落基山脉的小字辈，但却独具魅力：它拔地而起，绝壁空灵，冰川与峡谷相望，雪原与碧湖交映，湖光山色，冰雪晶莹，景色蔚为壮观。

分析：这是一则特顿山的英文介绍，原文将"glaciers" "canyon" "snowfields" "lakes" "range" "foothills"等地形风貌——罗列，注重信息传达的准确性和实用性，较为客观，个人感情色彩不如中文景点介绍那么强烈。汉语景物介绍则不同，用词华美，常常将主观感情融入客观对象，虚实相生，情景交融，意境致上。因此，英译汉，可用汉语四字格，将英语罗列的"形象"转化为汉语的"意象"，如"峡谷相望" "碧湖交映" "湖光山色" "冰雪晶莹" "拔地而起"等，化英文之"形象美"为汉语之"意象美"。

例2. 殿内香烟袅袅，晨钟暮鼓，僧诵阵阵，佛像栩栩如生。

译文：The Haibao Pagoda is between Daxiong and Weituo palaces, with vivid Buddhas and fragrant incense. The bell and chanting can be heard from time to time.

分析：原文描绘了海宝塔殿的景象。汉语较多使用四字格，其英韵美感体现在叠音词上，读起来朗朗上口，创造意境之美，给人带来听觉和视觉上的冲击感和画面感，将读者代入了一幅绝妙的佛教寺院意境图。译文注重客观景物的再现，重在景物外在的"景"，而非景物内在的"意"，仅使用几个名词和形容词，便将中文中的意象转为英文中的形象，给人一种直观的画面感，而非似是而非的"朦胧感"。

例3. 每当夕阳晚照，<u>鞭身涂金</u>，<u>熠熠闪光</u>，<u>瑰丽夺目</u>，<u>构成一幅奇特壮美的"夕阳金鞭图"</u>。

译文：In the late afternoon sunshine, it glitters with brilliance as if glided with gold, creating a <u>miraculous</u> and <u>grand</u> scene of "Golden Whip in Sunset".

分析：原文连用数个四字词语，为读者展现了一幅美丽而壮观的金鞭溪美景图，营造出一种意境美，让游客不仅爽心悦目，更要感慨万千，而外国游客却无法体会其中的美感。因此，译文仅使用个别具有感染力的形容词，借助现在分词连接句子，将汉语渲染的意象转化为英文实实在在的景象。

例4. 冬天，<u>飘飘洒洒</u>的冬雪把整个西岭雪山装点成一个银白色的<u>童话世界</u>，只见<u>银蛇狂舞</u>，<u>蜡象飞驰</u>，<u>玉树琼花怒放</u>，<u>飞瀑流泉凝固成冰的音符</u>，演绎出<u>晶莹剔透</u>的西岭之冬。

译文：In winter, snowflakes turn the mountain into a white wonderland. Mountains become silver snakes or wax statues while the ice in the trees looks like jade flowers. The waterfalls become frozen, like silent music and present a diaphanous and snow-caped winter.

分析：原文是对冬天西岭雪山的描述，大量使用四字结构，形式对称，对景物进行了超越现实的描写，追求虚实不定的朦胧美，符合汉语旅游景点介绍善用修辞、辞藻华丽渲染的文本特点。译文删略了原文中过于渲染的词语，以"旁观者"的身份对景物进行临摹，语言质朴，呈现的是一种画面可感的景象，而不是意境。

2. 静态与动态的转换

英语偏"静态"，多用名词、形容词，通常以谓语动词为中心，通过大量反映形式关系的动词不定式、分词、介词、连词、关系代词、关系副词等把句子其他各个成分层层搭架，呈现出由中心向外拓展的树形空间结构。一个完整的英语句子中往往只有一个谓语动词，再用其他成分层层链接，名词、介词、形容词的变化相对较稳定。汉语偏"动态"，喜用动词，且没有形态上的变化，动态特征明显，句式一般是通过多个动词连用，按照时间或事理推移的方式，把事情一件一件地交代清楚，呈现出线性的"排调式结构"（曾剑平，2017：197）。英汉互译应掌握两种语言的表达习惯，做到"静态"与"动态"相互转化。

例1. Within sight are the forested stone peaks and steep cliffs, densely growing jade-green plants, birds soaring and flowers in full blossom, and the stone caves, valleys and streams which are honeycombing all over the forest park.

译文：奇峰林立，怪石嶙峋，树茂林丰，溶洞群布，沟壑纵横，溪水潺潺，珍禽竞翔，奇花争妍。

分析：英文主句使用"be动词+名词"形式，罗列具体景物，使用名词、形容词、介词，后面使用的定语从句也是"be动词+名词"形式，整个句子属于静态描写。译文使用8个主谓结构动态性四字词语，化静为动，注重动态描写，符合汉语行文习惯。

例2. 这里三千座奇峰拔地而起，形态各异，有的似玉柱神鞭，顶天立地；有的像铜墙铁壁，巍然屹立；有的如晃板垒卵，摇摇欲坠；有的若盆景古董，玲珑剔透。

译文：3,000 crags rise in various shapes—pillars, columns, walls, shaky egg stacks and potted landscapes—conjuring up unforgettably fantastic images.

分析：原文景物描写大量使用动词，如"拔地而起""顶天立地""巍然屹立""摇摇欲坠"等，整个句子呈现动态特征。英文以一个谓语动词"rise"为中心，通过反映形式关系的分词、介词、连词架构整个句子，如"in various shapes""conjuring up…"等，使用大量名词罗列景物，如"pillars""columns""walls"等，整个句子偏静态。

例3. 峰峦叠翠，林海莽莽，各种附生、腾生、灌生、乔木纵横交错，遮天蔽日，各种珍禽异兽嬉闹林间，生机盎然。南国天池在海拔800米的高度上托起一泓碧波，水光山色，交相辉映。

译文：Here green mountains and forests exist almost everywhere, and all kinds of epiphytes, lianas, shrubberies and arbors crisscross, and all kinds of animals and birds live happily. "The Hanging Lake in the South" is the lake on top of the mountain, 800 meters above the sea level with tree reflected in the lake.

分析：原文用词华丽铺张，音韵谐美，追求的是景物内在的"意"。除了极具动态的四字词语，"托起""辉映"等动词也呈现中文动态的美感。译文则偏重客观再现，景物描写平铺直叙，实景实写，具体而形象；"be动词+名词"属于英文静态描写形式，后半句为介词短语，均呈静态色彩。

例4. 这里有丰富的自然奇观，山高谷深，河床叠跳、飞流跃涧，形成道道瀑布；河流两岸，乔灌丛生，柳桦榆荟郁郁葱葱；好一幅万泉争涌、浪击石鸣、飞流直下、两岸对峙的动人画卷。

译文：A plenty supply of natural wonders are also present: towering mountains, precipitous valleys, terracing riverbeds, bubbling gullies, flying cascades, clustering shrubs, gushing springs, surging waves, resounding rocks—all these work together to bring up an imposing and appealing panorama of natural beauty.

分析：原文景物描写虚实相生，达到一种抽象的意境，多动词，偏动态。译文在景物描写上平铺直叙，用语简洁，偏重客观再现，将中文中朦胧的"意象"转化为英文中直观的"形象"。译文将汉语前半句处理为"be动词+名词"形式，将汉语四字格处理为英语"形容词+名词"形式，整个句子偏静态，将汉语的动态转化为英语的静态。

3. 简约与华美的转换

从语篇审美的角度看，英文语篇最突出的三个特点是直观美、逻辑美和简约美，其中简约美最能代表英文美篇。汉语对景物的描写崇尚一种"化实为虚"的境界，而英语写景则要求描述真实，以达到"观物"而非"融情于物"。汉语写景抒情喜欢虚幻空灵、用词华丽、文字洗练，常采用四字结构和排比手法；而英文行文则讲究简洁明快、逻辑严谨、文风质朴。旅游景物描写的英汉互译应注意这些差异，根据译入语的审美和语言习惯做出相应的变通和调整（潘莹，2009：

106）。英译汉，应尽量观照中文读者的审美需求，将英语的"简约美"转化为汉语的"华美"；汉译英，应尽量观照英语的表达习惯和审美需求，将汉语的"华美"转化为英语的"简约美"。

例1. 峨眉山月<u>清凉皎洁</u>，<u>光华如洗</u>，<u>熠熠生辉</u>，<u>丝丝扣人</u>。

译文：The moon over Mount E'Mei is charmingly shimmering, giving off its coolly pure and silk-slim moonlight.

分析：原文描写峨眉山月光。汉语四字格形式整齐悦目、音调抑扬顿挫，营造出情景交融的意境美。译文则采用副词、形容词形式描写景物，借助现在分词连接句子成分，简洁流畅，逻辑清晰，符合西方民族强调模仿和再现的审美要求，体现了英文重形式、重写实、重理性的特点。

例2. 西海群峰<u>千姿百态</u>，<u>云雾缥缈</u>，<u>万壑深渊</u>，<u>似有群仙游荡</u>，<u>变幻莫测</u>。

译文：The Xihai Peaks are of <u>various shapes</u> with <u>deep ravines</u> in between, all shrouded in <u>clouds</u> that are always moving and changing, as if carrying immortals on their wonderings.

分析：原文景物描写虚实相生，情景交融，运用比喻和大量四字词语，主观色彩浓厚。译文将原文的华美辞藻转化为具体而形象的景象，用语简洁，使用名词、介词、形容词，借助连词、代词连接起整个句子，逻辑清晰，语言自然流畅，具有英文的简约、客观、理性之美。

例3. 沿湖四周，<u>花木繁茂</u>；群山之中，<u>溪泉竞流</u>；亭台楼阁，<u>交相辉映</u>；湖光山色，<u>千古风情</u>，如天上人间，令多少人<u>流连忘返</u>。

译文：The <u>causeways, bridges, pavilions, springs, trees and flowers</u> in and around the West Lake make it a paradise on earth, where one can't tear himself away.

分析：原文大量使用四字格和排比，辞藻华丽，营造出一种情景交融、意境和谐、诗情画意的风景图。译文将原文意象的表达转化为形象的罗列，将汉语的各种词组转换成英语中的词、词组、分句，使用名词、介词，借助连词、代词架构整个句子，将汉语的"华美"转换为英语的"简约美"。

例4. 秋季，各种林木的树叶<u>变成了</u><u>红色</u>、黄色，<u>形成了</u>"万山<u>红遍</u>，层林<u>尽染</u>"的奇观，红叶<u>点缀</u>着层林，甚为亮丽，似一幅美丽的油画<u>展现</u>在眼前。观西岭雪山秋天景色，<u>奇妙无比</u>，<u>令你流连忘返</u>。

译文：In autumn, all the leaves change to red or yellow, <u>creating</u> a gorgeous spectacle of "all the mountains <u>turning red</u>, while all the trees <u>having been dyed</u>". It is really a wonderful experience to see this scenery, <u>decorated and splashed with color</u>, which looks like a perfect oil painting. The landscape of autumn makes you <u>reluctant to leave</u>.

分析：原文使用动词和四字词语，用词华丽，文字洗练，整个句子偏动态，描绘出一幅生机盎然的风景图。译文则较多使用名词、形容词，整体偏静态，将原文景象具体罗列，描写真实自然，将汉语的"华美"转化为英语的"简约美"。

四、景物说明性文本的翻译

景物说明性文本以信息功能为主，介绍景点的位置、风格、形态、历史沿革、文化背景、民俗风情、社会影响等基本信息。中、英文景物说明性文本有共同的特点：语言简明朴实，以说明为主，注重实用性和知识性，具有较强的逻辑性，但也有不同之处。英文说明性文本一般比较客观，注重事实的陈述，而中文说明性文本不仅陈述事实，有时还引经据典或用名人典故，甚至引用诗歌加以描写，文中出现大量的人名、地名、朝代、官职等文化负载词。因此，景物说明性文本的翻译不仅要将眼前所见之景描绘清楚，更要将景点背后隐藏的历史、文化告诉游客，让他们理解景点背后的意义。

通常情况下，景点说明性文本的翻译应与原文的内容和风格保持一致。汉语景点介绍常引用古诗词、俗语、名人典故，仿佛这样更能显示自己的文采，殊不知英语读者会觉得这样的文字有很多是多余的，会让他们觉得"too poetic（太华丽）"了，因此可省略不译（杨山青，2016：49—52）。但是，如果景点说明文本涉及历史文化背景，游客无法理解时，译者应找出原文本中缺失的部分，并将其增补出来。对原文中文化信息的增补尤为重要，具体包括增词、加注、解释等（刘春华，2019：141）。

中、英文句子在结构上也存在差异，翻译时还应尽量按照译语的表达方式重新组织信息，使译文连贯流畅，层次清晰，便于读者理解。景物说明性文本的翻译与景物描写性文本的翻译一样，需在"形象"与"意象"、"静态"与"动态"、"简约"与"华美"之间进行转换，可使用直译、重构、增译、省译等多种翻译方法。

1. 直译法

直译法，从字面意思上讲，就是按句子顺序翻译，在译文中尽量保持被译句的原有内容及原有表达方式。景物说明性文本多为信息型文本，很多汉语句子在语言表达上与英语有相似之处，特别是连动句、流水句。有些汉语句子看起来松散，分句较多，仍可采用直译法，不会影响英语读者的理解。总的来讲，景物说明性文本的英汉互译应采取直译优先的原则，尽量保持译文与原文在结构、语言风格上的一致。

例1. 那里有一片坂楼仙境。你看，祥云飘荡，紫气升腾，云上一群楼高耸，玉柱林立，仿佛仙山琼阁，海市蜃楼。

译文：There is a Wonderland of Jade Tower. You can see auspicious clouds floating, purple air rising, the buildings towering on the cloud, jade columns standing everywhere, as if it is a wonderland mountains and jade tower or a mirage.

分析：译文采用的是直译法，没有改变或调整原文语句的结构，顺句顺译，在结构上，总体上保持了译文与原文一致。

例2. 从茶地坪至两溪口，你可以到达低山区的花石峪景区。这是一条纵贯3.7公里的曲折而幽深的溪谷，两岸青山，峭壁对峙，成片的翠竹、山杨、野葡萄、山核桃、七里香、迎春花、映山红和不知名的奇花异草，交替怒放，香气袭人。

译文：The path from Chadiping to Liangxikou takes you to the Huashiyu Scenic Area at the lower part of the Mountain. It is a 3,700-meters long valley, winding its way through the quiet and green mountains and steep cliffs. Bamboo, arbutus, wild grapes, walnuts and other unknown plants bloom fragrantly along the valley.

分析：原文是一则景物说明性文本，属于信息型文本。译文采取直译法，未改变原文的结构顺序，尽量保留了原文的内容和表达方式，行文简洁流畅，符合景物说明性文本直译优先、顺译优先的原则。

例3. 树正瀑布是九寨沟四大瀑布之一，落差11米，宽62米，正如其名所示，与树正群海相连。

译文：The Shuzheng Falls, with a 11-meter drop in height and 62 meters in width, is one of the four largest waterfalls in Jiuzhaigou. As the name implies, they lie next to the Shuzheng Lakes.

分析：原文是景物说明性文本，简要介绍树正瀑布的情况。除一句插入语外，译文基本上采用了直译法，按照原文的语序、结构译出，保留了原文的内容，做到了译文信息与原文信息等量交换，不增不减。

例4. 五彩池海拔3010米，深6米多，面积5600多平方米，位于长海之下，深藏于挺拔参天的翠林之中。

译文：Multi-hued Lake is situated 3,010 meters above sea level at the lower reaches of the Long Lake, and has an area of more than 5,600 square meters and an average depth of over 6 meters.

分析：原文是一则信息文本。译文采用直译法进行翻译，保留了原文的内容和表达方式，和原文一样为一个独立的长句，句意简洁明了，结构紧凑严谨。此句采用重构法翻译，将地点状语主位化。

2. 重构法

英汉句型结构有相似之处，如连动句、流水句等，但汉语为意合句，比较松散；英文为形合句，结构严谨。由于英语和汉语句型结构存在重大差异，句式不可能完全对应，这就要求翻译时重组原文信息，重构原文结构。汉译英，应借助连词、关系代词、关系副词将分散的句子衔接起来，"以形显义"；英译汉，应尽可能省译英文连词、关系代词、关系副词等，摆脱英语句式结构的束缚，按照汉语的表达方式重组英文句子，"以意统形"。

例1. 阿斯哈图花岗岩石林分布在大兴安岭最高峰北约40公里，海拔1700米左右的北大山上，石林沿山脊从北向东分布，面积约5平方公里。

译文：Ashatu Granite Stone Forest stands on Mount Beida that is 1,700 meters in altitude and about 40 kilometers north of the peak of Greater Khingan Mountain. The Stone Forest covers approximately five square meters and extends from the north to the east along the ridge.

分析：此句为景物说明性文本，介绍阿斯哈图花岗岩石林的地理位置、海拔高度。原文句子比较松散，分句之间逻辑关系不强。译文采用结构重组法，将句子译为两句，重组各部分的词序，使用连接词连接各个部分，使句子层次分明、逻辑清晰。

例2. 泾县位于中国安徽南部风景如画的黄山脚下，面积2000多平方公里。从泾县向西南约40公里处就是桃花潭。镇子里有上百幢画龙雕凤的古民居，其中既有中国最古老的会馆，也有被专家题名为"天下第一祠"的祠堂。

译文：Jingxian county, <u>covering an area of 2, 000 square kilometers, lies at the foot of the scenic Mt. Huangshan in southern Anhui Province</u>. 40 kilometers southwest of the county seats the town of Taohuatan, <u>site of over a hundred ancient folk dwellings with carved beams and painted pillars</u>. It also boasts the oldest guildhall in China, and a famed ancestral temple.

分析：这一部分为景物说明性文本，介绍了泾县的地理位置、建筑风格等。中、英文均为三个句子，但各部分词序有很大区别。译文使用了较多名词、介词、连词、分词架构句子，将原文各部分的词语、小句重新组合成符合英文结构的词语和语序，层次分明，结构严谨。

例3. About 16 kilometers southeast of Red Wing is Frontenac State Park, one of the premier bird-watching sites along the river, where over 260 species pause on their journeys north and south every year.

译文：芳堤那州立公园坐落在雷德温市东南约16千米处，是密西西比河沿岸观察鸟类的首选地点之一，超过260种鸟类在每年的南北旅程中都会在此停留。

分析：此为景物说明性文本，首先介绍了芳堤那州立公园的地理位置，再说明该公园为观鸟胜地，各种鸟类在此聚集。原文地理位置信息的介绍采用倒装、同位语，并用状语从句对信息补充说明，整个句子主次分明，逻辑关系明确；译文以话题为龙头，采用流水句的形式重组原文信息，无一连接词，以意合的方式组织句子。

例4. 晋祠大门上方有一牌匾，上面写有"晋祠"二字，是陈毅1959年5月22日来晋祠视察时所写。

译文：A horizontal tablet is over the new temple gates Two words — "Jinci" (Jin Memorial Temple) were inscribed in it. They were written by Chen Yi, who used to be our nation's famous marshal. On May 22nd, 1959, he visited Jin Memorial Temple.

分析：此为景点说明性文本，介绍晋祠大门牌匾的内容和由来，注重信息的实用性和知识性。原文为一句，译文分为三句，按照英文句式结构架构句子，重组原文信息，结构严谨，语义层次分明。译文还采用增译法，解释说明晋祠中出现的历史人物。

3. 增译法

由于文化差异和知识局限，游客对历史文化知识缺乏足够的了解，从而限制了他们接收旅游景点信息的能力，影响他们的旅游兴致。对此，译者应增补旅游景点的相关信息，尤其文化负载词的翻译，需增加必要的解释，以突出文本的"信息"功能，方便目标游客了解旅游景点的基本信息（刘倩，2018：65）。译文通过加注或语义拓展，增加背景知识或相关资料，对历史文化信息添加必要的解释，有利于跨文化交际（石佳星，2015：6）；而汉语意合句向英语形合句转换时，也需要语法性增译。

例1. 大殿雄伟壮丽，门额上悬挂有"人文初祖"四字大匾。

译文：Above the door of the magnificent main hall is a large horizontal board with a four-character inscription: "Ren Wen Chu Zu" (Founder of the Human Civilization).

分析：此为黄帝陵的景点说明词，属于景点说明性文本，介绍大殿门前"人文初祖"匾额。由于外国游客无法理解匾额背后的文化内涵，因此译文增补信息，解释说明了"人文初祖"的文化内涵。

例2. 怀化名胜古迹有芷江受降坊、溆浦向警予故居、黔城芙蓉楼、通道马田鼓楼、沅陵龙兴讲寺、芷江天后宫等。

译文：The historical attractions across Huaihua City include the Shouxiangfang (the original site of China's accepting Japan's surrender in the War of Resistance Against Japanese Aggression) in Zhijiang, the former residence of Xiang Jingyu (an outstanding communist fighter and revolutionary martyr) in Xupu, the Hibiscus Pavilion in Qiancheng, the Matian Drum Building in Tongdao, the Longxing Temple in Yuanling, and the Goddess Temple in Zhijiang, etc.

分析：此句属于景物说明性文本，介绍怀化主要名胜古迹。原文中的人文景点富有历史文化色彩，但如果只罗列其名称，对于不了解中国历史的外国游客来说，会造成理解障碍，影响他们的旅游体验。译文通过增译法增加了历史信息，弥补了原文和译文之间的"文化空缺"。

例3. 山峰上尖下圆，单看俏似莲瓣，双看又宛若并蒂；若从整体看来，它又颇似一朵盛开的莲花。

译文：The peak-tops look very much like pinnacles whereas they are round at the bottom. If you look at them separately from one to another each and every of them seems to be a petal of a lotus flower but if you look at them doubly they are like twin-lotus-flowers on one stalk and still if you look at them as a whole they seem to be a lotus-flower in full bloom.

分析：汉语描写景物时重在抒情，"以意统形"，可不用形式连接手段。英语"以形统意"，多用关系词、连词、介词等作为连接手段。原文中有两个小分句，无一连词衔接句子。译文为了语义衔接，增译了多个连词，使句子前后逻辑紧密，语句通畅自然，符合英文形合句的表达方法。

例4. 跨进瓦屋山门，就进入了双洞溪，长约2公里，由从大法洞和三星洞两个大溶洞流出的山泉交汇而成，故而得名。

译文：Walking through the gateway of Mount Wawu, you will arrive at the Shuangdong Stream (Double-cave Stream). The stream is about 2 kilometers long, made up of two springs which flow from Dafa Cave and Sanxing Cave, hence the name Double-cave Stream.

分析：原文是"意合"语言，注重隐性连贯，"以意统形"，句与句之间没有连词连接；译文增译了主语"you"和连接词"which""hence"，均属于语法性增译，以厘清句子之间的逻辑关系。

4. 省译法

旅游景点，特别是中国的旅游景点包含厚重的历史文化因素，包括地名、人名、诗歌、楹联等。若直接译出，反而会给不了解中国历史文化的游客带来理解困难。中外大多数游客为普通游客，阅读景点介绍是为了了解风土人情，增加乐趣，不是为了考古或研究（刘倩，2018：65）。因此，为了让游客有更好的旅游体验，不能为了原文与译文的"对等"而增加游客的阅读负担，可删减对普通游客来说的"冗余"信息，传递景点的实质信息即可，汉译英尤其如此。

例1. 翠屏学馆始建于<u>清咸丰八年</u>（1858年），为义塾，对外收徒，培养出多位学人义士。因遥对台儿庄南部翠屏山，故取名"翠屏学馆"。辛亥革命志士尤民，运河支队创始人<u>孙伯英、赵静波，诗人贺敬之，戏剧导演郑亦秋</u>，曾在这里就读。该学馆1938年毁于战火，后于原址重建，现为私塾文化、古玩字画和古本图书展示区。

译文：Cuiping School was first built in 1858 in the Qing Dynasty. As a free private school, it admitted students openly and trained <u>many scholars and righteous persons</u>. Located opposite to the Cuiping Mountain south of Taierzhuang, it was thus named Cuiping School. Now it serves as Exhibition Hall for Culture of Old-style Private Schools, Antiques, and Ancient Books.

分析：该文为景物说明性文本，介绍了翠屏学馆的历史沿革、文化背景。景点中列出的人物比如孙伯英、赵静波，外国游客不必过多了解，可采用省译法，删去不译，用概括性短语"many scholars and righteous persons"译出。为了传达实质性信息，译文仅保留原文中的公元纪年，对于皇帝年号、纪年这些多数外国游客来说的"冗余"信息也省略不译。

例2. 湛山寺山门一对石狮子，雕琢精细。寺外建有"药师琉璃光如来宝塔"，简称"药师塔"。

译文：In front of the gate of Zhanshan Temple stand a pair of exquisitely carved stone lions. By the side of the temple there stands the Yaoshi Pagoda.

分析：原文为景物说明性文本，介绍湛山寺的石狮和药师塔。汉语景点中有一些文化负载词，如"药师琉璃光如来宝塔"，即使原文作者也不一定理解；对于对中国传统文化知之甚少的外国游客来说，译出来他们也不一定能理解、欣赏，反而有可能造成理解障碍，故译文省译了容易造成理解障碍的复杂信息"琉璃光如来"，只译出核心信息"Yaoshi Pagoda"。

例3. 每逢空山新雨，阳光映照，可见石色洁白如玉，恰似一幅幅浓淡相宜的山水丹青，故有"南溪玉屏"之称，在清代续八景中被称为"南溪新霁"。

译文：Whenever it rains the hill under the sunshine is afresh with the cliff washed white as a piece of jade, making the hill look as though it were an ink-and-wash picture, hence known as "Jade Screen on Nanxi Hill." In the sequel to the Eight Scenic Attractions in Guilin of Qing Dynasty it is called "Nanxi Hill After Rain."

分析：译文采用了省译法，省译了原文中的"浓淡相宜"。在描述景物时，中文常用四字词语渲染景点的画面感，但在西方读者眼里，并没有太多实际意义，会干扰他们的理解，因此省略不译，反而提高了译文的可接受性。

例4. 风景秀美的大观园规模巨大，占地8公顷，建筑面积8000平方米。花木树丛之中，亭台楼阁，星星点点，曲径幽洞，隐隐约约，假山庭园，婀娜秀丽。

译文：The Scenic Grand View Garden is a large-scale garden, covering an area of 8 hectares with a floor space of 8,000 square meters. Amidst the beautiful views dotted with pavilions, chambers, towers, rockeries and winding paths.

分析：原文是对大观园的介绍，多用四字词语，虚幻空灵，用词华丽，"化实为虚"，追求的是一种意境美、朦胧美；英文追求的是"观物"，行文简洁明快、文风质朴，故译文采取省译法，将汉语中重复累赘的词汇删除不译，使译文简洁明快。

本章小结

旅游景点介绍文本分为景物描写文本和景物说明文本。英、汉的思维差异对景物描写的翻译策略和方法产生重大影响。汉语描写文本多用词华美以渲染描绘，注重情景交融的意象，句子多呈现动态特征。英语描写文本追求自然真实，用词简洁朴实，注重再现景物实实在在的景象，多使用形容词、名词，句子呈现静态特征。翻译景物描写性文本，译者应注意英汉不同的审美观照，使译文符合目标语读者的审美观照，获得美好的旅游体验；翻译景物说明性文本，译者应按照译入语的表达习惯重组句子结构，适当增补或省略信息，利于游客理解，避免冗余信息影响旅游者的体验。翻译旅游景点介绍，译者应注意两种语言和审美的差异。中、英旅游景物描写的翻译过程实际上就是"形象与意象""动态与静态""简约与华美"之间的转换过程。

翻译实践

一、热身练习

翻译下文，并对译文做简要分析。

1. 红日初升时，水面波光粼粼，浮光跃金，云蒸霞蔚，如梦如幻。

2. The West Thumb is about the same size as another famous volcanic caldera, Crater Lake in Oregon, but much smaller than the great Yellowstone Caldera which formed 600,000 years ago.

3. 枫泾古镇景区水网密布，河道纵横，素有"三步两座桥，一望十条巷"之称。

4. The British Museum was the first of a new kind of museum — national, belonging to neither church nor king, freely open to the public and aiming to collect everything.

5. 峰下蟾池，石均似蟾，或高或低，或相视鼓噪，或蹲而欲纵，栩栩如生，相映成趣，令人遐想万千……怪不得国画大师蒋兆和先生曾赞誉道："石如玉，山似蟾，奇峰妙景甲川南。"

6. The sky reflected in the water turned the Seine into a lovely shade of blue which trembled in the hazy sunshine filtering through leafy branches of the trees lining the river's edge.

7. 道升酒坊始建于清朝乾隆五年（1740年），是兰陵酒厂的门户酒坊。该酒坊通过公开展示酿酒工艺，使兰陵美酒通过运河渠道销往南方。

8. Founded as a trading post in 1842, La Crosse emerged as a key railroad junction after the Civil War.

9. 那泉水形如雪豹，飞吼着从78米高的山凹处飞扑下来。一里之外，就能听见它的吼声，回荡在山谷中。飞泉跌下山涧，卷起朵朵雪花，寒气袭人，不敢在此久留。

10. When the British Museum opened in 1753, it was the world's first national public museum, free (as it still is) to all "studious and curious persons." It contains a breathtaking collection of over 8 million objects that paint a portrait of the world's cultures.

二、巩固练习

翻译下文，并对译文做简要分析。

1. 广宗寺，始建于明正德二年，坐北朝南，占地2912平方米。

2. 楚国是一个充满乐舞旋律的国度，既有大众喜爱的《下里》《巴人》，也有曲高和寡的《阳春》《白雪》，音乐、舞蹈都具有很高的水准。

3. 明太祖得知后，曾三次请他出去做官，但都被他婉言谢绝了。他死后，明太祖敕封他为上海城隍神。

4. 笔架山位于渤海湾北部，登临远眺，景点美妙，山门奇特，岩石洁白。雨后天晴，光彩耀眼，上有"光耀家国"四个大字。

5. 被誉为长城脚下天然园林的长寿山，层峦叠嶂，怪石林立，古木参天，柳泉飞瀑直泻谷底，自然胜境令人叹为观止。

6. 粼粼碧波之中，一岛屹然，是为杏花岛。岛上遍植杏树，每至春风送暖，红杏带雨绽放，色泽娇艳，恍若云霞。杏花岛四面环水，环境幽静，无尘嚣之乱耳，有世外桃源之况味。

7. 碧霞元君又称送子娘娘，传说她统摄东岳神兵，明察人间善恶，掌管生儿育女，保佑儿童健康，在北方地区享有盛誉。

8. 青海湖位于青海省东北部大通山、日月山和青海南山之间，古称"西海"，是我国最大的咸水湖，其面积大约4626平方公里，湖面海拔3196米，湖水最深处38米。此湖地处高原，气候寒冷，水中含氧量低，故水面漂游生物少，湖水终年保持着清澈透明，呈现出青蓝色，青海省也因此得名。

9. 谈及海南传统佳节"三月三"时，描述如下："三月三"，自古以来是黎族人民喜庆新生、赞美生活、追求爱情的传统节日……在传统乐器的奏鸣声中，小伙子引吭高歌，纵情欢跳，姑娘们躲在绿树丛中，手持带香味的树叶半遮着面，悄悄窥视意中人。

10. 唐朝有位诗人张继，在一个秋夜，乘船停泊在枫桥下，独坐孤舟，面对着霜天、残月、栖鸦、渔火、红枫、山寺，不禁游子情思联翩，写下《枫桥夜泊》一诗："月落乌啼霜满天，江枫渔火对愁眠。姑苏城外寒山寺，夜半钟声到客船。"这首诗写景抒情清丽淡远，传为千古名篇。

三、阅读翻译

阅读下文，重点翻译下画线部分。

木格措

木格措，即野人海，又叫"大海子"，是川西北海拔2000米以上地区最大的高山湖泊，长5公里，宽1.5公里，总面积近4平方公里，湖水最深处达70余米。野人海环绕红海、白海、黑海等多个卫星湖，犹如众星捧月。<u>湖对面是红海草原，蓝天白云下，辽阔的草原一直绵延至塔公景区。</u>出海口左面有一山峰，名犀牛峰，月明星稀的夜晚，如水的月光泻在山峰上，朝天的犀牛角会发出银色的寒光；出海口右面山上可观"卧虎观月"景观。

野人海群山、森林、草原环抱，一日气象万千，景色多变。<u>清晨，雾气弥漫，水面乱雾翻滚，烟波浩渺，神秘莫测。红日初升时，波光粼粼，浮光跃金，云蒸霞蔚，如梦如幻。</u>待到晴空万里、风和日丽时，蓝天白云、山林花草、鸟兽虫鱼，真切可见，环海景物，清晰地倒映在如镜的海面。傍晚时分，夕阳余晖洒满海面，流光溢彩，群山沉寂，林木肃立，游人如置身仙境。

寒暑变换、四季轮回。奇山异石，叠瀑飞泉，水雾烟霞，更是组成野人海一幅幅风格迥异的奇观，如"双雾坠海""木格夕照""木格潮汐"等。盛夏的野人海，海滨沙滩上可以悠然地享受日光浴；深秋的野人海，四周层林尽染，野果飘香；隆冬的野人海，银装素裹，玉树琼枝，宽阔的海面结上厚厚的冰层，可以在上面尽情地溜冰滑雪。

七色海为野人海风景区重要景点之一，形似一弯新月，又如一位蜷身而卧的睡美人，恬静地躺在茂密的森林与碧绿的草坪之间。这里天气变幻莫测，好像天宫中的画师不慎把巨大的调色板掉入七色海中，所有颜料顿时混在一起，湖水或蓝或紫，或红或绿，五光十色，千变万化，如梦似幻，使人拊掌称绝。朝晖夕阴时，七色海时雨时雾，可见"莲花雾绕""莲花夕照""驼峰倒影"等佳景。

七色海是冷泉与温泉交融的共生湖。湖右侧水底，温泉热雾缭绕，水温最高达67摄氏度，是洗浴疗疾的好地方。海中水族嬉戏悠游，海上山鸟振翅翱翔；岸边树林里鸟雀啁啾，野花飘香。登一叶轻舟，从容摇桨，推开涟漪千重，穿破蒙蒙烟雾；环顾四周，湖光山色尽收眼底，赞叹"造化钟神秀"，体味"山光悦鸟性，潭影空人心"。

杜鹃峡蜿蜒六公里，东连七色海，西接野人海。峡谷中溪水时缓时急，缓时从容自在，如闲庭信步；急时飞珠溅玉，从山石上倾泻而下，形成美丽的叠瀑。峡谷两岸，林木苍翠，花草美丽。原始杜鹃林漫山遍野，聚集着杜鹃花族中68个品种。从4月中旬直到7月，都有不同品种的杜鹃花次第开放，使峡谷成为一片花海。各种高高矮矮的野花野草，或险踞山崖，或闲处密林，或迎风舞动，或寂然肃立。花朵或红或白，或蓝或紫，花团锦簇，不一而足，令人眼花缭乱，目不暇接。林中飞禽走兽，时隐时现，呈现出一派盎然野趣。

第八章　景点导游词翻译

导游词泛指物化的导游文字，它包括导游图、交通图、旅游指南、景点宣传画册、旅游产品目录、旅游广告、旅游纪念品等材料中的介绍文字，以及景点现场对相应的景物、遗迹、文物等所标识的文字说明（李良辰，2013：51—54）。导游员是语言表达的主体，游客是导游词的受众；旅游景观是导游词最基本的内容。导游词是导游员与游客交流思想、情感，传播知识文化的载体，类型丰富多样，在很大程度上不同于一般旅游资料或见闻，也不同于旅游景区的景点介绍。从语言编码、解码的角度，导游词的翻译也是一种编码、解码过程，即从源语作者创作的导游词到导译人员翻译成其他语种导游词的编码、解码过程（胡鲁飞，2013：113—116）。

图8.1　图示理论下的导游词翻译

一、导游词风格类型

根据讲解时空，导游词可分为景点导游词和途中导游词；根据导游词风格，可分为幽默型导游词、煽情型导游词、审美型导游词；根据导游词内容，可分为自然景观导游词和人文景观导游词。自然景观导游词包括对山、水、植物、动物、气候等的描写，多用白描、细描、衬托、烘托、渲染、对比等修辞手法；人文景观导游词包括对宫殿建筑、亭台楼榭、碑林墓塔、洞窟摩崖、风土民情、实物展品等的描写，多用较严谨的笔法和准确的语言。根据导游讲解语言，可分为中文导游词和外语导游词；从口语和书面语言角度，导游词还可以分为口语体和书面体，而口语体又可分为演说型、介绍型、解说型和描写型四种类型。

（1）演说型。突出"演"，句式整齐，音节和谐，节奏波浪起伏，多用于导游大赛；

（2）介绍型。突出"说"，多用于介绍景观外形、性能、功用和行程安排等；

（3）解说型。突出"解"，多用于解释专用名词、科技术语和景观的文化底蕴等；

（4）描写型。突出"描"，把看似普通、平淡的景观描绘得美妙无比，充满神奇色彩。

1. 幽默型导游词

美国心理学家赫布·特鲁说：幽默是一种最有趣、最有感染力、最具有普遍意义的传递艺术。旅游是寻找快乐的旅行。在旅游过程中，人们大都期望"旅"得轻松，"游"得愉快，这就要求导游翻译能恰当地运用意味深长的幽默语言，为游客创造富有魅力和活力的语言氛围，使游客获得精神上的快感。西方的游客多喜爱幽默，恰如其分地使用幽默的语言会使导游词既生动风趣，又富有感染力，让外国游客"知之""乐之""好之"。导游词增加幽默感的方法多种多样，有谐音法、拟人法、顺口溜法、歇后语法等（汪亚明，王显成，2012：11）。

比如，长途旅行时遇到路途颠簸，如果导游适时地说："It's time to enjoy Chinese massage, and it's free of charge!"（"现在开始免费中式按摩啦！"）游客们定会在欢笑中暂时忘却颠簸之苦。又如游客指着一盘醋熘西葫芦问这是什么菜，如果导游不知如何准确表达，便可急中生智地说："This is cucumber's cousin."游客便会哄堂大笑，点头称是，因为西葫芦和黄瓜的外观和口感都十分相似，将西葫芦说成是黄瓜的表亲很形象，但导游还必须将西葫芦的正确名称"vegetable marrow"告诉游客。（李承燕，盛夏，2017：13）

又如，飞机误点，客人纷纷向导游投去询问的目光，这时幽默的导游会镇静地说："Now please fasten your seat belts."当航班因天气原因推迟起飞后，导游又叹口气："Fail to plan, plan to fail."（文字游戏幽默，可译为："人算不如天算，人不留人天留人。"）从一定程度上会给游客些许慰藉，失望之余，找到暂时一点儿轻松（尹燕，2007：58）。

但是翻译幽默段子也不能一味取悦游客，要做到"幽默不俗"。幽默一定要贴切、自然，不要造作，有些中国式的"冷笑话"未必能被西方游客所理解。有些"中国式的幽默"增加了导游词的幽默感，但扭曲了中国人的价值观，不符合中国传统美德。

又如，杭州灵隐寺前飞来峰石像最有名的要数弥勒佛像，雕工精美，栩栩如生。有的人把弥勒佛译为"Beer Belly Buddha"，再加上一句中国俗语"A carefree mind and of a fatty kind"，并配上一句欧美家喻户晓的广告词："It's a Kodak moment."自己以为轻松、诙谐，能博游客一笑，但殊不知在寺庙将"弥勒佛"比喻为"啤酒肚"是对佛教的大不敬，有可能引发宗教纷争；用中国俗语"A carefree mind and of a fatty kind"来描写佛像也很不妥，西方人忌讳"胖"这个字眼，这也不符合西方人士的审美观。增加导游词的幽默感不能违反宗教政策，不能有损国家形象。以下为幽默型导游词的译例。

例1. 现在，大巴转右弯了，正行驶在光明路上。你们为啥回头看呢？在看谁呢？哇，原来在看路过的藏族美女。丹巴盛产美女，嘉绒妹子天生丽质，远近闻名。

译文：Now, our coach is turning right. We're traveling on the Guangming Road. Why are you looking back? Who are you looking at? Wow, you're looking at the beautiful Tibetan girls walking past. Danba is famous for producing a lot of beautiful women. The Jiarong women are all born beauties.

分析：该段导游词通过设问的方式一问一答，接连提出两个问题"Why are you looking back?""Who are you looking at?"通过"为啥回头看呢""在看谁呢"两个设问，加强了导游与游客之间的互动。爱美之心，人皆有之。导游以幽默的口吻、轻松的语气与游客调侃，通过"丹巴藏族美女""嘉绒天生丽质"这一话题,引起游客的注意,给旅途增添了不少趣味。

例2. 现在我们的大巴正沿着沱江前行。沱江是内江的母亲河,蜿蜒穿过城市,将整座城市分为两部分:市中心和东兴区。内江人爱吃蜜饯,我也一样。瞧,我的脸白皙姣好,滋润甜美。每天吃蜜饯能美容,你的脸也会像我的一样甜美。信不信由你,反正我是信了。

译文:Now, our coach is running along the Tuojiang River, the mother river of the city. It meanders through the whole city and divides it into two parts: the downtown district and Dongxing District. The natives in Neijiang love eating candied fruit, and so do I. You see, my face looks sweet and fair. The candied fruit may beautify your skin if you eat it everyday. Believe or not! Your face will look sweet and fair, just like mine.

分析:该段导游词轻松幽默,恰到好处地宣传了内江的特产蜜饯和内江"甜城"绰号的由来。"爱美之心,人皆有之"。导游"自夸"吃蜜饯能使人脸颊甜美,"调侃"自己的皮肤白嫩来吸引游客的注意力。幽默只有适当加入一些个人感情色彩,融入个人的真情实感才能打动人。导游用自己的亲身体验和个人感悟,营造出幽默轻松的旅行氛围,潜移默化中加深了游客对内江的美好印象,丰富了游客的旅游体验。

2. 煽情型导游词

翻译煽情型导游词,以目标游客为中心,从游客视角介入,使用第二人称,或从导游视角介入,使用第一人称,以达到情景交融;在修辞方面,使用比喻、排比、拟人等手法,移情也煽情;在措辞方面使用描述性形容词和动词、形容词最高级,双重否定表示肯定,以达到渲染、呼唤功能;句型使用祈使句和感叹句,增强动态感和现场感,以达到"动其容,悦其心"的效果(朱华,2016:22)。导游词的用语是一种表达力丰富、生动形象、具有感染力的语言,直接影响游客的心理活动,因此,导游词的用语应煽情、移情,在语言艺术的"达意"和"舒适"上下功夫,在"雅"字上做文章,寓情于景,情景交融,打动游客。

例1. 亲爱的游客们,你们有谁能描写一下心中的月牙泉是什么模样呢?有人说,月牙泉让他们想起女子的眼眸;有人说,此泉更像她的无名指;也有人说,它像一块香甜可口、嫩美多汁、晶莹剔透的香瓜。在我看来，它更像是一弯掉进沙漠的新月，月牙泉因此得名。今天月牙泉还能汩汩涌出泉水，清澈透明，不愧为"沙漠第一泉"。

译文：Ladies and gentlemen, anybody can tell me what the Crescent Spring looks like? Some say the Spring reminds them of the eye of a woman. Some say it looks more like her ring finger. Some of our guests said it looks like a slice of lush, sweet and crystal cantaloupe, but I imagine it was a crescent fallen down into this desert. The Crescent Lake is so called because of its crescent shape. Today, the Spring still gurgles and gushes clear water, and remains worthy as the "first spring in the desert".

分析：本篇导游词一切景语皆情语，丰富了游客的情感，文本的诱导功能、呼唤功能都很强，体现了导游词应有的情感与温度，是一则典型的煽情型导游词。首先，本篇导游词的语言感染力强，用"香甜可口""晶莹剔透""清澈透明"等四字词语来描写人物、景物，译文则采用感染性较强的形容词，"sweet""crystal"，用具象型动词，"gurgles""gushes"等，感染读者，给游客带来美的感受；其次，导游词使用了排比、比喻、拟人等修辞格，如"有人说……""有人说……""也有人说……"；"像……眼眸""像……无名指""像……香瓜"等，译文对等译出所有中文导游词的修辞格，移情也煽情；最后，导游词以导游视角介入，使用了第一人称，用"我的看法""我的评价"影响游客的认识和判断，文末又用评价性语言"沙漠第一泉"等进一步影响游客，通过评价性语言吸引游客前往月牙泉游览。

例2. 我们终于登上了天游峰一览台，史密斯先生和佩妮太太数得最精确，石阶总数是826级。大家可以在一览台上俯瞰群峰拱卫，云雾之上，只露峰顶，<u>宛如点点小岛</u>，峰下九曲萦回，武夷山水，尽收眼底。

现在请大家跟我到天游观后面看红豆树。这红豆并不是我们吃的那种红豆，它的果实鲜红艳丽，象征爱情。每当成熟季节，很多人会到这里捡拾红豆。中国古诗中，红豆常常是相思之物。最有名的要数王维的《相思》了："红豆生南国，春来发几枝。愿君多采撷，此物最相思。"

译文：<u>Congratulations</u>! Mr Smith and Ms Penny have got the number correct.

It is 826. Now we are standing at *Yilan Tai*, or Bird's Eye Lookout. You can enjoy the panoramic view of the surrounding peaks and hills and also the winding Nine-bend River below. <u>The peaks practically look like islands in the sea of mist and cloud.</u>

<u>Let's go behind the Tianyou Temple.</u> This is an ancient ormosia tree. It bears hard and bright red beans. We call them Hongdou in Chinese, meaning "red bean", but they are not the red beans that we eat. They have become a symbol of love for Chinese. When the seeds are ripe, people like to search under the tree hoping to collect some fallen red beans. Some old Chinese poems relate red beans to lovesickness, as described by the poet Wang Wei in the Tang Dynasty.

分析：导游词描述天游峰一览台时，用比喻修辞煽情，"宛如点点小岛，峰下九曲萦回"，译文将其译为"The peaks practically look like islands in the sea of mist and cloud"，优美的语言陶冶了游客的情感，丰富了游客的游览体验；为了增加煽情效果，译文在句首增译了感叹句"Congratulations!"，使用祈使句"Let's go behind the Tianyou Temple."，进一步增强了文本的感染功能。中文导游词还引用了古典诗使导游词具有移情功能、审美功能，"愿君多采撷，此物最相思。"用王维的《相思》来讲述景点中的红豆树，既煽情，也移情。但是，由于中、英审美差异，中文引用诗歌可以移情、煽情，用在英文中未必有此功效，故可省略不译，或释译、编译，只译出诗歌的大致意思即可。

3. 审美型导游词

旅游观光是一种综合性审美活动，集自然美、艺术美、社会美与生活美之大成，涉及审美的一切领域和一切形态。根据接受美学理论，读者在阅读作品之前都具有"期待视野"，即读者原先各种经验、趣味、素养、理想等综合形成的对文学作品的一种欣赏水平，在具体阅读中表现为一种潜在的审美期待。译者对译文必须具有高强度的语感，具备敏锐的鉴别力、创造力，"吾身入乎其中而涵泳玩索之"，以充分驰骋想象去品"味外之味"，去寻"象外之象"，发现其"语不接而意接"的审美空间（屠国元，2006：15—16）。审美型导游词多为书面体或半书面体，具有山水游记或散文体风格。在翻译过程中，译者用丰富的语言、不同的句式、多种修辞格激活语言的审美信息，调动接受者的审美体验，使接受者的审美体验与原作者的审美体验熔于一炉。

例1. Extraordinary temples done in wildly flamboyant architectural styles <u>centuries-old cities</u> of powerful, long-gone empires; <u>fruit-laden boats</u> gently row down calm canals; <u>caparisoned elephants</u> heading parades in northern villages <u>multicolored kites</u> fluttering below clear blue skies; lush paddy fields being worked by plow-pulling oxen; and expansive plantations of rubber trees, coconut palms, and bananas.

译文：非凡的庙宇，建筑风格狂野华丽；强大、逝去的帝国留下了<u>历尽沧桑的世纪老城</u>；平静的运河上轻轻地行走着满载水果的船只；<u>披挂着装饰的大象</u>，成群结队行走于北部乡村；清澈的蓝天下，<u>飘着五彩风筝</u>；水牛，在郁郁葱葱的田里辛勤拉犁；广阔无垠的种植园里满是橡胶树、椰子树和香蕉树。

分析：导游词介绍柬埔寨圣剑寺，用景物罗列的方法呈现旅游景观，属于审美型导游词，如"centuries-old cities" "fruit-laden boats" "caparisoned elephants" "multicolored kites"等。在所有的名词前面几乎都使用了描述性较强的形容词。翻译此类审美型导游词，译者需根据中文读者的审美观照，将英文中罗列的"形象"转化为"意象"，主要方法是将英文单词或词组译为中文四字格，或用四言八句、排比、对偶的形式，如译为"历尽沧桑的世纪老城" "满载水果的船只" "披挂着装饰的大象" "飘着五彩风筝"等，烘托旅游气氛，创造一种景物的"意象美" "朦胧美"。此外，在英文"形象"向汉语"意象"的转换过程中，译文还需实现"静态"向"动态"的转换，以满足汉语"动态美"的审美观照。

例2. 每年冬春之交，玉局峰顶常会出现一朵孤单的白云，<u>上下飘动，若顾若盼</u>。继而转为乌云，形如一位身着黑服的女性。此时狂风大作，湖上波涛汹涌，这就是"望夫云"。夏秋雨后，一缕浮云轻轻飘起，绵延数十里，如玉带一般束于山腰上，称为"玉带云"。

译文：Every year when winter is changing into spring, a lone cloud will emerge over the top of Yuju Peak, <u>drifting up and down, casting glances about</u>. Then, it suddenly turns into a dark cloud, <u>resembling a woman in black</u>. At this very moment, a gale will howl and cause rolling waves across the lake. After rain in summer or autumn, a cloud will drift up slowly in the sky, stretching out kilometers around <u>like a jade belt round the mountain</u>; this is called "the Jade-like Belt of Clouds".

分析：导游词介绍大理苍山玉局峰的自然风景，辞藻华丽，语言夸张，景物与主观情感交融，极尽渲染之能事，反映了中国人的审美心理。如"上下飘动，若顾若盼"，营造一种朦胧的意象；而西方人的审美与中国人的审美不同，在景物描写上偏重客观再现，实景实写，追求的效果是实实在在的形象，而非中国人追求的华美，因此译文用英文质朴的语言将其译为"drifting up and down, casting glances about"；原文使用比喻修辞格，将"乌云"比作女性，将"浮云"比作"玉带"，英文则分别译为"resembling a woman in black" "like a jade belt around the mountain"，保留了明喻，再现了原文的审美和感染力。对比中、英文导游词审美，两者都擅用修辞格和极具感染力的词汇，但中文辞藻华丽，偏重借景抒情；而英文语言质朴，偏重景物再现。

二、导游词翻译原则

有人说："祖国山河美不美，全凭导游一张嘴。"但是如果没有高质量的导游词预制文本，即使导游口才再好，也无法达到预期的讲解目的和效果。英文导游讲解比中文导游讲解难度更大，更应做好导游词预制文本的翻译工作，优秀的英文导游对于同一景点甚至会准备不同风格的导游词。导游词的翻译与一般翻译不同，是一项充满挑战性的工作，需从受众（游客）的角度出发，注重生动性、实用性和交际性，忠实原文又不拘泥于原文，以提高译文可读性与接受性为要旨（王青，2010：166—169），采取"创译""变译"等翻译方法。为了提高译文可接受性，译者不能按部就班，而应发挥译者的主体性，对原文某些信息进行调整、删减、改写，甚至忽略不计（陈小慰，2000：10—12）。由于导游词多用于导游现场讲解，现场化、口语化、故事化、生活化的"创译"是必须遵守的翻译原则，应以现场化、口语化、故事化、生活化的语言译出。

1. 口语化原则

导游讲解是一门口语艺术,用于导游讲解的导游词应通俗易懂、生动形象,并能从多方面吸引旅游者的注意力、激发游兴。导游词翻译后大多数是供导游员进行导游讲解使用的,因此,导游词预制文本在表达知识性和趣味性的同时,应具备轻松活泼、通俗易懂、口语化的特点。口语化的导游词具有良好的表意传情功能,避免讲座式、书面化的描述(赵琳琳,李家春,2009:110—111)。如果导游词预制文本学究气十足、死板呆滞,甚至故弄玄虚,导游员即使将导游词背得滚瓜烂熟,使出浑身解数,也很难吸引旅游者(林竹梅,2014:42)。

例1. Hello! Welcome to the breathtaking town of Suffolk. My name is John Locke and I'm the gatekeeper here at Vir-Ren Castle. I'd like to take you for a tour of the beautiful Vir-Ren Castle here in Suffolk. We townsfolk are quite proud of her ...

译文:大家好!欢迎来到激动人心的萨福克郡。我叫约翰·洛克,是维伦城堡的看门人。我将带领大家游览萨福克美丽的维伦城堡。我们萨福克市民为这座城堡感到非常自豪……

分析:导游词使用第一人称叙事,如 "My name..." "I am..." "I would like to..." "We townsfolk are...",平易近人,拉近了与游客的距离;大量使用口语化词语,如 "Hello" "Welcome to..." "here at..." "I'd like to...",通俗易懂;一改英语"树状句"的特点,连续使用四个单句,便于快速传递信息;运用拟人手法,如 "We townsfolk are quite proud of her ...",亲切自然;通过重复 "Vir-Ren Castle" 景点名称,加深游客印象。译文采用直译法,使用短小精悍的句子,语言平和、亲切自然,体现了原导游词口语化的特点。

例2. 普陀山是我国四大佛山之一,位于浙江省东北部的普陀岛上,风景秀丽,东西宽约3.5公里,南北长8.6公里,主峰海拔291.02米,山上有著名的三大佛寺,为普济寺、法雨寺和慧济寺,另外还有一个古洞,名曰"潮音洞",传说观音菩萨曾在此现身说法。

译文一:The scenic Putuo Mountain, one of the four great sacred mountains of the Buddhist faith in China, stands on the Putuo Island off the northeast coast of Zhejiang Province. The mountain is, in extent, about 3.5 kilometers from east to west and 8.6

kilometers from north to south, with the highest peak at the elevation of 291.2 meters. On the mountain stand three famous temples called Puji, the Fayu and Huiji. There is also an age-old cave in the mountain, called the Chaoyin Cave, where Guanyin (the Goddess of Mercy) is said to have preached Buddhism in the incarnation of a human form.

译文二：The Putuo Mountain is one of the four great sacred mountains of Buddhism in China. It stands on the Putuo Island off the northeast coast of Zhejiang Province. The scenery is beautiful. It is about 3.5 kilometers in width from east to west. It is 8.6 kilometers in length from north to south. Its highest peak rises at 291.2 meters above sea level. On the mountain stand three famous temples, they are the Puji Temple, the Fayu Temple, and the Huiji Temple. There is also an old cave in the mountain. It is called the Chaoyin Cave. It is said Guanyin (the Goddess of Mercy) once appeared in the cave to preach Buddhism.

分析：译文一为导游词预制文本，偏书面体；译文二为即席文本，偏口语体。在预制文本中，"古洞"译为"an age-old cave"，"现身"译为"incarnation into a human form"；在即席文本中，"古洞"和"现身"简单译为"an old cave"和"appear"。通过译文一和译文二对比可以看出，导游词的预制文本与即席文本之间的区别不仅在于使用的文字不同，句型转换、衔接方式也不同。译文一个别地方的书面语言可改为口语体或半书面体，但译文二语言简单，句式过于单一，衔接不连贯，也应修改，这样才能体现导游词的移情功能、美学功能、呼唤功能。由此可见，导游词的翻译需在口语体和书面体之间保持平衡，既不能过于学究，也不能过于直白。

2. 现场化原则

导游词应具有较强的现场感，这是因为导游词的讲解主要在景点、途中、购物等场所，特别是集中在景点讲解和途中讲解阶段。导游词的现场感主要用设问、现场导引词和表现现场感的词语三种方式来实现。

（1）设问

设问就是直接向旅游者提出问题，但并不要求回答，其目的在于集中旅游者的注意力,引导旅游者,保障导游讲解顺利进行。

例:Ladies and gentlemen, have you ever heard of a dune that echoes to the sound of sand as you slide down its slopes? Can you imagine a limpid lake in an area of desert for thousands of years? Here in Dunhuang, you have the chance to enjoy such a wonderful spectacle—the Mingshashan and the Crescent Spring?

译文:游客朋友们,听说过从山丘上往下滑,脚下的沙子会沙沙地发出回响声吗?你能想象一泓清澈的湖泊在沙漠中千年都不枯竭吗?在敦煌,你就可一览这样的胜景——鸣沙山、月牙泉!

分析:本篇导游词开门见山,抛开一切繁文缛节,直奔主题。开篇气势不凡,连用三个设问将导游讲解推向了高潮,现场感极强,仿佛身临其境。"Have you ever heard of...?" "Can you imagine...?" "You have the chance to enjoy such a wonderful spectacle..." 三个设问并不一定要求游客回答,目的在于吸引游客的注意力或制造悬念,为后续讲解鸣沙山、月牙泉的成因打下伏笔。

(2)现场导引词

所谓现场导引词,是指对进行旅游者提示或引导的一些词语。使用现场导引词,可使导游词的灵活性与现场感更加明显。

原文	译文	分析
They have been apprised of your coming by the Medici family and will be most happy to talk with you. Feel free to look around.	已通知梅第奇家人你会来。他们将会很高兴与你交谈。你可以四处走走看看。	本例中"feel free to look around"为现场导引词。
Speak softly because we are now at the Sleeping Dragon Lake...	说话轻声点儿,我们正在睡龙湖……	本例中,"speak softly"为现场导引词。

(3)表现现场感的词语

一般来说,用来表现现场感的词语主要包括下面几类。

a. 指示代词,如this, that, these, those等。

b. 地点副词,如here, there, over there等。

c. 时间副词,如today, now, right now等。

在导游词中运用上述表现现场感的词语可随时随地吸引游客的注意力,并为游客带来一种身临其境的感觉。例如:

原文	译文	分析
The theater over there took about 20 years to come to life.	远处的剧场是20年心血的结晶。	本例中,地点副词 over there 是表现现场感的词语。
Now, we are at the entrance gate of the park.	现在,我们是在公园的正门。	本例中,时间副词 now 是表现现场感的词语。

3. 故事化原则

中国有句古语:"山不在高,有仙则灵。"对于自然景观的描写,中国文人常寓景于情或引经据典,以讲故事的手法道出景点后面的人文知识和名人轶事。所谓故事化,就是导译人员围绕参观的景点,介绍一些与景点相关的历史典故、神话传说,用故事化的方式讲解景点。这种方法对于来自不同文化背景的游客理解景点中的中国历史文化会起到一定的辅助作用。例如,参观成都武侯祠刘备殿时,可讲"三顾茅庐";参观静远堂时,可讲"空城计";参观三义庙时,可讲"桃园三结义"等历史故事和事件。通过讲故事,在游客领略我国名胜古迹的同时,增加他们对景点、景物的理解。讲故事是一种娓娓道来、引人入胜的叙事方法,更能增加游客对景点的关注,激发他们的游览热情和兴趣,也是中文导游词重要的特点之一。

例1. 大家注意喽,我们的大巴正行驶在旌阳大桥上,正前方约30公里处便是白马关了。德阳是三国文化旅游线重要的旅游城市之一,有许多三国历史遗迹,两千多年前的三国时代便封存于此地,位于白马关的庞统祠便是最著名的旅游景点。我给大家讲一段这位英雄豪杰的故事吧。214年,刘备率军进攻德阳突遭敌军袭击。为了保护主公,庞统用自己的胭脂马替换刘备的大白马。敌军误以为庞统是刘备,乱箭射死庞统,此地便成了庞统的长眠之地。庞统生前绰名"凤雏",后来,人们将这个地方称为"落凤坡"。

译文:Dear friends, our coach is driving across Jinyang Bridge. Ahead of us is Baima Pass (Pass of the White Horse). It is about 30 kilometers ahead. Deyang is one of the important tourist cities on the itinerary of Three-kingdom Culture. There are many historic sites of Three Kingdoms around 2,000 years ago. Pang Tong Shrine at the Baima Pass is the most famous one. In 214, Liu Bei and his army suffered a surprise attack at Luofengpo when they launched a campaign against Deyang. To safeguard his Lord, Pang Tong exchanged his rouge-hued horse with Liu's white horse. The enemies mistook Pang Tong for Liu Bei and shot Pang Tong dead with hundreds of arrows. Later, Pang Tong was buried where he died, and the place where he lost his life was called "Slope of Falling Phoenix", because Pang Tong was nicknamed "Young Phoenix".

分析：白马关是德阳三国历史遗迹，景点特色不多，但蕴含三国历史文化，与之相关的就有三国历史人物刘备、庞统以及历史遗迹庞统祠、落凤坡等。导游通过讲故事的方式追溯了该地的历史人物事件，讲解了刘备入川、庞统白马救主的故事，以及落凤坡地名的由来，增强了旅游景点的人文色彩，有利于游客感受中国的历史文化，情景交融，思绪回到点火纷飞的三国时代。

例2. 游客朋友们，我们的大巴开了34公里的路程，正在经过飞沙关。1952年以前，这里是仅容一马通过的关口，关口悬崖上刻着三个字"飞沙关"，为唐朝著名诗人李白题写。据说，唐玄宗爱妃杨玉环前往长安时在此歇息。当晚皓月当空，曲曲清流，于是她走进河中沐浴。不一会儿，杨贵妃发现一男人竟在窥视她沐浴，顿时恼羞成怒，一把沙土撒向偷看的男人。霎时间，天昏地暗、尘土飞扬，狂风吹个不停，竟吹了数百年。如今此处的关口已被拆除，新建了一条高速公路隧道。

译文：Dear friends, after a 34-km drive, we're now passing through the Feisha Pass. Before 1952, there was a pass that only a horse could walk through. On the precipitous cliff of the pass were three Chinese characters:飞沙关 (*Fei Sha Guan*, Whirling Dust Pass). They were inscribed by the famous poet Li Bai in the 8th century during the Tang Dynasty. It was said on the way to Chang'an, Yang Yuhuan, a concubine of Emperor Xuanzong stopped over at Feisha Pass. Looking at the clear water and the bright moon, she walked into the Minjiang River to have a bath. After a while she found a man peeping at her. She was so angry that she threw dust at the man. Suddenly the dust in the area whirled up. The strong wind has been blowing here for hundreds of years since then. Today, the pass has been dismantled and a highway tunnel was built here.

分析：本篇导游词预制文本的撰写采用了"故事化原则"。飞沙关没有什么风景，经过飞沙关，为了避免枯燥乏味、平淡无奇，导游通过讲故事、道传说的方式来增强导游词的艺术感染力，实际上也是采用"虚实结合"来构建即席导游词。此处的"实"是"飞沙关"场景，"虚"是"贵妃抛沙"的故事。导游词以"实"为主，以"虚"为辅，"虚"为"实"服务，以"虚"烘托情节，以"虚"加深"实"的存在和现场感，通过虚实结合、故事化的方式，将无情的飞沙关变成"贵妃抛沙"有情有义的导游词。

4. 生活化原则

由于地理、历史、民族、文化、社会制度以及宗教信仰的不同，导游员要想将每个旅游景点向来自不同的国家、不同的年龄层次、不同的社会背景的旅游者讲解得生动活泼，一听就懂，一看就明白，并非一件容易的事情。因此，导游员应采取生活化的原则创作、翻译导游词，增加一些生活元素，如通过寒暄、劝导，告诉游客在游览过程中要注意安全、增减衣物、避免走失等。寒暄功能不在于交流信息，只是人们常用的交际套语，对接受者产生某种影响（丁大刚，2008：70）。导游词的生活化还可运用类比法，让游客通过自己熟悉的人物、事件、环境对比当前的景点、人物、景物，从译出的"陌生化"到译入的"熟悉化"，使游客更接近自己的生活环境。

例如，游览天安门时，导译人员常将天安门比喻为"国门"，导译人员可用欧洲人熟悉的凯旋门（Arch of Triumph）来作比较，用外国人熟悉的生活环境或事物类比当前的环境或事物。翻译紫禁城建筑年代和它的建筑面积，可与欧洲人熟悉的凡尔赛宫对比，译为"The Forbidden City was built in 1417, 207 years ealier than the Palace of Versailles"，就比直译为"It was completed in the 15th year of Emperor Yongle"更具体化、生活化，更亲近外国游客。

例1. 游客朋友们！松潘海拔约3000米。现在是深秋时节，寒气袭人，记得添加衣物、披上披肩，御寒保暖哦。看看右边窗外。大家看见古城门口松赞干布和文成公主的雕像了吗？为什么这里会有藏王和汉公主的雕像呢？为什么藏王会迎娶敌国公主呢？稍后我会为大家讲解。公元639年，吐蕃王松赞干布发兵20万攻打松州，战争在川主寺地区爆发，最终吐蕃战败，唐军获胜。

战争结束后，吐蕃派使者求和，于是唐太宗决定与吐蕃政治联姻，这又是为什么呢？因为唐太宗认为政治联姻可以巩固唐朝与吐蕃的关系。正如欧洲国家间的政治联姻一样，英国国王娶了德国公主，西班牙王子娶了奥地利公主，最终文成公主嫁给了松赞干布。这次政治联姻不仅为两国带来了近三十年的和平与安宁，同时也促进了两个民族之间的文化交流。

译文：Ladies and gentlemen! Songpan is about 3,000 meters above sea level. It is cold in the late autumn. You may put on more clothes or put on shawls to keep warm. Look out of the window on your right hand! Have you seen a statue of Songtsen Gampo and Princess Wencheng at the entrance to the ancient town? Why was the statute of a Tibetan king and a Han princess put here? Why did the Tibetan king marry the princess of his rival? I'll tell you about it later. In 639 during the Tang Dynasty, the chieftain of Tubo Kingdom Songtsen Gampo sent 200,000 soldiers to attack Songzhou. The war broke out in the area of Chuanzhu Temple, but the Tang army won the war.

After the war, Tubo sent the envoy to make a negotiation with the Tang Dynasty. Emperor Taizong decided to establish the political marriage alliance with Tubo. Why? Because Emperor Taizong believed the political marriage could reinforce the stability of the border. Just like the political marriage alliances in Europe, King of England married Princess of Germany, and the Prince of Spain married Princess of Austria. Eventually, Princess Wencheng married Songtsen Gampo. This political marriage alliance not only brought the peace between Tubo and the Tang Dynasty, but also promoted the cultural exchange between the two nationalities for about 30 years.

分析：松潘地处高原，海拔约3000米，深秋时节，寒气袭人，导游提醒游客增添衣物，披上披肩，"put on more clothes or put on shawls to keep warm"，体现了导游词生活化原则，增强了导游词的寒暄、劝导功能；导游词采用设问，向游客连提三个问句，提醒注意古城入口处的吐蕃王和唐公主雕像，并将两人的政治婚姻与英国国王娶德国公主、西班牙王子娶奥地利公主的政治联姻进行了类比，让导游词更加贴近外国游客感兴趣的生活话题，增强了旅游的人文气息，符合导游词故事化、生活化的原则。

例2. 现在我们离德阳还有大约三十分钟的车程，我给大家科普一些德阳的小知识吧。"德阳"这个名字来自中国一句话"德阳如政"，高度赞扬许逊执政爱民，许逊对待咱们老百姓就如同阳光一样温暖人间。许逊何许人也？且听我慢慢道来。西晋时期，许逊是德阳的一名县令，那时的德阳还不叫这个名字，正是许逊"德阳如政"，此地才改名为"德阳"。1863年，美国总统亚伯拉罕·林肯在葛底斯堡发表演讲时曾说过："民有、民治、民享。"许逊为民便是这句话的最好体现。从这一点上讲，许逊是提倡"民有、民治、民享"的先驱，林肯还是小字辈呢！

译文：Ladies and gentlemen! After about 30 minutes' drive our coach is approaching Deyang. The name Deyang comes from a phrase which highly praises Xu Xun's political feats: 德阳如政 (De Yang Ru Zheng), which means that service Xu Xun offered the people is just like the sun shining on the people. Who is Xu Xun? He is the magistrate of Deyang in 4th century during the Western Jin Dynasty. Because of his service for the people, the county was named "Deyang". Compared with the Abraham Lincoln' address in Gettysburg in 1863, "the government of the people, by the people, and for the people", Xu Xun's policy shows he is a pioneer of "for the people" while Lincoln is a successor.

分析：该段导游词主要讲述"德阳"地名的由来。导游词通过"德阳如政"用典，采用比喻修辞格，将许逊执政爱民比作阳光温暖人间，高度赞誉了许逊的政绩，寓意隽永。许逊的"为民"（for the people）与林肯的"民享"（for the people）有异曲同工之处，因此导游词采取类比法，将"德阳如政"与"民有、民治、民享"进行了类比，用西方游客的文化语境解释中国用典"德阳如政"，使游客产生了联想，从而更能理解德阳地名的含义。最后一句还对中外两个人物进行了对比："许逊是提倡"民有、民治、民享"的先驱，林肯还是小字辈呢！"导游词需要接近游客生活环境，采用生活化的翻译原则。

三、导游词翻译方法

导游词主要用于导游景点讲解或途中讲解，让游客在游览过程中获得美好的旅游体验。导游词的翻译是忠实原文，与原文"对等"，还是让导游词通过导游员的讲解让游客产生最佳的旅游体验和反应，这是一个值得探讨的问题。我国传统的翻译理论强调"信""达""雅"，作者的地位是至高无上的，原文是神圣不可侵犯的，"信"（"忠实原文"）是翻译必须遵守的第一原则；而功能翻译理论认为"忠实原文"并不是译者必须遵守的第一原则，好的译文并不是"原文至上"，而是能在读者身上产生最佳的阅读体验和最佳反应。

由此可见，传统译论强调"对等"；功能翻译理论重"反应"。导游词翻译属于应用型翻译，游客的"反应"显然比与原文的"对等"更重要。因此，导游词的翻译应"创译为上"，采取与传统翻译不同的"创造性的译写策略"（陈刚，2010：111），对原文进行以导游讲解为目的的改写和编译。对于原文内容的取舍，译者应"点面结合""以点带面"、"故事化""生活化"，而不是面面俱到，全文翻译；对于原文的语言和表达，则需将其转化为符合导游或游客所能接受的话语，做到"口语化""现场化"。

下面以乐山大佛中文导游词的改写、编译为例，以案说法，探讨中文导游词"创译"的策略和方法。

乐山大佛

各位游客：

大家好！

欢迎各位到乐山大佛景区来观光旅游。现在我们看到的就是举世闻名的千年古佛——乐山游大佛。它是世界上最大的一尊石刻弥勒佛，通高71米，肩膀的宽度是24米，头宽直径10米，耳朵有7米长，眼睛的宽度是3.3米，鼻子的长度是5.6米，颈高3米，指长8.3米，从膝盖到脚背28米，脚背宽度是8.5米，头上的发髻有1021个。乐山大佛雄伟壮观，人们形容它："山是一尊佛，佛是一座山。"

乐山大佛始建于唐玄宗开元初年（也就是公元713年），竣工于唐贞元十九年（公元803年），大家可以计算一下，乐山大佛屹立于此已经1200多年了。

现在请大家看一看大佛两侧的岩石。这种岩石叫红砂岩，是一种质地疏松、容易风化的岩石，乐山大佛就是在这种岩石上雕刻而成的。那么大佛为什么能历经1200多年而"风雨不动安如山呢"？首先我们看一下大佛所处的位置。大佛位于凌云山西面的阴坡上，加之佛体周围林木稠密，地质结构稳定。佛身处于江弯地段，隐藏于山体之中，减少了风雨侵蚀和水流冲刷，因此岩石风化较缓慢。不仅如此，乐山大佛还有非常巧妙的排水系统。在大佛身后，有左右相通的排水洞穴，可以避免山泉对佛像的侵蚀；大佛头上发髻的第4层、第9层、第18层各有一条排水道与佛体衣服折皱连成排水渠道网，也避免了雨水对佛体的侵蚀。可见，乐山大佛的设计是非常科学的。除此之外，在竣工之后，还曾经修造了一个高13层的楼阁覆盖大佛，可惜毁于明末的战乱。

虽然乐山大佛有着十分完善的保护系统，然而在一千多年的漫长岁月中，它仍免不了遭到各种各样的破坏，有自然的，也有人为的。因此，各个朝代、政府都对它进行过维修。特别是中华人民共和国成立以后，乐山市政府曾对乐山大佛进行过多次维修，其中工程较大的是1963年的维修。1982年，乐山大佛经国务院公布成为国家重点文物保护单位。1996年峨眉山——乐山大佛被联合国教科文组织列入《世界自然与文化遗产名录》。目前，乐山大佛的保护工作已经引起了全世界人民的关注，乐山大佛已成了全世界人民的一笔宝贵遗产。

那么，是谁为我们创造了这笔财富？当初修大佛的目的是什么？带着这些问题，我们一起去参观海师堂。海师堂里的三尊塑像就是修建乐山大佛的功臣。首先我们看中间这一位，大佛的始建者——海通禅师，他是贵州人氏，当年在凌云山上结茅为僧。

古代的乐山是三江汇流之处，水势相当凶猛，经常发生船毁人亡的事件。海通禅师大发慈悲，准备修建大佛来镇水患。于是他四处化缘，筹得不少的钱财。当时有一个贪官见钱眼开，准备敲诈勒索他，海通禅师义正词严地说："自目可剜，佛财难得。"意思是说，我自己的眼睛可以挖下来给你，但你休想得到这笔佛财。那个贪官居然蛮横无理地要他试一试，海通禅师大义凛然地一手捧盘，一手挖出了自己的双眼。贪官吓坏了，从此再没为难他。海通禅师造佛时年事已高，当大佛修到肩部的时候，他就圆寂了，大佛的修造工程也因此停了下来。大约过了十年的时间，剑南西川节度使章仇兼琼捐赠俸金20万两，继续修造乐山大佛。由于工程浩大，需要巨大的经费，于是朝廷下令赐麻盐税款，使工程进展迅速。当乐山大佛修到膝盖的时候，续建者章仇兼琼迁任户部尚书，到京赴任，工程再次停工。

40年后，剑南西川节度使韦皋捐赠俸金50万两继续修建乐山大佛。在三代人的努力之下，前后历经90年时间，乐山大佛终于彻底完工，并且通体施金，华丽的佛衣和宝相庄严的佛体交相辉映。

现在大家对大佛已经有了一个初步的了解，接下来我们一起通过九曲栈道到大佛脚下看全景。我们脚下的九曲栈道是同乐山大佛一起修建的，共有173个台阶，最宽的地方是1.45米，最窄的地方仅有0.6米。大家沿途可以欣赏一下崖壁上留下的石刻佛龛。这些佛像神态各异，工艺精妙，可与中国四大石窟的佛像相媲美，遗憾的是它们的风化现象非常严重。

谢谢大家聆听！

点评分析：本篇中文导游词"以点带面"，从大佛像到海师堂，经九曲栈道下山，再观大佛像，运用故事法、名人法、问答法、引用法等，数字讲解法是一大亮点，但存在以下三个缺点：一是讲解对象发生移动，从大佛像跳跃到海师堂，而海师堂不在游客可视范围内，在景区的另一处，有隔空喊话之嫌；二是内容比较宽泛，重点不突出，没有围绕大佛这个"点"，深入挖掘博大精深的中国文化内涵；三是导游与游客虽有互动，但没有通过大佛像细部的讲解"以点带面""点面结合"，因而不能抓住游客的注意力。此外，本篇中文导游词的一些内容可能不适合外国游客，或不能引起他们的游览兴趣，如红砂岩体、排水沟、"自目可剜"、剑南西川节度使以及历代大佛修建的长篇大论；而过多的数字讲解，如果没有形象对比，也会让他们感到枯燥无味。因此，针对外国游客的英文导游词需对源语进行符合目的的改写、编译、"创译"。

创译导游词：

Leshan Giant Buddha

Ladies and gentlemen! We've arrived at the feet of the Leshan Giant Buddha. The statue of Giant Buddha is 71 meters high. More than 100 people could stand on each of

his 8.5 meter-wide instep. In 1996, the Giant Buddha was inscribed on the List of World Natural and Cultural Heritage sites. It is one of seven wonders in China, a wonder among world wonders.

Maybe you'll ask me a question: There are numerous Buddhist mountains in Sichuan. Lingyun Mountain is only 448 meters above the sea level, but why was the Giant Buddha chiseled here? A good question! In ancient times, Leshan frequently suffered from the floods and a lot of fishermen lost their lives. Haitong, the abbot of the Lingyun Temple began to raise money to chisel a giant Buddha statue out of the precipice at the confluence of the Minjiang, Qingyi and Dadu rivers. He hoped the rocks chiseled from the cliff would still the water and improve the channel safety.

Dear friends, let's appreciate the majesty of the world's largest statue of Giant Buddha. One eye is 3.3 meters wide. One ear is 7 meters long. One hair curl is larger than a dining table. Together there are 1,021 bobs on his head. From his head to his feet Giant Buddha is the length of a Boeing 747. The Statue of Liberty Goddess in New York only reaches up to his shoulders. You can park a bus on each of his shoulder; 50 soldiers can stand between his legs. His finger is about 8.3 meters long; three Yao Mings are shorter than any of his fingers. His instep is 8.5 meters wide; over 100 Shaquille O'Neal can stand on it. It is the largest Maitreya Buddha statue in the world.

There goes a saying: "The hill is a Buddha and a Buddha is a hill". Actually, the statue of Giant Buddha was chiseled from Linyun Mountain. On each side of the mountain stands other two gorgeous mountains. The unique contour of three mountains presents us a landscape of "Sleeping Buddha". Linyun Buddha in the middle is just seated in the bosom of the "Sleeping Buddha". What a mysterious landscape! A sleeping Buddha hugs a sitting Buddha. It presents us a miracle of "a Buddha within a Buddha". You can appreciate the miracle on the travel boat from another angle.

Dear friends, please look at the Giant Buddha's face carefully. His face is 10 meters wide and 15 meters long. A small dot between his eyes represents the third eye, a symbol of spiritual enlightenment. Worshipers think it is a symbolic hope for the bright future.

Look at his eyes. A pair of large eyes is half open, half closed. Maybe he is sitting in meditation or chanting scriptures. Look at his ears. A pair of big ears is very long, and the long ears demonstrate his extraordinary listening perception. Here is the sacred place for Buddhist believers. I'd like to repeat: Don't say anything profane about Buddhist gods. Believe it or not, his long ears may hear you even when you whisper. That's what Buddhist believers told me many times.

Well, what is the posture of this Giant Buddha? Different from the statue of cross-legged Buddha in other places of the world, his feet are not cross-legged, but flat on the ground. Such a posture shows the Chinese culture has been melted into Buddhist culture in the late years of Tang dynasty. The Chinese "Bag Buddha" and "Laughing Buddha" are good examples.

Now, we have 10 minutes to walk around. You may as well hug the leg of Giant Buddha if you could, but "don't hug Buddha's leg at the last minute" as the Chinese elderly blame the young. It will be too late to take remedies if you don't have preparations for it. This is the lesson I learnt from watching the Giant Buddha.

Thank you for your attention.

点评分析：本篇英文导游词与中文导游词一样，都是采取"点面结合""以点带面"的方式，但对中文导游词采取了符合目的的改写和编译，使之符合英语受众的阅读体验，更有利于英语导游员使用。

一、中文导游词内容繁杂，描写过于跳跃，一些段落过多或过于集中在"面"上讲解。因此英文导游词没有全文翻译，而是按照"点面结合""以点带面"的方式选取原文内容，避免由于内容过于分散、跳跃，给人"东拉西扯""滔滔不绝"的印象。

二、删除了外国游客可能不感兴趣或难以理解的内容，如红砂岩体、排水沟、剑南西川节度使以及历代建造大佛的过程。海通禅师"自目可剜"的故事过于血腥，可能引起外国游客不适，因此采取了缩译。导游词译与不译，如何译，取决于翻译目的和翻译效果。

三、围绕大佛像这个"点位"，增译了"a Buddha within a Buddha"（"佛

中有佛"）、"the third eye"（"第三只眼"）、"a Buddha within a Buddha"（"佛中有佛"）、如"cross-legged"（"跏趺坐"）等与大佛本身相关的中国文化内容，做到重点突出，避免蜻蜓点水。

四、海师堂离大佛像较远，不在游客可视范围之内。中文导游词这一段的讲解有不见其景，隔空喊话的弊端。为了避免景点之间"点位"的移动，符合景点导游词站立式讲解的要求，译文省译了海师堂的内容，仅用寥寥数语带过。

五、中文导游词运用了数字讲解，英文导游词也运用了数字法，但增译了数字比较的对象，使导游词讲解对象更加具体、更加形象，符合导游词创译生活化、故事化的原则。

六、与中文导游词一样，为了增加互动，英文导游词使用了设问句、祈使句，并以第一人称"I"和第二人称"you"交替叙事，增加了英文导游词的亲和力、感染力。与中文导游词相比，英文导游词更注意导游与游客的互动，寒暄功能、祈使功能更强。

七、英文导游词对于注意事项等程式化的问题也处理得很好，在介绍大佛巨型耳朵时插入，而不是导游词开始时进行，亲切自然而不露程式化的痕迹："I'd like to repeat：Don't say anything profane about Buddhist gods. Believe it or not, his long ears may hear you even when you whisper."

八、本篇英文导游词的结尾更是别出心裁，用了一句中国俗语："don't hug Buddha's leg at the last minute"（"不要临时抱佛脚哦！"），以"我"这个导游员经常讲乐山大佛的人生感悟作为本篇导游词的结尾，可谓寓意深长。

从以上点评可以看出，导游词创译的"点"要有"深度"，就像淘金一样不断地向深处挖掘，不能蜻蜓点水、浅尝辄止；创译的"面"要有广度，可采用概括式讲解历史沿革、名称来历等，或做专题介绍景点的品位、声誉等。"面"不能离开"点"，而是"以点带面""以点拓面"，将"点"不断放大，产生更广泛的影响。比如乐山大佛预制文本的创译，可选的"点位"很多，灵宝塔、凌云寺、海师堂、东坡楼、璧津楼、大佛像、九曲栈道、乌尤寺、麻浩崖墓等，但如果全部翻译，"点位"太多，而且会产生景点之间的移动，混淆景点讲解（位置不移动）和途中讲解（边走边讲）两种讲解方式的界限。由此可见，导游词的翻译并不是"忠实原文"的翻译，而是在原文的基础上进行以导游讲解为目的的改写或编译。

四、面中取点、点面结合

导游词的创译，"面中取点"必须在游客的可视范围之内。"选点"就像使用圆规一样，把带有针的一端固定在一个地方，作为圆心（点），再用尺子量出圆规两脚之间的距离作为半径，画圆的过程中两脚距离不能随意改变。这里的"距离"是指导译人员翻译、讲解的可视距离，不能不见其物，隔空喊话。至于在旅游景点众多的"点位"中哪里取"点"，如何挖掘景点内涵，如何"以点带面""以点拓面"，突出面上的中心思想，则由导译人员自行决定。

翻译一篇优秀的导游词必须向"深"度挖掘，向"高"度建树，因此"选点"是导游词创译的核心问题之一。除了"选点"，还有一个"带面"的问题。"面"就是景点内容的广度和内涵。导游词翻译"面中取点""以点带面"不能仅仅停留在"点"上，而是通过"点"来"带面""拓面"，扩大导游预制文本的范围和内容，翻译出景点"人所不知"的品位，翻译出游客"知之不详"的精彩，翻译出人生感悟和情怀。

"点面结合"在导游词中最重要的体现就是围绕一个"点"，翻译"人所不知""知之不详"。翻译"人所不知"需要导游挖掘景点的背景材料，而不能人云亦云。当今我们已进入大数据时代，要翻译"人所不知"实属不易；但要翻译"知之不详"，导游掌握的资讯较多，变"不详"为"详尽"还是比较容易的。翻译"知之不详"，实际上就是要求突出重点，而突出重点则要求"点面结合""以小博大"。一名出色的导游应当博学，"知之详尽"，而不能只翻译个"大概"。例如，翻译乐山大佛导游词预制文本，很少见到有人翻译"佛中有佛""布袋和尚""第三只眼""临时报佛脚"等内容，那么，何不选取这些与大佛相关，且更能体现中国文化的内容，创译一篇"点面结合""以小博大""人所不知"的导游词呢？

当然，由于英语导游的服务对象是外国游客，什么是"人所不知""知之不详",不能以中国人的认知标准,而应以服务对象的思维和文化背景选择翻译、讲解材料,全面翻译中文导游词是不可取的,因为"人所不知""知之不详"对于不同文化背景的游客,特别是外国游客也许完全不一样,不同年龄、文化层次的人对景点的理解也会有所不同。对于外国游客翻译"人所不知",不能"故弄玄虚",让人"摸不着头脑";翻译"知之不详",不能滔滔不绝,"信息轰炸",让人应接不暇。导游词的翻译、内容的取舍必须考虑外国游客的文化差异和信息接受能力。同样是翻译"七擒七纵""挥泪斩马谡",外国游客和中国游客的接受程度和反应是不一样的,必须懂得取舍、详略得当,而且用词得当。

案例研究

原文: 九寨沟

亲爱的游客朋友们,欢迎来到九寨沟!

九寨沟位于四川省阿坝藏族羌族自治州,距离成都450千米。"九"是数字9,"寨"意"村落",由于沟里分布着九个藏族村落,故名"九寨"。1992年,联合国教科文组织将九寨沟列入《世界自然遗产名录》。1997年,联合国将它列为"人与生物圈自然保护区"。与美国黄石公园相比,九寨沟奔放的藏族风情、神奇美丽的传说,更令游客心驰神往。

译文: **Jiuzhaigou National Park**

Ladies and gentlemen, welcome to Jiuzhaigou National Park!

Jiuzhaigou is located in the Aba Tibetan and Qiang Autonomous Prefecture in Sichuan Province, about 450 kilometers away from Chengdu. "Jiu" literally means "nine" while "Zhai" means "village". The Park is named after nine Tibetan villages scattered throughout the valley. In 1992, it was inscribed on the List of World Natural Heritages by UNESCO. In 1997, it was accepted as the Man and Biosphere Nature Reserves by the United Nations. Compared with the Yellow Stone Park of the United States, it is more appealing to the tourists because of its legends and the customs that Tibetans practice.

第八章　景点导游词翻译

评析

> 　　该导游词按导游词典型的开篇布局，撰写九寨沟地理位置、名称由来、品位和旅游价值。预制文本"面"上写得非常生动，与美国黄石公园进行了类比，使导游词接近受众的生活环境，拓展了九寨沟的想象空间和品牌价值，是"以点带面"成功的典范。此处不足百字，作者就用了两种讲解方法：解释法和类比法，难能可贵。

原文：现在我们到了一个岔口。之前我和你们说过，九寨沟呈"Y"字形，有三条沟，分别是树正沟、日则沟和则查洼沟。则查洼沟在你们左手边，右手边是日则沟。我先要带你们去树正沟和日则沟，原路返回再游览则查洼沟。在则查洼沟，你们会看到九寨沟海拔最高的高山湖泊——长海，全程约四个小时。昨晚下了场雨，栈道曲折，路面湿滑，小心脚下，不要跌倒。

译文：Now, we've arrived at a fork on the road. As I told you before, Jiuzhaigou takes the shape of the letter "Y", and consists of three beautiful gullies: Shuzheng Gully, Rize Gully and Zezhawa Gully. On your left is the Zezhawa Gully; on your right is the Rize Gully. I'll show you around the Shuzheng Gully and Rize Gully, then travel back along the same route to the Zezhawa Gully. There you'll see the highest alpine lake in Jiuzhaigou—the Long Lake. The tour will take about four hours. The winding and narrow path is slippery because it rained last night. Please watch your steps when you walk on the plank walkway.

评析

> 　　此段介绍旅游线路和注意事项，但打破常规，与"程式化"线路和注意事项放在与游客见面时宣布完全不同。九寨沟呈"Y"字形，本次旅游将从这里开始，在此介绍旅游线路和注意事项亲切自然，一点儿也没有一般导游词"程式化"的痕迹，是本篇导游词处理"程式化"的高妙之处，也是导游词生活化、现场化在旅游翻译中的运用。

原文：亲爱的游客朋友们，游完树正沟的诺日朗瀑布，现在我们来到了日则沟，前方便是隐匿在丛林之中的高山湖泊——镜海。你们看，镜海湖面平静如镜，波澜不惊。蓝天、白云、远山、近树水中清晰可见，"鱼在空中游，鸟在水中飞"，让人叹为观止。大家安静点儿，不要大声说话，不要向湖中扔石子。要是不小心打碎了这面鬼斧神工的"镜子"，那镜湖就不叫"镜湖"了。

译文：Dear friends, after we tour the Nuorilang Waterfall in the Shuzheng Gully, we've arrived at the Rize Gully. In front of us is the Mirror Lake, which is an alpine lake tucked away in the forest. Look, the lake looks exactly like a mirror. It is still and smooth, reflecting the landscape nearby flawlessly: the blue sky, the white clouds, the distant mountains and nearby trees. It presents us a magnificent view: "fish swimming in the air while birds flying at the bottom of the water". What a beautiful landscape it is! Be quiet! Don't speak aloud, or throw pebbles in the lake! Or, you might have broken the mirror of Nature, and the lake might have not been called Mirror Lake anymore.

评析

> 导游词将诺日朗瀑布一笔带过，切入镜海作为本篇导游讲解的"点"，围绕这个"点"描写九寨沟的自然风光。导游词运用拟人、虚拟、感叹句、祈使句，借景抒情，天人感应，与游客心心相印，感情交流与自然美景融为一体。蓝天、白云、远山、近树，湖面如镜面，无声胜似有声，导游词预制文本能描写得如此细腻，达到如此出神入化的意境，实属不易；翻译能用寥寥数语将中文导游词的"华美"转换为英文导游词的"简约"，也难能可贵。

原文：亲爱的游客朋友们，相信镜海已经净化了你们的心，咱们更加心安神定了。走近再看看，淡黄色、翡翠色、深蓝色，湖光山色，色彩斑斓。第一眼，没准你们还以为湖里倒满了颜料呢。再仔细看看，水底长满各种水藻、苔藓，呈现不同的颜色。天气在变，沉淀物颜色也在变；水深不同，色彩也不同。同一天，湖水色彩千变万化，稍不留神，你们就会错过那奇光异彩。快拿相机吧，捕捉斑斓世界中一纵即逝的时光!

译文:Dear friends, I think your souls might have been purified, and your minds might have been more peaceful. Please take a closer look at the lake! The lake has different colors: light yellow, emerald, deep and dark blue. At the first sight, you may think the lake is full of different pigments, but you'd better look at it more carefully! Many types of algae and bryophytes grow on the bottom of the lake, and present different colors in the water. What's more, the tufa sediments change the colors when the weather changes. Different depths of the water also present different colors. Even in a day, the lake presents ever-changing colors you might miss in a second. Why not take your cameras to capture the moment of the mosaic world now?

评析

此处导游词采用了"递进式"的写作方式,仍然围绕着镜海这个"点",重点挖掘景点深层次的内容,特别是镜海颜色形成的原因。作者连用两个"look",增强了游客与导游之间的互动。翻译镜海颜色成因很难,要翻译得如此生动活泼更难!作者综合多种翻译手法,化无生命之平淡为生命之神奇。最后一个反问句更是妙笔生花,将镜海的五彩斑斓定格在游客的相机镜头之中!

原文:实际上,镜海是由地震落石和石灰岩沉淀形成的堰塞湖。传说很久以前,英俊潇洒的男神达戈爱上了美丽的女神沃诺色,送给她一面镜子作为定情信物,他们决定在此定居生活,却惹恼了这里的妖魔鬼怪,被驱赶出此地。战乱中,沃诺色的镜子掉在山谷里,碎裂成108个大小不一、色彩斑斓的海子,其中的一个就是镜海。最后,妖魔鬼怪被打败,被埋葬在巨石下。还记得吗?就是九寨沟入口处你们见过的那块宝镜岩。

译文:Actually, the Mirror Lake is a barrier lake because of rock falls of earthquakes and travertine sediments. Long long time ago, a handsome god Dage fell in

love with a beautiful goddess Wonuose. He gave the goddess a big mirror as a token of love and decided to settle in this beautiful valley when the evil was irritated and drove them away. A war broke out. In a hurry, Wonuose dropped her mirror into the valley below, and it was broken into 108 lakes of different sizes and colors. One of the 108 lakes was just the Mirror Lake in front of us. Finally, the evil was defeated and buried in a huge rock. What is it? Right, it is the Precious Mirror Cliff you've seen at the entrance to Jiuzhaigou.

 评析

"山不在高，有仙则灵"。作者在叙述九寨沟海子成因的基础上，用故事法讲解了达戈与沃诺色的爱情故事，给景点赋予了浪漫的人文色彩，符合导游预制文本故事化原则；同时采用了回叙的方法，在尾篇提及九寨沟入口的宝镜岩。这就比按线路顺序、按部就班翻译讲解旅游线路上的景点更具戏剧性，也做到了首尾兼顾，前后呼应。

原文：与镜海相比，珍珠滩则惊艳得让你们感到窒息，甚至让你们欢呼雀跃。咱们稍事休息再去参观，这段行程会比您见过的诺日朗瀑布更激动人心。电视连续剧《西游记》就在此地拍摄。

译文：To the contrast of the Mirror Lake, the Pearl Shoal will take your breath away, and certainly make you shout for joy. Let's take 10 minutes rest before we go to the Pearl Shoal. It's an more exciting excursion than the Nuorilang Waterfall you've been. A TV series—*The Pilgrimage to the West* was just filmed there.

原文：谢谢大家。

译文：Thank you.

评析

> 导游词结尾别出心裁，不按常规导游词那样简单地写道："我们要去的下一个景点是珍珠滩"，而是拿眼前的镜海与下一站的珍珠滩做了一个拟人化的对比，并与第一个景点诺日朗瀑布做了比较，还用《西游记》拍摄地做衬托，寥寥数语，就达到"点面结合""以点带面"的效果。如此精彩结尾，终成导游词创译的经典。

总体评价

本篇导游词横向有广度，纵向有深度，点面黄金分割比例恰当。导游词翻译"面中取点"，以画龙点睛之笔介绍了九寨沟这个"面"以后，便以镜海为切入点，细致入微地翻译介绍了九寨沟"鱼在空中游，鸟在水中飞"的奇特景象。围绕镜海这个"点"，导游采用了"递进式"翻译讲解方式，重点挖掘，深入讲解，科学地介绍了镜海五彩斑斓的成因，而达戈和沃诺色的爱情故事又为九寨沟的自然风光增添了丰富的人文色彩，符合导游词预制文本故事化的原则。

五、以点带面、以小博大

导游词"以点带面""以小博大"应在游客可视范围内选一个看得见、摸得着的物象作为讲解对象，如一副联、一块匾、一方碑、一尊像、一座鼎等，在有限的时间内围绕这个点不断地挖掘景点的内涵，而不能"天马行空"，让人感到隔空喊话，只闻其声，不见其物。同时，翻译景点导游词，导译人员还应"以点带面""以小博大"，在一个"点位"上前伸后引，谈古论今，将导游词中的一个"点"不断放大，将"点"放在相关的历史、文化背景之中，提升景点的内涵和品位，引发游客的思考和想象。

翻译"面"要有广度，一般采用"概括式"的编译，翻译景点的历史沿革、旅游资源等，或用"点睛法"介绍景点最具价值的、独特的称谓、等级、评价等，但这个"面"不能离开"点"，而是"以点带面""以点拓面"，将这个"点"不断放大，产生"蝴蝶"效应。翻译"点"一定要有"深度"，要像淘金一样不断向深处挖掘，不能蜻蜓点水、浅尝辄止。例如翻译武侯祠"攻心联"预制文本，导游应围绕"攻心"这个"点"，深度翻译"攻心为上""攻城为下"，挖掘"攻心联"的内涵，并通过这个"点"，"以点带面""以小博大"，可翻译"七擒七纵""挥泪斩马谡"等。"以点带面"，导游词旁征博引，但翻译必须突出重点，要在"点"上不断挖掘，将"攻心联"的深厚哲理和文化底蕴译得入木三分、引人入胜。

导游词的翻译需"以点带面""以小博大"，还应遵守导游词"程式化"的结构和要求（见表8.1）。当然，如果按照导游词"程式化"的结构翻译，导游词格式又会千篇一律，有经验的导游不会削足适履，生搬硬套，而是根据讲解对象，翻译出自己风格独特的导游词。总之，对于程式化部分的翻译，导译人员应当"以点带面""点面结合"，处理好"点"与"面"的关系。还是一句话，以目标游客为导向、优美隽永的英文、突出的个人风格等仍然是导游词翻译的灵魂。

表8.1 景点讲解程式化要求

项目	内容
景点的导向性知识	景点所在的位置
	游览景点的注意事项
	景点的参观游览线路
景点的说明性知识	景点的历史沿革（科学成因）
	景点的风景或文化特色
	有关景点的历史故事（传说、神话、典故等）
	有关景点的名人、名家、名言、名句或后人的评说

案例研究

Nanjing Road

南京路

原文：亲爱的游客朋友们！南京路是"中华商业第一街"，在上海不是建成最早的,也不是最广的,但却是最有名的。鸦片战争后,上海成为通商口岸,欧洲殖民者按照他们家乡的建筑风格在这儿建造了各式各样的欧式建筑。南京路曾经以"东方华尔街"闻名于世,也是上海殖民时期的缩影。

译文:Ladies and gentlemen, Nanjing Road is known as "China's No.1 Business Street". It is neither the first road constructed in Shanghai, nor the widest one, but it is the most famous one. After the first Opium War in 1840, Shanghai became a commercial treaty port, where the European colonialists built the city with the architectural style of their hometowns. Known as the "Wall Street of the East", Nanjing Road is a historical miniature of the Shanghai in the colonial period.

评析

> 本篇导游词开篇用了南京路的两个响当当的名片:"中华商业第一街"和"东方华尔街",一下就提高了南京路的旅游价值和品位。导游将南京路历史沿革的介绍放在鸦片战争后上海成为通商口岸的历史背景下,从而为"面中取点""以点带面"翻译讲解南京路的历史文化奠定了基础。

原文:这里是外滩上的和平饭店,我们将从这儿沿南京路步行5.5公里前往静安寺。如果遇上下雨,可在步行拱廊下避雨。时光荏苒,南京路已修葺重建,发生了巨大的变化。为了方便游客购物,南京东路段修建了步行拱廊。如果你们游得太累,或不想走路,可以乘坐无轨观光车。南京路上现有六百多家商店,商品琳琅满目,品牌众多,款式新颖,质量上乘。一百多家传统店铺和特色商店销售丝制品、玉器、刺绣、羊毛制品以及钟表等商品。

译文:Here is the Peace Hotel at the Bund. We'll walk along the 5.5-km long Nanjing Road to the Jing'an Temple. You may take shelter from the rain under the pedestrian arcade. Over time, Nanjing Road has been restructured and undergone a significant change. For shopping convenience, its eastern end has an all-weather pedestrian arcade. A trackless sightseeing train provides a comfortable tour when you are tired or you don't want to walk. Today, over 600 businesses on the Nanjing Road offer countless famous brands, superior quality, and new fashions. About a hundred traditional stores and specialty shops still provide choice silk goods, jade, embroidery, wool, and clocks.

评析

> 导游词"取点"放在和平饭店，介绍了旅游线路、旅游交通和旅行方式，语言自然亲切，没有显露"程式化"介绍的痕迹，实为导游词处理"程式化"翻译的范例，值得借鉴。

原文：和平饭店是"装饰艺术风格的杰作"，上海地标性建筑，老派建筑的魅力与新上海的荣耀交相辉映，相得益彰。与其他欧洲建筑相比，和平饭店在这"万国建筑博览会"众多杰出的建筑中独树一帜，别具一格。南京路因此声名远播，可以说是当之无愧。大家看看你们周围的建筑群，这些建筑都具有显著的欧洲文艺复兴时期的建筑风格：哥特式、巴洛克式、罗马式、古典主义和文艺复兴风格，不一而足。上海是当今亚洲最繁忙的港口之一，酒店、银行和写字楼比比皆是，满足上海金融、贸易之需。

译文：Peace Hotel is a "luxurious Art-Deco masterpiece", a landmark building where old-fashioned glamour sparkles with a new luster in Shanghai. Compared with other European buildings, it is unique, but only one of numerous finest buildings in the "World Architecture Show", for which Nanjing Road is well-deserved. Please look at the building complex around us. They have striking European architectural features of the Renaissance Period. The styles of the buildings include Gothic, Baroque, Romanesque, Classicism and Renaissance. Today, the hotels, banks and office buildings serve the financial and trade needs of Shanghai, one of the busiest ports in Asia.

评析

　　和平饭店是上海艺术装饰风格（Art-Deco）地标建筑，从地标建筑这个"点"将景点翻译介绍到上海"世界建筑博览会"这个"面"上，展示了上海欧式建筑林林总总、风格各异的面貌，是导游词"以点带面"创译的成功之道。

　　原文：南京路不仅因古老的欧式建筑闻名于世，也是购物者的天堂。在这里只有您想不到，没有您买不到。和平饭店位于著名的外滩，在这里您可以一览上海风光，但如果想一探世界时尚与奢华，南京路才是不二之选。与巴黎的香榭丽舍大街、纽约的第五大道一样，南京路也是商店林立，商品琳琅满目。现代化的购物商场、品牌专卖店、电影院、国际大饭店鳞次栉比，应有尽有。

　　译文：Nanjing Road is not only famous for the old buildings of European styles, but also known as the paradise for shoppers, where you can buy what you want in any parts of the world. Peace Hotel is situated at the famous Bund where you may go sightseeing, but Nanjing Road is the perfect place to explore the world's fashions and luxuries. Like the Champs Elysees in Paris and the Fifth Avenue in New York, Nanjing Road is packed with rows of shops arrayed with large collections of goods of various kinds. Modern shopping malls, specialty stores, theatres, and international hotels have mushroomed on both sides of the street.

 评析

　　和平饭店位于上海传统的商业区、观光旅游区，但南京路才是购物者的天堂。导游词不仅将南京路与和平饭店做了对比，而且与巴黎的香榭丽舍大道和纽约的第五大道做了比较，进一步拓展了南京路的商业价值和旅游价值，成功地运用了"以点带面""以点拓面"的翻译方法。

　　原文：南京路也是美食家的天堂。这儿有上百家餐馆，可以品尝到16种不同风味的中国菜，如川菜、粤菜、鲁菜、扬州菜等。这里也有来自法国、俄罗斯、意大利、英国、德国、日本、印度等国家的美食,其他地方的风味佳肴、清真食品以及素食风味也可一一品尝,肯德基、麦当劳、必胜客及其他有名的美食店更是遍布街头巷尾。如果您觉得和平饭店的饭菜不合胃口,还可以在南京路品尝来自各国的美味佳肴。

译文:Nanjing Road is also a paradise for gourmets. There are hundreds of restaurants serving the famous 16 styles of Chinese food, such as Sichuan food, Guangdong food, Shandong food, Yangzhou food, etc. There are also French, Russian, Italian, English, German, Japanese, Indian and other kinds of foreign flavored cuisines, and Muslim food and vegetarian food. KFC, McDonald's, Pizza Hut, and other world-famous food vendors line both sides of the street. If our chefs in the Peace Hotel cannot satisfy your appetite, you can have a taste of different kinds of food from different countries on the Nanjing Road.

评析

南京路也是美食者的天堂。如果仅仅翻译介绍南京路上世界各种风味食品和菜系,还未真正做到"以点带面";导游词翻译讲解上海美食时与和平饭店大厨的饭菜对比,就完美地做到了"以点带面"。最后一句话将和平饭店美食与南京路的佳肴做了一个假设性的对比,实为点睛之笔。

原文:现在,夜幕降临,华灯开启,霓虹灯熠熠闪光,将宏伟的建筑群照得光彩夺目,上海的夜空灿若星辰,使这座城市更显活力四射。无轨观光车正从熙熙攘攘、人声鼎沸的街道穿过。在上海这样的大都市,在露天酒吧小酌一杯,耳畔萦绕着街头歌手的音乐声,真是赏心悦目、心旷神怡,对吧?

译文:Now, it is getting dark. Flashing neon signs illuminate the magnificent buildings and decorate the night skyline of this lively city. The trackless sightseeing trains are driving through the street in the hustle and bustle of the crowd. To enjoy a cup in the open-air bars and listen to the lingering sounds from street musicians is an especially refreshing feeling in a big metropolitan like Shanghai, isn't it?

原文：走吧，去乘这趟无轨观光车，去领略一下上海南京路上的夜生活。如果累了，咱喝上一杯咖啡。

译文：Let's take the trackless sightseeing train to see something of night life on the Nanjing Road in Shanghai. When we're tired, we'll have a cup of coffee in the open air.

原文：祝大家玩得开心！

译文：Have a nice day!

评析

> 在南京路上喝上一杯露天咖啡，在南京路上欣赏流行音乐，在霓虹灯下享受上海夜生活，体验与住店不同的生活，也是"以点带面""以点拓面"的翻译方法，拓展了导游词翻译讲解的内容。这里虽然没有提及和平饭店，但实则是与和平饭店进行了不留痕迹的对比，是不同旅游体验的真实写照。

总体评价

南京路的翻译讲解可采取两种方式：一是固定位置翻译讲解，二是边走边翻译。本篇导游词预制文本采用的是第一种方法。边走边翻译的优点是随机取景，触景生情，但南京路是"中华商业第一街"，也是历史街区，短短5分钟要翻译、讲解那么厚重的历史文化会造成信息分散，重点不突出。以固定的位置翻译导游词最大的优点是重点突出，能够"以点带面""以小博大"，适合短时间或有时空限制的翻译讲解。要翻译讲解好一条5.5公里的"中华商业第一街"难度不小，而"以点带面""以小博大"的方式正好弥补了这一短板。程式化导游词规定"固定式讲解""讲解不能移动"，而本篇导游词竟做到了"以点带面""以小博大"，将南京路的历史文化翻译讲解得栩栩如生，实属不易。

导游词"取点"上海外滩的和平饭店，将南京路的翻译放在上海成为通商口岸、南京路成为"东方的华尔街"的历史背景下，并通过和平饭店的建筑延伸到南京路上形形色色的欧式建筑，有哥特式、巴洛克式、罗马式等，堪称"万国建筑博览会"，是一种"以点带面"的翻译讲解方式；接着导游将南京路与巴黎的香榭丽舍大道和纽约的第五大道进行对比，这就大大拓展了南京路的价值空间和想象空间；然后导游又翻译介绍了南京路上的商业、美食，特别是翻译了法国菜、日本菜、俄国菜、美国菜、意大利菜以及中国四大菜系，呈现出上海南京路欣欣向荣的商业气象。导游词的翻译并没有局限在和平饭店这个"点"上，而是"以点带面""以小博大"。结尾翻译讲解夜上海，导游巧妙地用了一个反问句，加强了导游与游客之间的互动，也拓展了上海生活的内容，展示了上海人的情怀。

本章小结

导游词是导游员与游客交流思想、情感，传播知识文化的载体，主要用于导游景点和途中讲解。根据导游词的风格，导游词可分为幽默型、煽情型、审美型等多种类型，也可分为预制文本导游词和现场讲解导游词。导游词的翻译与一般翻译不同，需从游客的角度出发，以提高译文的可接受性为要旨，采取"创译"的方法，现场化、口语化、故事化、生活化的"创译"是必须遵守的翻译原则。导游词的"创译"不以原作为导向，而是根据受众的文化背景、对目的地文化的可接受程度以及景区的时空布局，对原文进行以导游讲解为目的的改写和编译。对于原文内容的取舍，译者应"点面结合""以点带面"，从原文中选取他们易于理解并乐于接受的旅游信息，而不是面面俱到，全文翻译；对于原文的语言和表达，需将其转化为导游或游客所能接受的话语，做到口语化、生活化、现场化。改写和编译是导游词"创译"的主要方法。

翻译实践

一、热身练习

根据百度百科剑门关介绍，创译一篇英文导游词。

旅游景点的翻译、讲解不同于途中翻译及其讲解，要求位置相对固定、"不移动""不走动"。如果要深度翻译、讲解旅游景点，站立式、"不移动""不走动"更符合要求。无论是站立式还是移动式，导游词预制文本的创译都要求根据"面中取点""点面结合""以点带面""以点拓面"，做到重点突出，双向互动。"点面结合""以点带面"的导游词，其最大的优势是翻译对象时间与空间融合，均在游客合理的可视范围之内，而"全景式""报站式"的翻译名为"全面""忠实"，实则片面，用于导游现场讲解不具有操作性，不能引发游客的预期反应，让游客产生美好的旅游体验。根据百度百科剑门关的相关介绍，创译一篇"点面结合"或"以点带面"的英文导游词。

二、巩固练习

翻译漓江导游词，并对译文进行点评。

Lijiang River

Ladies and gentlemen! Welcome on board for cruising the beautiful Lijiang River. Please sit back and relax. Our boat is going to leave the Zhujiang port. This cruise will take us about four hours to reach Yangshuo. I believe the gorgeous karst peaks will give you surprises at each bend of the limpid river under the blue sky. You'll see water buffalo patrolling the fields, peasants reaping rice paddies, school kids and fisherman floating by on bamboo rafts. The scenery along the Lijiang River is a taste of life far away from the concrete jungle of the city. And the ever-ceasing landscape and country scenery will never disappoint you.

Now we can see the river rushing to the steep Bat Hill. The two peaks with flat yellow cliffs look like two flying bats. The nine peaks on the right look like nine cattle plowing the land. The five peaks on the left look like five running horses. If you look carefully, you will find out two peaks ahead like two lions playing with an embroidered ball and looking around the three islets.

Ladies and gentlemen, our boat is entering the Caoping Scenic Area. The mountain in front looks like a golden crown of the Han Dynasty, so it is called Crown Hill. There is a grotto called Guanyan Grotto at the foot of the hill. It is the exit of an underground river with a different source from the Lijiang River. Some people had tried to look for its source, but they failed. In 1987 Sino-British Team dived 24 meters underwater and found that the fish there were more than one meter long. But they still failed to discover the source of the underground river. It remains a mystery of the Lijiang River.

Now, our boat is going to arrive at Yangdi. The stretch of river from Yangdi to Xingping is the most excellent part of our cruise. It is the climax of the musical movement that we are enjoying. Down stream from Yangdi to Xingping, the river passes an endless procession of distinct peaks and bamboo groves and stunning landscapes. The marvelous landscape will present you a painting in a poem and a poem in a painting.

Look ahead! On the upper right, the steep peaks and flowing clouds create a mysterious atmosphere. The eight peaks over there are eight immortals in a famous Chinese legend. The immortals originally lived in Penglai, Shandong Province. But why did they come here? It is said that the eight immortals came to Guilin and were attracted so much by the beauty of the place that they decided to stay here. So, the scene is named "Eight Immortals across the River."

Ladies and gentlemen, the most exciting memento on our cruise is coming. The hill in front of us is the famous attraction—Nine-horse Painting Hill. The huge cliff with rich colors looks like an enormous piece of Chinese landscape painting. Now the boat is coming close to the hill. You will be surprised to find out that nine handsome horses were painted on the cliff.

Now, our boat is entering Yangshuo. Please get ready to get off the boat. We'll go shopping in the West Street. At 4:00 p.m. we'll take coach back to Guilin.

Have a good time!

三、阅读翻译

阅读下文，重点翻译下画线部分。

黄山北海景区

各位朋友：

　　大家好！欢迎来到黄山北海景区参观游览。①北海景区（包括西海）位于黄山中部，是一片海拔在1600米左右的高山开阔区域。北海景区，汇集了石、松、坞、台、云等奇景，色彩变幻莫测，构成一幅幅伟、奇、幻、险的天然画卷，是黄山的风景窗。北海景区是黄山最重要的景区，这里集合了黄山的四绝胜景，大家是绝对不能错过的。

②请大家再看山峰顶侧的这株松树，它横于悬崖石壁之中，在树干20厘米处分两支盘曲生长，伏卧昂首，人们给它取名为"卧龙松"。请再顺着卧龙松往下看，这株松树树冠平整，极像迎客松，最下一侧枝的长度几乎是树高的一倍。此枝向谷中伸出，当云雾在山壑间弥漫飞腾时，伸出的侧枝犹如凌波探海，所以人称"探海松"。

③黄山以奇松、怪石、云海、温泉"四绝"而闻名天下。奇松遍布黄山峰谷，但是尤以始信峰的松树最为独特，因而有"不到始信峰，不见黄山松"的说法。黄山松的主要形态特征为：枝叶短粗而稠密，叶色绿，枝干曲生，树冠扁平，盘根于石，傲然挺立。我们现在看到的是黄山名松之一的黑虎松。松高15米，胸径达65厘米。这边这棵松树叫龙爪松。从树形、树龄看并无突出之处，但却成为黄山一景。大家仔细看，此松主根深扎地下，另有五根粗壮的支根全部裸露在外，状似苍龙之爪，所以人们给它取名为龙爪松。

④大家请看前方，这里是黄山著名的始信峰，位列黄山三十六小峰第十五。峰名得来十分独特：相传古时有人从云谷寺游山至此，如入画境，似幻而真，始信黄山风景奇绝。

⑤请大家小心脚下。我们正在经过的这座长4米、宽1米的桥名为仙人桥，又名渡仙桥，意为渡过此桥，即入仙境。过了这净土门，就真正登上了始信峰绝顶了。古诗有"山登绝顶我为峰"之说，此时我们已站在了海拔1668米的始信峰山顶了。

第四篇

游后文本翻译

第九章 旅行后文本的翻译

旅行后文本可以是记者或作家撰写而成刊登于旅游杂志或报纸的文章，也可以是旅游者游后在博客或旅游网页写下的旅行见闻或评论，常常是图文结合，主要目的是记录和分享旅行体验，最贴近生活，属于个人作品。旅行后文本往往带有个人印记，也是个人旅行经历的最好见证。我国学界对旅行后文本的翻译研究较少，只有少数学者在研究旅游翻译的著作中提到过旅行后文本，但篇幅简短，通常一笔带过，并未深入研究（王宪，2016：120）。

旅行后文本的翻译是旅游翻译服务的重要组成部分，也是旅游对外宣传的方式之一，因此有必要研究旅行后文本的文本特点，通过对比旅行前、中、后文本的语言和篇章结构，探索针对性的翻译方法。学习旅行后文本的翻译策略和方法，不仅能提升译者翻译旅行后文本的能力，也能提高其游前、游中旅行文本的翻译水平；通过阅读、欣赏旅行后文本及其译文，有助于丰富译者的文化知识，提高文学修养，反过来促进译者的学习能力、翻译能力、鉴赏能力和文艺批评能力。

一、旅行后文本的分类

根据不同旅行阶段，旅游文本可划分为旅行前文本、旅行中文本和旅行后文本。旅行后文本主要指旅行见闻、报告、评论、游记、博客等，取材范围十分广泛，既可描绘客观景物，如大自然的瑰奇景色、现代城市中的人文景观、古时遗留下来的文明奇迹和夕阳下的断壁残垣等，也可记录个人旅游体验，如对异乡的民俗民风、奇闻轶事和旅途中的所思所感等，体裁包括但不限于散文、记叙文等。从内容来看，旅行后文本可分为以写人记事为主和以咏物描写为主两大类。

1. 记叙型旅行后文本

以记人、叙事为主。这类旅游文本由时间、地点、人物、事件等因素构成，侧重于从一个角度选取题材，从叙述人物和事件的发展变化过程反映事物的本质，记录旅游地的自然地理、风土人情和历史文化。为了记叙生动，需辅之以描写表达方式；为了记叙过程流露感情色彩，需辅之以抒情表达方式；为了记叙的人和事有意义，需辅之以议论表达方式；在记叙的过程中，有些地方需要说明，需辅之以说明表达方式。灵活运用不同的记叙方法，可以使记叙型旅行后文本更有表现力，更具感染力（冯雪燕，2016：67）。

例1. The number of islands encountered during the day proved so troublesome that we were compelled to crawl cautiously along at a snail's pace. The peaceful prospect which had dominated the scenery farther back was now shattered by the near approach of gigantic mountain peaks towering far into the clouds, while on the river's banks hung low-lying vapors of dank moisture.

译文：白天经过的群岛十分难走，<u>我们</u>不得不像蜗牛一样小心翼翼地沿着岸边慢慢爬行，眼看即将踏上坦途，可好景不长，迎面高耸入云的大山又让先前的希冀化为泡影，祸不单行，河岸边低悬的阴云还氤氲着层层水汽，预示着大雨即将来临。

分析：这是一则游记，作者以第一人称 (We approach) 讲述自己的坎坷旅途，叙事性、故事性强。"...we were compelled to crawl cautiously along at a snail's pace" "on the river's banks hung low-lying vapors of dank moisture" 记叙了此次旅途的艰难历程，让读者不禁为作者感到担心，也是在为潜在的游客旅行提供警示；作者夹叙夹议，"劫后余生"的旅行经历又让探险旅游者产生非去不可的逆反和挑战心理。

例2. A young man can only marry if he or his family has enough cows—no cows, no wife. Usually, it is about the five to twenty-five cows that the girl's family expects. Of course, the exact number always depends on the social status of the candidate. Many men cannot afford a wife. The parents also have a great say in choosing the partner. By the way, that does not just happen in the bush, but almost all over Uganda.

译文：一个年轻男子想要娶妻，除非他本人或者他家里奶牛够多。<u>换句话说，没有奶牛，就没有妻子</u>。通常，女方家希望男方家能给5到25头奶牛，至于具体数目，要看男方的社会地位，但现实中很多男人娶不起妻子。父母在为子女选择伴侣方面也有很大的发言权。顺便说一下，这种结婚风俗不是只有这个村子才有，整个乌干达地区都是这样。

分析：这是一则游记，主要记叙了作者在非洲乌干达的一个村子里了解到的婚俗。"no cows, no wife" "depends on the social status" "Many men cannot afford a wife"表明当地的婚俗与一个人的经济、社会地位有很大关系。很多男子娶不上妻子，从一个侧面反映出当地的贫困、落后。最后一句，"By the way, that does not just happen in the bush, but almost all over Uganda"，在记叙过程中辅之以说明，说明这种婚俗在乌干达是普遍现象。

例3. I went to Chengdu for a few days last week and felt the charm of the food capital. The most memorable thing is this mother's hoof flower. The soup is delicious and mellow; the pig's hand is soft and rotten, and the hot and sour water is used to eat two dishes. A variety of different tastes have greatly satisfied my taste buds!

译文：上周我去成都待了几天，感受到了这个美食之都的魅力。最难忘的当属老妈蹄花，汤香四溢，可口醇厚，猪脚炖得很烂，蘸水酸辣爽口，可蘸两个菜。众多口味极大地满足了我的味蕾！

分析：这是一则旅游博客，记录了作者在成都旅游时品尝老妈蹄花的经历和感受。作者站在第一人称的角度，对老妈蹄花这一美食作了个性化的评论和描述，是作者主观性的评价，表达了作者对成都美食的喜爱之情。不过作者将"老妈蹄花"描写成"mother's hoof flower"让人忍俊不禁，正确的译法应是"the stewed pig hoof in bean soup"。

例4. I booked this tour last minute and did not regret it! The cost was minimal compared to the fun I had! First we toured the Forbidden City and our guide, Leo, was wonderful! He shared great knowledge and gave us time to explore on our own. Next we went to the Jade factory and was given a short tour followed by lunch there. The dining experience was wonderful and delicious. We then headed to the Great Wall and it was amazing! Although our time there was limited to two hours, it was just almost perfect. We ended the day with a tea sampling and shopping. I couldnt have asked for a more perfect first tour of China.

译文：就在一分钟前，我报名参加了这次旅行，我一点儿也不后悔！这些成本费远远不及快乐重要！我们首先参观了故宫，导游Leo真是太棒了！他分享了丰富的知识，给我们时间自己参观与探索。随后我们去了玉石工厂，在那里吃了午饭。食物很美味，用餐体验也很棒。然后我们去了长城，真的太精彩了！虽然我们只在那里待了两个小时，但一切都几近完美。在一日游的尾声，我们还品了茶，购了物。没有比这更完美的中国之行了！

分析：作者以第一人称的口吻讲述了自身在游前报名参加旅游团的心路历程，游中所经之地、所见之感，对整个旅行经历非常满意。在记叙过程中辅之以情（我一点儿也不后悔！导游Leo真是太棒了！真的太精彩了！）；辅之以议论（虽然我们只在那里待了两个小时，但一切都几近完美。没有比这更完美的中国之行了！）

2. 描写型旅行后文本

以写景、状物为主。这类旅游文本按照时空变换顺序，运用移步换景的方法，以作者的情愫作为"文眼"，把事物的变化作为"文脉"（张子泉，2006：149）；常用渲染、衬托、对比、铺垫、象征、比喻、拟人等手法，往往形成如诗如画的意境。生动的景物描写沁润着作者的心绪，文字中的情意萦绕着读者的心扉。作者以景语传达情语，在"文眼"和"文脉"引导下写景、状物，或借景寓情，或寓情于景，将个人情感寄予山川名胜、自然景物之中，感情真挚，情景交融，具有较强的艺术感染力。

例1. The fierce lightning twitched, as it danced in and out the crevices—inwards, outwards, upwards, then finally lost in one downward swoop towards the river.

译文：猛烈的闪电抽搐着，随着它在缝隙中来回跳动——时而藏于其中，时而炸裂开来，时而直上云霄，最终却在奔流直下的猛扑中迷失了方向。

分析：作者描述了作者晚上乘船渡长江，暴风雨来临时的闪电景象，言辞优美，特别是使用了"inwards""outwards""upwards""downward"

等,极具音乐感、画面感,属于旅行后文本描写型文本。译者对原文中"inwards""outwards""upward"这三个副词进行了词义转换,将副词分别译为动词,即"藏于其中""炸裂开来""直上云霄",并连续使用排比句式"时而……""时而……""时而……",这样一来,"化静为动",译文自然流畅,同样也产生了游记的音乐美、画面美,这样的描写方法有助于提高读者的审美情趣。

例2. The precipitous mountains stretches to the north and east, covered with long, coarse, dun-colored grass and the occasional patch of stunted scrub, and with a multitude of waterfalls dashing down granite ravines. It was a daunting landscape, far from the touch of man.

译文:陡峭的山脉向北、向东蜿蜒伸展着,上面覆盖着黑乎乎的草,又长又毛糙,偶尔还会有一片片矮小的灌木丛。山上还有众多瀑布从花岗岩峡谷冲流而下。这里人迹罕至,风景让人望而生畏。

分析:该文段描写的是故事中主人公探寻自身周围环境时所看到的景致。其中,"touch"本是"触碰"的意思,但是如果将"far from the touch of man"直译为"远离人类的触碰",读者必然是一头雾水。通过阅读原文的描述,知道该地地势险要,环境恶劣,绝大多数人都不会来这种地方,故译为"人迹罕至"。这一处理使译文更具可读性,也很好地体现了原文的文学性。

例3. 再往前走去,走到林子尽头,当前是平坦的原野,望见了村舍,初青的麦田,更远处三两个馒头形的小山掩住了一条通道。

译文:The trail eventually led me out of the woods and into an open field. A cluster of country cottages stood in the distance amid wheat fields, which had just begun to turn green. A country road stretched all the way to the foot of a couple of round-shaped hills.

分析:作者以自身的视角,由近及远,描写了旅途中作者看见的景象。"平坦的原野""初青的麦田""馒头形的小山"等描写语言清丽,清新自然,画面感很强;译文全部采用非人称主语,物象一一排列,体现了英文旅行后文本描写景物的风格之一:清丽隽秀。

例4. 桥的两端有斜倚的垂柳与掩荫护住。水是彻底的清澄,深不足四尺,均匀地长着长条的水草。

译文：At both ends of the bridge are weeping willows with curtains of drooping branches and rows of cypress trees that provide cool shade. Water is crystal clear. It's no more than four-foot deep. Waterweeds stick out their long, slender leaves; they are evenly spread.

分析：这一段属于景物描写，作者使用形象贴切的形容词，将所见之景进行了详细的描绘，让读者跟随自身的视角对景物细致玩味；译文语言清新自然，描写景物长短句结合，多用具象的名词和形容词。

二、旅行后文本的特点

从语言来看，英文旅行后文本和其他旅游文本一样，文体大多比较简约，用字简练，直观具体，在客观事实的基础上抒发个人感情；中文旅行后文本在主观意愿下描写客观事物，常用渲染、夸张的词汇描写事物，寓景于情，语言生动、隽永；就篇章结构而言，中文旅行后文本多先写景、后抒情；英文旅行后文本则大多开门见山，语言前景化，然后再叙事或描述事物。旅行后文本记录作者的心绪和经历，作者身份可识别度高，融地域性、知识性、文学性为一体，对旅游者而言，更有说服力，可读性更强。

1.可识别性

旅行后文本属于个人写作，作者地位和其他旅游文本相比更为突出，常以作者视角介入，使用第一人称写作，常采用夹叙夹议，或寓景于情，或托物言志，文本中有个性化的描述与评论，包含个人主观因素和审美情趣，表达个人在旅行过程中的心声，分享自己的旅行体验和感悟，具有个性化的特点，作者身份的可识别性很高，这与匿名性的其他旅游文本大不相同。

例1. My partner and I walked to the Banff sign and on our walk back we saw the trail and decided to take it. It took us about 45 minutes because we stopped a lot to take photos and we saw soooo many elks. It was amazing to watch them graze. Being from the city, we don't get to see many wildlife, so we appreciated the wildlife.

译文：我和同伴来到了班夫标志，在我们回来的路上，看到了Fenland Trail这条徒步小路，于是我们从这条小路走回来。大约花了45分钟，因为我们一路都在拍照，走走停停，还看到了非常非常多的麋鹿。我们看着它们吃草，简直太不可思议了。我们生活在城市里，无法见到这么多野生动物，所以我们见到这些野生动物时十分欣喜。

分析：这是一则旅行评论，作者以第一人称（We approach）的口吻描述了在Fenland Trail徒步小路上的见闻和感受，从当事人、见证人角度出发，叙述真实、亲切、生动，拉近了与受众的关系。作者用"soooo many elks""amazing""appreciated"等表明这次旅行是一次愉悦的体验，用第一人称叙事则表明旅行后文本的作者身份，可信度高，更能引起其他潜在游客的注意。

例2. Take a stroll around the area whist staying in Banff. The walk consists of woodland, wetland and riverside trails. We couldn't help but marvel at the sparkling crystal clear water of the river, however, we were disappointed by the distinct lack of wildlife in the area. We saw and heard nothing, well, that was except mosquitoes. If we paused for a moment they were upon you, therefore, we kept moving. At another time of year, or with a lot more spray, maybe we would have got more out of the area.

译文：在班夫的惠斯特区逛了一圈。我们走过了林地、湿地和河边小路，禁不住惊叹于河水的清澈明净。可惜，这个地方没什么野生动物，我们对此有些失望。我们的所见所闻除了蚊子，什么也没有，如果稍停片刻，这些蚊子就会盯上你，所以只得片刻不停地往前走。若我们选择其他时间来这里，或者多喷一些驱蚊喷雾，或许能更好地领略此处的自然之美。

分析：这是一则旅行评论，作者简短地分享了自己的旅行体验。用第一人称（We approach）的口吻展开叙述。"couldn't help but marvel at"写出了作者对此处自然之美的赞叹，而"disappointed""except mosquitoes"写出了此次旅行不愉快的地方，旅行后文本作者身份可识别性明显。或许作者去那里时并不是最佳的旅游时间，野生动物少，蚊子多，这也能给其他潜在游客提个醒。

例3. Thunder frightened me. I dropped my folded pajamas on the bed, grabbed the room key dangling from its heavy antique brass bobble, and hurried out to the courtyard lobby without stopping to look for my flip-flops. The old-fashioned ceramic floor tiles felt cool and hard against my bare soles. I reached the main court of the house just in time to see razors of lightning silver the sky above into a thousand shards. For an instant, silence. And then a roaring waterfall of late monsoon rain began pouring down.

译文：我被雷声吓坏了，将叠好的睡衣扔到床上，一把抓起挂在沉重古董铜球上的钥匙，顾不上停下来找人字拖，便急忙跑到了院子大堂。脚下的老式陶瓷地砖又冰又硬。我来到院子的正堂，恰好看到闪电劈下，天空碎成了千万片。顷刻之间，一片沉寂。不一会儿，便下起了瓢泼大雨。

分析：这是一则游记，作者以第一人称 (I approach) 叙述，描写生动形象，极具画面感。"Thunder frightened me"写出了作者受到惊吓的心理，开门见山，吸引读者眼球，勾起读者的好奇。"dropped""grabbed""hurried out"几个动词生动描述了作者当时受惊的情景，读者也能从文字中感受到作者内心的惊恐与慌乱，读者带着紧张的情绪沉浸到文本里。"cool and hard""a roaring waterfall"使当时的整个情景跌宕起伏，画面也定格在此处。

例4. 站在月台上，北方的风吹过来，带来秋日森林的气息和微微的凉意。在蓝天和日光下安静又美好。虽然从小生活在丘陵区，这样的山脉和森林也是抬头不见低头见，但是大兴安岭的山林，依然有着独特的魅力，让人一见就喜欢不已。

译文：Standing at the railway platform, I was greeted by wind of the North, which brought smell of autumn forest and a little bit of coolness. Opposite to the railway line was a stretch of rolling mountains, which seemed tranquil and beautiful under the blue sky and sunlight. Although I grew up in hill area, such mountains and forests can be seen everywhere, yet the mountains and the forest of the Greater Khingan Mountain still have unique charm, which I fell in love with at the first sight.

分析：这是一则散文游记，描写了作者在月台上的所见所感，表达了对大兴安岭景色的喜爱，语言优美，具有一定文学审美价值。中文游记中没有出现作者的身份，但从描写中能看出"站在月台上""从小生活在丘陵区""一见就喜欢不已"就是作者本人，因此译文以作者视觉介入，使用第一人称"I approach"，突显了旅行后文本作者的身份。译文偏口语化,娓娓道来,亲切自然。

2. 地域性

地域文化是特定区域的生态、民俗、传统、习惯等文明表现,它在一定地域范围内与环境相融合,打上了地域的烙印,具有独特性,是吸引旅游者的重要因素之一。旅行后文本是对一次出行、游览的记录,也是对旅程中的所见所闻、独特感受的记述,旅游者(作者)的旅游轨迹表现出不同地方的旅游地理特征。这些地理特征是多方面的,既强调地质地貌的特殊性,也突出民俗风情的独特性,还展示古今建筑的民族特色与地方特色(丁大刚,2008:189)。旅行后文本承载着旅游地的地理、历史、文化和风土人情等信息,读者会从旅行后文本中感受到当地独有的地质地貌、文化传统和民族风情,因此旅行后文本一般都具有很强的地域性。

例1. The state of woman among them was also much exalted over that seen in the regions through which we had heretofore been traveling. Women seemed to be on terms of equality with the men, mixed and talked freely with them, and evidently had a share in the government.

译文:与我们之前到过的地区相比,这里的女性地位更高,似乎和男性平等。她们可以和男性自由地交谈、相处,在政府也享有一席之地。

分析:这是一则游记,主要叙述作者在阿昌族地界了解到的当地妇女社会地位的情况。"much exalted""be on terms of equality with the men""mixed and talked freely with them""evidently had a share in the government"等描述表明当地女性社会地位较高,与作者到过的很多地区情况是不一样的,体现了当地人民和政府尊重女性和男女平等的观念,旅行后文本所展示的人文地理特征明显。

例2. 花园中部有墨池一方,水榭临池巧架,池东曲廊环绕,池北古树参天。

译文:In the center of the garden lies a small ink pond, a pavilion ingeniously built nearby, a zigzagging corridor to the east, and an ancient towering tree to the north.

分析:这是一则游览苏州园林的散文游记。"墨池一方""临池巧架""曲廊环绕""古树参天",短短几个词就将花园中墨池、水榭、曲廊、古树等景观一览无遗，江南私家花园的特征十分明显。作者以"墨池"为叙述起点，将其他三者的位置与墨池联系起来，"巧架""环绕""参天"则是三者的修饰成分，译文则将其处理为"ingeniously built""zigzagging""towering"，总体风格贴近原文，突出了苏州园林的布局特点。

例3. When it was time to say farewell, I bought a large pack of biscuits for the girl and the boy to thank them for the boat ride. They were happy about it. The girl even <u>knelt down</u> in front of me and kissed my hand.

译文：临走时，我给小女孩和小男孩买了一大包饼干，感谢他们带我乘船游玩。他们对此非常开心。这个小女孩甚至<u>用当地最高的礼仪</u>跪在我面前，亲吻我的手，<u>以示感谢</u>。

分析：这是一则游记，叙述了作者在非洲旅行的一段经历。原文有一个理解难点，即"knelt down in front of me""kissed my hand"，译文增译了"用当地最高的礼仪""以示感谢"。"下跪吻手"是当地独具特色的传统习俗，表达感谢，增译后能让读者更好地了解非洲乌干达地区的风土人情，文本中的人文地理特征十分明显。

例4. 俄罗斯族是<u>一个很懂得美化居住环境的民族</u>。屋前的院子里都<u>栽种着漂亮的鲜花</u>，房间的窗台上也都<u>摆放着花盆</u>。小院里，常可以看到<u>木制的秋千</u>飘飘荡荡。小屋里面和外面总收拾得很整洁。

译文：Russian is a really nation <u>knowing how to beautify the living environment</u>. <u>In front of the house yard</u> are <u>a variety of beautiful flowers</u> and <u>on the room windows</u> are also <u>placed some flower pots</u>. <u>In the yard</u>, a wooden swing floating can be seen often. <u>Either the inside or outside</u> is always tidy and clear.

分析：这是一则游记散文，从"一个很懂得美化居住环境的民族""栽种着漂亮的鲜花""摆放着花盆""木制的秋千"等描述能看出俄罗斯人民对生活品质的追求，呈现出俄罗斯的人文地理特征。译文地点状语"In front of the house yard""on the room windows""In the yard""Either the inside or outside"等被主位化，使俄罗斯院子的整体布局这一信息被突出出来，带有明显的地理空间描写，有利于读者了解后叙的新信息，为游记后面的描述做了铺叙。

3. 知识性

旅游活动是旅游者与外界信息进行接触、认知、交流、传播的过程。亨利·杜南曾说过,旅行是真正的知识最伟大的发源地。身体和灵魂,总有一个在路上。旅行后文本的知识性与地域性密切相关。"读万卷书,行万里路。"除了对旅行所见所感的记录,旅行后文本也涉及旅游地的历史、地理、建筑、美食、民俗、节庆、歌舞、风物等各个方面的知识,这些知识有助于潜在旅游者在今后真实的旅行过程中更好地适应所处的时空环境。旅行后文本的作者对游览地当地民俗的观察和理解,可以帮助游客充实自己的人文地理和自然地理知识。

例1. 与其说"丰夏"是个大都市,不如说它是个小城镇,大半是<u>两三层楼高的欧洲风格的建筑</u>。<u>店面接着店面,一座座是半圆形的拱门</u>,挂着<u>一盏盏带玻璃罩的煤气灯</u>。木质方格子的老式橱窗,配着一座座<u>厚重殷实的刻花木门</u>,挂着<u>深黄色的铜门环</u>。古意盎然、幽暗的<u>大吊灯</u>,白天也亮,照着神秘的大厅堂。古旧的气味,弥漫在街头巷尾。城内也没有柏油路,只是石板路上没有生青苔而已。

译文:Rather than a metropolis, Funchal was a small town, over half of which were <u>European-style buildings with two- or three-stories</u>. Store were next to stores. Past the overhang were semicircle arches, hung with gaslights covered in glass. <u>Old-fashioned wooden square windows</u> were matched with <u>thick solid engraved wooden door</u>, which hung with <u>dark yellow bronze door knocker</u>. Gloomy chandeliers, full of ancient charm, were lighted in the days and lit up the mysterious large hall. The smell of antiquity permeated the streets and lanes. The city had no tarred road, just stone roads without moss.

分析:这是一则游记,作者从个人视角对"丰夏"这座古城的建筑风格、氛围进行了描述,让读者对"丰夏"这个城市有了初步的了解。这则游记文笔细腻,极具文学价值和美学价值。其中涉及一些建筑方面的词汇表达,如"两三层楼高的欧洲风格的建筑""半圆形的拱门""一盏盏带玻璃罩的煤气灯""老式橱窗""厚重殷实的刻花木门""深黄色的铜门环"等描写,呈现出城市的古香古色,体现了旅行后文本知识性的特点,可能帮助读者了解当地的建筑。中文重"意象",英文重"形象",译文用名词词组罗列形象描写古城建筑,如

"European-style buildings with two- or three-stories" "Old-fashioned wooden square windows" "thick solid engraved wooden door",让外国读者尽可能按照自己的认知和审美方式体验"丰夏"建筑之美。

例2. In the morning, I drove on to St. David's, on the westernmost point of the Welsh mainland, above the rolling surf and crashing waves of St. Brides Bay. St. David's boast is that it is Britain's smallest city, which is really just another way of saying that it is the smallest place that has a cathedral. By any other measure, it's a village, but an adorable one, on a hill a little inland from the sea. It is very pretty and prosperous, with a butcher's, a National Trust shop, a tiny bookshop, several cafés.

译文：早上，我开车前往圣戴维。圣戴维位于威尔士的最西端，建在海浪翻滚冲击的圣柏瑞德斯海湾（St. Brides Bay）上。圣戴维值得夸赞的原因是它是英国最小的城市，也就是说此处是有大教堂的最小的地方。用另一种方式衡量，这里是一座村庄，但是这座村庄很可爱，在离海不远的一座小山上。这里很美，也很繁华，有一家肉店、一家国家信托商店、一家小书店、几家咖啡馆。

分析：这是一则游记散文，其中涉及一些人文地理知识，具有旅行后文本知识性的特点，"on the westernmost point of the Welsh mainland" "above the rolling surf and crashing waves of St. Brides Bay"等介绍了圣戴维的地理位置；而"... it is Britain's smallest city" "...it is the smallest place that has a cathedral"等对圣戴维的人文地理做了介绍，增加了游客对旅游目的地旅游自然环境和人文环境的认识。

例3. The suspended temple is spectacular from a distance. It consists of 40 cave rooms carved into limestone, fronted with wooden facades, columns, and tiled roofs, all connected by a series of catwalks and bridges perched on jutting beams and posts socketed into solid rock.

译文：从远处看，这座悬空寺让人叹为观止。寺庙有40个嵌入岩石的洞穴，前方是木质外墙、柱子和青瓦盖的屋顶，由一些狭窄过道和木桥连接起来，这些窄过道和木桥搭在嵌在坚硬岩石里突起的梁木和柱子上。

分析：这是一则游记，是对悬空寺的描述，涉及一些建筑学相关的词汇，如"cave rooms" "wooden facades" "columns" "tiled roofs" "catwalks" "bridges""jutting beams""posts"等，介绍了悬空寺的建筑特点，体现了旅行后文本知识性的特征。在句法方面，作者用过去分词短语作定语，如"carved into...""fronted with...""connected by...""perched on..."，简化了句子结构，利于读者了解寺庙的建筑构造。

例4. We were only planning to stay a couple of days in the small town of Dali and ended up staying for four days. Dali is <u>a very old town</u> where the first settlements are <u>dated from 3,000 years ago</u>. <u>Located at 1,900m high</u>, <u>near the lake Erhai</u>, the town is <u>surrounded by mountains up to 4,000m high</u>. It just an awesome place and you can judge by yourself when looking at the photos we took.

译文：我们本打算在大理这个小镇待几天，最终待了四天。大理是<u>一座古镇</u>，历史悠久，这里最早的定居点可以<u>追溯到3000年前</u>，<u>海拔1900米</u>，<u>靠近洱海</u>，<u>四面高山环绕</u>，<u>这些山高达4000米</u>。大理是<u>一个诗情画意的地方</u>，在欣赏我们拍的照片时，你可以给出自己的答案。

分析：这是一则旅游博客，简单介绍了大理这座古镇的历史、地理位置和地貌，把它描写成"一个诗情画意的地方"。"a very old town""dated from 3,000 years ago"说明了大理悠久的历史。"Located at 1,900m high""near the lake Erhai"等地点状语主位化，突出了大理古镇的位置。"surrounded by mountains up to 4,000m high"描写了大理的地理环境，所有这些都体现了大理的自然风貌和人文气息。

4. 文学性

一些旅行后文本，如旅行见闻、游记、博客等，会以偏散文化的手法撰写，以散文形式记写游踪、描摹景观、议论旅行游览中的所见所闻，寄情于山水之间，抒发个人情感，体现作品的文学性。与普通的景点介绍、导游词相比，旅行后文本，特别是游记散文更灵动，更富有感情色彩，处处彰显着旅游地的自然美、人文美、生活美。语言美、文辞美、意境美成为游记散文的一大特色，也因此而常被称为"美文"。汉语旅行后文本常寓情于景，以达到诗情画意的"朦胧美""意境美"；英语则通过罗列客观的具象来表达实实在在的景物，追求的是

"简约美""自然美"。因此,旅行后文本的英汉互译要尽量做到原文与译文在形象与意象、具体与抽象、动与静之间的有效转换,呈现不同语言的文学性。

例1. Every moment they are furrowed by vivid lightning. The rain—icy rain—lashes and smites us. At intervals the thunder mingles its formidable voice in a thousand ominous sounds.

译文:每时每刻,它们被闪电划破,留下几道明晃晃的印记。冰冷的雨狠狠地打在我们身上。时不时地,一千种不祥的声音交织在一起,形成了雷电那令人畏惧的声响。

分析:该文是旅行后文本中的游记,是主人公对出海时分的情景描写。作者以第一人称的口吻记录了雷雨天气的景致,仿佛读者身临其境一般,能够感受到出海时阴晴难测的不易与艰辛。原文使用非人称主语,通过客观的具象"lighting""rain""thunder"等描写雷雨交加的场景,颇有"白描"的写作手法,体现了英语重客观写实的"简约美"。汉语旅游景观描写多寓情于景,客观景物与主观情感融为一体,使用渲染性的词汇描写景物。译文用似人修辞,使用具有主观感情色彩的形容词"明晃晃的",副词"狠狠地";用对比修辞手法,如"每时每刻……""时不时地……",体现了中文旅行后文本浓郁的文学色彩,引发读者的共鸣。

例2. 攀援而登,箕踞而遨,则凡数州之土壤,皆在衽席之下。其高下之势,岈然洼然,若垤若穴,尺寸千里,攒蹙累积,莫得遁隐。萦青缭白,外与天际,四望如一。

译文:After struggling to the top we squatted down to rest. The fields of several districts lay spread below my seat. There were undulating slopes with gaps and hollows, as well as mounds and burrows. A thousand *li* appeared like one foot or one inch, so compact that nothing escaped our sight. Encompassed by white clouds and azure sky, the hill merged with them into one single whole.

分析:作者一路攀登,居高望远,山丘宛若"坑洼",反衬西山之巍峨,远近风景,尽收眼底,一览无余。为了突出"萦""缭"景象,作者有意把"主谓式"变为"动宾式",并用比喻、对比、反衬、夸张等修辞手法描写登顶风景,情景交融，意境相谐。译文则按西方人士的审美，使用名词和名词词组罗列物象，如"gaps and hollows""mounds and burrows"，呈现或临摹西山自然景观，没有像汉语那样抒发强烈的个人情感。原文中的古汉语是意合文体，高度依赖上下文，英译时译者进行了必要的语法性增译，使用"After""as well as""so"等连接词，体现了英文形合句的逻辑美。对比原文和译文，汉语辞藻华丽；译文用词简洁，形象具体。

例3. Light seeped dimly to the berth, and the sounds of the wind in the rigging and the rhythmic crash of the sea were almost as nerve-spasm as the constant jerk and tumble of the hull.

译文：灯光昏暗朦胧，从泊位处映射出来。绳索在风中摇曳，海浪有节奏地碰撞，发出声响。这些跟船体持续不断的颠簸与摇晃一样，让人心烦意乱。

分析：该文是作者在一整天忙碌的航海旅途之后对夜景的描写。英文为一个独立句子，由"and"连接，语义连贯，逻辑清晰。汉译时，译者将其切分成四个意象句，把灯光、绳索、海浪、船分别以小句的形式展现出来，化英文之"形象"为汉语之"意象"，体现了汉语的意合性。原文中的英语是静态语言，如"sounds were as...as..."是典型的主系表描述性句型，汉译将其拆分开来，译成动态的多个小句，用兼动和联动手法，化静为动，使用"昏暗""摇曳""碰撞""颠簸""摇晃"等带有负面情绪的词语，烘托出"让人心烦意乱"的情绪，寓景于情，文学色彩很浓。

例4. 悠悠乎与颢气俱，而莫得其涯；洋洋乎与造物者游，而不知其所穷。饮觞满酌，颓然就醉，不知日之入。苍然暮色，自远而至，至无所见，而犹不欲归。心凝形释，与万化冥合。

译文：I felt I was mingling freely with the boundless expanse of heaven, and lost myself in the infinity of nature. In utter content I filled my cup and got drunk, unaware that the sun had set. Dark night came from afar and soon nothing could be seen, yet still I was loath to leave; for my heart seemed to have ceased beating and I felt released from my body to blend with the myriad forms of created things.

分析：中文为典型的中国文言文，具有中国古典文学的形式美、音韵美，如

"悠悠乎""洋洋乎",读起来朗朗上口,富有美感,给读者传达出一幅朦胧缥缈的意象。这些词语对于中国读者极具文学感染力,但由于中西方审美的差异,外国游客却很难理解。英译时,译者化虚为实,客观、真实地呈现了自然景观,具有临摹、素描的写作特点。如原文"苍然暮色,自远而至,至无所见,而犹不欲归"表达出作者被美景吸引、流连忘返的心境;译文则仅用"came from afar"三个词表现出暮色由远及近的场景,用"loath"一词便是体现了作者对自然风景的喜爱与不舍。又如,译者用"mingle with..."一词写出了作者与自然融为一体的愿景;而"boundless expanse of heaven"以及"infinity of nature"分别与"涯"和"穷"对应,自然之景,恢宏气势,跃然纸上,体现了英美文学的写作特点。

三、旅行后文本的翻译

中国人在撰写旅行后文本时,注重以主观的感觉和好恶为判断标准,常运用具象思维使概念生动,从而产生联想意义。中文"意在言外""意出言表",注重语言背后的"象"和"意",将意象看得比语言本身更重要(余静娴,2014:57)。中文思维具有主观性,常用主动式、意念被动句和人称主语表达法,从自我出发来叙述客观事物;而西方注重客观描述和理性判断,以景物的实际景观和价值为取舍标准,通过近于白描的手法,较为客观地描写景物事物。非人称表达在旅行后文本中较普遍,常使用被动句,以较为理性的口吻表达客观事实(康春杰,陈萌,吕春敏,2016:328),语言规范,文风质朴,逻辑性强,文理清晰,多复杂长难句(张文英,张晔,2015:280)。

此外,英语常采用动词名物化、分词化,动词同源形容词表达动词意义;善用名词、形容词、介词,有时甚至占主导地位(杨莉等,2020:133);英语忌讳重复,常用代词或其他手段来代替需要重复的词语。在句子结构上,英语以主语和谓语为核心,利用显性连接词、屈折词缀等手段来连接句子,形成"树杈形"句式结构(涂靖,2016:13);一个完整的英语句子中一般只有一个谓语动词,其他动词多作非谓语形式处理;而汉语善用动词,动词重复或叠加,形成连动式或兼语式句子;一个句子会出现多个动词,连词成句、行为铺排,不求句法形式完备，依赖顿悟式理解句段之间的隐性衔接（杨元刚，2008：257）。

总体上讲，中国人注重悟性，重直观经验、顿悟和整体综合，带有模糊性思维，具有典型性艺术家素质（连淑能，2010：340）；西方人重逻辑推理，从某一角度考察事件本质，演绎推理出最终的结果，具有演绎型思维，具有典型性科学家素质（张善城，许共城，1994：205）。英语偏"客观"，汉语偏"主观"；英语偏"静态"，汉语偏"动态"；英语"形合"，汉语"意合"；英语"简约"，汉语"华美"。翻译旅行后文本应注意这些差异，在"形象"与"意象"、"简约"与"华美"、"静态"与"动态"之间进行合理转换，可采用词语转换、句型转换、语义引申、语义整合等翻译方法。

1. 词语转换

在中文旅行后文本中，四字格较为普遍，语音悦耳、形式整齐（黄忠廉，任东升，2014：79）；而英语重简洁、自然，忌重复、冗余。翻译中文四字词语，需删除四字格中重复的语义，多用形容词+名词代替四字格，不必全部译出。英语根据词句中所表现的"形态"判断词性，而汉语根据词的"句法功能"判断词性（祈阿红，2019：147），词语转换也包括其词性转换。汉译英，可将汉语的动词转译为英语的名词、形容词、副词、介词或介词短语，化动为静；英译汉，可将英语中的名词、形容词、副词、介词或介词短语等转换为汉语动词，化静为动。

2. 句型转换

汉语受归纳型思维的影响，强调"从多归一"的思维方式，句型结构以动词为中心，横向铺叙，层层推进，归纳总结，形成了"流水型"句型结构；多主动句，展现主观顿悟的思维特点。英语受演绎型思维的影响，强调"由一到多"的思维方式，句型结构以主谓为核心，由主导词层层叠加，结构复杂，形成"树杈形"句式结构，多被动句，展现了客观陈述的思维特点（夏增亮，2016：45）。旅行后文本的英汉互译，应根据英语"形合"和汉语"意合"的句型特点，对句子进行重构，包括主动与被动、"形合"与"意合"、"分总"与"总分"之间进行转换。

3. 语义引申

英、汉词汇既存在对应关系、包孕关系，也存在空缺关系，包括文化空缺，翻译时需要语义引申。语义引申包括语境引申和艺术引申。语境引申指的是"以原文特定的语言环境为依据，适当转换原有表达形式，译出原文的内涵意义和联想意义，译出原文的情感色彩和语气特征"（边立红，黄曙光，2016：67）。译者需分析话语产生的语言语境和心理语境，认真揣摩字里行间可能产生的情感意义，译出原作的内涵意义和联想意义。艺术引申根据词语本身的形象和特点，把握原作潜在含义，刻意传达原作所营造的神韵和意境（周文，2013：153）。由于中、英语言形式不同，译者需发挥译入语的优势，使用译入语读者喜闻乐见的语言以及比喻、拟人、排比、夸张等修辞手法，使译文产生艺术感染力。

4. 语义整合

汉语句子受阴阳逻辑制约，句子重语意，不关心结构上的完备性，只需符合阴阳对立即可；英语句子主要受形式逻辑制约，语言审美在于主、谓、宾齐全，句子成分齐全就能满足英美国家的语言心理（马秉义，2000：73）。因此，汉语句子"形散神聚"，流散铺排，自然洒脱，重整体感悟意义；英语句子结构严谨，具有严格的组织性和规范性，重逻辑推理表达意义。因此，汉译英需"以形统意"整合英文的语义；英译汉需"以意统形"整合汉语的语义，在方寸之地"左右"逢源，"流散"和"聚集"相互转换，表现出旅行后文本不同体裁的形式美、语言美、意境美。

例1. 是日也，<u>天朗气清</u>，<u>惠风和畅</u>。仰观宇宙之大，俯察品类之盛。所以游目骋怀，足以极视听之娱，信可乐也。

译文：It is such a wonderful day, with <u>fresh air</u> and <u>mild breeze</u>. Facing upwards to the blue sky, we behold the vast immensity of the universe; when <u>bowing</u> our heads <u>towards</u> the ground, we again satisfy ourselves with the diversity of species. Thereby we can refresh our views and let free our souls, with luxuriant satisfaction done to both ears and eyes. How infinite the cheer is!

分析：这是一篇脍炙人口的记叙散文。开篇记叙了集会当日的天气情况。"天朗气清""惠风和畅"为中文四字语言，用词清丽典雅，林语堂仅用"fresh air""mild breeze"两个形容词+名词短语，即传情达义，词语转换亲切自然，完美地体现了英语的简约美。名句"仰观宇宙之大，俯察品类之盛"出自《兰亭集序》，对仗工整，表现出作者的广阔视野和阔达心态，一"仰"一"俯"极具动感，林语堂将其处理为"facing upwards"和"bowing towards"，而非"looking"或"bending"，以身体部位作为动词，更能突显其动作，与原文意义贴切，且兼顾了对称的形式。汉语重意境烘托，语句高度"意合"，而英语注重逻辑衔接，因此译文添加了主语"we"，将原文中隐藏的人称代词显化出来，"以形统意"，符合英语SVO（主谓宾）句型结构；又增译了"the blue sky"和"the ground"进行语义引申，且形式对仗。文末，作者辅之以抒情，直抒胸臆，将所有的感受归化为"乐"，而林语堂将此句抽离，将原本语气平和的"也"字句转化为感叹句"How infinite the cheer is!"成功地进行了艺术引申，强化了译文的感染功能。

例2. 若夫霪雨霏霏，连月不开；阴风怒号，浊浪排空；日星隐耀，山岳潜形；商旅不行，樯倾楫摧；薄暮冥冥，虎啸猿啼。

译文：During a period of incessant rain, when a spell of bad weather continues for more than a month, when louring winds bellow angrily, tumultuous waves hurl themselves against the sky. Sun and stars hide their light. Hills and mountains disappear. Merchants have to halt in their travels. Masts collapse and oars splinter. The day darkens and the roars of tigers and howls of monkeys are heard.

分析：原文出自《岳阳楼记》，属于旅行后文本的描写型文本。全文由四字格堆砌而成，用词凝练华美，通过对岳阳楼和洞庭湖的景物描写，表达了作者的政治抱负和人生感悟。本段游记以"若夫"开头，埋下了"哀愁"的感情基调，选取"霪雨""阴风""浊浪"等意象，展现出恶劣的天气环境，再配以"隐耀的日星""潜形的山岳"等景物描写，以及被大雨耽误的商旅和破败的船楫，从天气到具体事物，层层渲染，虽无一颜色、感情用词，却展现出一副天昏地暗、朦胧不清、人心惶惶的画面，极具艺术感和朦胧美。译文对"霪雨""阴风""浊浪"的翻译，选取了"incessant""louring""tumultuous"三个具有感染力的形容词，修饰后面的名词，体现了英文"情感+形象"的文学色彩。对于恶劣的天气，译者增译了"spell"一词。该词本有"咒语"之意，用在此处仿佛天空被神灵施了咒，是恰当的语义引申，加重了哀愁、阴郁的感情色彩。游记后半部分采用数个四字格，节奏紧凑，短小精悍，"以意统形"；译文则"以形统意"，用主谓短句（简单句）译出，但又用了"hurl""hide""disappear""splinter""darken"等做谓语，表现一系列动作，使译文体现出明快有力、仓促紧凑的特点，句型转换非常成功，且保留了原文的音韵美，让人感受到游记所渲染的沉闷阴郁的色彩。译文还将"虎啸猿啼"转译为被动句，使得原文明快有力的节奏感被打破，但并不伤英文大雅；此句也可译为主动语态，译为"the tiger roars and the monkey howls"，似乎更有韵味。

例3. My spirit and my senses were heightened. I was keenly aware of the world, eager to experience it. My senses were willing to be gratified by their fullest exercise. Hence my eyes were sharp, but so were my ear and my nose, I was open to experiencing aesthetically. And on the way, I did take minor pleasure in a bird's song, a tree's sway, and a cloud's contortion.

译文：我精神抖擞，感官敏锐。我真切地感受到周围的一切，急于体验这一切，渴望在最充分的感官体验中得到最大满足。因此，我不但目光敏锐，听觉和嗅觉也十分灵敏——我敞开心扉，尽情地体验着美的滋味。沿途所见所闻，哪怕是一点儿小小的愉悦，鸟雀鸣唱，树影婆娑，云卷云舒，都着实让我动情。

分析：原文是典型的记叙型旅行后文本。作者以第一人称介入，记叙了作者登上山顶后的感受和体验。从当事人的角度叙述会更亲切自然，拉近与读者的距离，体现出旅行后文本较强的身份可识别性，使文本更具权威性、诱导性。原文一大特色是使用"无灵主语+有灵动词"主谓结构，如"my spirit and my senses were heightened""My sense were willing to...""my eyes were sharp..."句式拟人化，表达生动灵活；汉语也有此种表现方式，如"什么风把你吹来了？"相对于英文，汉语较少使用。总体上讲，英文比较客观理性，多使用非人称主语；译文没有亦步亦趋，而是转"客观"为"主观"，体现了中文"万事皆备于我"的特点，如译文将原文几个"无灵主语+有灵动词"的搭配译为偏正结构的四字格，如"精神抖擞""感官敏锐""目光敏锐"，词语、句型转换非常成功，提高了中文的审美和感染力。文末，译者对于几组名词的处理更是惟妙惟肖，分别将"a bird's song""a tree's sway""a cloud's contortion"译为中文动宾短语，如"鸟雀鸣唱""树影婆娑""云卷云舒"，化英文之"简约"为中文之"华美"，化英文之"静态"为中文之"动态"，一幅生机勃勃、生意盎然的画面跃然纸上，实现了原文与译文"简约"与"华美"、"静态"与"动态"之间的转化，突出了旅行后文本的审美功能。

例4. At the heart of the sanctuary is Loch Coruisk, fed by the cold river's waters that drain from the ridge. The water of the loch alters color, too, depending on one's angle of vision of its surface; black when you are beside it, sky-blue when you are on the peaks and ridges above it, and a caramael brown when you are in it.

译文：圣地的中心是科鲁伊斯克湖。冰冷的河水从山脊缓缓流下，滋养着科鲁伊斯克湖。湖水的颜色随着观看的角度产生变化：身处湖畔，湖水呈黑色；站在湖上方的山峰和山脉往下看，湖水呈天蓝色；置身湖中，湖水呈棕色。

分析：原文是一篇描写型散文游记。作者运用白描手法，从不同角度描写了自己看到的科鲁伊斯克湖湖水的颜色，没有使用过多的华丽辞藻和修饰，仅用三个平行结构"black when...""sky-blue when...""caramael brown when..."便勾勒出湖水不同角度呈现的色彩，体现了英文散文的用词和句型特点。游记开头将地点状语主位化，突显了科鲁伊斯克湖的地理位置，符合英文的行文特征。"fed by..."用得十分巧妙，将河流拟人化，河流如母亲般哺育着科鲁伊斯克湖，而译文译为"滋养"进行艺术引申，不可谓不妙。作者以第二人称介入，仿佛是在与读者对话，增强了游记的交际功能；译文则采用直译法，按原文的篇章结构译出，但"以意统形"，隐去了英文中的三个人称主语"you"，使用汉语排比句进行语义整合，如"身处……""站在……""置身……"，巧妙地转英文之"形合"为汉语之"意合"，且化英语之"静态"为汉语之"动态"，行云流水，甘洌回甜。

例5. 再循溪下，溪边香气袭人，则一梅亭亭正发。

译文：While I continued my walk along a stream, something fragrant greeted my nose. It came from a tall blossoming plum by the bank.

分析：中文句式结构常为"话题与说明"，依赖于语义分解，"以意统形"，此为一例。原文出自柳宗元《游黄山日记之徽州府》，以"香气"作为话题，意在突出梅花和芬芳，短短的三个小句便描写了"溪""岸""香"和"梅"。游记首句用一个"再"字暗示读者旅游的线路，句尾又用一个"则"表示强调和确认的作用，提示读者"香气"来自盛开的梅花，读者跟着作者一起可探寻梅花芬芳。英文与中文不同，常采用SVO（主谓宾）句式，依赖句子成分释义，"以形统意"，因此需对原文进行语义整合。译文把三个小句按照语义重心译为两个独立的句子，在"While"引导的状语从句中增译了第一人称"I"，以示旅行后文本的作者身份；在主句中使用非人称主语"something fragrant"，突出梅花香气袭人，句式符合英文客观、写实的行文特点。译文不仅将中文"意合"句转换为英文"形合"句，还增译了地点状语"by the bank"，与上一句"along a stream"相呼应，完整地体现原文的空间意境。两个小句之间既有主次之分，也有呼应之处。

例6. 洞庭湖衔远山，吞长江，浩浩汤汤，横无际涯。朝晖夕阴，气象万千。

译文：Carrying distant mountain in the mouth and swallowing the Yangtze River, the vast and mighty Dongting Lake stretches endlessly. It turns brilliant in the morning and gloomy at dusk. The scenery abounds in changes.

分析：原文为描写型旅行后文本，使用中文三字、四字连珠句，一"衔"一"吞"，气势连贯，体现了中文喜"动态"、重"意合"的语言特点。"浩浩汤汤，横无际涯"，使用叠字词，即言水波壮阔；"朝晖夕阴，气象万千"，概括说阴晴变化，简练生动。前四句从空间角度，后两句从时间角度，尽写洞庭湖的壮观景象，展现了中文的"音律美""意境美"。"朝晖夕阴，气象万千"描写洞庭湖的气象，具有旅行后文本知识性的特征，有利于读者、游客了解洞庭湖的天气变化，择选出游时日。但如果按照中文四字格句式译出，译文可能会词语堆砌，而且还有可能逻辑混乱。因此，译文将"衔""吞"分别处理为现在分词

"carrying""swallowing"修饰谓语"stretches"作伴随状语,而不是译为汉语的连动句,句型转换自然。

例7. 再有一次是更不能忘的奇景,那是临着一大片望不到头的草原,满开着<u>艳红</u>的小花,在青草里<u>亭亭</u>的像是万盏的小灯,阳光从褐色云里斜着过来,<u>幻成</u>一种异样的紫色,透明似的不可逼视,刹那间在我<u>迷眩</u>了的视觉中,这草田变成了……不说也罢,说来你们也是不信的!

译文:I had another <u>surreal</u> experience when I found myself amid a boundless meadow dotted with red flowers like hundreds of thousands of tiny red lanterns. The sun, which was about to set, squeezed through thick dark clouds, and enveloped the world with <u>otherworldly</u> purplish but transparent light. A <u>mirage</u> emerged, and I was left <u>dazzled</u>. All of a sudden, my surroundings were transformed into… something I'd better not reveal. You won't believe me!

分析:原文语气亲切自然,整个语篇未用显性衔接词,全凭意境和画面构成语篇。文末的一段"对话"——"不说也罢,说来你们也是不信的",恍若跳脱出文本与时空的桎梏,与读者进行了亲切的互动,让读者有一种身临其境的感觉,也体现了游记文本的作者身份,可信度高。中文游记采用了一些渲染性较强的文学词汇,如"艳红""亭亭""幻成""迷眩",使描写的景色具有虚幻空灵之感,营造出一种朦胧的"意境美"。译文采用了第一人称叙事,采用显性衔接,包括连接副词和定语从句,进行语义整合,句型转换自然、流畅。译文文字简洁、质朴,但也采用了文学性的词汇,如"surreal""mirage""dazzled""otherworldly"等,感情深厚,文学色彩浓郁,传递出作者的个人情感,让读者感受到了作者见到情景时的心境,不禁亦啧啧称奇。

例8. 梁之上有丘焉,生竹树。其石之突怒偃蹇,负土而出,争为奇状者,殆不可数。其嵚然相累而下者,若牛马之饮于溪;其冲然角列而上者,若熊罴之登于山。

译文:And beside this rose a knoll, grown over with bamboos and other trees. It had countless rocks of fantastic shapes projecting from the ground: here a chain of boulders like cattle trooping down to be watered, there crags rising sheer like bears toiling up the hill.

分析：此段为柳宗元代表作《永州八记》中第三篇《钴鉧潭西小丘记》中对于景物的描写，属于描写型旅行后文本。内容言简意赅，形式高度意合，为中国古代山水游记范文。第一句，杨宪益采用倒装句，用"grown over with bamboos and other trees"修饰主语"knoll"，是典型的英文形合句；中文第二句、第三句、第四句均为"其"引导的排比句，其中古汉语中的"者"与"之""乎""也"一样，是判断句的标志词，而译文仅用一个冒号便整合出三句话的语义，解释说明山石之形状，运用的是英文典型的"先总后分"篇章结构；"殆不可数"没有译为"I could not possibly enumerate them all"，不刻意在言辞上做过多渲染，译者只用了一个形容词"countless"，可谓将英文用词之"简约"发挥到了极致，与中文用词之"华美"形成鲜明对比。整个译文用词精练，句式规范，突显了英文散文游记的魅力。

例9. Looking down at my feet, I think I discern stars reflected in a pool of water beside the path. I peer up to confirm this impression, but there is nothing to be seen. I cannot even see through the canopy of trees. Curiosity aroused, I crouch on my hands and knees to examine the pond. I distinguish bluish pinpricks, not a metre from my face, sheltered from heavy globs of falling water by overhanging roots and earth. The mysterious blue sources of light appear to be the eyes of little fairies. I wave one hand towards them to see if they scare, but they stay motionless, unafraid. They are glow-worms, little two-centimetre critters, dangling sticky phosphorescent fishing lines to attract moths. In the silence of the gloomy damp rainforest, the unexpected apparition seems explicable as an assembly of fairies, even if I do know what they really are.

译文：低头看的时候，我发现小道边的一处水洼似乎倒映着星光。我抬头看天，但是看不到星光，在树木的遮盖下，我甚至看不到任何东西。受好奇心的驱使，我手脚并用地匍匐前行去看那个小池塘，发现了很多蓝色的小点，距离我的脸不足一米，被悬着的树根和泥土保护着而没被水滴砸中，这些神秘的蓝色小点就像是小仙女的眼睛。我向它们挥手，看看它们会不会害怕，但是它们保持不动，也不害怕。它们是蓝光萤火虫，两厘米长的小生物，正摇晃着沾着荧光素的发光器吸引飞蛾。在安静、昏暗又潮湿的雨林中，这些意想不到的小东西似乎真的是聚集在一起的小仙女，尽管我确实知道它们原本是什么东西。

分析：本篇游记文风清新自然，语言凝练隽永，描写了作者在树林里发现蓝光萤火虫时所观察到的情景。作者将萤火虫这些可爱的小生命比作小仙女，字里行间洋溢着"我"对萤火虫的喜爱之情，是作者对自然美的捕捉，体现了作者的审美情操，也给读者带来了美好的阅读体验，仿佛读者也一下子爱上了这些美丽的"蓝色小不点"。在修辞手法上，作者运用了比喻和拟人的写作手法进行艺术引申，如"The mysterious blue sources of light appear to be the eyes of little fairies.""the unexpected apparition seems explicable as an assembly of fairies"，表达作者热爱生命的感情。译者捕捉到作者这些情愫，将两句话译为"这些神秘的蓝色小点就像是小仙女的眼睛""这些意想不到的小东西似乎真的是聚集在一起的小仙女"。"小东西""小仙女"译得尤其传神，体现了游记亲切自然的语言特点。在本篇游记中，作者以第一人称叙事，处处"我"字当头，分享了自己的旅行经历和人生感悟，带有强烈的个性化色彩。在遣词造句方面，译文没有使用华丽的中文四字词语，而是使用清新隽永的语言，体现出当代游记另一类风格。由此可见，原文与译文之间是否需要从"简约"到"华美"、从"静态"到"动态"的转换，还得考量使用何种语言或文体，什么样的翻译方法更能表现原文的意境和情趣。

四、游记翻译欣赏

游记是旅行后文体中最重要的一种文体。游记，顾名思义，就是对一次出行、游览、参观、考察等的记录。"游"的含义有多种，如游历、游玩、游览、参观、访问、考察等。在古代，"记"是一种文体，分为游记和碑记（朱成广，2007：195）。游踪、风貌和观感是游记的三个基本要素。游记分为很多种，以记录行程为主的是记叙型游记；以描写景物、景观为主的是写景型游记；以抒发感情为主的是抒情型游记；通过游记来说明一个道理的，是说理型游记。但是，不论哪一种游记，都是通过对自然风光、风景名胜、城市景观、景观中的人与事进行描绘，来达到记事、抒情、说理的目的。游记一定要有"游"的记录；没有"游"，也就不会有"游记"（申玉辉，2006：174）。

旅行后文本之美，特别是游记散文之美体现在其情味、韵致、意境之美，语言朴素、自然、流畅、平实之美。与诗歌语言相比，游记可能平淡无奇，但由于经过了作者"情感的渗透、写意的磨炼"（胡显耀、李力，2009：178），其中的一个个字，必沁润着作者的心绪，宛如烟雾，轻轻地环绕，纠缠着读者的心扉，让读者充分领略其中的功夫、其中的品位以及其中精致的语言（李明，2010：105），因而有着无限的艺术之美。旅行后文本的翻译，包括游记散文的翻译，就是要以精湛的语言艺术，再现文本中的意境和情趣，表达作者的情感，再现文本中的音韵美、修辞美、篇章美。

但是，由于中西文化、历史背景不同，中、英文游记在表达意境和情趣的方法上也有所不同。汉语受儒、释、道的影响，重意念、悟性，用词华丽缥缈、虚幻空灵，善用修辞格，主观色彩浓厚，营造出一种"朦胧美""意境美"；英语受亚里士多德形式逻辑和欧洲理性主义的影响，主客分明，重写实，不刻意在言辞上做过多渲染，用词简洁，文风质朴，呈现的是一种"简约美""自然美"；汉语重"意合"，善用连动句、四字格，语言偏动态；英语重"形合"，多用连词、介词、不定式和分词结构，语言偏静态。掌握中西游记散文在语言特点、风格特征、篇章结构上的差异，对旅游散文，包括游记、旅行见闻和其他旅行后文本的翻译和评价，大有益处。

1. A Village Lunch at Weifang

Those on a day tour, as I was, can also partake of one of the most interesting lunch stops in China, in a farm house at Shijia Village, south of Weifang, where a family prepares a lavish banquet in their tiny kitchen. Our lunch consisted of mounds of jiaozi (steamed buns filled with vegetables and meats) and big bottles of local beer, served up at the kitchen table by Mr. and Mrs. Shi. Shijia Village contains all of 304 households, with a per capita income of about RMB 5,000. The village also maintains a dozen different small factories and vegetable farms. We each had to sign a temporary resident permit before the meal. The village also offers visitors overnight stays with families arranged by the Weifang CITS.

Most day Adsits also include a lively circle dance put on by the villagers, who, donning capes and costumes, stilt walk and ride stick horses around the main square. Foreigners are free to join in, and some try out the stick horses. All in all, this is one of the happier lunchtimes I've spent in China.

In the evening, Weifang conducts lavish opening ceremonies in its new Olympic-size outdoor stadium, which seats 50,000. Entertainment consists of a parade of colorful floats and marching bands, a soccer match featuring local celebrities, and a fireworks show.

An unforgetable trip in Weifang, Shandong, isn't it?

参考译文：

潍坊的乡村午餐

参加一日游的人可以像我一样，进入中国最有趣的午餐站之一，它位于潍坊南部史家村的一间农舍里。厨房虽然狭小，但一家人可以在里面准备一顿丰盛的午餐。我们的午餐是一桌子饺子（其实就是包着蔬菜和肉的馒头）以及大瓶的当地啤酒，史先生夫妻俩会把菜端到客人桌上。史家村共有304户居民，人均收入约5000元。村里还有十几家各具特色的小工厂和菜园。吃饭前，每个人都得签一份临时居住证明。该村还为游客提供由潍坊国旅安排的家庭夜宿服务。

这儿活动丰富多彩，几乎每天都有。村民围成一圈，莺歌燕舞。他们个个身着披肩，装束整齐，在广场中央表演踩高跷、骑木马。外国人可以随意加入，有些人还试骑了木马。总之，我在中国度过了一个快乐难忘的午餐时光。

晚上，潍坊举行了一场盛大的运动会开幕式。此次开幕式在潍坊一座崭新的户外体育场举行，规模足以举办奥运会，可容纳5万人。娱乐活动包括花车巡游和仪仗队表演，观看当地名人参加的足球比赛，还有一场烟火表演。

这真是一次难忘的山东潍坊之旅啊！

2. Setting Sails to Hangzhou

Suzhou is a romantic place to begin a Grand Canal cruise. Known as the "Water City of the East", Suzhou rose to prominence by shipping its silk embroidery up the canal to China's imperial courts, establishing a high reputation in the arts that it never relinquished. Square bricks from Suzhou's kilns paved the Forbidden City. An inner moat encases this city of interlaced canals; a gated outer waterway connected Suzhou to the Grand Canal.

Panmen, the old water gate in the southwest of Suzhou, consists of two sections: an inner brick gate 12 feet wide and an outer granite gate 9 feet wide. The walls between were used to entrap and inspect canal ships that called upon the city. The Panmen Water Gate is still in place, as is the nearby Wumen Bridge, one of the largest arched stone bridges on the canal and now the entryway to Suzhou's wharves. Suzhou has everywhere the marks of a Grand Canal city. The white-washed houses of Suzhou still have crimson doors that open on the inner waterways that feed the Grand Canal. You can cross more than a hundred bridges in Suzhou: arched stone bridges, ladder-shaped bridges, even house-spanning bridges (*lian jia qiao*) that connect two parts of a dwelling.

Two miles west of the city, the Grand Canal sweeps by Cold Mountain Temple, jogging inland to join Suzhou's city moat to the southeast. This is where poet Zhang Ji, arriving at the temple by canal boat during the Tang Dynasty, wrote this delicate passage:

> Moon sets and crows caw in the frosted sky,
>
> River maples and the lights of fishing boats break into my troubled sleep.
>
> Beyond Suzhou lies Cold Mountain Temple,
>
> At midnight the clang of the bell reaches the traveler's boat.

I did not hear the clear bell in the frosted sky clanging in Cold Mountain Temple as I embarked on the canal boat at Suzhou. Instead, I heard the horns of two dozen nearly identical canal boats as they backed out from the piers to begin their journeys to Hangzhou. These are not dainty vessels, outfitted to resemble the elegant dragon boats of the emperors who once sailed the Grand Canal. Nor are the modern ferries, comfortably tailored for the international tourist. They are rusty steel double-deckered passenger boats that have worked hard and long. Their deluxe staterooms are simple, crude, deteriorating closets with a set of narrow bunk beds, a nightstand, an oil heater, and a spittoon on the floor. They have windows to let in the breeze and glass doors that open directly onto the outside deck. Although the knob was missing from my door, I could still lock it from the inside. But alas, the real drawback is that these ferries cruise by night. We departed in the late afternoon, with only a few hours of daylight on either end. I tried to make the most of the light, clinging to the railing above the bow.

The city moat where we pushed off is exceedingly narrow. The ship must pivot neatly and precisely to begin the journey. I was surprised but fascinated when three of these bargelike flat-bottomed passenger ships undocked together. The vessel on our port side was the only one using its engines. The deck hands, leashing and unleashing the ropes that held the three ships together, maneuvered us into the middle of the canal so that we drifted into a staggered line. Then the crew hooked us together, end to end, using an iron pole on a swivel to lash stern to bow. My canal boat was second in line. The lead boat does all the work. We were gently towed forward, the black smoke of the first canal boat streaming back on us.

Setting sails, our boat began to voyage to Hangzhou.

参考译文：

驶向杭州

苏州是游览大运河的浪漫之地，有"东方水城"之称。当时丝绸、刺绣经运河送到宫廷后，声名鹊起，在艺术领域颇具盛名，从未逊色。紫禁城地面便是由苏州窑的方砖铺砌而成的。内护城河环绕着这座运河交错的城市，一个封闭式外水道将苏州和大运河相连。

苏州西南部的旧水门，由两个部分组成：一个内砖门，约12英尺（约3.7米）宽；一个外花岗岩门，约9英尺（约2.7米）宽。它们之间设有一墙，是用来停泊和检查到访城市的运河船只的。盘门水门至今还在,附近的乌门大桥也是运河上最大的石拱桥之一,如今是苏州码头的入口。苏州到处都是大运河城市的标志,白房子仍然有深红色的门,面对大运河的内河水道。在苏州,你可以游览一百多座桥:石拱桥、梯桥、甚至屋桥(连家桥),它们连接了住宅的两个部分。

城西两英里(约3.2公里)处,大运河穿过冷山寺,向内陆延伸,与东南的苏州护城河相连。唐代诗人张继曾乘运河船来到这里,写下了一段优美的文字:

月落乌啼霜满天,江枫渔火对愁眠。

姑苏城外寒山寺,夜半钟声到客船。

我在苏州上了船,没有听见霜天寒山寺那清脆的钟声。然而,当二十多艘几乎一模一样的运河船从码头启航前往杭州时,我听到了船只的鸣笛声。这些船只都不是特别精致,也不是为国际游客量身定制的现代渡轮,它们更像是古时曾在大运河上航行的皇家龙舟。双层钢客船早已生锈,好像已经使用了很长时间,已经有了磨损的痕迹。豪华特等房间简单破旧,只有一张狭窄的双层床、一个床头柜、一个油加热器和地板上的痰桶。玻璃门正对着外面的甲板,风从窗户透进来。虽然门把手不见了,但我还是可以从里面把门锁上。真可惜,这些渡轮是夜间航行。傍晚时分我们出发,再过几个钟头天就要黑了。我抓住船头上方的栏杆,借着暮色,努力地打探周围。

我们出发时经过的那条护城河非常狭窄,船必须小心地航行才能通过。当三艘类似驳船的平底客轮一起驶离码头时,我既惊讶,又着迷。靠左舷的那艘船是唯一使用发动机的船,甲板上的水手们把连接三艘船的绳索拉拉放放,把我们推到了运河中央,形成了交错排列的线。然后,船员又用一根装在转盘上的铁杆把两艘船钩在一起,把船尾和船头拴牢。我乘坐的船居中,领头的船包揽了所有的活儿,我们被轻轻地拖着向前走,领航船的黑烟向我们飘了过来。

我们扬帆起航,驶向杭州。

3. Temple of the Liao

It is a remarkable temple, quiet and unassuming, but survives on a scale rare in modern China. During the Liao and Jin dynasties, Huayan was the central temple of its own school of Buddhism (later known as Kegon Buddhism in Japan). Huayan Buddhism, based on the Garland Sutra, upholds the essential sameness of all things. In keeping with this doctrine, the temple in Datong takes austerity to a high level.

After my visit to the temple, I returned to the streets of Datong, where I overtook handcarts of coal pucks on their way to makeshift sidewalk ovens consisting of loose bricks. At the Hongqi Market, I bought soda pop and strawberries from a bicycle cart. Toddlers were racing around Post Office Square on electric-powered miniature army jeeps and jet fighters, their grandparents running behind them to catch up.

I next passed by the wooden gate to the Nine Dragon Screen (Jin Long Bi), the city's most famous sight—a ceramic mural 150 feet long portraying nine dragons rising from the sea in pursuit of the sun. It was created in 1392 as the spirit wall for the mansion of the provincial viceroy Zhu Gui, 13th son of the first Ming emperor, but its setting doesn't suit it (it's in a vacant lot).

I turned east down a backstreet and came out at the entrance to the old city wall. The Datong city wall is as old as the famous city wall of Xi'an. A general of the early Ming empire oversaw its construction, of stamped yellow earth, in 1372. Much of the 4-mile circumference remains, though most of it is neglected, exposed, and subject to erosion. Here, renovation is under way New stairs lead to the top of a section of the wall that has been freshly bricked in. Sections that haven't are often used by locals as storage cellars, earthen caves dug into the walls of the city.

参考译文：

辽代的寺庙

这座寺庙引人注目，万分静谧，规模庞大，如今实属罕见。辽金时期，华严是其佛教学派（后在日本称为盖根）的中心寺庙。华严宗以《加兰经》为基础，主张万物本质上的同一性。大同寺升华了这种"朴实"的理念，传承了华严宗的佛道。

参观完寺庙，我回到大同的街道上，在那里，我碰见了装煤球的手推车，在散砖堆成的行道上,朝着煤炉推去。在红旗市场,我在一推车摊买了汽水和草莓。小孩子坐在外观类似于军用吉普和喷气式战斗机的电动车里,在邮局广场上追逐打闹,后面紧跟着他们的祖父母。

我随后经过木门来到了九龙壁,这幅陶瓷壁画长150英尺(约46米),当属这座城市最为著名的景观,画中有九龙,从海里腾空而起,追风逐日。该墙建于公元1392年,当时是省督朱桂府的灵墙,他是明朝第一个皇帝的第13个儿子,但在当时,此设置不是很恰当(灵墙位于一个空旷的地段)。

我向东拐进一条后街,来到老城墙的入口处。大同城墙和西安著名的城墙一样古老。公元1372年,在明朝早期一位将军的监督之下,用黄土建造了这座宫殿。如今大部分建筑因暴露在外而受到侵蚀,但仍有一部分古迹被保存了下来。受损的部分正在翻修,新楼梯通向一面新砌成的墙的顶部。当地人把不常使用的地方作为储藏室——也就是城墙上挖出的土洞。

4. Nanjing Road to the Bund

Of course even the old Shanghai, on the west side of the river, has modernized considerably in the past few years, and this is still the place to spend the most time, largely because it has a romantic past that is still accessible. Until 1999, old Shanghai was nearly impassable, a patchwork of torn streets and detours, demolitions and new construction sites, but today downtown Shanghai no longer resembles a giant erector set dropped from the sky. Ian Buruma, writing for the *New York Times* in the mid-1990s, called Shanghai's reconstruction perhaps the greatest urban transformation since Baron Haussmann rebuilt Paris in the 19th century, much of the preliminary work, at least, has already been completed.

Shanghai is again a city to walk. I begin my explorations at Shanghai Centre, a complex of offices, apartments, and shops that are still the most prestigious business address in the city. It's located 2 miles west of the Huangpu River up Nanjing Road, Shanghai's main street. Shanghai Centre is a city within the city, a joint venture opened in 1990 that has become the emblem of the new international Shanghai. Its 472

Western-style apartments house many of the city's high-rolling foreign business people, requiring rents that used to exceed those in Tokyo, London, and New York, although recent competition has lowered prices. Inside you'll find a shopping mall, supermarket, preschool, health club, theater, exhibition hall, and plenty of pricey restaurants, lounges, and even an espresso bar. Some foreign residents scarcely venture out into the city streets, but they are missing nearly everything the city has to offer.

The length of Nanjing Road east from Shanghai Centre to the Bund promenade on the river front shows what's happened. I know the road well, having strolled it frequently since 1984, but it now looks like the main route through an entirely different city. There are plenty of new office and shopping complexes, most following the modern Western model inside and out. Within minutes I passed the massive Westgate Mall and a sidewalk arcade featuring fast-food chicken from KK Roasters, as well as pizza and cappuccino from the Gino Cafe. A Burberry of London is followed by a Nautica outlet store and finally a shop that a decade earlier would have been unthinkable anywhere on Nanjing Road, anywhere in China: a thriving Playboy Store, its bunny logo gracing a variety of upscale merchandise.

参考译文：

从南京路到外滩

当然，即使是位于长江西岸的老上海，在过去的几年里也变得极其现代化，一直以来是人们消磨时光的好去处，很大程度上是因为它有着一段浪漫的过往。直到1999年，老上海一直都几乎无法通行，街道和弯路支离破碎，拆迁场地和新的建筑工地混杂在一起，但今天，上海市中心不再像一个突兀的、巨大的建筑工地。20世纪90年代中期，伊恩·布鲁玛在《纽约时报》撰文称，上海的重建也许是自奥斯曼男爵（Baron Haussmann）在19世纪重建巴黎以来最伟大的城市转型。至少，大部分前期工作已经完成。

上海再次成为一个主打步行的城市。我的探索之旅从上海中心开始。这里是一个由办公室、公寓和商店组成的综合体，是上海最负盛名的商业地址，位于上海主干道南京路黄浦江以西2英里（约3.2公里）处。上海中心是一个合营企业，成立于1990年，好比一座城中城，如今已经成为国际化新上海的象征。它囊括472套西式公寓，可供众多阔气的外商居住，尽管最近的竞争导致价格降低了，但租金曾远超东京、伦敦和纽约的水平。这里不仅有购物中心、超市、幼儿园、健身俱乐部、剧院、展览厅，以及许多高档餐厅、会所，还有一个意式咖啡厅。一些外国居民不怎么来这里，没有享受到这座城市提供的众多福利。

南京路从上海中心往东一直延伸到外滩滨江步行街，沿途可以一览城市街景。我很熟悉这条路，自从1984年我就经常在这里散步，但现在它已然是连通各个城市的通衢广陌。这里新建了许多写字楼和购物中心，里里外外很多项目都采用的是现代西方的经营模式。仅需几分钟，便经过了巨大的梅龙镇广场（Westgate Mall）和一个人行道拱廊，拱廊上有KK Roasters的快餐鸡肉，还有Gino Café的比萨和卡布奇诺。接着是伦敦的一家巴宝莉（Burberry）专卖店，还有诺蒂卡（Nautica）专卖店，最后一家是生意红火的花花公子专卖店，其售卖的各类高档服饰上都装饰着标志性的兔子图标。这要在十年前，不管是在南京路，还是在中国其他任何地方，都是无法想象的。

本章小结

旅行后文本由旅游者自己撰写而成，通常以第一人称的口吻叙述，与他人分享自己的旅行体验，属于个性化作品，文本中多有主观性的评论和描述，作者身份可识别性高；旅行后文本通过作者的游踪描写旅游目的地的人文地理、民族风情，其地域性特征也十分明显；旅行后文本记叙旅游目的地的自然地理和人文地理，也有可能涉及当地的历史、地理、建筑、民俗、节庆、风物等，知识领域广泛，因此旅行后文本也有地域性、知识性等特征；语言美、文辞美、意境美是多数旅行后文本的一大特色，因此旅行后文本多为"美文"。旅行后文本虽为个人作品，描写的是个人旅游体验，但由于比较真实，不同于旅游广告，因此最能感染潜在的旅游者。现实中，有很多读者正是由于阅读了旅行见闻、报告、评论、游记、博客等旅行后文本，受到启发、感染，才决定前往某地旅游，也才有通过网络搜索等方式获取相关旅游目的地资料的后续行为。翻译旅行后文本需了解中、英旅游文本的语言差异和不同的审美观照,主要翻译方法有词语转换、句型转换、语义引申、语义整合等。

翻译实践

一、热身练习
翻译下文,并对译文做简要分析。

1. So, Durham Cathedral, like all great buildings of antiquity, is essentially just a giant pile of rubble held in place by two thin layers of dressed stone. But—and here is the truly remarkable thing—because that gloopy mortar was contained between two impermeable outer layers, air couldn't get to it, so it took a very long time—forty years to be precise—to dry out. As it dried, the whole structure gently settled, which meant that the cathedral masons had to build doorjambs, lintels, and other horizontal features at slightly acute angles so that they would ease over time into the correct alignments. And that's exactly what happened. After forty years of slow-motion sagging, the building settled into a position of impeccable horizontality, which it has maintained ever since. To me, that is just amazing—the idea that people would have the foresight and dedication to ensure a perfection that they themselves might never live to see.

2. 一石一径,一亭一阁,一草一木,都自然而然,没有一点儿烦琐堆砌、娇揉做作之感,或许这正契合了园主耿直的气节和脾性。

3. Qinghai Lake as it is known by the local people is a salt lake and it is the biggest lake in China. It has got also a Bird Island where many species of birds live. I love the spectacular mountain scenery and the mix of Tibetan, Mongolian, and Muslim culture. Qinghai Lake is over 3,000 meters above the sea level and the beauty of traveling to Qinghai Lake is the immense space, little population, and a bit of loneliness which is what I like to find when I travel.

4. 枕席而卧,则清泠之状<u>与目谋</u>,潺潺之声<u>与耳谋</u>,悠然而虚者<u>与神谋</u>,渊然而静者与心谋。

5. The old stone walls and small canals were nice and it reminded me a little bit of the water town I had visited near Shanghai, a good few years ago. There were lots of cute, little shops along this street and we spent a while browsing in them. I loved that there were lots of small side streets to explore. The traditional feel here was nice and so different from where I live, which is modern. It was on a wander down one of these side streets that we came to the Couple's Garden Retreat. We couldn't tell much about it from the outside, so rapid the entrance fee to see what was inside. While this place looked small and unassuming from the outside. Once we got inside and consulted the map we were a little shocked to see how big the garden was. There was lots to explore. The garden has been in existence since the Qing Dynasty, and has underwent several names, owners and transformations. It had been a private residence until 1980, when it was opened to the public. The garden and buildings are very peaceful and there weren't too many tourists there. We spent a good couple of hours and wandering around and taking it all in. The attention to detail was amazing. This place was really beautiful and incredibly well maintained.

6. 伦敦眼，如其名，是伦敦泰晤士河两岸一道道古迹中的画龙点睛之笔。虽是现代风格，却与四周的壮丽古迹出奇地融合，是旅客镜头下不可或缺的部分。

二、巩固练习

翻译下文，并对译文做简要分析。

Sunday Market in Kashi

Every cart and camel on the Silk Road seems to pour into Kashi on Sunday for one of the largest open-air markets in Asia. It's open daily, but Sundays. It is in full swing and the horse traders come into town. By dawn, the donkey carts start arriving from the desert and the mountains, converging on Aizilaiti Lu on the eastern side of the Tuman River. The larger carts and trucks carry upward of 20 people standing on their belongings. Herds of sheep, goats, cows, and horses make their way through the city to separate trading compounds. The market radiates out for a dozen blocks and is packed with farmers, merchants, and traders, as well as whatever foreign tourists and business travelers happen to be in town. The crowds are immense. I've seen estimates ranging from 50,000 to 150,000 people, all converging at the Sunday Bazaar.

I entered the market from the east, shouldering my way past the carts and animals, past large lumberyards and lovely Uygur homes with ornate columned balconies and shuttered windows lining the upper floors. Sidewalk merchants line the highway for a half mile down to the river. There are straw mats unrolled on the dusty street next to tables of pots and pans pounded out of metal. There are knives and jeweled scimitars, high sheepskin boots and long scarves, and table after table of fresh oasis melons and bagel-shaped breads. There are woven carpets, embroideries, tapestries, and clothing such as the people themselves wear: hats, scarves, veils, jackets, coats, dresses, all dyed in rainbow colors in an endless arabesque of geometric and floral patterns. Several roadside alcoves are filled with hundreds of straw brooms, hand-woven and tied. There are shoemakers stitching without machines, and barbers in belted black tunics and black wool caps trimmed in white fur at work in the shade of white umbrellas, their customers bolt-upright on plain wooden chairs waiting nervously for a close shave.

In the formal market grounds by the river, corrals hold livestock. Sheep, horses, cattle, and donkeys have their own yards. Within each arena, families or clans rope off their animals from those of competitors. Animals and people crowd together, bartering and braying and neighing, while on the periphery of these pungent pens vendors serve up hot noodles, flat breads, goat soups, milky teas, jars of yogurt, and ice cream. The ice cream is served on sticks or in bowls, kept chilled by enormous blocks of ice wrapped in cloth and delivered by pushcarts to the stands.

On the fringes of the market there are streets devoted to vegetables, hauled in from the farms in gunny sacks; to debarked, unmilled shanks of lumber, shining white; to saddles, bridles, and harnesses; to sheepskins and felt carpets draped over donkey carts;

to baskets woven from red twigs; to songbirds in cages. In the shadow of a new gallery of empty shops built by the Chinese government, there is a street of used clothing, of worn shoes and patched coats, of discards that belong in the dump. There is also a square where dogfights were once held and where occasional cockfights still break out when officials are looking the other way.

This market has met in Kashi for 1,500 years. Walking in the streets, squares, and alley arcades, I constantly brushed up against donkeys, sheep, horses, and wooden carts. The sun through the dust gives the market an ancient patina. There are con men squatting low, playing a shell game. There are old men in black, experts in horseflesh, puffing on long, thin pipes. Across the river, above the market swirl, I could see the old town of Kashi on a hillside, its square huts and houses packed together like crates, a city of unpainted mud and brick, the single color of desert sand, with no hint of the modern world east of the desert or west of the mountain snows.

三、阅读翻译

阅读下文，重点翻译下画线部分。

Forest of Lions Garden

When I first saw the private gardens of Suzhou, they looked to me like large estates consisting of pavilions and open halls, unpaved and irregular pathways, small labyrinths of walls and screens, and <u>heaps of grotesque rocks.</u>

There were few flower beds, no manicured lawns, and an absence of logical order. While I could immediately admire their quiet beauty, any deeper design or effects remained obscure. <u>A quick tour of a celebrated garden can be disappointing to an inexperienced visitor from abroad, but with a little patience a Suzhou garden opens up an entirely new vision of the world.</u>

The first Suzhou garden I ever toured was the Forest of Lions Garden at 23 Yulin Lu. It was founded in 1342 by a Buddhist monk and last owned by relatives of the renowned American architect L. M. Pei. The garden consists of four small lakes, a multitude of buildings, and random swirls of rockeries. Its elements are strange to those unaccustomed to Chinese gardens.

<u>The principles of garden landscape design in China are often the reverse of those in the West.</u> A classic Chinese garden expresses man's relation to nature, not his control over it. The symmetry and regularity we expect in a garden have been replaced by an organic, spontaneous pattern.

The Chinese garden is a manifestation of the essential (even mystical) order of nature, in all its shiftings of vitality and vista. This is the way of nature itself expressed by the garden at every turn. For this reason, the cult of the lawn never developed in China because the emphasis was always on the spirit of nature, uncultivated and various. As one Chinese critic wrote, the large lawns in an English garden, "while no doubt pleasing to a cow, could hardly engage the intellect of human beings."

Neat flower beds and trimmed hedge borders are likewise eschewed in the traditional Chinese garden, since they are too obviously artificial, too unnatural. Many human elements in the garden—the halls, verandas, and bridges are regarded as points of intersection with the natural realm rather than the interventions of a superior human hand. It is ultimately the task of the garden artist to arrange courtyard and screen, lake and path, rock and shadow organically in obedience to the rhythms and patterns of a purely natural world, heightened in a garden for human contemplation.

While Tai Hu rocks and honeycombed rockeries seem more bizarre than evocative at first, the Chinese landscape artist regards them as an essential component of nature. The Forest of Lions Garden contains the largest rocks and most elaborate rockeries of any garden in Suzhou. This garden was designed specifically to emphasize the role of mountains in nature. These miniature monoliths recall the sacred mountains of China's past and the twisted, gouged-out morphology of the quintessential Chinese landscape common to scroll paintings. Mountains are also emblems of the Way (Dao), that process of transformation and transcendence in nature that Daoist monks and hermits achieve in their quests for immortality.

It took repeated visits to Chinese gardens before I developed a feel for these rocks, which I can now contemplate with interest. The Qing Dynasty emperors Kangxi and his grandson Qianlong were far more knowledgeable in such matters: they valued the rockeries of the Forest of Lions Garden so highly that they used them as a model for those in the Summer Palace in Beijing.

The finest of the expressionistic slabs in Suzhou's Forest of Lions Garden came from nearby Lake Tai (Tai Hu). Since the Tang Dynasty (A.D. 618—907), connoisseurs have been selecting the best Tai Hu rocks for the gardens of emperors high officials, and rich estate owners. During the Song Dynasty(A.D. 960—1279), rock appreciation reached such extremes that the expense of hauling stones from Lake Tai to the capital is said to have bankrupted the empire.

The Forest of Lions Garden is open daily 8:30am to 5pm; admission is RMB 40 ($5.78).

第十章　旅游文本中的诗歌、楹联翻译

诗歌是用凝练的语言反映个人情感和社会生活,并有一定节奏和韵律的文学体裁,以诗歌作为吸引物的旅游形式被称为"诗歌旅游"(尹向东,2004:87)。中国历史悠久,旅游景点常引用诗词歌赋描写景物;山水游记、导游词等旅游文本更是热衷于运用古诗词,营造出一种诗情画意的意境。这些古诗词四言八句,形式工整,或托物言志,或寓情于景,具有强烈的个人感情色彩。中、英语言文化不同,诗歌的形式、韵律、节奏差异很大,几乎到了"不可译"的程度。关于诗歌的"不可译",路易斯·昂特迈耶(Louis Untermeyer)曾引用美国诗人罗伯特·弗罗斯特(Robert Frost)说过的一句话形象地进行了说明:"Poetry is what gets lost in translation. It is also what is lost in interpretation."("诗就是翻译中丧失的东西,也是在解读中丢失的东西。")(Untermeyer,1964:469)

楹联是中国诗歌的一种浓缩形式,是诗中的精品(黄中习,2005:100),字数相等、词性相当、结构相称、节奏相应、平仄相谐,可谓字字珠玑,在翻译和解读的过程中"丢失"的东西可能更多,难度更大,是翻译界迄今为止面临的最大的难题之一。楹联翻译不仅需要扎实的语言功底,还需要超乎常人的悟性、丰富的翻译经验以及广博的学识(叶文学,2017:159—160)。与诗歌辞赋翻译一样,楹联的翻译既可采用语义翻译,也可采用交际翻译;既可省译,也可全译;既可以诗译诗,注重形式、音韵、节奏对等,也可意译、释译、缩译。旅游文本中诗歌、楹联翻译与纯文学翻译不一样,不一定遵守中国古典诗歌翻译的"三美原则"。译与不译,如何译,主要取决于文本类型和翻译目的,是希望突显旅游文本的信息功能,还是旅游文本的呼唤功能,或是文本的美学功能。

一、诗歌、楹联在旅游文本中的作用

中文旅游文本中出现大量诗歌、楹联，或审美、或移情、或增加人文背景和历史信息，作用和功能不同。如果旅游文本中的诗歌、楹联是为了增加旅游文本的美感，增强文本的呼唤功能、审美功能，或增加人际互动，则可采用许渊冲诗歌翻译"三美"原则，尽量做到"意美""音美""形美"；如果是为了增加景点的人文背景或补充历史信息，补充、说明文本信息，则可采取意译、编译，译出主要信息或实质信息即可。

旅游文本作为一种大众化的通俗读物，主要目的就是让普通游客读懂看懂，并从中获取相关的自然、地理、文化、风俗等方面的信息（谢建平，2008：249），因此旅游文本中的诗歌、楹联翻译与纯文学中的诗歌、楹联翻译不同，不能完全以形式、格律对等为取向，而应以文本的功能为导向，重信息、重意义，兼顾形式和内容，尽量做到功能对等。旅游文本中的诗歌、楹联主要用于增补信息、呼唤诱导和移情审美，在文本中的功能和作用不同，翻译标准也不同。

1. 信息功能

中文旅游文本中的诗歌、楹联具有移情、审美的作用，使旅游文本文诗情画意，具有浓郁的人文色彩，但英文旅游文本大多重写实、求本真，注重信息的准确性、实用性。此外，中文旅游文本中的一些诗歌、楹联并不一定完全是为了移情审美，而是对景物描写进行说明或总结，增加的是文本的信息功能。在此情况下，译者也可采用"异功能"的翻译方法，将文本中的审美功能、呼唤功能转换为信息功能。

2. 呼唤功能

呼唤功能也称"诱导功能"，中文旅游文本中的诗歌、楹联大多数都有呼唤功能。在汉语旅游宣传材料中，作者喜欢用诗歌、楹联或名人名言等来点缀行文，增加当地景点的文化底蕴，以此激发游客参观景点的兴趣。中、英文旅游文本中的诗歌、楹联也有相似之处，如使用比喻、拟人、排比等修辞格，使用具有积极意义的形容词，使文本产生诱导作用，但中文旅游文本更善用修辞格，辞藻华美，文本的呼唤功能比英文更强。

3. 美学功能

中文旅游文本大量运用诗歌、楹联，形成了中文旅游文本的风格特色，借助这些中国特有的文化烘托出一种"诗情画意"或历史氛围，主观色彩非常浓厚。英文景物描写侧重完美再现客观事物，以不妨碍真实情景、再现事实为限，表达客观具体，没有汉语那么强烈的主观情感色彩，旅游文本中很少出现诗歌、楹联。中文诗歌、楹联追求的是一种"意象美"，英文诗歌更多体现的是一种"自然美"，诗歌、楹联英译应符合英文读者的审美需求。

例1. 水水山山处处明明秀秀，晴晴雨雨时时好好奇奇。

译文：With waters and hills, every place looks bright and beautiful; Rain or shine, every moment appears pleasant and wonderful.

分析：这是西湖的一则楹联，被誉为西湖第一奇联。原句上下联各用五组叠字成句，相互对仗。最妙之处还在于该联使用了回文的修辞手法，字词位置不变，从末尾至开头又是一副可以诵读的楹联，这是中文特有的语音和词汇特点，翻译时很难将这一形式表现出来。译文采用意译法，在内容上反映了该楹联的原意；同时也尽量模仿原句的结构，押尾韵，突显了文本的美学功能。

例2. 桥面的西半边属于满城的范围，桥面的东半边属于大城的范围。清人的《竹枝词》曾对此有过颇有微词的形容："右半边桥作妾观，左半边桥当郎看。筑城桥上水流下，同一桥身见面难。"

The west half of the bridge was under the jurisdiction of Manchu City, while the eastern half of the bridge was part of the larger city. One Qing author expressed his discontent with the layout in a *Bamboo Branch Verse*：" A woman gazes from the right side, a man looks back from the left side. With a fort above and a river below, the lovers cannot meet with a sigh."

分析：该诗出自清代诗人杨燮《锦城竹枝词》，描写了晚清成都满城水关（即半边桥）的独特景象以及半边桥上一对男女近在咫尺却不能相见的郎情妾意。译文在传递原文信息的同时,在形式、节奏和韵律上与原诗保持了一致。译文句子长度控制在7—8个字,与原文七字句看齐,力争做到"齐言";"右半边"对"左半边"("from the right side" vs "from the other side");"妾"对"郎"("a woman" vs "a man"),"上"对"下"("above" vs "below"),句式对仗工整;翻译"观""看""见"时,特选用英文单音节动词"gaze""look""meet",节奏明快,朗朗上口,与原文平仄相交的节奏有异曲同工之妙,也反映了原诗"顿"的节奏;一二四行与原诗一样押尾韵,韵律十足。

例3. 名城首受降实可知扶桑试剑富士扬鞭还输一着,胜地倍生色应推倒铜柱记功燕然勒石独有千秋。

译文:Our accepting Japanese aggressors' surrender here marks the complete failure of war of aggression launched by Japanese militarists; The historical event gives added significance to Zhijiang and is worth inscribing on stone tablet for permanent remembrance.

分析:此联为怀化芷江和平公园的受降纪念坊的两副对联中的一副。"燕然勒石"指的是东汉著名史学家、文学家班固随大将军窦宪出征匈奴的故事,对联用典,译成英文需要较长的篇幅才能解释清楚,用有限的字数译成英文对联更是难上加难。因此,译文重在原文信息的传递,旨在突出文本的信息功能,采取了编译的手法。

例4. "借得西湖水一圜,更移阳朔七堆山;堤边添上丝丝柳,画幅长留天地间。"叶剑英委员长的诗句高度浓缩了星湖的万种风情。

译文:A poem written by Ye Jianying sums up the appeal of the Star Lake. It says: with waters borrowed from the West lake, seven hills transferred from Yangshuo, what an exact depiction!

分析:译者调整了诗句的语序,将原文蕴含的文化信息进行了重组,介绍了肇庆星湖的魅力。前两句全译,体现了美学功能;后两句采用释译法,译为"what an exact depiction!"概括了"堤边添上丝丝柳,画幅长留天地间"所描写的诗意。第一种译法呈现了文本的美学功能;第二种译法呈现文本的信息功能,

第十章　旅游文本中的诗歌、楹联翻译

两种译法相得益彰，既体现了中文旅游文本的特点，又避免译文过分"诗情画意"，造成读者理解障碍。

例5. 慕才亭楹联：湖山此地曾埋玉，花月其人可铸金。

译文：Here the jade was buried around the lake and hill; Where the beauty was cast into a gold statue.

分析：上联从景入手，湖山虽美，佳人如玉，"埋玉"在此，使湖山增色；下联"铸金"出自《吴越春秋·勾践》，以越王勾践铸范蠡金像于座侧来感念其平吴之功，意谓苏小小虽为花月中人，但品格高洁，以金铸其像也无不可。译文力图重现原句的形式美，在语言方面尽量做到短小精悍；在形式方面尽量做到对仗；在节奏方面尽量做到节奏轻快鲜明，突显楹联的美学功能。

例6. 乐山水光山色独特，地理环境优越，素有"绿杨夹岸水平铺"之称，举行龙舟竞渡得天独厚。

译文：Famous for its "tranquil river fringed with rich vegetation", Leshan in Sichuan Province has the ideal setting for its Dragon Boat Festival.

分析：该诗句出自清代诗人李嗣沆《五桥杂咏诗》："垂杨夹岸水平铺，点缀春光好画图。烟火万家人上下，风光应不让西湖。"中文景点介绍引用该诗句为之增色，其实也就是表达乐山"水光山色独特，地理环境优越"之意。由于诗句与原文前半句意义重合，有两种处理方法：一是省译诗句，译出前半句的描写；二是译出诗句大意，呈现文本的信息功能，而非其美学功能。总之不必全文照译。

例7. 峰峦或再有飞来坐山门老等；泉水已渐生暖意放笑脸相迎。

译文：Let us sit and wait upon the threshold, where we shall see another peak flying from afar; Let us welcome a spring with a smile as the snow melts and the brook starts to flow once more.

分析：此句来自灵隐寺天王殿正门楹柱的对联，共24个字，以弥勒菩萨的口吻讲述了飞来峰和冷泉亭的故事。上联写或许会再飞来一座灵峰，所以"坐山门老等"；下联写因为冷泉已渐生暖意，所以"放笑脸相迎"。楹联情景契合，诙谐幽默，对仗工整。译文使用了两个排比句，"Let us sit and wait upon the threshold..." "Let us welcome a spring with a smile..."；断句也恰到好处，将上联和下联拆分为两个结构相似的形合句，用连接副词"where""as"衔接，基本上做到了"内容相关""对仗工整"，突显了楹联的美学功能。

例8. 成都著名文士刘师亮有《竹枝词》写道："聚丰餐馆设中西，布置精良食品齐。偷向玻璃窗内望，何人依桌醉如泥？"

译文：Famous Sichuanese scholar Liu Shiliang composed a Bamboo Branch Verse to describe it: "Jufeng Garden is where China meets the West, all the finest fares are perfectly prepared. Through the glass window, I try to peer, who is leaning on the table drunken here?"

分析：从节奏和韵律上来看，原文是一首打油诗。译文第一句"West"与"prepared"押辅韵，两者虽有清音和浊音的区别，但读起来也别有韵律感；第二句中"peer"和"here"押[ə(r)]韵，且"finest fares"和"perfectly prepared"押头韵，完美地呈现了英美诗歌的韵律；原诗第一小句的重音在"设"字，第二小句在"齐"，第三小句在"望"，第四小句在"醉"，译文每一小句的重心都与原文一一对应，即"meet""prepared""peer""drunken"，呈现了原诗的节奏，即呈现了中文诗歌中的"顿"或"逗"（中国古典诗歌一般由两个音节组成"顿"，其中最显著的那个"顿"被称为"逗"。一句诗须有一个"逗"，"逗"把诗句分成前后两半）。此外，译文把每一小句的字数控制在7—8个英语单词，形成两个相似的句长，基本上做到了"齐言"。这首诗的翻译，无论是韵律、节奏、齐言，都呈现了诗歌的美学功能。

二、诗歌、楹联的翻译策略

中文旅游文本中使用大量国人耳熟能详的诗歌、楹联，以增加文本的知识、权威和人文色彩。恰当使用与景点特点相匹配的诗歌、楹联，能够补充旅游景点内容，增添旅游地的文化气息。但是由于中外游客在文化、思维、认知、语言等方面存在差异，中文旅游文本中的诗歌、楹联无法在英文中找到对应的表达，因此翻译这些诗歌、楹联时很难做到在语言、形式、节奏、韵律上对等。再者，旅

第十章 旅游文本中的诗歌、楹联翻译

游文本的读者是普通游客,因此旅游文本中诗歌、楹联的翻译应有别于纯文学中的诗歌、楹联的翻译。在多数情况下,首先是传递旅游文本中的信息,其次是呈现其美学功能,能两者兼顾更好。

旅游文本中的诗歌、楹联翻译根据文本功能和翻译目的可采用语义翻译策略或交际翻译策略。语义翻译注重原文与译文在内容、语言、形式、音律、风格等方面的动态对等,力争表现原文确切的语义,尽可能地贴近原文的词汇和语法结构,再现原文的"意美""音美""形美",多用直译法;交际翻译用符合译语规范和文化标准的语言形式来传递原文的意义,关注的重点是译文要在目的语读者身上产生最佳的阅读反应,多用意译法。旅游文本中的中国诗歌、楹联英译,无论是表情,还是达意,主要采用交际翻译策略。过于"忠实"原文,将"没有实质意义的"信息全文译出,反而会影响旅游景点信息的传递(张美芳,2004:98)。

例1. 水映山容,使山容益添秀媚;山清水秀,使水更显柔情。有诗云:"<u>岸上湖中各自奇,山舣水酌两皆宜,只言游舫浑如画,身在画中元不知</u>。"

译文:The hills overshadow the lake, and the lake reflects the hills. They are in perfect harmony, and more beautiful than a picture.

分析:译文与原文变化很大,原来的诗句不复存在。译文对诗句进行解释性的翻译,采取交际翻译策略,使之成为一句白描。虽然译文篇幅大大缩短,但仍然能够将水天一色的景观呈现在游客面前。由此可见,旅游文本中的诗歌翻译与纯文学翻译不同,可省译或意译,传情达意即可。

例2. "<u>寺前有冷泉,飞来峰诸胜</u>。"据说苏东坡守杭时,常携诗友来此游览,并曾在冷泉上"画扇判案"。

译文:...It is said that the Northern Song Dynasty poet Su Dongpo when he served as governor of Hangzhou, used to go to the temple with his friends and subordinates for a visit. And he is said to have handled a court case in the Cold Spring for the owner of a fan shop, for Su was a famous painter, calligrapher as well as a poet.

分析:原文虽引用诗句,但仍然是信息型文本,讲的是苏东坡携友到冷泉、飞来峰游玩以及"画扇判案"的故事,"寺前有冷泉,飞来峰诸胜"这句诗在文

中的美学功能不强，又未增强原文的信息功能，因此译文采取交际翻译策略，省译了诗句，但不影响"画扇判案"的叙事。

例3. 自古以来，无数诗人对泰山日出都有过生动的描述。宋代诗人梅圣俞题诗一首："晨登日观峰，海水黄金熔。浴出车轮光，随天行无踪。"

译文：Since ancient times, countless poets have vividly described the sunrise on Mount Taishan. Mei Shengyu, a famous poet of the Song Dynasty, wrote a poem, "I climbed to the Riguan Peak, or Sunrise-viewing Peak, to watch the sunrise in the morning. What a magnificent view to see the rising sun gilding the sea!"

分析：原文选自介绍泰山的一篇导游词，引用了一首五言诗。结合本篇旅游文本的语篇来看，前面讲到很多诗人赞美泰山，随后就引用了一首诗进行举证，属于信息性增补，因此只译出全诗的大概内容即可。从格律、节奏、音韵来看，译文都不是诗歌，更像是记叙文，突显的是诗中的信息，但使用了祈使句，因而带有较强的呼唤功能，采取的是交际翻译策略。

例4. 几百年人家无非积善，第一等好事只是读书。

译文：A time-honored family of wealth is built on nothing but accumulating charity; The best of all things in the world lies in nothing but reading books.

分析：上联"几百年人家"与下联"第一等好事"对仗，采用名词词组相对应，译文则采用"a time-honored family of wealth"和"the best of all things in the world"两个英文词组与之相对应；"accumulating charity"和"reading books"与"积善"和"读书"相对应；"nothing but"双重否定结构与原文"无非"和"只是"语气、结构也基本一致。译文采用语义翻译策略，全文译出，基本上做到了内容与形式上的对等，楹联的意境美和形式美都表现出来，是楹联翻译的佳作。

例5. 人日游草堂的习俗来源于清代学者何绍基的对联："锦水春风公占却，草堂人日我归来。"

译文：The custom of paying a visit to Du Fu's Thatched Cottage on the Renri (the seventh day of the first lunar month) originated from the couplet written by scholar He Shaoji of the Qing Dynasty:

You enjoy the spring breeze over the Jinjiang River,

I come back to visit on the seventh day of New Year.

分析：此联为清咸丰年间，时任四川学政的何绍基书写的一副对联。译者将"人日"释译为"the seventh day of the first lunar month"，清除了跨文化交际障碍，采取的是交际翻译策略；第一人称"I approach"和第二人称"You approach"交替使用，形式对仗，押尾韵，尽量接近原文的风格和体例，审美、移情功能都很强。

例6. 花径公园是庐山旅游景点的一颗明珠，唐朝大诗人白居易在此游览时曾写下："人间四月芳菲尽，山寺桃花始盛开。长恨春归无觅处，不知转入此中来。"园内有白居易堂、觅春园、孔雀馆等参观项目，是集山水、人文、古代、现代为一体的综合性公园。

译文：The Floral Path Park is a pearl among Mt. Lushan's scenic areas. Bai Juyi, a famous poet of the Tang Dynasty, after visiting the path, wrote a famous poem: <u>In April all the flowers are withered. But the peach flowers near the mountain temples are in full bloom. Long regretting that spring has passed. Surprised, I see that spring reappears here</u>. It is a comprehensive park with hills and waters centuries of ancient and modern times concentrated.

分析：如果单从诗歌翻译的角度来看，这句诗全译无可厚非，但具体从旅游文本中的诗歌翻译策略和方法来看，是否需要全译就值得商榷了。一方面，此诗内容与景点描写关联性不强；另一方面，作为旅游景点的附加信息，此诗的信息功能也不强，故大可不必全文译出。从"三美"角度来看，此诗的翻译难度较大，译文也没有达到"意美""音美""形美"，文本的美学功能也没有体现，"译"不如"不译"，如果非要译出，可采取交际翻译策略，用翻译的方法译出。

例7. 望江公园得名于建于清代的，也是清代成都的最高建筑望江楼，而望江楼的本名是崇丽阁，并不叫望江楼。崇丽阁得名于晋代著名文学家左思《蜀都赋》中的名句："既丽且崇，实号成都。"本来是既有诗意，又喻寄托，是一个很不错的名字，可是为什么成都人都不叫它崇丽阁，而要叫望江楼呢？我以为并不是成都人缺乏诗意，而是因为那个"江"字和江上的那个"望"字。

译文：Wangjiang Park is named after the Wangjiang Tower, the highest building constructed in Chengdu in the Qing Dynasty. The tower was originally called Chongli (meaning lofty and pretty) Pavilion, deriving from the text that "beautiful and lofty, it is hailed as Chengdu" in Zuo Si's *Shu Capital Rhapsody*. Chongli is not only a poetic name but also embodies the aspiration for a better life. Why was it changed to Wangjiang (literally overlooking the river) Tower? I don't think it is because Chengdu people are not fanciful, but because they want to look far beyond the river.

分析：原文出自文学家左思的《蜀都赋》，译文采取语义翻译策略，根据原文的语序和结构，将两个并列的形容词"beautiful and lofty"放在句首，突显文本中成都"丽"和"崇"的美学功能，句式对仗，句意十足，增强了辞赋的美学功能。

例8. 特别是在抗日战争时期（为了躲避日本空军的轰炸，1939—1943年迁到新繁龙藏寺办学），蜀中进步人士将其称为"四川陕北公学"，成都流传着"要革命，读协进；要救国，到陕北"的顺口溜。

译文：To avoid bombings during the War of Resistance against Japanese Aggression, the school moved to a more remote area of the city, holding classes in Xinfan Town's Longcang Temple from 1939 to 1943. Particularly during this period, progressives in Sichuan referred to the school as "Sichuan Shanbei School" (i.e. the Northern Shaanxi School of Politics and Law), and those in Chengdu would recite this rhythmic chant: "To join the revolution, study at Xiejin; to save the nation, go to Shanbei."

分析：此文出现地名、专用名词等，如"抗日战争""龙藏寺""四川陕北公学"以及"要革命，读协进；要救国，到陕北"的顺口溜。翻译顺口溜，译文采取语义翻译策略，注重结构和韵律的对等，并运用不定式加强语气，读起来朗朗上口，体现了楹联、俗语、顺口溜的形式美、节奏美、音韵美。

例9. 正门匾额"草堂"二字，是清代康熙皇帝的第十七子、雍正皇帝的弟弟果亲王所书。"万里桥西宅，百花潭北庄"这副对联是杜甫诗句。

译文：Over the Front Gate is a horizontal board with two Chinese characters 草堂 (Cao Tang) written by Prince Guo, the seventeenth son of Emperor Kangxi and the younger brother of Emperor Yongzheng of the Qing Dynasty. The couplet "To the west of Wanli Bridge; To the north of Baihua Pond" is taken from a poem composed by Du Fu.

分析：这首楹联出自成都杜甫草堂正门，讲的是杜甫草堂的地理位置正好位于万里桥的西边，百花潭的北边。译文采取语义翻译策略，对仗工整，"west"对"north"；"bridge"对"pond"，内容和形式与原文对等，信息功能和美学功能都很强。

从以上译例可以看出，中、英在语言、审美方面存在巨大的差异，很难做到内容、形式、节奏、格律完全对等。形式上，英文单词长短不一，音节多寡不定，因而造成英文诗歌句式长短不一（邓乔彬，2013：96）；中国古典诗歌对仗工整，依靠规范的整齐性建构语篇，重视"齐言"，每行字数都有规定，格律诗分为二言、三言、四言、七言等。节奏上，英文诗歌节奏建立在轻重音节上，即在音步中有规律地配置，形成抑扬、扬抑、抑抑扬、扬抑抑等格律（刘新民，2006：185）；而汉字是单音节字，一般由两个音节组合成"顿"，在"顿"中确定一个"逗"，逗把诗句分成前后两半，且"平仄递用"，即平声的长调与仄声的短调交替使用（王力，1979：6）。在韵律方面，英语诗歌有阳韵、阴韵之分，押头韵、腹韵、尾韵，诗律由长短音交替或轻重音间隔构成。中文诗歌则既可押同步平声韵，又可押相邻相近异步平声韵；既可一韵到底，也可以换韵（韩陈其，1995：320）。中、英诗歌互译，因需兼顾形式、节奏、格律，在内容上必须有所取舍；在翻译方法上可全译，也可编译、省译。

三、诗歌、楹联的翻译方法

文学翻译体裁中诗歌翻译最难，汉语诗歌中的典故、绝句、楹联、神话故事、历史人物都会构成翻译的难点（刘宏义，2013：32）。诗歌、楹联本身意义深奥，要求意境营造、情感延移，尽量做到"境中有意，意中有境"（肖乐，2011：66）。但是旅游文本中的诗歌、楹联主要用于烘托景点的意境或补充旅游信息，其翻译是一种特殊的翻译，针对的是一般读者和游客，与纯文学翻译的方法不同，不一定要求内容、形式、格律完全对等，许渊冲提倡的诗歌翻译"三美"原则并不完全适用于旅游文本中的诗歌、楹联翻译。旅游文本中的诗歌、楹联翻译采取什么样的翻译方法取决于文本的类型、功能和翻译目的，在语义翻译和交际翻译策略的指导下可全译（偏语义翻译）、编译（偏交际翻译），也可省译或"零翻译"。

1. 全译

全译是一种追求风格近似的思维和语际活动，是将文化信息由一种语言转化为另一种语言的活动（刘丽，2015：93—94），但是由于多种因素的制约影响，在形式、内容和风格方面，诗歌、楹联的译文与原文只能最大限度地接近，而非完全等同。全译与编译、省译不同，应在保持原文结构的基础上，实现"三似"：1.译文与原作形式基本相似；2.在风格上与原作最大限度相似；3.在与原作内容、风格相似的情景下，尽可能发挥译入语的优势，超越原作，此为"胜似"。

例1. 浣花溪两岸风光秀丽，曾经江阔水深，能行大船，杜甫在《绝句》中生动地描述了这一景色："两个黄鹂鸣翠柳，一行白鹭上青天。窗含西岭千秋雪，门泊东吴万里船"。

译文：The Huanhua Brook has fine scenery on each side and used to be a river deep enough for ships to sail on. Du Fu vividly describes the scene in a quatrain:

    Two yellow orioles chirp in the green willows,

    White herons flutter into the blue sky in a row.

    The Snowy Xiling enframed in my windows,

    Boats from Dongwu anchor outside my abode.

分析：这是一则杜甫草堂的介绍，语篇的重点是描写浣花溪两岸的风光。齐言是中国诗歌的第一要素。译者采用全译法，对仗工整，排列整齐，每行字数基本相同，力争做到中国古典诗歌要求的"齐言"；每行押尾韵，节奏明快，做到中国古典诗歌要求的音韵"和谐"；意象生动，描写极具画面感，将黄鹂鸣柳、白鹭展翅、窗含西岭、门泊大船的田园景色呈现在游客面前。

例2. 成都从来不乏文人骚客的溢美词句："桑麻接畛余无地，锦绣连城别有春""成都海棠十万株，繁华盛丽天下无"。

译文：Chengdu has never been short of compliment from the literati, as it is hailed in the following poems:

> Mulberry & hemp fields extend beyond paths there,
> Flowers present a special landscape in spring here.

> Myriads of crab apple trees are planted everywhere,
> Flowering scenery in Chengdu is beyond compare.

分析：原文引用了两首诗赞美成都，考虑到文本的重点信息都在诗歌里，且行文以诗歌的形式单独排列，只有将诗歌的内容和画面感全部译出来，才能让游客体会到古代成都繁花似锦的美丽，因此译者在这里采用全译法，每一行诗均押尾韵，无论在内容上、形式上、音律上都遵循了"三美"翻译原则，行文工整，声律对仗，做到"意美""音美""形美"。

2. 编译

编译是一种翻译方法，属于交际翻译策略，也有意译、缩译之称。纽马克认为编译属于交际翻译，"是一种最自由的翻译形式"（Newmark，1988：22）。诗歌、楹联使用编译，需要译者在一定程度上创造性地改变原文的内容与形式，达到相应的翻译目的和效果。旅游文本中使用编译，可实现互换型功能的目的。

例1. 黄汲清给后人留下的最著名的一句话刻在他自己使用的地质锤上："生不愿封万户侯，但愿一敲天下之石头。"

译文：However, the most famous sentence Huang Jiqing left to future generations was that "I would rather just hammer away at the rocks in the world than seek for the fame and fortune." This sentence had been engraved onto his personal rock hammer.

分析：黄汲清是中国著名的大地构造学家、石油地质学家，他借用李白"生不用封万户侯，但愿一识韩荆州"的诗句，改编后刻在自己使用的地质锤上，用来鞭策自己和后人。这句诗的意思是"我活着的时候不在乎官职，只希望勘测世界上的石头",体现了地质学家黄汲清淡泊名利、甘愿奉献的精神。译文采用编译法,没有直译原文中的"万户侯",重在传递原文中的实质信息,符合交际翻译的策略和方法。

例2. 李白在《蜀道难》中所写的"尔来四万八千岁,不与秦塞通人烟"夸张、不符合历史真实。但是他所写的因为付出了"地崩山摧壮士死"的代价,终于换来了"天梯石栈相钩连"的栈道交通,却是符合历史真实的,因为他是蜀人,他走过蜀道。

译文:Although Li Bai's description of the isolation of the Sichuan Basin in his poem *Hard Road to Shu* is exaggerated ("Up to present, it has been forty-eight thousand years, and Shu has no communication with Qin"), the opening of the Shudao system at great costs as demonstrated by his line is real ("earth collapsed, mountain got destroyed and heroes died; then heaven ladders and stone trestlework hooked and connected with each other"), because Li Bai, a native of Sichuan, travelled along this route.

分析:译者采用编译法,将极为夸张的"尔来四万八千岁,不与秦塞通人烟"的诗句在译文中用简洁明快的语言体现出来。中文诗句晦涩难懂,而译文通俗易懂,便于外国游客理解,符合交际翻译策略。"地崩山摧壮士死,天梯石栈相钩连",也采用了相同的翻译策略。此处对李白诗句的处理也可省译,避免信息量过重影响读者的阅读体验。试将括号中的诗歌译文删除,整个译文是不是更流畅呢?

3. 省译

与全译相比,"省译"其实也就是"减译"。"省译"需做到对原文删减后读者仍然能从译文体会到原文的基本意义,即做到减词不减意。游客接受旅游文本信息有短时性、片段性的特点,大篇幅的译文可能会增加游客接收信息的负担,甚至会使其放弃接受信息,此时译文删繁就简就成为旅游文本翻译的关键所在。如有必要,甚至可以整段不译,采取"零翻译"。

例1. 在一块雕塑上,写着春熙路名字的由来,原来是出于老子《道德经》:"众人熙熙,如享太牢,如登春台。""春熙"一词,后来也见于唐宋诗句,如李崎的"莺喜春熙弄欲娇"（《人日侍宴大明宫恩赐彩楼人胜应制》）、欧阳修的"民物含春熙"（《南獠》）。一条街道的名字竟然是如此有典有据，这在全国都是不多见的。成都人的古为今用，真可谓古今皆然。

译文：There is a sculpture with inscriptions telling us that the name Chunxi (spring brilliance) comes from a verse in Laozi's *Tao Te Ching* that speaks of the pleasures of the common people. "Chunxi" was also found in Tang and Song poems and lyrics. There are not so many roads or streets across China like Chunxi Road that has a classical allusion. Chengdu is really a model in drawing inspirations from past.

分析：原文引用诗词是为了突显春熙路的悠久历史，表明在很多年前就有"春熙"这两个字了。译者省译了《道德经》中的引文和其他唐宋诗句，目的是让读者把注意力放在春熙路名字的由来上，而不是过多地放在诗句的内容上；换句话说，本文引用的诗歌不是重点信息，而是次要信息，一笔带过就可以了。

例2. 当时的书店都是开架经营，读者可以自由翻阅，一些书店还挂着"欢迎看书"的牌子，甚至免费供应开水，故而每天都有不少爱书人在此阅读学习。《锦城旧事竹枝词》中这样描述："琳琅满目读书香，不逛公园逛店堂。开架任君随意取，一卷忘饥坐中央。"

译文：Bookstores at that time were all open shelf, meaning that customers could browse freely. Some bookstores even posted a sign of "you're welcome to read" and offered free boiled water. Many book lovers would spend all day reading and studying in the shops—as described in *Memories of Old Jincheng Bamboo Branch Verses*.

分析：原文引用《锦城旧事竹枝词》中的诗句来说明这家书店书籍很多，"开架运营"，书籍可以随意拿取，读书氛围很自由，体现了这家书店的经营风格。很明显，诗歌在原文中仅是一种补充说明，信息功能不强。由于前文已经说明了这家书店"开架运营"的经营方式，因此译文省译全诗，重点翻译原文中诗歌前两句对书店的介绍内容，符合交际翻译策略。

四、旅游文本中的诗歌翻译

旅游诗歌是旅游文学中历史最久、数量最多的一种样式，在旅游文本中使用得当，往往会让旅游者产生一种诗情画意、音形意美的效果。中国古诗讲究平仄、对仗，节奏以顿歇为节奏点，节奏单元就是意义单元，要求押尾韵，具有抑扬顿挫的节奏美和韵律美；英语格律诗的节奏主要体现在音步上，各行诗都要讲究一定的音节数，行末押韵或不押韵，交错排列（吴燮元，2014：26）。中、英诗歌在文法、句式、修辞、格律等诸多方面形成各自的特点，存在不可通约性，这些都给中、英诗歌互译带来了巨大的挑战。此外，旅游文本中的诗歌与纯文学中的诗歌不同，在文本中所起的作用和功能不同。根据诗歌在旅游文本中的不同功能（信息功能或审美功能），可全译，也可省译；可编译，也可"零翻译"。

例1．杨贵妃名叫杨玉环，唐开元年间人，是蜀州司户杨玄琰的女儿。相传，贵妃出生时，左肩上隐有"太真"二字，因名"玉环"。玉环天生丽质，姿容绝艳。滴泪，好似红冰；浸汗，有如香玉。容貌之美，到了"回眸一笑百媚生，六宫粉黛无颜色"的程度。

译文：Yang Yuhuan (A.D. 719—756) was the daughter of a local official in Sichuan in the Tang Dynasty. She grew up to be a rare beauty, and later became an imperial consort of the emperor.

分析：这是华清池旅游景点介绍，使用大量专用名词，并引用诗歌，讲述中国美女杨玉环的故事。文中引用的诗歌信息功能不强，与信息型文本功能也不太吻合，故译文省译了该诗句和文中过于夸张的描述，化中文之"华美"为英文之"简约"，将中文近于工笔的细腻描述以及"诗情画意"的诗句提炼为一句话："She grew up to be a rare beauty"。

例2．整座水乡古镇似诗如画，人处其间，恍然桃源琼瑶，不知是人在画中游，还是画在心中移。

译文一：The whole old town is like a poem and a picture. In this town, people will feel that they are seemingly in an earthly paradise. It is hard to know that people exist in the picture of picture exists in the heart of people.

第十章　旅游文本中的诗歌、楹联翻译

译文二：The whole old town is like a poem and a picture. In this town, people will feel that <u>they are seemingly in an earthly paradise</u>.

分析：译文一采用"全译法"，全文译出"不知是人在画中游，还是画在心中移"；译文二采用"零译法"，未译诗句，但游客阅读体验更佳，因为"they are seemingly in an earthly paradise"已有"桃源琼瑶"之意，后文引用诗歌不过是对前文的补充，且主观性极强，与信息文本写实风格也不符，不如不译。

例3. 黄鹤楼是一座具有悠久历史的名楼。许多文人骚客都在这里留下了流传千古的绝句……后来，李白在此送别好友孟浩然，写下了"<u>故人西辞黄鹤楼，烟花三月下扬州。孤帆远影碧空尽，唯见长江天际流。</u>"

译文：Yellow Crane Tower is a famous and historic tower, attracting many men of letters to travel and compose poems handed down for generations. One was written by Li Bai, a major Chinese poet of the Tang Dynasty (around 618—907) on the occasion of seeing his friend off at this tower.

分析：这是一段关于黄鹤楼的景点介绍，引用了李白的诗句，补充说明景点背景知识，即黄鹤楼是一处名胜古迹，历史悠久，许多文人留下了描写它的名句。旅游景点介绍是以信息型、操作型为主，兼具其他功能的混合型文本，翻译此类混合型文本首先要厘清其主要功能，其次译文需契合翻译目的和译文的整体风格，故此处引用的诗歌可省译。

例4. 清晨……如诗所云："<u>山光悦鸟性，潭影空人心。万籁此俱寂，唯闻钟磬音</u>"，你一定会一见钟情。

译文：In the early morning...<u>The birds are gladdened by the mountain light; shaded pools bring your heart to peaceful climes. All fretful stirrings of the world now hushed, you only hear deep bells and tingling chimes.</u> You will be sure to grow fond of the poetic scenes instantly.

分析：原文诗歌的尾部不押韵，译文从音韵的角度考虑，按照英文诗歌的韵律，采取二、四句押韵的方式，第一句的"climes"和第二句的"chimes"押韵。译文采用全译法，其主要目的是用诗歌的形式美和韵律美打动读者、感染读者，以实现文本的审美功能、移情功能、呼唤功能。由此可见，旅游文本中的诗歌翻译采用什么翻译策略和方法,是全译、编译、省译或"零翻译",主要取决于翻译目的和希望实现的文本功能。

例5.古人留下的描绘成都的著名诗句很多,在这里,我们应当日日念诵的是李白的名句:"濯锦清江万里流,云帆龙舸下扬州。"

译文:Among many poems describing Chengdu, we should bear Li Bai's line in mind, and recite it daily:

Washing brocade, Jinjiang meanders miles and miles.

Setting sails, boats voyage to beautiful Yangzhou in a line.

分析:原文中的诗句相对独立,"日日念诵",其重点是诗,故采用全译法。译文每一句都押尾韵,结构对仗,韵律优美,读起来朗朗上口,实现了与原诗的动态对等,为读者呈现出锦江绵延万里、龙舸成排驶向扬州的壮阔场景,基本上做到"意美""音美""形美"。

五、旅游文本中的楹联翻译

由于中、英文化差异,文法、句式、修辞、格律等的不可通约性,翻译楹联能做到"内容相关""词性相同""结构相应"实属不易,要做到韵律、节奏、修辞对等更是难上加难。因此,楹联的翻译最重要的是根据外国游客的认知和审美,在尽可能照顾到楹联的结构特征的同时,将蕴含在楹联背后的人文知识表现出来,起到移情、审美、传递信息的作用。

例1.承前祖德勤与俭,启后孙谋读与耕。

译文:Succeed to the ancestor's virtues of diligence and frugality; Encourage the young generations to take up literacy and farming.

分析:此联讲的是传承祖辈勤俭节约的美德,教育后代子孙需勤奋读书。译者用"succeed to"和"encourage"两个动词翻译"承德"和"启后";用"diligence"和"frugality"翻译"勤"与"俭";用"literacy"和"farming"翻译"读"与"耕",词性相同、结构相应,形式工整对仗,符合中国楹联翻译的基本要求,较好地传达了楹联的内涵和意义。

例2. 非必丝与竹，山水有清音。

译文：Fine music comes from strings and flutes; As well as from mountains and waters.

分析：这是无锡寄畅园匾额上的楹联，出自左思的《招隐》，意为无须箫管和丝弦，山水之间自在清乐，放在无锡寄畅园内，十分贴切。由于原文没有上下文，是一句孤例，因此译文采用了全译法。译文保留了原楹联的句法结构，基本上做到了"词性相同""结构相应""节奏相称"，重现了楹联的意境和情趣，表现出无声的泉水在寄畅园八音涧化为有声流水三叠的情境，体现了中国园林的诗情画意，增强了文本的美学功能。

例3. 忠烈祠对联：马革裹尸，千载岳云留浩气；羊碑堕泪，万年湘水吊忠魂。

译文：Soldiers had sacrificed in the war, while their spirits existed forever and ever; Steles were built for the heroes, yet people remembered them all the time.

分析："马革裹尸"是一个成语，意指用马皮把尸体包裹起来，多指军人战死沙场，形容为国作战、决心为国捐躯的意志。羊公碑又名"堕泪碑"，位于湖北襄阳，是当地百姓怀念西晋著名政治家、军事家羊祜而立的碑。从忠烈祠这副对联可以看出，中文对联的用词大多与浓厚的历史文化背景有关，是逐字翻译所不能体现的，对联中的四字格翻译也是较难处理的一部分，因此译文省译了夸张、冗长、晦涩的信息；用简洁的英文对楹联进行了解释性的翻译，尽可能保持对联"内容相关""结构相应"。

例4. 1936年9月27日，四川各界人士公祭于6月14日辞世的章太炎先生，李植撰写的集句联被誉为当代最佳名联之一："富贵不能淫，贫贱不能移，威武不能屈；泰山其颓乎！梁木其坏乎！哲人其萎乎！"

译文：On September 27, 1936, the people of Chengdu held a memorial service for Zhang Taiyan, who had passed away on June 14; the elegiac couplet composed by Li Zhi for that occasion has been praised as one of the best in contemporary times: "Not corrupted by wealth or honors, never deterred by destitution, unable to be subdued by force. Mount Taishan has collapsed! The pillars have buckled! The great sage has passed away!"

分析:"富贵不能淫,贫贱不能移,威武不能屈"出自《孟子·滕文公下》,意思是贫贱时不要改变自己的意志,威武时不能做理亏的事,这样才是大丈夫。"泰山其颓乎!梁木其坏乎!哲人其萎乎!"出自《礼记·檀弓上》,孔子歌曰,子贡作答是孔子的一句话,意思是"泰山将要崩塌,那么我将瞻仰什么?栋梁将要倒塌,那么我住在哪里?贤能的人枯萎,我们还仿效什么?"译文每一句开头使用了不一样的动词"Not corrupted""never deterred""unable to be subdued";后面连用三个感叹句,在结构上与原文相对应,但用词又富于变化,基本做到了"内容相关""结构相应""节奏相称"。

本章小结

中文旅游文本常引用诗歌、楹联,以增强文本的感染力;而英文旅游文本重写实,很少引用诗歌、楹联,没有汉语那么潇洒随意和强烈的主观情感色彩。旅游文本中诗歌、楹联的翻译,大致可分为三种翻译方法,分别是全译、编译和省译。考虑到文本的功能不同、侧重点不同、读者对象不同,翻译方法也有所不同。如果是为了突出景点历史文化信息,通过诗歌、楹联提升景点的品位和知名度,可采取编译法;如果是引用诗歌来烘托旅游景观,托物寄情、咏物言志,提升文本的移情功能、美学功能,则可采用全译法,起到诗歌移情、审美的功能和作用。翻译楹联应尽量做到与原文"内容相关""字数相等""词性相同""结构相应""节奏相称""平仄相对",将蕴含在楹联背后的人文知识展现给读者;翻译诗歌,应根据翻译目的和诗歌在文本中的作用,正确处理"译"与"不译"的关系,而不局限于在语言、形式、节奏、韵律上的一致或对等。

第十章　旅游文本中的诗歌、楹联翻译

翻译实践

一、热身练习

翻译下文，并对译文做简要分析。

1. 明代大旅行家徐霞客曾经说过："薄海内外无，如徽之黄山，登黄山，天下无山，观止矣！"后人据此又归纳为："五岳归来不看山，黄山归来不看岳。"

2. 1963年郭沫若老先生游览灵渠时，为灵渠写了《满江红·灵渠》，称："灵渠与长城南北相呼应，同为世界之奇观。"

3. 从上海到南京旅游，能体验到与上海不同的古都魅力。"六朝金粉地，金陵帝王州。"

4. "邢客与越人，皆能造兹器。圆似月魂堕，轻如云魄起。"这首唐诗反映的是当时邢窑白瓷与越窑青瓷南北对峙、平分天下的局面，曾经的南方青瓷一枝独秀不复存在。唐宋更替，定窑取代邢窑，白瓷在烧制上精益求精，影响不断扩大。

5. ……时至傍晚，又是另一番景象。"暮从碧山下，山月随人归，却顾所来径，苍苍横翠微"是阿里山落日的绝美写照。

6. 雍容华贵的高山杜鹃、晶莹剔透的冰凌花、金黄娇艳的凤毛菊，红灿灿的百合、紫盈盈的龙胆、矮墩墩的石松，一片生机盎然。有诗为证：百花争艳不觉奇，姹紫嫣红香万里。置身花间云飘处，疑似天堂花园里。

7. 华清池内有一贵妃池，相传是杨贵妃当年沐浴的地方。唐代著名诗人白居易的《长恨歌》中有"春寒赐浴华清池，温泉水滑洗凝脂"的诗句。

8. 个园，中国四大名园之一，全国重点文物保护单位。依苏东坡"宁可食无肉，不可居无竹"之意，园内遍植翠竹。因竹叶形似"个"字，故名。

9. 飞升台台高两米，台面九米见方，青石砌筑，四周有白色石栏。台壁刻有八仙图，间以太极八卦图案。台上立石坊一座，石坊两侧石刻"修真句曲三峰顶，得道华阳八洞天"，此楹联为已故全国道教协会会长黎遇航所书。

10. 新西湖十景之一的吴山天风，山巅建有"江湖汇观亭"，亭前楹联沿用明代文人徐文长的题词："八百里湖山，知是何年图画；十万家烟火，尽归此处楼台"，点明了"吴山天风"的意境。

二、巩固练习

翻译下文，并对译文做简要分析。

1. 子曰："假作真时真亦假，无为有处有还无。"

2. 克敌受降威加万里，名城览胜地重千秋。

3. 石狮上有朱德手书"风景如画"，是他1963年观看黄山摄影展时所书。玉屏峰顶有毛泽东手迹"江山如此多娇"，气势磅礴。

4. 汉正街博物馆墙上的"汉正街地形图"向世人很好地展现了当年大汉口——汉正街"十里帆樯依市立，万家灯火彻宵明"的繁华景象。

5. 柳州市区青山环绕，水抱城流，被誉为"世界第一天然大盆景"。唐代诗人柳宗元诗中"岭树重遮千里目，江流曲似九回肠"，明代地理学家徐霞客笔下"千峰环野立，一水抱城流"，便是柳州城市风貌最为形象的写照。

6. ……让你全身心享受"疏松影落空坛静，细草香闲小洞幽"的恬静。

7. 然而，她的真实形象，诚如《诗经》描写美女之"巧笑倩兮，美目盼兮"一样，后人对这位瓷器王国的绝代佳人，钦羡仰慕而不能窥其全貌。著名的法门寺地宫出土晚唐秘色瓷文物，为人们提供了认识唐代越窑秘色瓷的标准器……

8. 泰安煎饼是泰山地区农家的主食。蒲松龄描绘煎饼时用了如下字句："圆如明月，大如铜钲，薄似剡溪之纸，色似黄鹤之翎。"

9. 但是，通过这个海交史陈列馆，我们不难想象当年"缠头赤足半蕃商，大舶高樯多海宝"的辉煌岁月。

10. 黄山四绝之一的怪石，其形态可谓千奇百怪，令人叫绝。似人似物，似鸟似兽，情态各异，形象逼真。黄山怪石从不同的位置，在不同的天气观看情趣迥异，可谓"横看成岭侧成峰，远近高低各不同"。其分布可谓遍及峰壑巅坡。或兀立峰顶或戏逗坡缘，或与松结伴，构成一幅幅天然山石画卷。

三、阅读翻译

阅读下文，重点翻译下画线部分。

杭州

意大利著名旅游家马可·波罗曾这样叙述他印象中的杭州："<u>这是世界上最美妙迷人的城市，它使人觉得自己是在天堂。</u>"在中国也流传着这样的话："<u>上有天堂，下有苏杭</u>。"杭州的名气主要在于风景如画的西湖。西湖一年四季都美不胜收，宋代著名诗人苏东坡用"<u>淡妆浓抹总相宜</u>"的诗句来赞誉西湖。杭州人观西湖却有自己的说法："<u>晴湖不如雨湖，雨湖不如夜湖</u>。"你在杭州，一定要去领略一下西湖的风韵，看看此说是否有道理。

第十一章 旅游文本中典故、专用名词等的翻译

中西文化不同,中、英旅游文本在内容、语言、叙事、审美等方面也不尽相同。中文旅游文本常借用名人名言、事典、语典,似乎没有这些就不足以体现旅游文本的价值(牛郁茜,韩文哲,2017:60)。中文旅游文本大量运用典故,引用名言、习语、俚语、典故、传说等,营造出一种厚重的文化底蕴,引经据典是常用的手法;而英文旅游文本很少引经据典,不像中文旅游文本那样旁征博引,翻译难以找到对应词或相应的表达方法(梁晓婷,2019:232)。中国历史文化悠久,中文旅游文本往往具有厚重的"历史感",其中的人名、地名、书名、称谓、官职、宗教概念、文化意象等蕴藏着深厚的中国历史文化信息,集中体现了中华民族的传统文化,有别于其他民族,这些独特的文化内容和语言表达方式是旅游翻译的重点,也是难点之一。

一、旅游文本中特殊的语言表达

1. 文化负载词概论

中国人文旅游景点的一些名称、习语、用典、表达方式沿用至今,是在漫长的中国历史发展进程中逐渐积累形成的,涉及中国政治、经济、历史、文化、风物等各个方面,是反映中国历史文化的特殊词汇。这些词反映了特定民族在漫长的历史发展进程中逐渐积累的、有别于其他民族的、反映民族独立的活动方式(廖七一,2000:232),是民族语言系统中最直接、最形象地反映民族文化和地域特色的"文化负载词"。除了景点地名、名称外,中国特殊的称谓、年代、官职、宗教概念、文化意象的表达方法不同于其他国家,也是中国文化负载词的重要组成部分。旅游文本中的文化负载词涉及面广,蕴藏着深厚的中国历史文化底

蕴，是中国文化"走出去"、构建中国话语的关键，也给翻译带来巨大的挑战。

2. 文化负载词译法

由于民族文化传统不同，不同民族的语言和文化存在或多或少的"不可通约性"，不可避免地存在"词汇空缺"或"文化空缺"，旅游文本中的典故、俗语、事典、语典、人名、地名等文化负载词蕴含着中国特有的意象形态、文体结构、修辞形式，很难用另一种语言符号全面呈现出来。翻译时，如果源语与目标语之间存在"词汇空缺"或"文化空缺"，可采取意译或音译+释义、直译+释义等方式，帮助读者理解；如果不存在，则可直译、替代、套译，以提高译文的阅读性、接受性。

文化负载词是传统文化最为核心的外在表现形式（郑德虎，2016：53—56），具有独特性、唯一性。翻译旅游文本中的典故、俗语、事典、语典、人名、地名等文化负载词，一方面应尽可能突显中国文化在目标语文化中的存在，体现中国的话语和核心价值观；另一方面也需考虑外国读者对中国语言、文化的接受能力以及译文的可读性。至于采取什么翻译方法，是直译、音译、音译+释义，还是意译、释译、套译，应综合考虑文本功能、文体风格以及读者的阅读体验和接受能力。

例1. 水利万物而不争。

译文：Great virtue is like water. Water nourishes all things and does not compete with anything.

分析：这是出现在桂林旅游网站上的一则语典，表达桂林山水养人、育人之意，以增加旅游景点的品位。"上善若水，水利万物而不争……"出自《道德经》，意为最大的善就如同水一样，水滋润万物却不与万物相争。译文采用增译法，增译首句"上善若水"，作为"水利万物而不争"的补充，帮助外国读者理解中国的道家思想，填补译文读者的"文化空缺"：水是如同大爱，是一种美德，因此才会滋润万物而不与其争。

例2. 少林寺是天下第一名刹，被统称为"禅宗祖庭"。

译文：Generally, Shaolin Temple, the first temple in the world, refers to the "ancestor court of Zen", a school of Mahayana Buddhism that originated in China during the Tang Dynasty as Chan Buddhism.

分析：这是河南嵩山少林寺的景区介绍。原文中出现了"禅宗祖庭"这一典故，指佛教开创各大宗派的祖师居住、布道的寺院。相传释迦牟尼的第二十八代佛徒菩提达摩历时三年到达少林寺，首传禅宗，影响甚大。但对于西方读者，如果直译"禅宗祖庭"而不通过阐释弥补中、英"文化空缺"，读者无法理解，是无效翻译。译文采用增译法，说明禅宗起渊于中国唐朝，属大乘佛教，便于外国游客理解。

例3. 郭柏荫故居……因郭阶三五子登科第，时人称此宅为"五子登科"宅。

译文：Former Residence of Guo Boyin... The property was known as "All Successful Candidates House" ...

分析：这是郭柏荫故居的景点介绍。"五子登科"是一则事典，也是中国文化负载词，讲述五代后周时期有个叫窦禹钧的人，五个儿子都品学兼优，先后登科及第，获取功名，故称"五子登科"。西方读者并不了解该习语蕴藏的故事和寓意，但若讲述整个故事又会使译文过于冗长，所以译文取其核心含义，直接表达出"五子登科"的核心含义，弥补了中、英之间的"文化空缺"。

例4. 在我国最早的典籍中，即有关于这条河的记载。《尚书·禹贡》："漆沮既从，洋水彼同。"《诗经·大稚》："洋水东注，维禹之绩。"说明洋水在远古就是一条著名的河流。

译文：Records about this river can be found even in the earliest Chinese classics, which prove that the Yang River had been well known since ancient times.

分析：这是对西安附近"八水"之一的"洋河"的景点介绍。原文出现《尚书·禹贡》《诗经·大稚》两部古籍，属于书名专用名词。原文引经据典，其目的是证明洋河悠久的历史，但对于外国游客来说是不必要的冗余信息，译出反而可能因信息负载影响读者对信息的理解和接收，故译文省译了两本书的书名及其引文，只概括地将其释译为"the earliest Chinese classics"。

例5. 气候特点是：冬长夏短，春秋相当。夏季气候凉爽宜人，平均气温23.7摄氏度，最高气温32摄氏度。三伏盛夏，午前如春，午后如秋，夜如初冬。有

"三伏炎热人欲死，清凉到此顿疑仙"之美誉。

译文：Every year there is a long winter and a short summer. The days of spring and autumn are equally distributed. In cool summer days the average temperature stays at 23.7℃ and the maximum is around 32℃.

分析：这是河南信阳鸡公山风景区气候情况的介绍。画线部分"三伏"和"三伏炎热人欲死，清凉到此顿疑仙"，一个是中国文化负载词，一个是中国谚语。由于前文已经翻译了鸡公山气候的基本情况，因此没有必要再对"三伏"进行释译，否则文化负载过重，影响读者的阅读体验；而谚语实际上是对前文的附加描写，信息性不强，故也可删除不译。

例6. "愚公移山"这个古老美丽的传说，让人们知道了王屋山。它是中国古代九大名山之一，又为道教十大洞天之首，也是传说中轩辕黄帝设坛祭天之所。

译文：The old beautiful tale of "How the Silly Old Man Removed the Mountains" makes people know Mt. Wangwu. It is one of the 9 famous mountains in China, the first cave of Taoist, as well as place where Xuanyuan Huangdi set up the platform to worship the God.

分析：这是河南王屋山风景区介绍，引用了"愚公移山"的寓言，以增强游客对旅游景点的兴趣。"愚公移山"的寓言蕴藏着丰富的文化意蕴，但译文没有过多地阐释其中的文化含义，而是从字面意思传达原文的主要信息，这是目的语不需要弥补"文化空缺"时翻译典故的方法。

例7. 孟姜女哭长城的故事旁证了建筑长城所付出的巨大代价——除了钱币，还有众多建筑者的躯体。

译文：The legend that the collapse of the Great Wall was caused by the cry of a woman named Meng Jiangnv, whose husband died in the construction of the Great Wall, is an evidence showing that the price of the building this wonder of the world was not only money, but also the lives of constructors.

分析：景点介绍中引用了"孟姜女哭长城"这一典故。典故的运用满足了游客对长城背后的故事的好奇心，增强了该景点介绍的吸引力。孟姜女的故事在中国家喻户晓，但外国人未必知晓。考虑到读者对象，译文对"孟姜女哭长城"

这一事典进行了解释性的翻译，而不在乎译文与典故名称在语言上、形式上的对等，重在讲故事。

例8. 刘三姐大观园山清水秀，有三姐与阿牛哥定情誓约的百年古榕；有集观赏性、参与性、娱乐性为一体的民族歌舞表演；还有<u>壮寨干栏、瑶寨木楼、苗族吊脚楼</u>等特色民族建筑及少数民族服饰。

译文：In the area an outstanding scenic beauty stands a century-old banyan tree, which is believed to have borne witness to the pledge of love made by Liu Sanjie and her lover Aniu. There are not only buildings and folk costumes bearing distinctive features of the Zhuang, Yao, Miao and other ethnic groups, but also performances of folk songs and dances that are appealing, participatory and entertaining.

分析："壮寨干栏""瑶寨木楼""苗族吊脚楼"这些都是具有民族特色的专用名词。很明显，译者没有将这些专用名词译出来，因为如果采取音译的翻译方法译出这些建筑名，既说明不了建筑的风格，解释起来又啰唆累赘，不如释译为" buildings... bearing distinctive features of the Zhuang, Yao, Miao and other ethnic groups"，更能传达原文的意思，便于外国读者理解。

二、旅游文本中典故、俗语的翻译

在中文旅游文本中，景点介绍、导游词、游记等最具旅游文本特色，也是旅游翻译的难点，主要体现在经常引用典故、俗语、习语、名人名言等。中文旅游文本大量引用典故、俗语、习语、名人名言，文意结合，通过典故、故事、俗语等增加旅游目的地的人文色彩，吸引游客前往旅游；而英文旅游文本很少像中文旅游文本那样运用典故、俗语、习语、名人名言等，形容事物往往不会故意夸大（汪庆华，2015）。因此，翻译旅游文本中的中国典故、俗语、专用名词等，需掌握中、英不同的语言特点，以读者接受、理解为要旨，可采取直译，也可意译。

第十一章　旅游文本中典故、专用名词等的翻译

1. 典故的翻译

典故是人们在谈话或写作时引用历史、传说、文学或宗教中的人物或事件（邓炎昌，1989：210）。汉语典故很多，汇聚了中国上下五千年中华民族历史长河中在农业、商业、战争、社会制度、礼仪风俗等方面所体现的智慧。典故可分为事典和语典、熟典和僻典、明典和暗典、人名典和书名典、正典和反典等，共11类。其中，旅游文本常用的典故有事典、语典、人名典等。典故的翻译要求中西文化融会贯通，根据文本的类型和功能采取针对性的翻译策略，一般采用音译、音译加注，也可意译，侧重呈现文本的信息功能。

（1）事典

事典，即来自古代的寓言、神话、传说和历史事件等。在旅游文本中，事典一般是对历史典故的运用，意在增加、补充文本的历史文化信息。事典多采用意译法、增译法，重在增加文本的信息功能。

例1. 历史上，除了文人骚客，新宁人对家门前这一片浪漫的山水并没有过多地留意，这里多的是揭竿而起的山民、除暴安良的绿林好汉。

译文：Ancient local people did not pay much intention to this beautiful scenery around, except to those famous literati. In the history, there are countless ordinary people who rose up to demand their rights and freedoms; there are many heroes of greenwood who weed out the wicked and let the ordinary people live in peace.

分析：原文中出现几个带有历史事件的成语，为文本增添了厚重的历史信息。"揭竿而起""除暴安良"分别出自司马迁《史记·秦始皇本纪》和宋代李昉《太平广记》，前者在书中的原句是"斩木为兵，揭竿为旗"，是陈胜、吴广不堪朝廷重负，奋起反抗的故事；"除暴安良"出自"舍之职责，在乎除暴安良"。以上事典成语在英文中多数没有对等或相似的表达，属于"文化空缺"，故译文采取意译法，将"揭竿而起"译为"rose up to demand their rights and freedoms"；将"除暴安良"译为"weed out the wicked and let the ordinary people live in peace"，重在传递信息，符合信息型文本中关于事典的翻译策略和方法。

例2. 关于"崀山"名称来源有两个。舜帝南巡路过新宁，见这方山水美丽，便脱口而出："山之良者，崀山，崀山。"

译文：There are two origins of Langshan Mountain's name "崀山": Emperor Shun passed by Xinning county on his southern tour. Words slipped from his mouth when he saw the beautiful landscape: "The finest mountain is 崀山（Langshan Mountain）." And the Chinese word 崀 consists of 良(fine) and 山(mountain).

分析：原文引用舜帝南巡的传说，用典给景区增添了一些神秘色彩。舜帝说："山之良者，崀山，崀山"，这句话对于中文读者来说，能从文字的结构上看出汉字"崀"是"山"和"良"的结合体，但英文读者不懂汉语，不可能像中文读者那样理解崀山文字的形状和意义，故译文采取中英结合，在中文"崀山"象形字上加上英文释义，"良(fine)""山(mountain)"，弥补了"文化空缺"；而"南巡"则采取直译法，译为"on his southern tour"。

例3. 这里又是典故之城……黄粱美梦、毛遂自荐、负荆请罪、完璧归赵等众多成语典故，脍炙人口，给人启迪。

译文：Being a town of allusions. This city is certainly has numerous greatly inspired allusions, such as "Golden Millet Dream (Pipe Dream)", "Mao Sui Recommending Himself", "Bearing the Rod for Punishment (In Sackcloth and Ashes)", "Returning the Jade Intact to Zhao", etc., which are widely loved and quoted by people.

分析：这是一篇关于历史名胜景点的旅游导读。原文材料中出现了"黄粱美梦""毛遂自荐""负荆请罪""完璧归赵"四个事典，属于中国文化负载词。如果从字面上翻译这四个事典，外国游客不能理解其意义，因为他们对这四个事典一无所知。翻译中国典故，如目标语有对等或相似的语言，可采用"套译"法，最能有效地弥补原文和译文之间的"文化空缺"，比如英文"Pipe Dream"用来指白日梦或空想，因此可将"黄粱美梦"译为"Pipe Dream"；"负荆请罪"与英文"In Sackcloth and Ashes"意义相近，都有"忏悔""悔恨"之意，故也可采用套译法；但对于中、英文没有对等的词语，则可采取意译法，传递原文主要信息即可，如本文中"毛遂自荐""完璧归赵"的翻译。

（2）语典

语典，即来自古代诗词、古籍中的词语等，相对于"事典"而言，但它不同于一般的词语，多有言外之意。旅游文本中的语典多采用意译、编译法，重在强

第十一章 旅游文本中典故、专用名词等的翻译

化原文本的信息功能或美学功能。

例1. 提名地保留了沿袭了几千年的农耕活动，成片的稻田随四季变化而呈现出春绿秋黄的田园风光，青瓦白墙、<u>小桥流水</u>的古式民居依山而建，古堡、山寨、寺院隐没山中……

译文：The nomination site followed the farming activities thousands of years ago. As the season changes, vast stretches of paddy fields show an idyllic scenery of green spring and yellow autumn. The ancient cottages with white walls and gray tile were built around the mountain, with <u>a small bridge over the flowing stream</u>, the ancient castles, stockades, temples were concealed in mountain, and everything is harmony in nature.

分析：这是一则对崀山风景区当地田园风光的描写。原文中的"小桥流水"出自马致远《天净沙·秋思》中的"枯藤老树昏鸦，小桥流水人家"。语典的使用除了使文本具有信息传递功能外，还使文本具有表达功能，这与引用"事典"的功能不同。原文小令中有众多密集的意象，表达作者的羁旅之苦和悲秋之恨，形象地勾勒了一幅静谧安详的画面，"小桥流水"就取自该句。翻译语典应根据原文的功能和文体，采取与原文一致的语言风格。"小桥流水"译为"a small bridge over the flowing stream"，文笔清丽流畅，重视的是画面的呈现而不是意象的烘托，符合英文"简约"的审美观照。

例2. 风和日丽时举目远望，佘山、金山、崇明岛隐隐可见，真有"<u>登泰山而小天下</u>"之感。

译文：Standing at this altitude on sunny days, one has the feeling that <u>the world below is suddenly belittled.</u>

分析：这句话出自《孟子·尽心上》，孟子曰："孔子登东山而小鲁，登泰山而小天下。"意思是说孔子登上东山，感到鲁国变小；登上泰山，天下变小。译文省译佘山、金山、崇明岛，避免因佘山、金山、崇明岛等地名的音译或过多的释义影响读者的阅读体验；后半句采取意译法，只译出诗句大意，言简意赅，文体简洁明快，全句用英文散文体译出，一气呵成。语典的译文应尽量契合原文的整体风格，不留翻译痕迹为上。

例3. 游人可泛舟于江上，赏"<u>风荷疏影</u>"；或策杖于古栈道，寻"大脚

印"，恋"古刹禅林"，聆听晨钟暮鼓，或登上三台阁，山川秀色，眺"天门晓日"叹"大江东去"。

译文：Tourists can take boats on the river, appreciating the sparse shadows of lotus in the breeze, or walk with sticks on the ancient temple, hearing the bells, or just climb Santai Loft to get a bird's eye view of the beautiful landscape, watch the sun rising from Mt. Tianmen, and view the river rushing eastward day and night.

分析：这是安徽省马鞍山的中文导游词，运用了多个语典，如"风荷疏影""天门晓日""大江东去"，都是名诗中提炼的语典，"泛舟江上""策杖古道""登阁远眺"是中国古代文人所喜爱的出游活动，而"风荷疏影""古刹禅林""晨钟暮鼓"也是人们最喜爱吟咏的景致意象，体现了文本的美学功能、呼唤功能、诱导功能。译文对语典词主要采用直译法，长短句结合，用英文的散文体将中文的语典融入英文自然清新的"简约美"。

（3）人名典

人名典是指文本中引用的古人名或称呼，而书名典是指旅游文本中引用的书名、篇名，均属于中国文化负载词。人名典多采用音译、音译加注，以帮助目标语读者理解为目的，重在体现文本的信息功能。但如果音译、音译加注影响读者的阅读体验，也可不加注，采取指代、统称的方法，以提高文本的可读性。

例1. 晚清时期，对新宁人来说，山留下的苦难记忆太多太深，而这一切都源于山那边出了个洪秀全，山这边出了个曾国藩。

译文：For people here, the mountain have made them suffered a lot, and all this should blame two famous men in Langshan Mountain, one figure is Hong Xiuquan (the leader of Taiping Rebellion), the other one is Zeng Guofan (an important officer in the late Qing Dynasty).

分析：原文中出现两个历史人物，向游客讲述了新宁的历史故事。中国游客知道洪秀全和曾国藩，前者是太平天国运动的领袖，后者是晚清名臣。考虑到外国游客不了解这两位中国历史人物，译文对人名典的翻译采取了音译加注释的方法，为游客提供了更多的人物背景信息。

例2. 从秦皇汉武到乾隆皇帝，从孔夫子登临的感叹到李白、杜甫的千古诗

第十一章 旅游文本中典故、专用名词等的翻译

篇，还有2200多年前的秦石刻，大字如斗的经石峪，错落分布的宫殿庙宇，比比皆是的古木题刻……悠久的历史，灿烂的文化，自然景观与人文景观的和谐统一，正是这些，吸引着中外游人络绎不绝地前来观赏。

译文：With the characteristics of a long history, a splendid culture and the harmonies integrity of natural landscapes and historical relics, Mount Taishan attracts tourists from all over the world. You will realize these from the frequent visits of emperors, emotional sighs of Confucius, verses of poets, stone sculptures of 2,200 years ago, and well-arranged temples and archways.

分析：这段文字是泰山的旅游介绍，运用了大量的人名典，构成排比句式。文中出现古代帝王秦始皇、汉武帝，唐朝诗人李白、杜甫以及"至圣先师"孔子等，增加了文本厚重的历史信息。人名典的使用突显了泰山的历史文化底蕴，但如果全文译出这些人名典，译文会变得很长，外国读者也未必能够理解这些历史人物，故译文只译出人物名称的统称："帝王将相""文人骚客"，分别译为"emperors""poets"，只保留外国人熟知的孔子英文名字Confucius。

例3. 晋祠，初名唐叔虞祠，是为纪念晋国开国侯唐叔虞而建。唐叔虞，姓姬，名虞，字子于，乃周武王之子，周成王胞弟。

译文：Jin Memorial Temple, originally named Tangshuyu Memorial Temple, was built to honor and worship Tangshuyu, who set Kingdom of Jin at the beginning. Tangshuyu, whose family name is Ji, given name Yu and courtesy name Ziyu, was a son of Emperor Wu of Zhou and younger brother of Emperor Cheng of Zhou.

分析：这是名胜古迹晋祠旅游介绍。原文提到了人名典"唐叔虞"，并以此介绍晋祠的由来，由浅入深，增加了文本的信息功能。译文对"唐叔虞"这一人名典采用了音译翻译方法，这是因为后文对这一历史人物有具体、翔实的介绍，根据上下文外国游客能够理解中国这一历史人物。对于人物的姓（"姬"）、名（"虞"）、字（"子于"），译文也采用音译法，但"周武王""周成王"人名典的翻译则在人名前加上称谓，以示其显赫的历史地位，也符合英文帝王将相称谓的表达方法。

2. 俗语的翻译

俗语，即在日常生活中广泛流行的定型的语句，具有形象生动、朗朗上口、易学易记的特点，反映人民的生活经验和愿望。一方面，俗语能在一定程度上概括景点的特色；另一方面，脍炙人口的俗语使文本内容更接地气、更贴近生活，增加文本的人际功能，使文本更活泼，具有生活气息。在中文旅游文本中，特别是在中文导游词里，俗语出现的频率非常高。旅游文本中也常见谚语。谚语与俗语相近，也是流传于民间、口口相传、言简意赅的话语。俗语、谚语的最佳翻译方法是套译法，也就是说用贴近目标语的最自然的语言表达原文中约定俗成的语言，也就是套译法，从原文语言的"陌生化"到译文语言的"熟悉化"。如果不能用套译法，则可用意译或编译法。

例1. 舜帝不仅被崀山的风景所陶醉，更对崀山血酱鸭赞不绝口，并钦点为宫廷御菜，从此崀山血酱鸭名声大震，曰："游崀山不可不呷血酱鸭。"

译文：Emperor Shun was not only attracted by the wonderful scenery but also spoke highly of Xue Jiang Ya, and had it cooked as an imperial meal. After that, this food enjoyed popularity. There is a saying, "It is in vain to visit Langshan Mountain without tasting Xue Jiang Ya (the Stew Duck with Duck's Blood)."

分析：原文中使用了当地一句俗语："游崀山不可不呷血酱鸭"，吸引游客品尝地方特色菜。对于中文游客来说，这一俗语具有较强的诱导功能，能唤起游客的好奇心，但对于外国游客，如果采用直译法，由于缺乏中国佳肴的背景知识，未必能使他们产生品尝血酱鸭的愿望。译文套用英文谚语："It is in vain to cast your net where there is no fish"，并采取音译加释义的方法译出"游崀山不可不呷血酱鸭"这一中国俗语，让译文读者产生了一种阅读本土谚语一样的亲切感。

例2. 在新宁旅游，你会经常听见当地人把"桂林山水甲天下，崀山风景赛桂林"这句话挂在嘴边，这句话是现代著名诗人艾青说的，艾青恐怕没有想到，自己随口说的一句话竟然会在半个多世纪后，成了当年他浪迹他乡的民谣。

译文：Travelling in Xinning one will often hear a saying "East or west, Guilin is the best, Langshan Mountain can be compared", which is said by the famous modern poet Ai Qing. It may not occur to Ai Qing that his throwaway remarks would become a folk song in other places after half a century.

分析：原文"桂林山水甲天下，崀山风景赛桂林"出自艾青之口，由普通民众传吟至今，已经被大众接受，成为口口相传的俗语，引用这一俗语使景点介绍更具有呼唤功能和人际功能。"桂林山水甲天下"这句话已有成熟的翻译，可借用西方的一句谚语"East or west, home is the best"的表达方法。译文采用套译法，为了押韵，后一句"Langshan Mountain can be compared"还省译了"with Guilin"，使译文更具节奏感和韵律感，信息功能、诱导功能都很强。

例3. 中国有句俗话"赶得早不如赶得巧"，赶上地坛庙会那就是巧。这里蕴含着浓郁的京味文化，叫北京人与外地人都喜爱。

译文：A Chinese saying goes, "Timing is everything" and this applies to Ditan Temple Fair (a temple fair held in the Park of Earth Temple), at which you will find everything concerned with culture of Beijing. Both insiders and outsiders of Beijing enjoy it.

分析：这是一则旅游宣传资料，引用民间俗语"赶得早不如赶得巧"，进而引入对地坛庙会的介绍，传递信息功能，也兼备诱导、呼唤功能，吸引游客前往参观旅游。译文模仿英文"Time is everything"的表达方法，把"time"巧妙地改译成"timing"，中文"早不如巧"的意思就这样自然贴切地在英文中"套译"出来了，有效地弥补了原文和译文之间的"文化空缺"。

三、旅游文本中地名、景点名称的翻译

专用名词是表示人、地方、事物等的特有名词。中国历史文化悠久，在历史的长河中积累了大量的专用名词，涉及政治、经济、文化、科技等不同领域，其中多数无法在英语中找到对等词，给旅游文本的对外翻译带来困难和挑战。旅游文本中的专用名词通常是中国文化负载词，带有中国独特的语言和文化特色，是旅游文本翻译的又一难点。当今，国际交流日益频繁，旅游文本中专用名词的翻译不仅要体现中国语言文化特色，讲好中国故事，更要传播中国的话语和核心

价值观。旅游文本中地名、景点名称等专用名词的翻译方法主要有音译、音译加注释，也可意译、释译，均取决于翻译的目的和文本的功能，并兼顾译文的可读性。

1. 景点地名的翻译

地名是历史的产物，是国家领土主权的象征，是日常生活的向导，是社会交往的媒介。在信息化社会中，地名在国际政治、经济、外交、外贸、科技、文化交流、新闻出版以及社会生活等方面都起着非常重要的作用。

如：同样是"东"字，"东宝兴路"译为"Dongbaoxing Road"，而"南京东路"译为"East Nanjing Road"。之所以有不同的翻译，是因为前一个地名是专有词汇，后一个地名属于非专有词汇。专有词汇需用拼音表示，非专有词汇则可以用英语直译。

（1）专名是单音节的英译

专名是单音节，通名也是单音节，这时通名应视作专名的组成部分，先音译并与专名连写，后直译。例如：

泰山Taishan Mountain

淮河Huaihe River

巢湖Chaohu Lake

渤海Bohai Sea

岷江Minjiang River

礼县Lixian County

（2）通名专名化的英译法

通名专名化主要指单音节的通名，如山、河、江、湖、海、港、峡、关、岛等。此类地名的翻译按专名处理，与专名连写，构成专名整体。例如：

绥芬河市 Suifenhe City（比较：Suifen River）

白水江自然保护区 Baishuijiang Nature Reserve（比较：Baishui River）

瓦屋山国家森林公园 Wawushan National Forest Park（比较：Wawu Mountain）

又如：蟒河风景区是集人文、山水、动植物等景观于一体的著名旅游区。

译文：Manghe Scenic Area with great fame has integrated resource including the humanity, landscape, plant and animal.

分析：这是关于蟒河风景区的景点介绍。译文采取音译+释义的方法翻译景点地名"蟒河风景区"。如果指"蟒河"河流，应译为"Manghe River"，但"蟒河风景区"通名成为专名的一部分，因此译为"Manghe Scenic Area"或"Manghe Resort"。

（3）通名是同一个汉字的多种英译法

通名是单音节的同一个汉字，根据意义有多种不同译法，在大多数情况下，这些英译词不能互相替换。例如：

山：

mount：峨眉山 Mount E'mei

mountain：天柱山 Tianzhu Mountain

hill：象鼻山 Elephant Trunk Hill

island：大屿山 Lantau Island

range：秦岭 Qinling Range

peak：扯旗山 Victoria Peak

rock：狮子山 Lion Rock

海：

sea：东海 the East China Sea

lake：邛海 the Qionghai Lake

horbour：大滩海 Long Harbour

port：牛尾海 Port Shelter

forest：蜀南竹海 the Bamboo Forest in Southern Sichuan

2. 景点名称的翻译

景点名称的翻译既可以音译，也可以直译、意译，还可音译+释义。为了文化输出、中国文化走出去，景点名称的翻译以直译为主，音译+释义为辅，也可适当意译，以便外国游客更好地理解景点名称蕴含的历史和文化，但直译、意译需合理使用。过多音译、直译，读者会因"文化空缺"无法理解；过多意译、释义，文化信息过载会影响读者的阅读体验。

例1.

三潭印月（西湖十景之一）　　　Three Pools Mirroring the Moon

寒山寺（佛教胜迹）　　　　　　Cold Mountain Temple

紫来洞　　　　　　　　　　　　Purple Source Cave

分析："三潭印月"可音译为"Santanyinyue"，"紫来洞"译为"Zilai Cave"，但不是旅游景点名称的最佳译法。从跨文化交际来讲，"紫来洞"含有"紫气东来"之意，译为"Purple source Cave"更好，而"三潭印月"译为"Three Pools Mirroring the Moon"更能被外国读者"知之""乐之""好之"。同理，"寒山寺"不一定非得音译为"Hanshan Temple"，也可采取直译法。由此看来，中国景点名称的翻译，是采取音译、直译还是意译，取决于跨文化交际目的以及目标语读者的接受能力。

例2. 展园"草堂品茗"坐落在公园的中轴线上，是以江苏泰州地方特色之一的茶文化为主题打造的，占地面积6600平方米。

译文：The exhibition garden "Tasting Tea in Thatched Hut" is situated on the axis of the park, focusing on the tea culture which is one of the local specialties of Taizhou city, Jiangsu Province and covering an area of 6,600m^2.

分析："草堂"俗名"茅屋"，即一种茅草盖成的简陋的小房子，意为"to describe a house with a roof made of straw or reeds"，译作"thatched hut"或"thatched cottage"比较贴切，著名景点杜甫草堂英译就有译文"Dufu Thatched Cottage"。"品茗"可译为"tasting tea"，也可译为"enjoying tea"，均采用直译法。直译形象直观，能够传达景点的意义和意象，更贴近读者，使译文更加流畅。

例3. 广西旅游胜地数不胜数，如南宁青秀山、桂林漓江、宁明花山、北海银滩、合浦星岛湖、灵川青狮潭等。

译文：There are numerous tourist attractions in Guangxi, such as Qingxiu Mountain of Nanning, Lijiang River of Guilin, Huashan of Ninming, Silver Beach of

Beihai, Xingdao Hu (Star Island Lake) of Hepu, and Qingshi Tan (Green Lion Pond) of Lingchuan.

分析：文中不同的景点名分别采用了音译、音译+释义等方法。由于英、汉两种语言中有的词和意象存在语义空缺，难以用一两个词表达，这时可直接把源语的发音转换为译语中相似或相同的语音，以保持译文名称的简洁性。如"青秀山""漓江""花山"采用音译，在专名上加一个表示地貌特征的通名，如"mountain""lake""river"等，便于读者记忆；对于一些含义丰富的景点名称，音译会造成语义缺失，这时可采用直译法，如"银滩"译作"Silver Beach"，形象直观，更加贴近译文读者；对于"星岛湖""青狮潭"这样意义丰富且有中国文化意象的景点名称，可采用音译+释义，如译为"Xingdao Hu (Star Island Lake)""Qingshi Tan (Green Lion Pond)"。音译+释义不仅保留了景点名称的读音，且译出了景点名称的文化内涵，知其意，晓其音，可谓一举两得，但需注意适用得当，过多使用会使译文文化信息过载，影响读者的阅读体验。

例4. 孔庙的第一座石坊叫"金声玉振坊"。"金声""玉振"表示奏乐的全过程，以击钟开始，以击磬告终，比喻孔子的思想集古圣先贤之大成。石坊上面莲花宝座上各刻有一个独角怪兽，称"辟邪"，也叫"朝天吼"，这是封建社会王爵府第才可使用的饰物。

译文：The Confucius Temple's first gateway is called Golden Sound and Jade Vibration Gateway. "Golden Sound" and "Jade Vibration" symbolize the whole process of playing music. The music starts with the beating of a drum and ends with the striking of an inverted bell. This means that Confucius' thoughts are a comprehensive expression of all previous saints' ideas. Unicorns called "avoiding evil spirits" or "growling towards the sky" are engraved on the stone gateway and lotus throne. These decorations were used only for the mansions of dukes in feudal society.

分析："金声玉振"比喻声音如金钟、玉磬般响亮，也形容人知识渊博。译文采用直译法，将"金声玉振坊"译为"Golden Sound and Jade Vibration Gateway"，与原文的结构形式一致，将中文的比喻意象移植到译入语，给读者带来一种新奇的感觉。由于译文在景点名称后对"金声"和"玉振"的意义进行了解释，译语读者完全能够理解其意，此处的景点名采用直译法是合情合理的。如果采用意译法仅译出其含义，剥夺原文的比喻，就会失去原文的文化意义和表达效果，难免"得意忘形"。"辟邪""朝天吼"是两个中国文化负载词，也是景点名称，译文采用直译法，与西方世界中的"unicorn"做了对比，也避免译文出现太多地名而增加读者的阅读负担，影响其阅读体验。

四、旅游文本中概念文化词的翻译

概念文化词是最能反映一个民族有别于其他民族意识形态的语言形式，分为本体概念文化词和附加概念文化词。"本体概念文化词"是指目标语与源语没有对应概念、目标语读者无法理解的词汇，属于"文化空缺"，一般采用音译+释义，也可意译。例如"春联"音译+释义，译为"chunlian (couplet scroll at the door)"，"北漂"意译为"Beijing Dream Pursuers"。"附加概念文化词"是指除了本体意义外，还附加了本民族特殊概念的词语，这类文化词不能直译，可意译或归化处理。例如，"我认识的几对老鸳鸯"，"老鸳鸯"意译为"old couples"；"你们约会，我不想做电灯泡"，"电灯泡"归化译为"the third wheel"。

从语际维度，文化负载词又可分为"封闭文化词""外流文化词"和"双源近似文化词"。"封闭文化词"是指还未传播到国外的文化词。"外流文化词"是指已经转播到国外的文化负载词（郑剑委，范文君，2018：127）。"外流文化词"，如"点心"(dim sum)，"太极"(Taiji)、"乌龙茶"(Oolong)等已经被西方读者接受，可直接使用。"双源近似文化词"是指源语的文化词与目的语的某一文化词存在部分概念对等的词汇，在不引起误解的情况下可直译或套译；如果产生歧义，需增加修饰语进行限定，如"凤凰"译为"phoenix"，"龙"则应译为"Chinese dragon"。

例1. 书舍主人区翰辉，因德而成三水岗头村<u>乡贤</u>梁知鉴的<u>妹夫</u>。清光绪年间，诰赠"<u>徽侍郎</u>"，成就了"<u>福缘善庆</u>"的传奇。

译文：The owner Ou Hanhui became the <u>brother-in-law</u> of the <u>county sage</u> Liang

第十一章　旅游文本中典故、专用名词等的翻译

Zhijian in Sanshui Gangtou Village by his good virtue. He was granted "Hui Shi Lang (a civil official)" during the reign of Emperor Guangxu of the Qing Dynasty and accomplished a legend of fortune and happiness.

分析：原文涉及诸多中国文化负载词，如"乡贤""妹夫""徽侍郎""福缘善庆"等，译者在处理中国文化负载词时，并没有选用单一的译法，而是采取多种译法。"乡贤""福缘善庆"属于"双源近似文化词"，英文中有类似的表达方式。译文采取直译法，分别译为"county sage""fortune and happiness"，读者可以直接理解。中国亲属称谓"妹夫"在英文中没有对应词，译文采用意译法，译为"brother-in-law"。对于"徽侍郎"这一极具中国特色的本体概念文化词，译文则采取音译+注释的翻译方法，译为"Hui Shi Lang（a civil official）"，进行了解释性的扩展，既有利于中华文化特色词汇输出，也有助于帮助外国读者理解，解决因"文化空缺"造成的意义或意象在翻译过程中的遗失问题。

例2．"嘎谐"是巴塘弦子的藏语全称，藏区其他地方的藏民称之为"康谐"，即康巴人的舞蹈，迄今已有1000多年的历史。

译文：Gaxie is a complete name of Xianzi dance in Batang. Tibetans from other areas call Batang Xianzi as Khampa shae, meaning the dance of Khampa people. Batang Xianzi has already existed for more than 1,000 years.

分析：这是康巴文化旅游外宣资料。"嘎谐""弦子"属于本体概念文化词，采用汉语拼音音译，拼写也采用汉语拼音，"康谐"则采用藏语音译和拼写，以便读者能脱离自身的文化认知语境理解康巴歌舞的内涵。对"康谐"的翻译，译文采用了藏语的音译和拼写，译为"Khampa shae"，不仅保留了藏族的语言特色，还在一定程度上避免了文化信息和语义的缺失，丰富了译入语词汇，增强了语言的活力。为了帮助译文读者理解，译文又通过释义，解释"康谐"之意："the dance of Khampa people"。英、美舞蹈取名倾向于地名与舞名相结合，故"弦子舞"译为"Batang Xianzi"。

例3．五供，古代象征性石雕祭器。中间是香炉，三足圆鼎形式，炉盖雕云龙。两侧是烛台和花瓶。

译文：Wu Gong (Five Offerings), the ancient symbolic sacrificial utensils carved out of stone: in the middle is an incense burner, a round tripod with dragon and cloud carved on the cover; on the two sides are candlesticks and vases.

分析:"五供"指的是中国民间祭祀时盛供品用的五件器皿,在道教中又称为"五献",工艺考究,造型古朴,由一只鼎、一对烛台、一对花觚组成。"香炉""三足圆鼎""烛台"等词蕴含着丰富的中国特色文化的信息,但目标语国家有相对应的概念,为"双源近似文化词",不属于"文化空缺",故"香炉"译为"incense burner","三足圆鼎"译为"round tripod","烛台"译为"candlesticks",不会造成跨文化交际障碍。"五供"是"本体概念文化词",目标语国家文化中不存在此概念,属于"文化空缺",故译文采取直译+释译法,译为"Wu Gong（Five Offerings）"。直译为"Wu Gong"是为了文化输出,加上释译"Five Offerings",是为了帮助译语读者更好地理解。

例4. 青城山三清殿中,供奉的是道教至高无上的三位尊神,即上清、玉清、太清。上清被称为"灵宝天尊",玉清被称为"元始天尊",太清被称为"道德天尊"。

译文:In the Trinity Hall on Mount Qingcheng, the three supreme Taoist divinities are enshrined and worshiped in it. The Trinity refers to "shangqing", "yuqing", and "taiqing", which represent the three states in three ages of the universe. "shangqing" symbolizes the era of Hong Yuan, the Flooding Era; "yuqing", the age of Hun Yuan, the Chaotic Era while "taiqing", the age of Tai Chu, the Beginning Era.

分析:道教神仙术语是中国特有的文化负载词,在民间被广泛使用,道教术语外译是一项充满挑战的跨文化交际活动,难度大,要求高。"三清殿"直译为"the Trinity Hall",是译者将中国道教"三清"与西方基督教"三位一体"对比思考的结果;而中国大多数神仙术语属于"本体概念文化词",多采用音译+释译,故原文中的"上清""玉清""太清"分别译为:"shangqing""yuqing""taiqing"并进行了释译:"shangqing" symbolizes the era of Hong Yuan, the Flooding Era; "yuqing", the age of Hun Yuan, the Chaotic Era while "taiqing", the age of Tai Chu, the Beginning Era 也可视为做了一文内加注。加注作为文化有效补偿手段,不仅可以使译文保留原文的语言和文化特色,也可以在一定程度上调整两种语言在文化上的差异，最大限度地弥补译文读者的"词汇空缺"和"文化空缺"。

例5. 有的制作了<u>水转玛尼筒</u>、<u>灯转玛尼筒</u>，自然力代替人念诵《<u>六字大明咒</u>》。

译文：Some people built <u>Water Wheels Turned by Flowing Water and Five Wheels Turned by the Heat of Candle or Electric Light</u> so that natural force could replace human to chant <u>Buddhist scripture (OM Mani Padme Hum)</u>.

分析：这是甘孜旅游外宣文本。原文出现了甘孜当地的"水转玛尼筒""灯转玛尼筒"《六字大明咒》等"本体概念文化词"，反映了当地的宗教信仰。"水转玛尼筒""灯转玛尼筒"是指装《六字大明咒》经卷的经筒，转动经文表示诚心向佛，故译文根据其转动的方式直译为："Water Wheels Turned by Flowing Water""Five Wheels Turned by the Heat of Candle or Electric Light"，便于读者直接理解；而对《六字大明咒》这一极富宗教文化的特色词，则采取直译+音译，译为"Buddhist scripture (OM Mani Padme Hum)"。《六字大明咒》是佛经特有的词汇，译文直接借用梵文发音，有助于外国游客直接了解佛教信徒诵经的声音。

例6. <u>天坛</u>是明清两代皇帝"<u>祭天</u>""<u>祈谷</u>"的场所。坛域北呈圆形，南为方形，寓意"<u>天圆地方</u>"。四周环筑坛墙两道，把全坛分为<u>内坛</u>、<u>外坛</u>两部分，总面积273公顷，主要建筑集中于内坛。

译文：<u>The Temple of Heaven</u> used to be the place where emperors of the Ming and Qing dynasties <u>worshiped Heaven</u> and <u>prayed for good harvests</u>. The northern part is circular while the southern part is square—symbolizing the ancient Chinese belief that <u>the heaven was round and the earth square</u>. The temple, covering an area of 273 hectares, is further divided into two parts, <u>the Inner and the Outer Altar</u> by two encircling walls, with major buildings in the Inner Altar.

分析：天坛景点介绍围绕古代帝王祭天祈谷的场所——天坛展开叙述，涉及众多文化负载词，具有深厚的中国文化内涵。中国古代哲学主张"天地人和"，中国文化中的"天"与西方基督教中的"paradise"概念不同，属于"附加概念文化词"，故中国哲学中的"天"只能译为"heaven"，不宜译为"paradise"，因此原文中涉及"天"的文化负载词均译为"heaven",如"天坛"("Temple of Heaven")、"祭天"("worshiped Heaven")等。"祈谷"是古代为了祈求谷物丰收的祭礼,译文处理为"prayed for good harvests"。"天圆地方"作为中国古代的一种哲学思想,运用到中国建筑领域,译为"the heaven was round and the earth square";而"内坛""外坛"属于"双源近似文化词",可直译为"the Inner and the Outer Altar",这是因为目标语不存在"词汇空缺",没有太大的理解障碍,不需要借助释译,读者也可理解。

例7. 金河又称金水河,是成都城内从西到东横贯全城的小河,是唐宣宗大中七年(公元853年),在当时的西川节度使兼成都府尹白敏中的主持下,在疏通城中小河的基础上修成的,其目的是给城内的大量居民提供生活用水的方便,也是为了向城外排出雨水与生活污水。因为是从西边入城,遂按古代五行学说中关于西方属金、金生水的说法,命名为金水河,简称金河。

译文:The Jinhe or Jinshuihe (meaning "river of golden water") is a small waterway that once flowed west to east across the entire city of Chengdu. It was constructed over existing channels in the city in the seventh year during the reign of Emperor Xuanzong (A.D. 853) under the direction of Bai Minzhong (who was both Military Governor of Xichuan and Magistrate of Chengdu Prefecture at the time) as a convenient source of water for a large number of city residents and means to discharge rainwater and sewage from the city. Because its source lay to the west, the river was named "Jinshuihe" or "Jinhe" for short, as traditional Chinese thought associates *jin* (gold/metal, one of the five elements) with the west.

分析:该段主要对金河的历史由来、功能效用展开描述,解释了金河的命名缘由,其中涉及多个文化负载词。译者在音译的基础上,解释金河名字的含义:"The Jinhe or Jinshuihe (meaning 'river of golden water')"。由于中国历代官职名称及职能变化较大,官职名称的翻译成为了文化负载词翻译的一大难事。译文采用"职能+泛称"译法,将"西川节度使"译为"Military Governor of Xichuan","成都府尹"译为"Magistrate of Chengdu Prefecture";"五行学说"是中国古代哲学的一个重要组成部分,认为世界上的一切事物都是由木、火、土、金、水五种物质之间的运动变化而生成的,属于"本体概念文化词",译文直译为"five elements",与"*jin* (gold/metal, one of the five elements)"相对应,是对"金"的一种补充性解释,让读者更好地理解"金河"这一地名的文化意蕴。

例8. "八宝"是在我国民间长期流行的多种吉祥物的总称,各地所指不尽相同,有如今天还在使用的<u>八宝箱</u>、<u>八宝粥</u>一样,基本上是一种表示其多的泛称。不过在民间工艺美术中一般都以宝珠、<u>方胜</u>、<u>玉磬</u>、犀角、古钱、珊瑚、银锭、<u>如意</u>为八宝。

译文:Throughout China's past, "<u>babao</u>" has been widely used to refer to different good-luck items, though the term has carried slightly different connotations depending on the setting. As with the <u>babao box (treasure chest)</u> and <u>babao porridge</u> we still have today, "babao" most often denotes a general wide-ranging assortment of treasures. But in the traditional arts, <u>it more often refers to eight specific treasures</u>: precious pearls, <u>*fangsheng* (a kind of jewelry with an overlapping pattern)</u>, <u>*yuqing* (an ancient percussion instrument made of jade)</u>, rhinoceros horn, ancient coins, coral, silver ingot, and <u>*ruyi* (a ceremonial S-shaped scepter)</u>.

分析:我国吉祥物"八宝"含义丰富,内涵深厚,属于"本体概念文化词","八宝"的翻译采取音译法,译为"babao",因为这一具有中国特色的汉语词在英语中没有对等词,采取异化翻译有利于中国文化对外传播,但在后段翻译"八宝"的内容时,译文做了释译:"it more often refers to eight specific treasures"。两种不同译法相得益彰,没有影响译文读者的接受和阅读体验。对于特别抽象的中国概念文化词,译文采取了音译+释译,将"方胜""玉磬""如意"等这类民间工艺专业词汇译为"*fangsheng* (a kind of jewelry with an overlapping pattern)""*yuqing* (an ancient percussion instrument made of jade)""*ruyi* (a ceremonial S-shaped scepter)",为不了解中国手工艺品的外国读者提供必要的文化背景知识,填补了他们的"文化空缺";对于"八宝粥"的翻译,由于不属于完全意义的"词汇空缺",译文采取了音译+直译的译法,译为"babao porridge",为译语文化注入新的内容,也是文化输出的一种方式。

例9. 风靡全国的蜀中名菜"夫妻肺片",原来是20世纪30年代郭朝华、张田政夫妇在长顺上街街边小摊所卖的麻辣肺片,因为滋味绝佳,遂被人们称为"夫妻肺片",有了名声之后,才发展成为一夫妻肺片小店。

译文:One Sichuan dish that would gain nationwide popularity started out as the *mala feipian* ("hot and numbing lung slices") sold by a married couple Guo Chaohua and Zhang Tianzheng at a small roadside stand on Changshun Upper Street in the 1930s. The dish gained popularity for its superior flavor, and people gradually began to call it *fuqi feipian* ("sliced lungs sold by husband and wife" or "sliced beef and ox tongue in chili sauce"). Their reputation growing, the couple was able to move their business into a small shop.

分析:中文菜名翻译不仅涉及菜品的原料、烹饪方法,还涉及人名、地名和一些独特叫法,属于"本体概念文化词",一般采取"烹制方法为主,原料为辅"的翻译方法。为了让外国读者理解中国菜的主料、作料、烹饪方式等,译文采取音译+释义的译法,"麻辣肺片"译为"*mala feipian* ('hot and numbing lung slices')","夫妻肺片"译为"*fuqi feipian* ('sliced lungs sold by husband and wife' or 'sliced beef and ox tongue in chili sauce')"。"夫妻肺片"后一种译法使用介词"in",是因为主料加配料,如果是汤汁或蘸料和主料分开,后浇在主菜上,则可使用介词"with";成都街道过长,当地人习惯分为上、中、下街,是当地具有特色的文化负载词,可采取专名+方位词+通名的译法,也可将方位词置于专名前面。

例10. 唐宋时期的科举考试以五经(即《诗》《书》《礼》《易》《春秋》)取士,每一经的第一名叫"魁首",共有五经魁首(今天人们饮酒划拳时喊的酒令中的"五魁首"就是这样来的)。这个"魁"就是来自古人对文运之神的崇拜。

译文:The imperial examinations in the Tang and Song dynasties selected scholars depending on the results of the examinations of *Five Classics* (i.e. *The Book of Poetry, The Book of History, The Book of Ceremony, The Book of Changes* and *The Spring and*

第十一章 旅游文本中典故、专用名词等的翻译

Autumn Annals), and the first one on the list of each of the five examinations was called "Kuishou" (this is the origin of the "Five Kuishou" in the drinking order that people shout when they drink and do Finger Guessing Game today). The Chinese character 魁 (*Kui*) just came from the ancient people who worshiped the Kui-star God in charge of literary fortune.

分析：该段主要介绍了唐宋时期的科举考试，涉及"魁首""五经魁首"等中华民族文化性极强的"本体概念文化词"。由于英文中没有对应词和相应的文化概念，属于"词汇空缺"和"文化空缺"，译文采取音译法，分别译为"Kuishou"和"Five Kuishou"，但没有释译，因为根据上下文可大概了解其意；对于译入语国家能找到对应词的词汇或意义相同或相近的表达方法，译文则采取直译法，如将"科举考试""酒令""划拳"等译为"imperial examinations""drinking order""Finger Guessing Game"；对于"五经"及其书名"《诗》《书》《礼》《易》《春秋》"的翻译，译文也采取直译法，译为"Five Classics"以及"*The Book of Poetry*""*The Book of History*""*The Book of Ceremony*""*The Book of Changes*""*The Spring and Autumn Annals*"，便于读者直接理解和接收。汉字"魁"采取了移译法，直接移入英文译文中，只加了一个拼音"*Kui*"，与后文中的"Kui-star God"翻译对接。由此可见，文化负载词的翻译需根据译文读者的文化背景、接受能力和阅读体验采取不同的翻译策略和方法。

本章小结

中文旅游文本常引经据典，引用典故、俗语、习语、名人名言等，以增强文本的知识性、趣味性；而英文旅游文本重写实，很少用典或引用名人名言。由于英、汉之间的差异，汉语中的典故、俗语、习语、名人名言、专用名词等蕴含着中文特有的意象形态、文体结构、修辞形式等，难以用另一种语言符号全面地呈现出来，也没有对等词，属于"词汇空缺""文化空缺"，翻译此类具有中国特色的旅游文本需采取针对性的翻译策略和方法，充分考虑目标语读者的接受能

力,如音译、音译加注释、增译、省译、套译等,处理好两种语言文化之间的差异,以弥补原文和译文之间的"词汇空缺""文化空缺"。翻译典故、俗语、人名、地名等是旅游文本翻译的难点,应以功能翻译理论为指导,正确处理字、词、句、语篇的转换,不可局限于在语言、形式上的一致或对等。

翻译实践

一、热身练习

翻译下文,并对译文做简要分析。

1. 巴彦淖尔,蒙语意为富饶的湖泊。

2. 大殿东侧有檀越祠、准提禅林,西侧有功德堂、尊胜院、水陆寺等。

3. 新春正月二十三,太上老君炼仙丹,家家户户贴金牛,一年四季保平安。

4. 岳庙始建于南宋嘉定十四年(1221年)初名"岳公行祠",是为纪念抗金名将岳飞而立。

5. 湘西人旧时所食多以杂粮为主,但逢年过节、红白喜事、待客之际,却颇有其民族地域特色。

6. "大唱"即"伊玛堪大唱",是指以说为主的表演,侧重和擅长表现英雄与传奇性的节目内容,如各种"莫日根"故事和赫哲族人的创世传说。

7. 《甘珠尔》,也称"正藏",是释迦牟尼本人语录的译文。《丹珠尔》,也称"副藏",是佛教弟子及后世佛教高僧对释迦牟尼教义所作的论述和注疏的译文。

8. 明代伟大的旅行家和地理学家徐霞客描述凤凰泉:"掏珠崩玉,飞沫反涌,如烟雾腾空,势甚雄历……"

9. 开封大相国寺位于开封市中心,红墙碧瓦,殿宇巍峨,霜钟远振,有"汴京八景"之"相国霜钟""资圣熏风",有"相国十绝"名誉天下。

10. 子曰:"兴于诗,立于礼,成于乐。"

第十一章　旅游文本中典故、专用名词等的翻译

二、巩固练习

翻译下文，并对译文做简要分析。

1. 在周易学说里，均有四大灵神，分别是青龙、白虎、朱雀、玄武，也称"四护卫神"。

2. 21世纪，武汉这座都市被商业占领着：步行街、司门口、新世界、武汉广场、庄胜崇光，以及遍布武汉三镇的大型商场、超市、商业街，琳琅满目的商品，随处涌动的人潮，令人叹为观止，精彩如购物天堂。

3. 关于河南婚嫁生育的民俗很有趣，如：新婚的当晚，洞房里要演出"撒喜床"，也称为"闹洞房"。

4. 位于南阳市西南的卧龙岗，相传诸葛亮曾躬耕于此，刘备"三顾茅庐"的故事也发生于此。

5. 这是新建的罗汉堂。中国的石洞和寺庙中有"十六罗汉""十八罗汉""五百罗汉"等。

6. 周武王灭殷7年之后，因病去世，其长子姬诵继位，是为周成王。因成王年幼，便由其叔父姬旦代行天子职权，史称"周公摄政"。

7. 梅里山庄整个木隔门及漏窗等处均镂空刻有卷草、花鸟、曲云图案和人物故事图案，如孔子讲学、八仙过海、岳母刺字、姜太公钓鱼、《西厢记》《红楼梦》等故事片段图案，还有喜鹊衔梅、鲤鱼跳龙门等，其雕刻内容之丰富、雕刻工艺之精湛，可谓美妙绝伦。

8. 两尊金刚居于左右，一哼一哈，令人生畏。中间是灵官护法，他额生竖眼，手执长鞭，显示出他的职责和佛法不可侵犯。

9. 在有着"桃源"美称的永春境内，四季水果飘香，农闲习武成风。

10. 太湖雷氏文化源远流长，太湖雷氏至今发展到26代之多，从第1代到第19代，据家谱记载，考取庠生（秀才）、举人、进士的达270余人，七品以上的官员7人。

三、阅读翻译

阅读下文，重点翻译下画线部分。

留园

<u>好了，我们继续往前。现在我们看到的这临水而筑的小屋，是赏春景的最佳去处——"绿荫"</u>。原来，小屋旁曾种有一棵老榉树、一棵老枫树，树枝像两把大伞遮在屋顶上，小轩处在这古树的绿荫之下，借此而得名。<u>轩名取自明代诗人高启的"艳发朱光里，丛依绿荫边"诗句</u>。在绿荫轩的后墙上有"花步小筑"四个字，为什么要写上这几个字呢？留园一带旧名"花步里"，"小筑"就是小的<u>建筑</u>，这是主人很谦虚的说法，意思是说我这个花园只是花步里边上的一处小建筑而已。

在绿荫轩欣赏完春景，现在我们来到涵碧山房，这三间卷棚硬山造建筑，是中部花园的主厅。<u>其名取自宋代文人朱熹的诗"一水方涵碧，千林已变红"。建筑面池而建，东临明瑟楼，隔水与小蓬莱相望</u>。周围山峦林木倒映在水清如碧的池中；每当盛夏时节，池内荷花盛开，荷香阵阵，这里便是赏荷的绝佳之处，所以又称"荷花厅"。

<u>循着涵碧山房西侧的爬山廊，我们来到中部花园中最高的建筑闻木樨香轩</u>。从建筑形式上看，这实际上是一个依廊而建的半亭。"木樨"就是桂花，这儿四周遍种桂花，每年中秋，丹桂飘香，晚上可以看到明月高悬，倒映水中，随波荡漾。因此，这儿是观赏秋景的地方。<u>轩前是一副对联："奇石尽含千古秀，桂花香动万山秋。"这是一副状景联。此处千姿百态的湖石在桂花树的掩映下，显得玲珑而古朴，而每到秋风送爽时，则满山荡漾着桂花的香气。这里的"动"字用得极妙，将"香味"这一园林中的虚景写活了。</u>

主要参考文献

[1] Brown, J. D. *China-the 50 Most Memorable Trips*[M]. San Francisco: IDG Books Worldwide, Inc., 2000.

[2] Dann, G. *The Language of Tourism: A Sociolinguistic Perspective*[M]. Oxfordshire: CABI Publishing, 1996.

[3] Davey, M. Gardens by the Bay: Ecologically Reflective Design[J]. *Architectural Design*, 2011(6): 108–111.

[4] DK. *EYEWITNEE TRAVEL USA*[M]. New York: DK Publishing, 2008.

[5] Else, D. etc, *Great Britain*[M]. London: Lonely Planet Publications, 2013.

[6] Getz, D. & Sailor, L,. Design of Destination and Attraction-specific Brochure[J]. *Journal of Travel & Tourism Marketing* 1993(2): 329–353.

[7] Halliday, M. New Horizons in Linguistics [C]. Halliday, M., Husan, R. *Language Structure and Language Function*[A]. Lyons: Penguin Books, 1970: 221–224.

[8] Mayhew, B. *Lonely Planet Nepal*[M]. Melbourne: Lonely Planet, 2006.

[9] Neubert, A., Shreve, G. M. *Translation as Text* [M]. Kent: Kent University Press, 1992.

[10] Newmark, P. *A Textbook of Translation* [M]. New Jersey: Prentice Hall International, 1988.

[11] Nord, C. Translating as a Purposeful Activity: Functionalist Approaches Explained [M]. Shanghai: Shanghai Foreign Language Education Press, 1997.

[12] Nida, E. A. *Language and Culture: Contexts in Translating*[M]. Shanghai: Shanghai Foreign Language Education Press, 2001.

[13] Pierini, P. Quality in Web Translation: An Investigation into UK and Italian Tourism Web Sites[J]. *Journal of Specialized Translation*, 2007(8): 113–115.

[14] Reiss, K. & Vermeer, H. *General Foundations of Translation Theory*[M]. Tubingen: Niemeyer, 1984.

[15] Snell, H. M. *Translation Studies, An Integrated Approach* [M]. 上海：上海外语教育出版社, 2001.

[16] Untermeyer, L. *Robert Frost: A Backward Look*[M]. Washington, D. C.: The Library of Congress, 1964.

[17] Venuti, Lawrence. *The Translator's Invisibility*[M]. London: Routledge, 1995.

[18] Yao, Chunyan. An Analysis of Differences between English and Chinese Tourism Texts[J]. *Open Journal of Modern Linguistics*, 2019:153–164.

[19] DK公司. 目击者旅游指南——美国[M]. 张寿峰, 李伟涛等译. 北京：中国旅游出版社,

2008.

[20] 柏舟. 旅游文化与翻译策略：以杭州西湖的匾额、楹联、诗词的翻译为例[J]. 现代城市，2009(03)：74-80.

[21] 边立红, 黄曙光. 大学科技英语翻译教程[M]. 北京：对外经济贸易大学出版社, 2016.

[22] 边立红, 郑橙. 旅游文本中诗歌引文英译的创造性叛逆[J]. 河北旅游职业学院学报, 2015(02)：72-75.

[23] 蔡玲, 许国新. 论旅游文化推介中中国古典诗词的翻译[J]. 扬州大学学报（人文社会科学版）, 2011(01)：123-128.

[24] 蔡小玲. 汉英旅游文本主要差异及其翻译[J]. 中国民航飞行学院学报, 2011(01)：62-65.

[25] 曹文刚. 汉英旅游文本翻译探析[J]. 湖北第二师范学院学报, 2014(10)：132-133.

[26] 常晖. 旅游资料文化翻译探析[J]. 四川外语学院学报, 2009(S2)：121-125.

[27] 陈白璧, 熊建闽. 旅游文本汉译英中"失当信息"处理[J]. 莆田学院学报, 2012(03)：53-56.

[28] 陈从周. 中国名园：汉英对照[M]. 上海：同济大学出版社, 2009.

[29] 陈刚. 旅游翻译与涉外导游[M]. 北京：中国对外翻译出版公司, 2004.

[30] 陈刚. 旅游英汉互译教程[M]. 上海：上海外语教育出版社, 2009.

[31] 陈刚. 旅游英语导译教程[M]. 上海：上海外语教育出版社, 2010：111.

[32] 陈刚. 旅游翻译[M]. 杭州：浙江大学出版社, 2014.

[33] 陈洪富. 福建省主要旅游景区景点英语导游词[M]. 厦门：厦门大学出版社, 2014.

[34] 陈金莲. 生态翻译学视阈下旅游翻译的三维转换[J]. 重庆交通大学学报（社会科学版）, 2016(01)：117-124.

[35] 陈莉. 中西旅游文化与翻译研究[M]. 北京：中国商务出版社, 2018.

[36] 陈敏. 旅游资料的翻译目的与译者主体性的发挥：以《怀化旅游指南》为例[J]. 怀化学院学报, 2013(06)：87-89.

[37] 陈水平. 旅游翻译的误区与价值伦理回归[J]. 中国科技翻译, 2012(3)：45-49.

[38] 陈思颖. 翻译目的论视角下的旅游文本英译实践报告[D]. 上海：上海师范大学, 2014.

[39] 陈小慰. 翻译功能理论的启示——对某些翻译方法的新思考[J]. 中国翻译, 2000(04)：10-13.

[40] 陈小慰. 对外宣传翻译中的文化自觉与受众意识[J]. 中国翻译, 2013(02)：95-100.

[41] 陈晓红. 德国功能翻译理论下的安徽旅游翻译探析[J]. 湖北函授大学学报, 2013(03)：142-143.

[42] 程珊珊, 夏赞才. 基于网络文本的文化主题景区旅游形象感知对比研究——以深圳、长沙世界之窗为例[J]. 旅游论坛, 2018(05)：111-123.

[43] 楚成东. 中国·青岛指南[M]. 青岛：青岛出版社, 2002(02).

[44] 褚琴. 江苏导游英语[M]. 北京：中国旅游出版社, 2016.

[45] 崔改丽. 英语旅游广告语言特点及汉译策略研究[J]. 佳木斯教育学院学报，2014 (02)：379–380.

[46] 崔刚. 广告英语3000句 选萃·分析·欣赏[M]. 北京：北京理工大学出版社，1993.

[47] 崔娟，李鑫. 变译理论视角下的旅游文体英译研究——以《中国烟台旅游指南》为例[J]. 鲁东大学学报（哲学社会科学版），2017(05)：50–55.

[48] 邓红顺. 旅游文本翻译与中国文化的传播[J]. 赤峰学院学报（哲学社会科学版），2010 (03)：49–50.

[49] 邓乔彬. 文化诗学[M]. 合肥：安徽师范大学出版社，2013.

[50] 邓炎昌，刘润清. 语言与文化——英汉语言文化对比[M]. 北京：外语教学与研究出版社，1989.

[51] 丁大刚. 旅游英语的语言特点与翻译[M]. 上海：上海交通大学出版社，2008.

[52] 丁姮. 旅游城市对外宣传材料的英译策略研究[D]. 哈尔滨：黑龙江大学，2013.

[53] 丁芸. 从"对等"论旅游翻译——以黄山旅游文本翻译为例[J]. 黄山学院学报，2016 (01)：75–78.

[54] 董踩. 翻译技巧与翻译方法、翻译策略的区别及其分类[J]. 湘潭大学学报（哲学社会科学版），2021(02)：186.

[55] 董晓波. 英汉比较与翻译[M]. 北京：对外经济贸易大学出版社，2013.

[56] 樊宁瑜. 浅析旅游翻译的特点及翻译技巧[J]. 新西部（理论版），2016(20)：98–99.

[57] 方婵. 从形合与意合谈《兰亭集序》的翻译[J]. 文学教育（上），2011 (03)：94.

[58] 方梦之. 译学辞典[M]. 上海：上海外语教育出版社，2004.

[59] 方幸娟. 旅游文本英译实践报告——以红色六安旅游文化宣传文本的英译为例[D]. 上海：上海师范大学，2018.

[60] 方宜庆. 新型大学英语作文技法[M]. 合肥：安徽科学技术出版社，1998.

[61] 丰文森，张建国. 翻译之美初探——以《徐霞客游记》大中华文库英译本用词为例[J]. 黑河学院学报，2020(06)：139–141+144.

[62] 冯娟，李佳. 功能对等理论视阈下西安旅游景点介绍的汉英翻译研究[J]. 海外英语，2015(22)：132–133.

[63] 冯庆华. 实用翻译教程：英汉互译[M]. 上海：上海外语教育出版社，2002.

[64] 冯秋怡. 旅游宣传文本英译汉中名物化词组的语言特点及其翻译策略[J]. 科教导刊，2018(8)：41–42.

[65] 付昱，郑景婷. 功能对等视角下《徒步穿越中国》的汉译本研究[J]. 英语广场，2020(31)：19–21.

[66] 傅燕. 跨文化交际与汉俄旅游翻译[D]. 上海：上海外国语大学，2007.

[67] 高飞雁，王莲凤. 旅游文本翻译策略与实例解析[J]. 广西教育学院学报，2019(06)：39–42.

[68] 高金岭. 从中西审美方式的差异看旅游资料中景物描写的翻译[J]. 山东外语教学，

2003(03)：100–103.

[69] 高珺. 从功能主义视角看文化翻译策略：以旅游文本翻译为例[D]. 哈尔滨：黑龙江大学，2010.

[70] 高士，奥罗宾多等. 20世纪印度比较诗学论文选译[M]. 尹锡南译. 成都：巴蜀书社，2016.

[71] 高吟. 功能目的论视角下平行文本在旅游文本英译中的应用研究——以福州旅游资料为例[D]. 福州：福州大学，2017.

[72] 高子越.《漫游意大利》旅游手册英译实践报告[D]. 哈尔滨：哈尔滨理工大学，2017.

[73] 龚珍.《梅山龙宫导游词》英译实践报告[D]. 长沙：湖南师范大学，2017.

[74] 谷向阳. 中国对联学研究[J]. 北京大学学报(哲学社会科学版)，1998(4)：129–136.

[75] 辜正坤. 中西诗比较鉴赏与翻译理论[M]. 北京：清华大学出版社，2010.

[76] 顾潇潇. 省译法在英译旅游文本翻译中的应用研究——以《神话世界九寨沟》序言翻译为例[J]. 英语广场，2018(10)：19–21.

[77] 郭建中. 翻译中的文化因素：异化与归化[J]. 外国语（上海外国语大学学报），1998(02)：13–20.

[78] 韩陈其. 中国古汉语学[M]. 台湾：台湾新文丰出版公司，1995.

[79] 韩竞辉，陈达，陈国庆. 跨文化旅游翻译中的归化与异化——以新疆旅游宣传资料为例[J]. 度假旅游，2018(01)：80–82.

[80] 韩荣良. 桂林导游（中英对照）[M]. 北京：中国旅游出版社，2004.

[81] 韩荣良，韩志宇. 江苏导游：汉英对照[M]. 北京：中国旅游出版社，2007.

[82] 韩志孝. 能力语文（下册）[M]. 郑州：大象出版社，2008.

[83] 何景芳. 关联理论指导下旅游手册的翻译[D]. 兰州：西北师范大学，2007.

[84] 何敏，李延林. 英文广告创作中的"三美"原则及其翻译[J]. 湖南城市学院学报，2006(06)：99–102.

[85] 何修猛. 现代广告学[M]. 上海：复旦大学出版社，2008.

[86] 何志范. 上海英语导游[M]. 北京：旅游教育出版社，2004.

[87] 贺一凡. 翻译伦理理论指导下旅游手册《意大利体验之旅》翻译实践报告[D]. 沈阳：辽宁大学，2019.

[88] 洪晓云. 目的论视角下旅游文本中文化负载词的英译策略——以闽南旅游文本为例[D]. 福州：福建师范大学，2018.

[89] 胡波，曹小露. 旅游景点介绍汉英翻译中的创造性——以泰州市天德湖公园为例[J]. 鸡西大学学报，2015(01)：90–92+100.

[90] 胡开杰. 外语教学改革与实践[M]. 北京：北京航空航天大学出版社，2006.

[91] 胡鲁飞. 图式理论下的英语导游词翻译[J]. 安徽文学，2013(09)：113+116.

[92] 胡显耀，李力. 高级文学翻译[M]. 北京：外语教学与研究出版社，2009.

[93] 黄成洲，谢同. 英语标示语的语言风格与翻译模式探讨[J]. 常州大学学报（社会科学版），2011(01)：91–94.

[94] 黄菲. 主题信息突出原则在旅游翻译中的应用[J]. 科技信息（科学教研），2007(35)：95–96+102.

[95] 黄小英. 目的论视角下旅游文本文化负载词英译研究——以河南旅游资料为例[D]. 福州：福建师范大学，2016.

[96] 黄艳群，项凝霜. 论译者注之阐释功能——以伍光建英译《英汉对照名家小说选》为例[J]. 西华大学学报（哲学社会科学版），2016(1)：106–109.

[97] 黄忠廉，任东升. 汉英笔译全译实践教程[M]. 北京：国防工业出版社，2014.

[98] 黄中习. 中华对联研究与英译初探[M]. 长春：时代文艺出版社，2005.

[99] 惠敏，张国霞，蒋云磊. 功能论视角下的泰山旅游资料的汉英翻译[J]. 山东外语教学，2014(03)：103–108.

[100] 霍洛韦, J. 克里斯托弗·旅游营销学(第四版)[M]. 修月祯等译. 北京：旅游教育出版社，2006.

[101] 纪俊超. 旅游英语翻译实务[M]. 北京：中国科学技术大学出版社，2014.

[102] 贾文波. 旅游翻译不可忽视民族审美差异[J]. 上海科技翻译，2003(01)：20–22.

[103] 贾文波. 应用翻译功能论（第二版）[M]. 北京：中国对外翻译出版公司，2012.

[104] 姜琳琳，陈立涛. 上饶灵山景区宣传册文化负载词分类及翻译策略[J]. 校园英语，2020(04)：251.

[105] 姜璇. 浅谈旅游文本汉英翻译的技巧——以《十八水原生态景区介绍》的翻译为例[J]. 佳木斯职业学院学报，2017(8)：326.

[106] 矫燕. "移情融合"视角下的译文审美再造[J]. 大理大学学报，2018(11)：62–66.

[107] 金春伟. 英语主述位理论中的状语主位化[J]. 福建外语，2002(01)：15.

[108] 金隄. 等效翻译探索[M]. 北京：中国对外翻译出版公司，1989.

[109] 金惠康. 跨文化旅游翻译[M]. 北京：中国对外翻译出版公司，2006.

[110] 景兴润. 英语旅游网站文本翻译策略[J]. 长春教育学院学报，2015(08)：49–50.

[111] 康春杰，陈萌，吕春敏. 基于错误分析理论的英语翻译教学研究[M]. 长春：吉林文史出版社，2016.

[112] 康宁. 从语篇功能看汉语旅游语篇的翻译[J]. 中国翻译，2005(03)：85–89.

[113] 李成明. 基于中西文化对比的旅游文本翻译[J]. 江汉大学学报（社会科学版），2012(05)：111–112.

[114] 李承燕，盛夏. 三峡景区英文导游词的撰写与解说[M]. 天津：天津大学出版社，2017.

[115] 李丹. 图式理论观照下的旅游景点导游词英语翻译[J]. 传播力研究，2020(18)：29–30.

[116] 李慧晓. 翻译为导向的文本分析模式指导下旅游指南英汉翻译实践——以《孤独星球·荷兰》翻译为例[D]. 西安：西安外国语大学，2018.

[117] 李鉴，曹容. 康巴藏区民俗风情的旅游资料翻译策略[J]. 北方文学，2012(08)：95–96.

[118] 李克兴. 论广告翻译的策略[J]. 中国翻译，2004(06)：66–71.

[119] 李莉，杨玉.翻译美学视角下宁夏旅游文本英译探究[J].宁夏师范学院学报，2018(06)：108–112.

[120] 李丽萍.旅游广告外宣翻译研究[J].教育教学论坛，2018(52):79–80.

[121] 李良辰.基于目的论的景点现场导游词英译[J].中国科技翻译，2013(02)：51–54.

[122] 李明.翻译批评与赏析（第二版）[M].武汉：武汉大学出版社，2010.

[123] 李明，李思伊.信息布局观照下英译文语篇的重构——以《〈岭南钩沉〉——2014中国印花税票》序言的英译为例[J].上海翻译，2017(06)：32–37.

[124] 李勤，杨博智.旅游广告的跨文化诉求[J].当代传播，2006(06)：58–61.

[125] 李雪丰.山水游记散文翻译风格对比研究——基于《永州八记》三个译本平行语料库的统计分析[J].翻译研究与教学，2020 (02)：129–136.

[126] 李艳.旅游广告语言风格与外宣翻译[J].语文建设，2012(20)：45–46.

[127] 李玉靓.从后殖民主义角度看辜鸿铭《论语》英译中的注释[D].成都：电子科技大学，2014.

[128] 李运兴.语篇翻译引论[M].北京：中国对外翻译出版公司，2001.

[129] 李泽，张天洁.迈向"花园里的城市"——新加坡滨海花园设计理念探析[J].中国园林，2012(10)：114–118.

[130] 连淑能.英汉对比研究（增订本）[M].北京：高等教育出版社，2010.

[131] 梁君华.平行文本与网络旅游广告英译[J].上海翻译，2012(02)：69–73.

[132] 梁丽清.旅游文化传播视角下推介佛山古村落的英文翻译探讨[J].无锡商业职业技术学院学报，2016(06)：38–40+53.

[133] 梁天柱，李海勇，鞠艳霞.外语翻译与文化融合[M].北京：九州出版社，2018.

[134] 梁晓婷.旅游文本特点及中英翻译策略——以广东旅游为例[J].北方文学，2019(03)：232+234.

[135] 廖七一.当代西方翻译理论探索[M].北京：译林出版社，2000.

[136] 廖七一.多元系统[J].外国文学，2004(04)：48–52.

[137] 廖素云，陶燕.翻译功能理论指导下的汉英旅游翻译[J].江苏技术师范学院学报（职教通讯），2008(06)：109–112.

[138] 林菲.新修辞视角下旅游网站文本的修辞分析与英译调适[J].合肥工业大学学报（社会科学版），2015(05)：76–80.

[139] 林红杰.《大兴安岭森林小旅行》汉英翻译实践报告[D].沈阳：东北大学，2015.

[140] 林莉.专门用途英语课程与教学研究[M].北京：中国商务出版社，2011.

[141] 林娜，陆世雄.文化语境视角下刘三姐旅游景点简介英译研究[J].河池学院学报，2020(02)：41–47.

[142] 林星平，叶苗.论翻译美学视角下旅游文本中古诗词的英译[J].牡丹江大学学报，2015(05)：150–152.

[143] 林竹梅.旅游翻译理论与实践[M].北京：对外经济贸易大学出版社，2014.
[144] 刘爱梅.关联理论视角下旅游广告的语言特点及其翻译[J].旅游纵览，2013(6)：9-11.
[145] 刘辰诞.教学篇章语言学[M].上海：上海外语教育出版社，1999.
[146] 刘春华.实用文体英汉互译教程[M].武汉：武汉大学出版社，2019.
[147] 刘法公.论广告词的汉英翻译原则[J].外语与外语教学，1999(03)：41-44+57.
[148] 刘宏杰.英语应用文文体分析（第1辑）[M].北京：知识产权出版社，2011.
[149] 刘宏义.论怀化旅游对外宣传资料中诗词楹联的英译[J].怀化学院学报，2013(07)：77-79.
[150] 刘季春.广告标题、口号的套译[J].中国科技翻译，1997(04)：44-47.
[151] 刘金龙，刘晓民.浅析旅游资料翻译的几种方法[J].山东教育学院学报，2006(01)：117-120.
[152] 刘军平.西方翻译理论通史[M].武汉：武汉大学出版社，2009.
[153] 刘兰，谭燕萍.接受美学视角下文学作品中的景物描写英译探究——以巴金小说《家》为例[J].岳阳职业技术学院学报，2018(02)：88-91+98.
[154] 刘丽.全译技巧在旅游文本中的运用——以2014青岛世界园艺博览会展馆解说词为例[J].常州信息职业技术学院学报，2015(01)：93-96.
[155] 刘伶.当代应用文写作[M].天津：天津大学出版社，2009.
[156] 刘梦.目的论视角下"晋祠名胜古迹"中文化负载词英译实践报告[D].大连：大连海事大学，2016.
[157] 刘梦璐.《环球游记——女子只身闯非洲》英汉翻译实践报告[D].唐山：华北理工大学，2020.
[158] 刘倩.中英旅游文本的文体差异及其翻译方法——以山东省台儿庄古城景点介绍为例[J].梧州学院学报，2018(05)：64-67.
[159] 刘文娟.旅游景点官网英译中的"归化"和"异化"——以清明上河园为例[J].企业科技与发展，2019(04)：234-236.
[160] 刘晓.旅游宣传手册翻译报告[D].济南：山东大学，2016.
[161] 刘新民.中英诗歌语言比较及翻译[A].刘重德.英汉语比较与翻译1（第2版）[C].上海：上海外语教育出版社，2006：184-194.
[162] 芦文辉.英汉互译中的直译与意译[J].晋中学院学报，2008(04)：122-124.
[163] 陆国飞.旅游景点汉语介绍英译的功能观[J].外语教学，2006(05)：80.
[164] 陆国飞.论汉语旅游景介英译策略——以海洋文化旅游文本的翻译为例[J].浙江海洋学院学报（人文科学版），2007(03)：100-106.
[165] 陆乃圣，金颖颖.英文导游词实用教程[M].上海：华东理工大学出版社，2000.
[166] 陆秀英.从文本功能对等角度探讨旅游文本的翻译策略——以庐山风景区的汉英翻译为例[J].华东交通大学学报，2006(03)：165-167.

[167] 罗丽莉. 浙江省旅游外宣翻译"文化流失"及其对应策略[J]. 宁波工程学院学报, 2015(04)：61–65.

[168] 罗珊珊, 林继红. 福建省5A级景区旅游文本英译研究——以生态翻译理论为视角[J]. 武夷学院学报, 2019(04)：41–46.

[169] 罗星星. Dann的旅游英语视角下桂林漓江和美国蛇江英文网站介绍对比分析[J]. 海外英语, 2020(09)：158–160.

[170] 罗艳. 旅游材料崀山景区介绍中典故的英译[D]. 湘潭：湖南科技大学, 2016.

[171] 吕焕. 旅游外宣文本翻译实践报告——以潜江旅游指南为例[D]. 上海：上海师范大学, 2021.

[172] 吕慧. 功能翻译理论指导下的旅游翻译[J]. 边疆经济与文化, 2007(03)：18–19.

[173] 吕俊. 翻译学——传播学的一个特殊领域[J]. 外国语（上海外国语大学学报）, 1997(02)：39–44.

[174] 吕政. 跨文化视域下的旅游广告翻译研究[J]. 上海翻译, 2016(01)：43–46.

[175] 马秉义. 英汉语句子结构常式比较[C]. 杨自俭. 英汉语比较与翻译3[A]. 上海：上海外语教育出版社, 2000：73.

[176] 马翠菊. 三维转换理论视域下的导游词英译分析——以拉卜楞寺导游词为例[J]. 甘肃高师学报, 2021(03)：40–44.

[177] 马国志. 英汉旅游景点介绍文本对比与翻译[J]. 天津市财贸管理干部学院学报, 2011(01)：65–66.

[178] 马玲玲. 旅游宣传文本的翻译策略初探：以美国的匹兹堡及其乡村地区与英国的哈伍德庄园两个文本的汉英翻译为例[D]. 上海：上海外国语大学, 2011.

[179] 马松梅. 一旅游景点的英译文引发的思考——谈汉、英民族不同的语言审美观[J]. 山东师范大学外国语学院学报（基础英语教育）, 2003(03)：109–111.

[180] 马文丽, 王利明. 网络本地化与新语言支持[J]. 中国科技翻译. 2005(04)：15–17+58.

[181] 梅休, 布拉德林. 尼泊尔[M]. 北京：生活·读书·新知三联书店, 2007.

[182] 孟琳, 詹晶辉. 英语广告中双关语的运用技巧及翻译[J]. 中国翻译, 2001(05)：49–52.

[183] 孟言. 旅游文本汉英翻译文化误译现象剖析[J]. 才智, 2015(08)：308.

[184] 穆慧琳. 浅析顺应论在汉语旅游文本翻译中的应用[J]. 江苏技术师范学院学报（职教通讯）, 2008(04)：105–108.

[185] 牛郁茜, 韩文哲. 旅游翻译文本中中英文语言特点及翻译策略[J]. 山西财经大学学报, 2017(C1)：60–61.

[186] 欧阳巧琳. 广告翻译中的顺应性[J]. 中南民族大学学报（人文社会科学版）, 2003(05)：177–179.

[187] 欧阳婉莹. 翻译美学视域下三毛散文《玛黛拉游记》英译实践报告[D]. 苏州：苏州大学, 2019.

[188] 潘莹. 从审美文化差异多视角看旅游翻译的读者观照[J]. 长沙大学学报, 2009 (04)：105–

107.

[189] 彭瑾. 关联理论与旅游手册的英译[D]. 西安：西安电子科技大学，2004.

[190] 彭萍. 实用旅游英语翻译：英汉双向[M]. 北京：对外经济贸易大学出版社，2010.

[191] 彭永生. 自然景观旅游解说汉英翻译：功能理论分析[J]. 重庆工学院学报（社会科学版），2008(09)：130–131+159.

[192] 平洪. 文本功能与翻译策略[J]. 中国翻译，2002(05)：21–25.

[193] 齐放. 英汉广告语修辞特征与翻译原则[J]. 呼和浩特：内蒙古农业大学学报（社会科学版），2009(01)：208–210.

[194] 祈阿红. 译海初探：实用翻译二十二讲[M]. 桂林：广西师范大学出版社，2019.

[195] 覃海晶. 平行文本比较及其对中文酒店文宣英译的启示[J]. 考试与评价，2014(01)：51–56.

[196] 邱冬娘. 从译者的主体性看客家土楼及其楹联的英译[J]. 齐齐哈尔师范高等专科学校学报，2019(01)：51–53.

[197] 裘禾敏. 操纵学派视角下旅游文本汉译英策略探幽[J]. 绍兴文理学院学报（哲学社会科学版），2008(02)：71–74.

[198] 任孝珍. 旅游应用文写作[M]. 北京：对外经济贸易大学出版社，2010.

[199] 撒忠清. 谈英汉旅游广告语的语言特色和创作[J]. 巢湖学院学报，2007(01)：107–112.

[200] 尚路平. 英国官方旅游网站研究[J]. 重庆理工大学学报（社会科学版），2014(03)：110–114.

[201] 申玉辉. 高考阅读——高考现代文阅读基础能力篇[M]. 重庆：重庆出版社，2006.

[202] 沈华丽. 语义交际翻译理论指导下旅游翻译策略——以庐山旅游景点为例[J]. 大众文艺，2020(20)：136–138.

[203] 沈继诚. 目的论与广告语篇汉英翻译的策略[J]. 浙江师范大学学报（社会科学版），2005(02)：69–74.

[204] 沈云. 旅游广告中英文体对比与翻译探讨[J]. 广西教育学院学报，2006(02)：142–145.

[205] 施志贤，陈德民. 从学生误译看翻译中逻辑思维转换的意义[J]. 集美大学学报（哲学社会科学版），2006(01)：87–92.

[206] 石佳星. 汉语旅游景点介绍交际翻译初探[D]. 南京：东南大学，2015.

[207] 舒娅. 《走遍中国：西藏》"西藏魅力速写"部分翻译项目报告[D]. 武汉：华中科技大学，2014.

[208] 司文凯. 游记文本中抽象语义的翻译——《通往涓涓细流之路》（第十四、二十五和二十六章）的翻译实践报告[D]. 大连：大连外国语大学，2019.

[209] 司显柱. 功能语言学与翻译研究——翻译质量评估模式建构[M]. 北京：北京大学出版社，2007.

[210] 宋燕，付瑛群. 从文本类型理论谈旅游文本英译汉翻译技巧——以Bountiful Bruges, a gem in Belgium为例[J]. 英语教师，2020，20(04)：134—136.

[211] 苏档. 英汉旅游手册语篇功能分析[D]. 长春：东北师范大学，2006.

[212] 苏淑惠. 广告英语的文体功能与翻译标准[J]. 外国语(上海外国语大学学报), 1996 (02)：51–56.

[213] 孙红梅. 汉英旅游景点介绍文本的对比分析与翻译[J]. 赤峰学院学报(哲学社会科学版), 2010(10)：125–127.

[214] 谭娟. 功能为先：析旅游文本翻译中的编译现象[J]. 湖北财经高等专科学校学报, 2009(03)：51–53.

[215] 谭卫国. 英汉广告修辞的翻译[J]. 中国翻译, 2003(02)：64–67.

[216] 谭业升. 旅游翻译中的"虚实"与移情[J]. 语言与翻译（汉文版）, 2014(04)：66–70+95.

[217] 唐沛. 英语旅游广告 基于Leech礼貌原则的分析[J]. 中国商贸, 2010(08)：163–164+166.

[218] 童庆炳. 文学理论教程（修订版）[M]. 北京：高等教育出版社, 1998.

[219] 屠国元. 三湘译论（第五辑）[M]. 长沙：湖南人民出版社, 2006.

[220] 涂嘉欣. 以目的论为指导的旅游文本英译实践报告——以《香港旅游手册》为例[D]. 上海：上海师范大学, 2019.

[221] 涂靖. 大学英语翻译教程[M]. 上海：上海交通大学出版社, 2016.

[222] 汪宝荣. 旅游文化的英译：归化与异化——以绍兴著名景点为例[J]. 中国科技翻译, 2005(01)：13–17.

[223] 汪萍萍. 论英文游记散文的翻译——以*The Wild Places*（节选）汉译为例[D]. 上海：复旦大学, 2014.

[224] 汪庆华. 旅游资料有意误译现象研究[J]. 贵州大学学报(社会科学版), 2015 (01)：169–172.

[225] 汪亚明. 导游词编撰实务[M]. 北京：旅游教育出版社, 2012.

[226] 王爱琴. 入乎其内，出乎其外——论汉英旅游翻译过程中思维的转换与重写[J]. 中国翻译, 2012(01)：98–102.

[227] 王才英. 旅游外宣文本的汉英翻译探析——以泉州地区旅游景点英译文本为例[J]. 怀化学院学报, 2009(10)：108–110.

[228] 王才英. 旅游指南汉英翻译的二元共存[J]. 厦门广播电视大学学报, 2014(04):42.

[229] 王菲. 德国功能翻译理论下的旅游文本翻译探析[J]. 湖北经济学院学报（人文社会科学版）, 2015(08)：128–129.

[230] 王芬, 谭波, 谭雅雯. 南岳名胜楹联特色及其翻译策略之探讨[J]. 湖南工业职业技术学院学报, 2017(06)：56–58.

[231] 王佳惠. 《中国旅游指南〈福建旅游指南〉》英译实践报告[D]. 哈尔滨：哈尔滨理工大学, 2017.

[232] 王浪. 中国著名旅游景区导游词精选（英汉对照）[M]. 北京：旅游教育出版社, 2010.

[233] 王力. 汉语诗律学[M]. 上海：上海教育出版社, 1979.

[234] 王露. 简析互文性视角下旅游广告翻译的语言特点[J]. 漯河职业技术学院学报, 2017(01)：76–79.

[235] 王青. 涉外导游词的翻译：归化？异化？[J]. 河北理工大学学报（社会科学版），2010 (06)：166–169.

[236] 王晴. 简论外宣翻译与文学翻译的区别：兼谈旅游外宣文本及诗词集的诗歌英译之异[J]. 浙江工商职业技术学院学报，2013(03)：83–88.

[237] 王晒存. 接受美学视角下《2016黄金海岸官方旅游指南》汉译实践报告[D]. 福州：福州大学，2018.

[238] 王婷，翟红梅. 旅游平行文本对比分析研究——以芜湖方特与加州迪斯尼乐园为例[J]. 山西农业大学学报(社会科学版)，2014(04)：392–396.

[239] 王伟. 旅游文本的英译原则：以武汉市旅游景点宣传资料英译为例[J]. 黄冈职业技术学院学报，2014(06)：69–72.

[240] 王先好，靳元丽. 徽州古民居楹联的文化内涵与翻译[J]. 巢湖学院学报，2018 (02)：132–135.

[241] 王宪. 论旅行后文本的写作与外译[J]. 集美大学学报（哲社版），2016(01)：120–121.

[242] 王小兵，倪娜. 浅谈旅游文本的语言特点与翻译[J]. 郑州航空工业管理学院学报（社会科学版），2013(02)：114–116.

[243] 王晓农，安广民. 山东省景区概览性旅游文本汉译英问题研究[J]. 唐山师范学院学报，2011(03)：40.

[244] 王学霞，温泉. 浅析关联论对长白山地域文化旅游翻译的影响因素[J]. 旅游纵览，2014（01）：78+81.

[245] 王玉慧. 以目的论为指导的旅游文本翻译实践报告——以《探访喀尔巴阡山的花园：罗马尼亚》为例[D]. 上海：上海师范大学，2018.

[246] 王佐良. 翻译：思考与试笔[M]. 北京：外语教学与研究出版社，1989.

[247] 韦忠生. 接受美学视野下的旅游文本翻译[J]. 安徽工业大学学报（社会科学版），2010(03)：64–67.

[248] 位巍. 青岛旅游手册的英译文本与英语旅游资料的对比分析[D]. 青岛：中国海洋大学，2006.

[249] 文红丽. 浅析英文广告创作中的修辞格运用及其翻译[J]. 中国科教创新导刊，2008(12)：171.

[250] 文军，邓春，辜涛，蒋宇佳. 信息与可接受度的统一——对当前旅游翻译的一项调查与分析[J]. 中国科技翻译，2002(01)：49.

[251] 文珍，荣菲. 谈现代英语旅游广告口号的功能特色与语言风格[J]. 北京第二外国语学院学报，2000(03)：70–77.

[252] 吴宝璋，何昌邑. 云南导游必备手册（中英双语）[M]. 昆明：云南大学出版社，1999.

[253] 吴朋. 形容词在旅游广告中的英汉对比及翻译[J]. 国际商务研究，2007(01)：58–60.

[254] 吴廷玉. 新编大学语文[M]. 上海：同济大学出版社，2006.

[255] 吴燮元. 实用口译教程[M]. 上海：复旦大学出版社，2014.

[256] 吴卓群. 目的论视角下英译游记散文——以《苏式的旅行》节选翻译为例[D]. 苏州：苏州大学，2017.

[257] 武萍. 从目的论角度分析旅游广告标语翻译：From the Perspective of Skopos Theory[D]. 青岛：中国海洋大学，2010.

[258] 夏康明，范先明. 旅游文化汉英翻译概论：基于功能目的论视角下的跨文化旅游翻译研究[M]. 中国社会科学出版社，2013.

[259] 夏瑛. 英语景物描写类旅游文本的特点及翻译方法初探[J]. 考试周刊，2015(92):78–79

[260] 夏增亮. 新编大学英语英汉互译实用教程[M]. 兰州：甘肃人民出版社，2016.

[261] 向程. 跨文化交际理论下的汉英旅游翻译策略研究——以巴中市旅游文本为例[J]. 重庆科技学院学报（社会科学版），2015(05)：75–79.

[262] 向程. 旅游文本中文化负载词的翻译及其补偿策略研究——以巴中市旅游文本为例[J]. 民族翻译，2015(2)：60–62.

[263] 肖乐. 旅游英语翻译中诗歌的处理[J]. 湘南学院学报，2011(04)：66–70.

[264] 肖卫国，刘跃斌. 国际商务管理[M]. 武汉：武汉大学出版社，2010.

[265] 肖新英. 广告翻译的科学性和艺术性统一[J]. 中国科技翻译，2012(02)：29–32.

[266] 谢建平等. 功能语境与专门用途英语语篇翻译研究[M]. 杭州：浙江大学出版社，2008.

[267] 谢晓朋. 文化视角下旅游文本的英译实践探讨[D]. 武汉：华中师范大学，2015.

[268] 熊力游. 旅游广告文汉译英方法探讨[J]. 中国科技翻译，2004(04)：36–39.

[269] 徐丹. 从归化策略看字幕翻译中汉语成语与谚语的应用——以《破产姐妹》为例[J]. 戏剧之家，2018(36)：227+229.

[270] 徐德宽，王平. 现代旅游市场营销学[M]. 青岛：青岛出版社，1998.

[271] 徐梦馨. 异化策略在游记文本翻译中的应用——以《徒步新西兰》为例[D]. 北京：北京外国语大学，2017.

[272] 徐志摩，蔡力坚. 我所知道的剑桥[J]. 中国翻译，2020(06)：153–158.

[273] 徐志摩，蔡力坚. 我所知道的剑桥（下）[J]. 中国翻译，2021(01)：178–184.

[274] 许宏宇. 游记类文本翻译中语用等值的实现——《通往涓涓细流之路》（第11章、第20章和第21章）的翻译实践报告[D]. 大连：大连外国语大学，2019.

[275] 许慎，汤可敬. 说文解字今释[M]. 长沙：岳麓书社，1997.

[276] 许琰. 旅游区（点）标准化管理[M]. 北京：中国工商出版社，2007.

[277] 熊力游. 旅游广告文汉译英方法探讨[J]. 中国科技翻译，2004(04)：36–39.

[278] 尹锡南译. 印度比较文学论文选译[M]. 成都：巴蜀书社，2012.

[279] 杨彬，孙炬，曹春春. 从评价理论看旅行指南的翻译——以《孤独星球：牙买加》为例[J]. 福州大学学报（哲学社会科学版），2017(01)：83.

[280] 杨丽华，王松林. 旅游语篇翻译的审美传达[J]. 山西农业大学学报(社会科学版)，2007(01)：73–75.

[281] 杨莉等. 跨文化交际翻译教程[M]. 北京：中国纺织出版社，2020.

[282] 杨林. 关联理论指导下旅游文本的改写[J]. 文学界（理论版），2011(07)：94–95.

[283] 杨柳青. 目的论指导下的旅游景点介绍文本翻译策略[J]. 山西煤炭管理干部学院学报，2013(03)：99–101.

[284] 杨萍，贺龙平. 论旅游翻译中译者主体性的限制因素[J]. 上海翻译，2012(02)：32–35.

[285] 杨秋怡. 关联理论和旅游翻译的"结缘"[J]. 科技信息，2010(07)：586+802.

[286] 杨山. 异化与归化在旅游资料四字格翻译中的运用[J]. 贵阳学院学报（社会科学版），2016(05)：49–52.

[287] 杨士焯. 简析纽马克的语义翻译和交际翻译理论[J]. 外国语言文学，1989(C2)：68–71.

[288] 杨贤玉，乔传代，杨荣广. 旅游英汉比较与翻译[M]. 武汉：武汉大学出版社，2014.

[289] 杨雁. 旅游广告英语的词法、句法及修辞特征[J]. 渝州大学学报（社会科学版），2002(01)：117–120.

[290] 杨永贤. 中文修辞句式在旅游英语翻译教学中的修辞审美差异探讨[J]. 成都教育学院学报，2005(08)：114–123.

[291] 杨元刚. 英汉词语文化语义对比研究[M]. 武汉：武汉大学出版社，2008.

[292] 姚宝荣等. 西安导游[M]. 北京：旅游教育出版社，1998.

[293] 姚友本. 如何调整旅游文本译文的篇章结构[J]. 湖北函授大学学报，2016(16)：180–181.

[294] 叶红卫. 旅游诗词翻译中的文化补偿[J]. 理论月刊，2010(06)：122–124.

[295] 叶文学. 浅析楹联翻译中的语言对等与意境契合[J]. 黑龙江生态工程职业学院学报，2017(06)：159–160.

[296] 叶欣.《中国消费的崛起》汉译实践报告——以Chapter 1 No Going Back为例[D]. 大连：辽宁师范大学，2014.

[297] 殷小娟. 云南民族村景点介绍的中英翻译效果：基于功能翻译理论的一个案例分析[J]. 重庆理工大学学报（社会科学版），2012(08)：76–80.

[298] 尹向东. "诗词旅游"探微[J]. 桂林旅游高等专科学校学报，2004(01)：87–89.

[299] 尹晓丹. 游记文本中文学性在翻译中的再现——《迷失岛》（第1至10章）的翻译实践报告[D]. 大连：大连外国语大学，2020.

[300] 尹燕. 英文导游词的创作与讲解[M]. 北京：中国旅游出版社，2007.

[301] 余芬. 异化为主的汉英文化旅游翻译策略研究[J]. 淮海工学院学报（人文社会科学版），2017(01)：65–68.

[302] 余静娴. 大学英语通用翻译教程[M]. 北京：对外经贸大学出版社，2014.

[303] 余英. 旅游文本《太湖志》英译实践报告[D]. 上海：上海师范大学，2020.

[304] 於丹丹. 交际翻译视角下的旅游景区外宣文本英译——以云南楚雄紫溪山景区为例[J]. 海外英语，2019(11)：177–178.

[305] 郁达夫. 钓台的春昼[M]. 成都：天地出版社，2013.

[306] 袁翠. 英汉汉英翻译实训教程[M]. 北京：对外经济贸易大学出版社，2012.

[307] 袁庭栋. 少城街巷志[M]. 朱华等译. 成都：四川文艺出版社，2022.

[308] 袁庭栋. 天府的记忆[M]. 朱华，张楠译. 成都：四川文艺出版社，2022.

[309] 袁晓宁. 翻译与英语语言研究[M]. 南京：东南大学出版社，2009.

[310] 袁晓宁. 以目的语为依归的外宣英译特质：以《南京采风》翻译为例[J]. 中国翻译，2010(02)：61–64.

[311] 袁晓宁. 论外宣英译策略的二元共存[J]. 中国翻译，2013(01)：93–97.

[312] 岳福曹. 译者主体性视域下的新疆高职院校旅游英语翻译教学探究[J]. 新疆职业教育研究，2020(01)：27–30.

[313] 岳中生. "桂林山水甲天下"翻译赏析[J]. 河南科技大学学报（社会科学版），2013(04)：71–74.

[314] 曾剑平. 文化认同和语言变异视角下的中国英语研究[M]. 南昌：江西高校出版社，2017.

[315] 曾利沙. 论旅游指南翻译的主题信息突出策略原则[J]. 上海翻译，2005(01)：19–23.

[316] 曾利沙. 基于实践的翻译批评应具学理性与客观论证性——兼论旅游翻译中的"商业伦理"[J]. 上海翻译，2009(02)：14–17.

[317] 曾咪. 旅游英语广告的文体风格[J]. 漳州职业技术学院学报，2009(02)：78–80.

[318] 翟晓慧. 克什克腾旅游文本的英译技巧及问题[J]. 赤峰学院学报(汉文哲学社会科学版)，2010(06):121–123.

[319] 詹红娟. 从接受美学谈旅游宣传广告的英译[J]. 牡丹江大学学报，2008(01)：83–84+97.

[320] 张戈. 从关联理论角度简析双关语在旅游广告英语翻译中的应用[J]. 和田师范专科学校学报，2015(02)：75–79.

[321] 张国良. 传播学原理[M]. 上海：复旦大学出版社，1999.

[322] 张鸿微.《杭州旅游指南》（节选）汉英笔译报告：旅游文本中文化负载词和长句的翻译难点及对策[D]. 杭州：浙江工商大学，2015.

[323] 张惠华. 英语写作基础教程[M]. 上海：复旦大学出版社，2008.

[324] 张基珮. 广告创作与翻译[J]. 中国科技翻译，2003(02)：41–43+40.

[325] 张建华. 旅游指南翻译技巧刍议[J]. 河北旅游职业学院学报，2020(02)：82–85.

[326] 张建平，俞惠. 功能目的论指导下的旅游文本英译[J]. 江西理工大学学报，2009(04)：92–94.

[327] 张娇娇. *The Rough Guide to Las Vegas*节选翻译报告[D]. 曲阜：曲阜师范大学，2014.

[328] 张姣. 英语旅游景点介绍文本的翻译[J]. 剑南文学(经典教苑)，2013(04):128.

[329] 张金红. 浅议英语广告中修辞的妙用[J]. 品牌，2015(04)：293.

[330] 张景霞. 翻译目的论引导下的旅游景点导游词英译研究[J]. 武汉商学院学报，2020 (05)：81–85.

[331] 张敬. 对文化语境的认知与广告语篇的英译[J]. 中国科技翻译，2009(02)：29–31+39.

[332] 张娟超. 连贯视角下旅游文本的翻译策略——以云冈石窟英译本为例[J]. 汉字文化, 2020(07)：116–117.

[333] 张可人, 黄芳. 接受美学视域下旅游文本英译策略探析——以天门山景区为例[J]. 文教资料, 2020（21）：55–57.

[334] 张琳. 中华文化特色旅游文本英译的语用学研究[J]. 海外英语, 2015(09)：154–155.

[335] 张露. 浅谈旅游网站英译汉文本的翻译策略[J]. 文艺生活(文海艺苑), 2015(10)：88+94.

[336] 张美芳. 编译的理论与实践——用功能翻译理论分析编译实例[J]. 四川外语学院学报, 2004(02)：95–98+113.

[337] 张瑞雪. 广告翻译中的互文性研究[J]. 科技展望, 2014(15)：65–66.

[338] 张善城, 许共城. 中华文化研究[M]. 厦门：厦门大学出版社, 1994.

[339] 张少兰. 论旅游翻译中的直译[J]. 广西教育学院学报, 2007(04)：138–140.

[340] 张双江. "旅游景介"汉英平行文本的比较及其翻译实践应用[D]. 福州：福州大学, 2014.

[341] 张思思. 图里翻译规范理论视角下泉州英语导游词研究[J]. 大学教育, 2018(12)：115–118.

[342] 张伟华. 主题相关信息突出原则在旅游资料翻译中的应用——实证分析瘦西湖旅游资料的中英翻译[J]. 牡丹江大学学报, 2007(10)：32–34.

[343] 张文英, 张晔. 英语科技应用文翻译实践教程[M]. 北京：国防工业出版社, 2015.

[344] 张心怡. 探析旅游文本汉英翻译中的文化交流与传播——从功能翻译理论指导角度探析[J]. 传媒论坛, 2021(02)：107–108+110.

[345] 张莹, 柴明颎. GILT本地化产业与翻译研究新动向[J]. 中国翻译, 2011(03)：77–80.

[346] 张芸. 《穿越未知的亚洲》第四章至第五章翻译实践报告[D]. 桂林：广西师范大学, 2016.

[347] 张正荣, 黄婷, 何姣姣. 简谈旅游资料翻译策略[J]. 开封教育学院学报, 2009(01)：54–56.

[348] 张子泉. 文学欣赏导引[M]. 北京：北京交通大学出版社, 2006.

[349] 赵爱萍. 英语广告词杜撰词、拼写变异及其修辞功能[J]. 齐齐哈尔医学院学报, 2008(23)：2900–2901.

[350] 赵春玉, 李春明. 旅游文本翻译浅析. 辽宁工业大学学报[J]. 社会科学版, 2010(06)：51–52.

[351] 赵红军. 英语翻译基础[M]. 沈阳：东北大学出版社, 2014.

[352] 赵琳琳, 李家春. 浅析涉外导游词的特征及翻译技巧[J]. 黑龙江教育学院学报, 2009(05)：110–111.

[353] 赵璐璐. 《里斯本旅游手册》英汉翻译实践报告[D]. 济南：山东大学, 2018.

[354] 郑德虎. 中国文化走出去与文化负载词的翻译[J]. 上海翻译, 2016(02)：53–56.

[355] 郑剑委, 范文君. 翻译思维、策略与技巧[M]. 武汉：武汉大学出版社, 2018.

[356] 郑丽娅. 《秦皇岛导游词》中四字格的英译[D]. 湘潭：湖南科技大学, 2016.

[357] 中国地图出版社. 经典中国游[M]. 北京：中国地图出版社，2008.

[358] 中国翻译协会. 中国翻译年鉴（2009–2010）[M]. 北京：外文出版社，2011.

[359] 周红. 本地化视角下的旅游网站英译标准刍议[J]. 绥化学院学报，2015(11)：60–63.

[360] 周建芝. 万变不离其宗——旅游文本中引文的英译策略探析[J]. 兰州教育学院学报，2017(10)：143–146.

[361] 周莉婷. 顺应论视角下导游词翻译实践报告——以"浙江著名景点导游词"的英译为例[D]. 南昌：江西师范大学，2018.

[362] 周锰珍. 基于目的论的对外宣传资料翻译[J]. 广西民族学院学报（哲学社会科学版），2006(06)：138–141.

[363] 周文. 浅谈文学翻译中的语义引申[C]. 石发林, 陈才. 外国语言文学论丛[A]. 成都：电子科技大学出版社，2013：153.

[364] 周星辰. 借宜造景理法研究——以杭州西湖风景名胜区为例[D]. 杭州：浙江大学，2019.

[365] 朱兵艳, 刘士祥, 姚立佳. 接受美学视角下的海南旅游景点翻译[J]. 郑州航空工业管理学院学报（社会科学版），2012(02)：120–123.

[366] 朱成广. 文言文全解[M]. 西安：陕西人民教育出版社，2007.

[367] 朱海玉. 目的论观照下的旅游文本翻译——以《岳阳旅游指南》翻译为例[J]. 湖北第二师范学院学报，2013(03)：117–120.

[368] 朱华. 四川英语导游——翻译、创作与讲解[M]. 北京：北京理工大学出版社，2016.

[369] 朱华. 旅游学概论(双语)（第二版）[M]. 北京：北京大学出版社，2014.

[370] 朱华. 模拟英语导游[M]. 北京：北京理工大学出版社，2022.

[371] 朱娟辉. 增译法在旅游英语翻译中的运用[J]. 云梦学刊，2009(02)：148–150.

[372] 朱梅. 旅游英语与翻译实践研究[M]. 石家庄：河北人民出版社，2017.

[373] 朱娉娉, 周海燕, 叶开艳. 互文性视角下旅游文本中的引用翻译研究[J]. 安徽职业技术学院学报，2020(02)：54–57.

[374] 朱全明. 大学英语写作与翻译：生成及其转换[M]. 苏州：苏州大学出版社，2009.

[375] 朱文艺. 黄石公园景点介绍汉译实践报告[D]. 上海：东华大学，2016.

[376] 朱义华. 外宣翻译的新时代、新话语与新思路——黄友义先生访谈录[J]. 中国翻译，2019(1)：117–122.

[377] 祝东江, 蒲轶琼. 改进旅游翻译，助推旅游发展[J]. 湖北师范学院学报（哲学社会科学版），2015(03)：83–85.

[378] 邹丹. 从目的论视角看旅游广告语的翻译[J]. 南华大学学报（社会科学版），2013 (02)：111–113+117.

[379] 邹璆. 从目的论角度看游记中隐喻的翻译方法[D]. 南京：南京大学，2014.

[380] 邹彦群. 游记在跨文化交流中的独特价值及其翻译[J]. 外国语文，2012(1)：91–95.

[381]《现在就开始》丛书编委会. 中国自助游，现在就开始（2018年第8版）[M]. 北京：旅游教育出版社，2018.

[382]《藏羚羊自助旅行手册》编写组. 旅游黄金线自助游手册 四川·重庆[M]. 北京：中国轻工业出版社，2002.

[383]《中国翻译》编辑部. "韩素音青年翻译奖"竞赛作品与评析[M]. 北京：译林出版社，2008.

[384] http://amazingthailand. org. cn, 登录时间2021.4.14

[385] http://language. chinadaily. com. cn/2017-07/30/content_30284397_3. htm, 登录时间2021.6.28

[386] http://tv. cctv. com/2019/08/21/VIDE2amIPgCRzSTExdcdaWLu190821. shtml, 登录时间2021.1.3

[387] http://wlt. sc. gov. cn/, 登录时间2021.5.7

[388] http://www. ahly. cc/, 登录时间2021.4.5

[389] http://www. dali. gov. cn/dlrmzf/c101684/yxdl. shtml, 登录时间2021.5.7

[390] http://www. doyouhike. net/special/singapore/, 登录时间2021.4.14

[391] http://www. fjta. com/scenic/208, 登录时间2011.10.7

[392] http://www. fjta. com/scenic/43, 登录时间2010.12.8

[393] http://www. fodors. com, 登录时间2021.4.14

[394] http://www. gardenly. com/index. php/jingdian/pic/page/117/i/14. html, 登录时间2021.3.3

[395] http://www. gdhotel. com. hk/en/discovery-hongkong/, 登录时间2021.4.14

[396] http://www. grandcanaltravel. com/, 登录时间2021.4.5

[397] http://www. liriver. com. cn/, 登录时间2021.4.5

[398] http://www. sxhm. com/, 登录时间2021.5.7

[399] http://www. szwwco. com/en/, 登录时间2021.5.7

[400] http://www. visitsingapore. com/, 登录时间2021.3.25

[401] https://www. visitsingapore. com/, 登录时间2021.3.6

[402] https://cn. tripadvisor. com/Attraction_Review-g297461-d488560-Reviews, 登录时间2021.6.27

[403] https://cn. tripadvisor. com/Attraction_Review-g297461-d488560-Reviews, 登录时间2021.6.27

[404] https://language. chinadaily. com. cn/a/202103/18/WS60530f4da31024ad0bab00f2. html,

[405] https://pic. sogou. com/, 登录时间2021.2.6

[406] https://singapore. com/museums/, 登录时间2021.4.5

[407] https://weibo. com/aishenghuodebianbian, 登录时间2021.6.20

[408] https://www. australia. com/en, 登录时间2021.4.5

[409] https://www. booking. com/hotel/gb/the-ritz-london. en-gb. html, 登录时间2021.1.6

[410] https://www. discoverhongkong. cn/china/explore/great-outdoor/great-outdoors-hong-kong/5-

377

senses/sight. html, 登录时间2021.5.7

[411] https://www. discoverhongkong. cn/china/greater-bay-area. html, 登录时间2021.5.7

[412] https://www. discoverhongkong. com/, 登录时间2021.5.7

[413] https://www. discoverhongkong. com/eng/explore/culture/hong-kong-locals-share-what-brings-them-joy-in-daily-life. html, 登录时间2021.4.5

[414] https://www. expedia. com, 登录时间2021.4.14

[415] https://www. huawei. com/cn/?ic_medium=direct&ic_source=surlent,登录时间05/07/2021

[416] https://www. huawei. com/en/, 登录时间2021.5.7

[417] https://www. ireland. com/en-gb/#, 登录时间2021.4.5

[418] https://www. nationalgeographic. com, 登录时间2021.4.14

[419] https://www. newzealand. com/, 登录时间2021.5.7

[420] https://www. newzealand. com/int/destinations/, 登录时间2021.4.14

[421] https://www. ourtour. com, 登录时间2021.4.14

[422] https://www. regentpalacehotel. co. uk/default. htm, 登录时间2021.4.6

[423] https://www. royallancaster. com/, 登录时间2021.1.6

[424] https://www. sydney. com/, 登录时间2021.5.7

[425] https://www. theritzlondon. com/staysafe/, 登录时间2021.1.6

[426] https://www. tourism. gov. hk/en/ , 登录时间2021.4.5

[427] https://www. tourism. gov. hk/en/, 登录时间2021.4.5

[428] https://www. tourismthailand. org/home, 登录时间2021.4.14

[429] https://www. tourtravelchina. com/top-china-tours/8-days-essence-of-china-tour/, 登录时间2021.9.7

[430] https://www. tourtravelchina. com/top-china-tours/8-days-essence-of-china-tour/,登录时间2021.9.7

[431] https://www. tourtravelchina. com/top-china-tours/8-days-essence-of-china-tour/,登录时间2021.9.7

[432] https://www. travelblog. org/Asia/China/Jiangsu/Suzhou/blog-1003847. html, 登录时间2021.6.28

[433] https://www. travelblog. org/Asia/China/Qinghai/Qinghai-Lake/blog-964151. html, 登录时间2021.6.28

[434] https://www. travelblog. org/Asia/China/Yunnan/Dali/blog-995864. html, 登录时间 2021.6.28

[435] https://www. tripadvisor. com/Attraction_Review-g154911-d2406648-Reviews,登录时间202.3.6

[436] https://www. visitabdn. com/, 登录时间2021.4.5

[437] https://www. visitlondon. com, 登录时间2021.4.14

[438] https://www. visitsingapore. com. cn/walking-tour/culture/city-hall-running-trail/#history 登录时间2021.1.11
[439] https://www. visitwales. com/, 登录时间2021.4.5
[440] https://zhuanlan. zhihu. com/p/349476180, 登录时间2021.6.20

后　记

　　本人祖籍安徽潜山，生于四川成都，长于偏远小城雅安。少时家境贫寒，家中排行老大，拾煤渣、担水、劈柴、洗衣、煮饭等重体力活全落在我的肩上。虽然生活贫困，但本人生性顽皮，时常上山捕蝉，下河捕鱼，林中捕鸟，游玩于山水之间。后学会拉京胡，出演京剧《智取威虎山》参谋长少剑波，拿今天的话来说颇有"文艺范儿"。本人开过520型机床，当过翻砂工，周公山放羊，天全县当"赤脚医生"，至今还会扎针灸、打吊瓶。高中毕业后本人到四川省雅安地区荥经县石家大队当了农民，常在煤油灯下读《红楼梦》《三国演义》等名著。日子过得很艰难，天天"劳其筋骨"，日日"饿其体肤"，夜夜"空乏其身"，但确有"动心忍性，增益其所不能"之功效，造就了一生"上下而求索"的精神。

　　改革开放以后恢复高考，1978年本人有幸以当年四川省"探花"的成绩（全省第三名）考上华东师范大学外语系，毕业后游历欧洲、北美、非洲、中东、东南亚数十国，历任译员、首席翻译、翻译组长，主持大型翻译项目6个，多次担任部长级会议翻译、陪同翻译、导游翻译，实现了"行游天下"的梦想。其实，翻译是一个很好的职业，早在30年以前国人还没有大众出游（指出境游），本人就已经"周游列国""行游天下"了。在中国经济日益繁荣、综合国力不断强大的今天，相信"行游天下"对很多中国人来说已经不是梦想，但是"行游天下"只是观光客的出行方式，对一个有理想、有抱负的中国人，应有更高的人生境界，那就是"写译人生"。

　　我是这样理解"写译"的。作为学者和作家，不仅要做学术研究，出版著作，编写高水平的国家级规划教材；还应当出版译著，宣传、译介中国的人文、历史、地理和文化，这是大国知识分子的历史使命，也是中国文化人个人的担当。"写译"也是一个人人生历程的演绎。当您出版一部甚至多部著作、译著以后，您的人生必然又达到了新的境界、新的高度，颇有"会当凌绝顶，一览众山

后　记

小"的感觉。当然，若没有"劳其筋骨，饿其体肤，空乏其身"的经历，没有"行游天下"的阅历，恐怕也难有"写译人生"的辉煌和荣耀。

本人学术研究横跨两个专业领域，旅游学、翻译学，属于"杂家"一类，系四川师范大学外国语学院和历史文化与旅游学院教授，带旅游管理和翻译专业两个不同学科的研究生，对旅游学和翻译学都感兴趣，出版过中文旅游著作，也写过英文著作，主编国家级规划教材8部，发表学术论文数十篇，但唯感翻译最难，也最有乐趣。本人从事旅游研究和旅游翻译数载，虽偶尔也有神来之笔，但从未有翻译大家所说的"得意忘言"，"化境"之说更是相形甚远，只有夜半三更，字斟句酌，唯恐得罪了作者，忌惮翻译理论家"拍砖"，更担心读者不满。爬完格子再睡回笼觉，已成"新常态"。

《旅游英汉互译》是本人多年从事旅游翻译教学和研究的成果，许多译例和翻译思考来自本人出版的《旅游学概论》《天府的记忆》《青羊街巷志》《美丽四川——最难忘的40个旅游胜地》《四川英语导游——途中讲解》等旅游专著和译著，也来自研究生旅游翻译课堂教学和翻译实践。何青青、王佳瑶、贺雯婧、田雨曼、代依洋、谢东芹、杨繁玉、李璟妍、宁颖、徐一丹、刘晓、陈钰婷、张芸、章文翌、梁琴、李蕊丹、张越、程娇娇、杨兰、向星宇、孙圳、古罗月、董丽、李欣雨、梁欢、夏玲玲、黄敏、刘乾懿、王靖文等研究生完成了布置的翻译练习，他们实践性的翻译作业丰富了本书的内容，并在一定程度上验证了本人主张的旅游翻译的策略和方法。

"读万卷书、行万里路"，这是历代中国文人的生活方式。"路漫漫其修远兮，吾将上下而求索。""行游天下"，世上游的地方还很多；"写译人生"，那是生命嬗变的过程。译无止境，没有最好，只有更好。

朱　华
写于2016年10月1日
修订于2022年5月29日
成都，龙湖